Welcome To Horlickville!
History of the Racine, Wisconsin
National Football League Franchise.
Horlick-Racine Legion 1922 1923 1924
Racine Tornadoes 1926

Horlick Athletic Field
~ Home Of The ~
Horlick-Racine Legion Football Team.

Welcome To Horlickville!
History of the Racine, Wisconsin National Football League Franchise
Horlick-Racine Legion 1922 1923 1924
Racine Tornadoes 1926

Matthew C. Snyder
Racine, Wisconsin

First Printing: 2014
ISBN   978-1-63452-368-4
Library of Congress Control Number 2014920591
Library of Congress
101 Independence Avenue, S.E.
Washington, DC 20540-4283
Matthew C. Snyder publishing
Racine, Wisconsin
Racine Legion Football Club- Matthew C. Snyder
RacineLegion@gmail.com
www.RacineLegion.com

Dedication

This book is dedicated to my family. You have each influenced my life in a positive way and therefore, you gave me the knowledge, tools, and drive to succeed.
Thank you!

Raymond E. McCarthy (1919-1992), My Grandfather. You taught me to appreciate all the great things about Racine, Wisconsin and you frequently shared the details of its rich history from an era long gone. I will always cherish the memory of our time spent motoring through the streets of Racine.

This is further dedicated to the following Family members, who contributed to the skills, drive and determination for me to succeed in the completion of this project.

Angeline Mc Carthy (1916-2013), My Grandmother. You taught me how to stay the course and never give up. David and Carol Snyder, My Parents. You showed me the way to find my success. Steve Snyder, My Brother. You and your family (Jane, Alexis and Sydney) showed me how to look at things from a different prospective. Victoria Snyder, My beautiful wife. You always encouraged me to never settle for second best. Cory, Nicholas and Jacob, My Sons. You reminded me that I need to be more patient and pay attention to the details.

Table of Contents

Acknowledgements

This book would have never been written without William Horlick, Sr., George "Babe" Ruetz, Hank Gillo, the Sports Writers of the Racine Journal News and Racine Times Call, the dedicated members of the American Legion Post No. 76 of Racine, Wisconsin as well as the Racine businesses and fans, who supported these teams.

First, my hat goes off to Mr. Horlick and his philanthropy. I am sure that we only know a portion of his generosity. Thank you for giving us NFL football in Racine, Wisconsin. You went above and beyond. Racine, Wisconsin is greater place because of you!

George Ruetz gave his knowledge, dedication and time in order to insure the success of the Horlick-Racine Legion and Racine Tornadoes professional football teams. Thank you for your drive for success, you ran the show like a Champion! You deserve to known as "The Father of Professional Football in Racine"!

Henry Charles Gillo, you wore the No. 1 jersey and deserve to be known as one the greatest to ever play the game. You set NFL records and you were the coach, captain and leader of both, the Horlick-Racine Legion and Racine Tornadoes. Thank you for representing Racine with style!

The American Legion Post No. 76 provided funds and administration to the football operations. Max Zirbes, L.A. McDowell and the other contributing post members, Job well done! Thank you for overseeing one of the best NFL teams in the country!

The Sports writers of the Racine Journal News and Racine Times Call kept the people of Racine, Wisconsin informed with accurate details. Thank you for your vision of Racine, Wisconsin professional football.

The Racine business community supported professional football and the fans cheered this team to victory. Thank you for your support of Racine, Wisconsin professional football!

The entire rosters of both, the Horlick-Racine Legion and Racine Tornadoes, you gave this great city, a fine brand of football and increased that star on the map. Thank you!

i

<u>Foreword</u>

Welcome To Horlickville! is a historical account of the Racine, Wisconsin National Football League Franchise. The Horlick-Racine Legion (NFL 1922, 1923, 1924) and Racine Tornadoes (NFL 1926) professional football teams participated in the National Football League during the early years of the League. This is a history of the true events as they were communicated by local newspaper sports writers and adapted to tell the complete history.

This never been told history of events includes the NFL Racine, Wisconsin franchise historical team facts, financial records, photos, team and individual statistical information as well as other uncovered facts. It is a close look inside the operations of an early 1920's NFL franchise with complete details.

George Halas, Paddy Driscoll, Curly Lambeau and Hank Gillo duke it out for the NFL title.

Horlick Athletic Field is one of the most famous football fields in the World! The early greats, who played on this football field included; Curly Lambeau, George Halas, Hank Gillo, Fritz Pollard, Ernie Nevers, Jim Thorpe and others!

This true history follows the franchise and tells the story which includes a record setting field goal by Racine football legend, Hank Gillo. There is a controversial call by referee Jim Holloway of Chicago, which changes the course of the team. The Racine fans are treated to a special halftime performance by Miss Ethel Dare as she jumps from a plane to the 50 yard line of Horlick Athletic Field. George Halas proclaims, the Horlick-Racine Legion as one of the best competitors as seen by his 1921 World Champions. Curly Lambeau is defeated by the passing game, which made him famous as a player. The first ever NFL Premium box seats were created by William Horlick, Sr. in order to give the fans an up close view of NFL football in Racine, Wisconsin at Horlick Athletic Field aka Horlickville!

Preface

Welcome To Horlickville! was inspired by a desire to research and preserve the history of Racine, Wisconsin professional football. This inspiration was brought forth by a love for the city of Racine as well as the game of football. Racine, Wisconsin is one of the most unique cities in the world. It is nicknamed the "Belle City" and also known as the "City of Invention". The growth of the invention of Malted Milk by William Horlick, Sr. is the reason why there was financial backing for this franchise to continue in the National Football League, as long as it did. Take a trip to the past, as you look into this "Uncovered History" of the Racine, Wisconsin NFL franchise and experience the beginning of organized professional football. This true account is filled with the historical detail of events surrounding these early NFL stars, who worked to make the professional football game, a permanent and exciting part of our culture.

WWW. RACINELEGION.COM

Introduction

The historical collection of facts forms a history of the Racine, Wisconsin football franchise, which participated in the National Football League during 1922, 1923, 1924 and 1926 seasons.

Welcome To Horlickville! follows the team as the events unfold around the franchise. A 1920's American city supports this up and coming professional sport as the nation reacts with mixed emotions.

William Horlick, Sr., a philanthropist, who owned the world famous Horlick Malted Milk Company provided the financial backing needed to sustain the operation of an NFL franchise in 1922. The American Legion Post No. 76 of Racine, Wisconsin, provided the leadership of a large organization, which was needed to professionally organize the day to day business operations. George "Babe" Ruetz, who owned/operated a local grocery store, brought military leadership skills as well as years of successful football playing experience. He would be their team manager but his knowledge of the game, along with the league made him invaluable. There were several soon to be football legends who would grace the football field of Horlick Athletic Field. Henry Charles Gillo would lead the team, which was made up of several college star football players.

Follow this professional franchise through a journey of twists and turns in an attempt to succeed in the National Football League during the early years.

Chapter 1:
Horlick-Racine Legion
1922 NFL season

The dust kicked up from the baseball field at Lakeview Park in Racine Wisconsin on a fall day in September of 1922. It was September 9th and the Horlick-Racine Legion professional football team was hard at work. They were preparing for their first game in the National Football League against the Chicago Bears on Sunday October 1st, 1922. Several months earlier in the spring of 1922, a merger took place between two Racine, Wisconsin professional football teams. Racine philanthropist, William Horlick, Sr., who owned the Horlick Malted Milk Company would join forces with the American Legion Post No. 76 of Racine, Wisconsin. The Horlick Standards and the Racine Legion combined to become the Horlick-Racine Legion professional football team. The management of this new franchise made George "Babe" Ruetz, their new team manager. Ruetz was the team manager and he also played reserve guard for the Racine Legion professional football team in 1921. The Legion was a 1921 associate member of the (APFA) American Professional Football Association. The APFA was created in 1920 and they changed the name to the National Football League in 1922. The 1921 Legion played a few games against the APFA league teams but Ruetz described the league as being a makeshift affair with a hit or miss schedule. This new Racine team wanted a dedicated schedule and they sent Ruetz to Canton, Ohio to secure a franchise in the newly named National Football League. George G. Ruetz paid the franchise fee on behalf of the Horlick-Racine Legion in order to join the National Football League. He made a motion at the NFL League meeting recommending that the League institute a "Closed game schedule". Ruetz was no stranger to the game of football. He played for several Racine football teams including the Racine Battery C football team, which was the 1917 Champions of Wisconsin.

William Horlick, Sr.

Horlick-Racine Legion Team Manager Ruetz became a member of the NFL league scheduling committee. While coordinating the 1922 schedule for the Legion, Ruetz boldly chose the 1921 World Champion Chicago Staleys for the Legion's first opponent. Starting at the beginning of the 1922 NFL season, the Staleys changed their name and they would be known as the Chicago Bears. George Ruetz was confident that the Legion would be able to play with any team that played in the National Football League

George G. Ruetz

and he was determined to prove this by taking on the Bears first. George G. "Babe" Ruetz would later be known as "The Father of professional football in Racine"

Under the direction of Coach O. D. Hollenback and Manager Ruetz, the players practiced 2 to 3 hours for four days a week. This would continue until the first game. Coach Hollenback held a management position at Racine Auto Tire Company and Manager G. G. Ruetz was the owner of a Racine grocery store, which bore his name. Therefore, the team practiced in the evenings and on the weekends. There were several players, who returned to the team from the previous season as well as some new players, who were brought in to add to the roster. Those early practices were also considered player tryouts. Capt. Henry Charles Gillo (Fullback, Kicker-Colgate All-American) returned to be a key player in this new franchise. He played with the Racine Legion in 1921. Gillo, as a collegiate player for Colgate University in 1919, once returned a punt the distance of the field for a game winning touchdown against the University of Illinois at Illinois. As a pro player, he was equally impressive. The real dope (information) about the style of player that Hank Gillo was on the field had been described as; *He was commonly known as "Line Plunging Hank" because he was one of the few men in football, who had developed the twisting run and spiral jump.* When Hank was at Colgate University, he and Jim Thorpe (The famous Carlisle Indian football player/NFL player) played for the football team and they both had the twist and spiral technique down to perfection. Gillo developed his running speed, when he ran the ball by using a bent over body motion similar to the takeoff of an aeroplane. He ran almost straight on his toes as a toe dancer would dance. The minute he was about to be tackled, he twisted his entire body to the left or right depending on the side on which, he was being tackled. If he was running into a play that involved several defenders, then he threw his body into a spiral shape and his head and arms forward. This gave him an extra gain of a yard or two, when he was being tackled.

George G. Ruetz
Racine Battery C team

Hank Gillo

Five players were battling it out for the tackle positions. They were several players from Marquette University such as Whitey Woodin, Frank Linnan, Fritz Roessler, George MaGill as well as Angus Look around (Carlisle) and Robert Johonnott (lineman). Norbert "Butts" Hayes and Elmer "Swede" Rhenstrom, both played the ends during the previous year in Racine. Wallie Sieb and Fritz Heinisch were substitutes at the end positions. Heinisch was a local Racine player, who played

2

with several local Racine football teams in the past. He would be a very valuable substitute for the Legion team. He had the ability to play several positions including quarterback and end on the offensive side of the ball. Dudley "Dutch" Pearson (Notre Dame) was practicing at the quarterback position and he was considered to be the most likely to be the starter for this team. Bob Foster and Irving Langhoff were practicing at the halfback positions.

As the baseball season came to a close, the NFL football season was fast approaching. The transformation of Horlick Athletic Field from a baseball field to a football field would take place in only a few days before the first game. Horlick Athletic Field was located at 1648 Forest Street (later to be known as North Memorial Drive) in Racine, Wisconsin. It was designed by architect Walter Dick in 1907 as a baseball park. It is surrounded by a stone wall and there were wrought iron metal gates at the entrances. A double window ticket booth was the main entrance. It included four gate openings, two on each side of the ticket booth as well as a single gate farther down on Forest Street. A double wrought iron gate allowed trucks and cars to enter the park on two different sides. It also featured a wooden covered grandstand with a booth on the roof for the field announcer, which was later expanded for other media personnel. There were also free standing uncovered bleachers. The players dressed in an area below the main grandstand. The clubhouse would have both dressing rooms and shower baths, added in 1923. It was originally known as Northside City League Park until October 19, 1919, when William Horlick, Sr. purchased the park and renamed it Horlick Athletic Field. Mr. Horlick invented the World Famous Horlick's Malted Milk and his company was located in Racine, Wisconsin. Aside from his company, he was involved in sponsoring many sports, such as baseball and basketball teams. He was true philanthropist to the city of Racine. He donated to several Racine, Wisconsin projects. Some of his donations were to the following: Memorial Hall, Horlick Athletic Field, Island Park, Racine Zoo, YMCA-Racine, construction of a Women's Health wing at St. Luke's Hospital as well as other major local donations.

Although the Legion and Standards both played at Horlick Athletic Field prior to the 1922 season, it would receive a major overhaul to prepare for the start of the National Football League season. This transformation would include added bleachers for expanded seating as well as the first ever NFL Premium boxes. There were forty boxes for premium seating built in 1922 at Horlick Athletic Field. Twenty boxes on each side of the football field. These boxes had board sides and a floor. They would accommodate up to eight people. On cold game days, straw would be tossed across the floor in order to help keep the feet warm of those watching the game from the box. Thirty men worked to upgrade Horlick Athletic Field for the 1922 NFL season.

Right-Premium Box seating similar to the original grandstand box seating was constructed at Horlick Athletic Field in preparation for the 1922 NFL season.

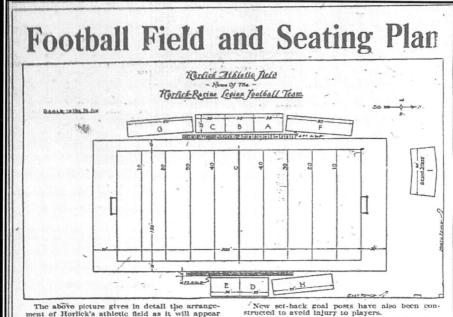

Football Field and Seating Plan

Horlick Athletic Field
~ Home Of The ~
Horlick-Racine Legion Football Team.

The above picture gives in detail the arrangement of Horlick's athletic field as it will appear October 1st for the football season.

Forty boxes will be constructed, twenty on each side of the field. The boxes will have board sides and floors and each will accommodate eight people. On cool days straw will be liberally strewn on the bottom to keep feet warm.

Reserved seats will be in sections A B C D and E. These sections are newly constructed.

Sections F G H and I will be general admission seats.

The playing field will be fenced in to avoid spectators getting on the field at any time.

Automobiles will not be allowed within the park. A welcome addition to the equipment is a new score board showing downs and distance.

New set-back goal posts have also been constructed to avoid injury to players.

All construction work possible is being done now and on the last three days of this month a great force of men will change the baseball field to a football field. Everything will be ready for the first big game, October 1st.

Every effort is being made to accommodate the public in the most comfortable manner.

Five admission coupon tickets for reserved seats as well as five admission coupon tickets for general admission will be sold in the big Legion Football Booster Campaign, Sept. 22nd to 30th.

Boxes for the season may be had from Max Zirbes.

Reservation of seats will be open four days before each game at Sam Smader's, 331 Main St.; Monument Cigar Stores; and Rehl's Cigar Stores on 6th Street and State Street.

Horlick Athletic Field 1648 Forest Street, Racine, Wisconsin Football Field New Layout with upgrades to accommodate the 1922 National Football League season for the Horlick-Racine Legion. 40 Premium boxes created along sidelines with up to 8 seats (wooden folding chairs) in each box. These upgrades transformed Horlick's Athletic Field to Horlickville.

Horlick Athletic Field
Racine, Wisconsin

Pictured above: An automobile is parked near the football field on the Horlick Athletic Field grounds. Starting with the 1922 NFL season, automobiles were no longer allowed to be parked inside the grounds of Horlick Athletic Field

The overhaul of Horlick Athletic Field for the 1922 National Football League season included a one of kind spectator experience. This unique football park raised the standards of viewing pro football for the fans. After this transformation, Horlick's Athletic Field became affectionately known as Horlickville.

Manager Ruetz was hard at work, attempting to get talented former college players to the Legion practices, in order to field the best team possible for the showdown with the Chicago Bears on October 1st. One notable player was Al "Rowdy" Elliott, who joined the Legion after playing his college career with the University of Wisconsin. He was an All-Western halfback. Elliott's main asset was the Chop knee run. He could run for large gains but the minute he was about to be tackled, his legs doubled up with his knees coming straight up in the air. This made it hard for an opponent to tackle him from the front or side because his knees hit the player trying to tackle him in the body. His first practice after joining the team, he took the ball on the first play of the scrimmage and ran down field for a 70 yard gain. He would end up being an outstanding contributor to the Legion line-up.

A football ticket drive was launched to kick off this first NFL season in Racine, Wisconsin. Fifteen teams of eleven members each would compete for the honor of having their team name engraved on a loving cup, which would be presented by the mayor of Racine at the first home game against the Bears. The team with the most tickets sold plus three tickets holders would be chosen for this honor. A scoreboard of the progress of each team would be displayed at the Monument cigar store in downtown Racine. The cup, which was going to be awarded to the winning team would ultimately be displayed in the trophy room at the new Memorial Hall that would be located in downtown Racine, Wisconsin. Before the end of the contest, the cup would travel to various businesses throughout the city of Racine for all to view. The schedule of the cup displaying was as followed:

September 20th, 1922	*Morning:*	H&M Body Corporation
	Afternoon:	Porter Furniture Company
September 21st, 1922	*Morning:*	Racine Rubber Company
	Afternoon:	Dan Metcalf Store
September 22nd, 1922	*Morning:*	Horlick's Malted Milk Company
	Afternoon:	Manufactures' Bank
September 23rd, 1922		
	Afternoon:	L&C Clothes Shop
September 24th, 1922	*Morning:*	Racine MFG Company
	Afternoon:	Rehl's Cigar Store (State Street)
September 25th, 1922	*Morning:*	Hamilton Beach Plant
	Afternoon:	Vandergrind & Dolister
September 26th, 1922	*Morning:*	S.C. Johnson & Son
	Afternoon:	Red Cross (Sixth Street)
September 27th, 1922	*Morning:*	Hartmann Trunk Company
	Afternoon:	Huber's Drug Store
September 28th, 1922	*Morning:*	Walker MFG Company
	Afternoon:	Bullock's
September 29th, 1922		
	Afternoon:	Monument Cigar Store

6

CHAMPIONS

of the
NATIONAL
FOOTBALL
LEAGUE

Pick Your Team and Boost for American Legion Football.

Racine Is Going After It!

That is why the American Legion has assembled for this year's team a great galaxy of football stars.

Every lover of good, clean athletics will want to have a good seat to see the thrilling runs of the Racine ends. The inspiring line plunges of the great Gillo.

What better enjoyment for the week-end than the thrill of the umpire's whistle, the struggle of 22 warriors for supremacy as aero passes are mixed with deceptive shift plays as the voice of the referee rings over the gridiron—last down—2 yards to go. The ball is set—4—11—61 the clock-like shift. The snap of the ball and Gillo goes over. It is the kind of amusement we need in Racine. It is hard to wait for the opening game of October first with the Chicago Bears.

YOUR PART

In the meantime, Racine people are going to play the greatest football game ever played in the history of the world. Every citizen is going to be able to assure successful football in Racine by buying reserved seats in advance.

There are a limited number but by buying now you can avoid the rush at the gate because your seat will be reserved.

So prepare to support your favorite team in the great Legion Football Booster Ticket Campaign, Sept. 22 to 30.

FIFTEEN TEAMS ARE COMPETING

These teams are composed of tackles, halfbacks and fullbacks from the business men of Racine. Each team will be competing to have its name engraved on the wonderful silver loving cup donated by the Mayor and Common Council. Buy your tickets early from your favorite team, as each ticket means a touchdown, a field goal, or a drop-kick on its percentage in the race for the cup. Yours may be just the ticket to give them their downs.

Aside from the team's name on the cup, you may be one of the three citizens of Racine who buy reserved seats that will win the great drawing contest to be staged at the opening game. The three winners of this contest will have their names engraved on the cup as typical Racine Boosters. The cup will be formally presented by the Mayor at the first game—October 1. The cup will be put in the Memorial Building Trophy Room.

1922 Newspaper Ad explaining Ticket selling campaign for Horlick-Racine Legion

The 1921 World Champion Chicago Bears were beaming with confidence. It was reported that the Bears were boasting about coming to Racine and defeating the Legion by four touchdowns. After that, they planned to run through the rest of the NFL teams and take another Championship.

On Sunday September 24, 1922, one week prior to the first game of the 1922 NFL season, the Horlick-Racine Legion football team held a morning practice at Lakeview Park in Racine, Wisconsin. They attracted more than 300 curious fans. The day before, the Legion scrimmaged with the Marquette University Golden Avalanche, up in Milwaukee, Wisconsin and they looked well prepared to face the Chicago Bears. The large crowd, who attended that practice saw a glimpse of Dudley "Dutch" Pearson and Moxie "Leather" Dalton, alternating at the quarterback position. Both men performed well and each would be equally capable of running the offense. The fans saw Norbert "Butts" Hayes and Elmer "Swede" Rhenstrom at the ends, Whitey Woodin and Frank Linnan playing tackle, Jack Hueller and Earl "Bud" Gorman in the guard positions and Vincent Shackelton playing center. In the backfield, Captain Hank Gillo was at fullback, while Bob Foster and Irv Langhoff filled in at the halfback positions. This team was settled and they were ready to compete in a professional football game.

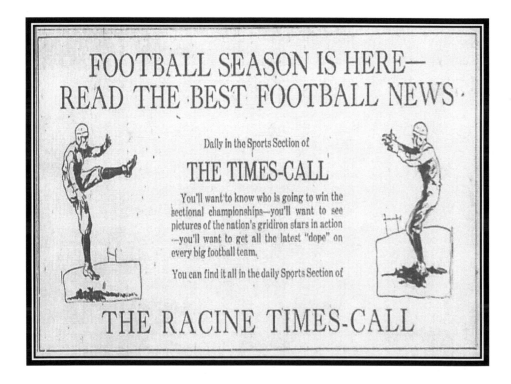

8

1922 Horlick Racine Legion Players

Dudley Pearson   **Moxie Dalton**   **Norbert Hayes**   **Elmer Rhenstrom**

Whitey Woodin   **Frank Linnan**   **Jack Hueller**   **Earl Gorman**

1922 Horlick Racine Legion Players

Vincent Shackelton   **Hank Gillo**   **Carl Baumann**   **Fritz Roessler**

Bob Foster   **Irving Langhoff**   **Al Elliott**   **Wallie Sieb**

1922 Horlick Racine Legion Players

Fritz Heinisch   **Angus LookAround**

    The Legion would not practice on Monday but the team would resume business as usual on Tuesday. The baseball season at Horlick Athletic Field was officially over on Wednesday September 27th, 1922 and there was not much time for Horlick's crew to transform his field for football. As this first game was fast approaching on Sunday October 1st, 1922, it was time to make some decisions as to who would be the first string players for this Legion team.

    Coach Hollenback, Captain Gillo and Manager Ruetz sat down together on Friday to decide who would make up the starting line-up. The NFL in 1922 required teams to be limited to 18 players on their roster after the first game. This gave the Legion some time to take another look at a few players but they needed to decide who would start against the Bears.

    There was no time to waste, the Legion needed to take care of some last minute preparations. Manager Ruetz and Supplyman (equipment) Hank Larsen went to Milwaukee to buy new brown jerseys for the players. Although the team already had uniforms, they needed to comply with an NFL rule that stated: *When the home and away team wear the same color jersey, the home team would have to wear a different color for the game.* The Chicago Bears and the Columbus Panhandlers both wore similar colors as the crimson red jerseys that were worn by the Horlick-Racine Legion. Therefore, the Legion needed to get an alternate jersey color for those home games. The Legion announced that uniforms for the game against the Bears would be khaki brown jerseys with 8" white numerals on the back and also black socks with white stripes. The socks had three white stripes and their helmets were black leather. Their football pants were made of canvas, which was a khaki brown color too.

The Legion practiced Friday before an estimated crowd of 1500 fans. This would be their last practice before the game Sunday against the Bears. Chicago was planning to arrive in Racine on Sunday morning and stay at a local Hotel.

Manager Ruetz announced that he was close to signing Robert J. "Duke" Dunne, who was a star player for the University of Michigan football team. He was a big All-American guard and a former captain of his college football team. He was also the son of the former governor of Illinois. Dunne was one of the greatest stars of the game and would be a fine addition to the Racine team. He had a lot of trouble trying to get his dad to consent to him playing pro football. When his dad heard that the Legion team was an all ex-service men team, then he finally did give his consent. While Dunne had not signed a Racine contract, Ruetz was certain that he would be in a

FOOTBALL

TOMORROW

Chicago Bears
National Champions 1921
vs.
Horlick Racine Legion

HORLICK FIELD

Kickoff 2:30

1922 Racine Newspaper advertisement for Horlick-Racine Legion vs Chicago Bears game

Horlick-Racine Legion uniform on Sunday. He would never make it to Racine, Wisconsin and after the Chicago Bears game on October 1st, he contacted Ruetz to tell him that he would not be playing professional football.

A celebration took place on Saturday in downtown Racine. The American Legion Post No. 76 football booster campaign ticket sale was complete. The team winner was announced as well as the names that would be inscribed on the loving cup. The trophy was set to be presented before the game on Sunday. The tickets for the Horlick-Racine Legion football games were available for sale at the following Racine, Wisconsin locations; Tommy Smader's Place, which was as a tavern on Main Street, as well as Monument Cigar Store (downtown Racine), and Rehl's Cigar Stores at both the State Street and 6th Street locations.

** GAME DAY **

Sunday October 1st, 1922 had finally arrived and the Legion would play their first
game in the NFL. Prior to the game, Mayor A.J. Hunt presented the loving cup
from the ticket campaign to the winners. H&M Body Corporation was the winning
team. In addition, Bill Higgins and Mr. Knutson were two of the individuals, who
would be honored on the trophy. This trophy would have a special place in the
trophy room at Memorial Hall in Racine, Wisconsin. The Bears brought the Famous
Harmony Four quartet of Chicago to play for the halftime entertainment and there
was also a planned performance by the American Legion Post No. 76 drum corps as
well as their jazz band. Mayor Alfred J. Lunt kicked the *Honorary first ball* to
signify the start of the game. More than 4,500 fans packed Horlick Athletic Field to
witness the first ever battle between these NFL teams. The kickoff was at 2:30 pm
and it was a hard fought battle right to the very end. Neither team could score a
touchdown. In the first quarter, the Chicago Bears were able to move the ball to
Racine 12 yard line and later in the third quarter, they would get as close as their 20
yard line but Racine would hold strong. The tough defense of the Horlick-Racine
Legion never allowed the defending World Champion Bears to ever get in the end
zone. Chicago played an equally tough defense and they never allowed Racine to get
any closer than Chicago's 38 yard line. The Legion would not be unable to score any
points against the Bears. The Bears had ten first downs on offense and the Legion
had five. Two field goals by Chicago's Dutch Sternaman, one from the 25 yard line
after ten minutes into the first quarter and a second from the 45 yard line in the 4th
quarter would give the Bears the victory with the score 6-0 over Racine.

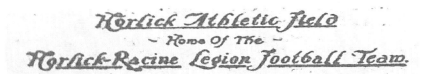

PLAY BY PLAY: **1922 NFL SEASON HRL GAME 1**
HORLICK-RACINE LEGION VS CHICAGO BEARS
Sunday: October 1st, 1922 2:30 pm
Horlick Athletic Field   Racine, Wisconsin

FIRST QUARTER:
Chicago's Garvey kicked off to Racine and it was received by the Legion's Hank
Gillo, who returned the ball to the Legion 25 yard line. On first down, the Legion
handed off to Rowdy Elliot, who ran the ball for a 5 yard gain. On second down, the
Bears were penalized 5 yards for an off sides penalty. This gave the Legion a first
down. The Legion gained 2 yards on a run. Racine handed ball off to Foster and it
resulted in a 5 yard loss. Pearson punted to Chicago. J. Sternaman, who received the
ball and it was downed the ball on the Bears 35 yard line. Dutch Sternaman and

Pete Stinchcomb, each ran the ball and it resulted in a total of a 4 yard gain. On third down, a hand off was made to Sternaman, who ran the ball, which resulted in another 4 yard gain as well as a first down. The ball was advanced to the Bears 47 yard line. On first down, a run by Lafleur resulted in a 5 yard gain. Stinchcomb's run resulted in a 2 yard loss. On third down, Sternaman launched a long pass to George Halas, who received it on Racine's 30 yard line and then he advanced it another 10 yards. Sternaman gained five yards on a run. The Legion sent Gorman into the game to substitute for Hueller. Lafleur ran for 3 yards. Sternaman ran off tackle and gained

1 yard. On fourth down and 1 yard to go from the Legion 12 yard line, the Bears opted to attempt a field goal. Sternaman dropped back to the Legion 25 yard line and sent a place kick squarely between the bars. The Bears took a 3-0 lead with ten minutes to go in the first quarter. _Score: Racine 0, Chicago 3._ Gillo kicked off to the Bears. The ball was received by J. Sternaman, who was tackled by Gorman. Sternaman gained 3 yards on first down. Pearson intercepted a Bears pass and advanced it to the 40 yard line. Gillo ran the ball through the line and it resulted in 3 yard gain. The Legion threw an incomplete pass. The third quarter ended with the ball on the 48 yard line.

SECOND QUARTER:

Pearson kicked to Stinchcomb, who was tackled by Gorman on the 20 yard line. The Bears kicked to the Legion. It was received by Pearson on the Legion 30 yard line. Pearson was stopped by Halas, who spurted around the end like a flash. The Bears substituted in the game, Scott for Englund at the left end position. "Rowdy" Elliot carried the ball for a 6 yard gain on an end run. Gillo ran the ball and gained 4 yards. Pearson kicked the ball to the Bears and Halas received the ball for Chicago. Rhenstrom was laid out on the play. A run attempt by J. Sternaman was nailed (stopped) by Gillo. A run by D. Sternaman resulted in a first down for Chicago. On the next play, "Rowdy" Elliott was tackled Stinchcomb, pulling him back a couple yards on the run attempt. The Bears pulled D. Sternaman out of the game and substituted Wolquist in at left halfback. Pearson completed a beautiful pass to Linnan but the Legion turned the ball over on downs. Elliott broke up a Bears pass attempt. Barry was substituted in the game for Linnan. Elliott helped stop the Bears at the line on a run attempt and Chicago turned the ball over on downs. Racine's Rhenstrom carried the ball and it resulted in a 9 yard gain. Two run attempts by Rhenstrom and Pearson were stopped at the line of scrimmage. Gillo kicked to Chicago. J. Sternaman, who received the ball on the 30 yard line and the half was over.

THIRD QUARTER:

Gillo kicked the ball to the Chicago and Wolquist received it on the 8 yard line. He was able to advance the ball 17 yards to the 25 yard line before being stopped. Lafleur gained 6 yards on a run. A run by Lanum gave Chicago their fifth first down. Garvey punted to the Legion. Pearson received the ball on the Racine 23 yard line. Elliot gained 2 yards on a run attempt. Elliott lost 1 yard after a Racine fumble. Not being able to covert the first down, Racine would be forced to turn the ball back over to Chicago. Pearson punted to Chicago. J. Sternaman received the ball and returned it 15 yards, where he was nailed by Barry on the Bears 45 yard line. Due to injury, Racine substituted Roessler in the game for Rhenstrom, who was originally injured in the second quarter. A run by Lafleur gained 5 yards. Lanum added 2 more yards on a run. A pass from Walquist to J. Sternaman netted 5 yards and a first down for the Bears. Two successful run attempts by both Lafleur and Lanum gave Chicago another first down, putting the ball on Racine's 18 yard line. The Legion substituted Linnan in the game for Woodin. Another run by Lanum, resulted in a 3 yard gain. Lafleur gained a total of 6 yards in two run attempts. Another Lafleur run attempt was stopped by Barry. J. Sternaman attempted a drop kick for field goal but it failed to go over the bar. The Legion substituted Foster in the game for Langhoff. Two run attempt gains by Gillo and a 5 yard penalty for being off sides by the Bears, gave the Legion a first down. Gillo added another 7 yard gain on a run attempt. The Legion could not make a first down, therefore the Legion punted. Pearson kicked to the Bears. Walquist received the ball on the 23 yard line. He advanced the ball 11 yards on the kick return. He was tackled by Roessler. The Bears would get one more play in before the quarter ended. Dutch Sternaman gained about 7 yards and the ball was on the 41 yard line as the quarter ended.

FOURTH QUARTER:

   With two runs by Lafleur and J. Sternaman, the Bears advanced the ball for a Chicago first down. Dutch Sternaman gained 15 yards in two run attempts. The ball was on Racine 40 yard line. Walquist gained 5 yards on a run attempt. Two Chicago passes went incomplete. Dutch Sternaman dropped back to the 45 yard line and sent a successful place kick across the bar. The ball struck the bar and bounced over. *Score: Chicago 6, Racine 0.* Racine substituted Dalton in the game for Pearson. Gillo kicked off to the Bears. Walquist received the ball on the Bears 8 yard line. Walquist advanced the kick return to the 33 yard line. The Bears were unable to complete their pass attempts and punted the ball to Racine. Elliott received the ball on the Racine 45 yard line. Racine started to open up the game. A short pass from Dalton to Elliott gained 5 yards for the Legion. A run by Gillo gave Racine a first down. Elliott ran the ball ran and it resulted in a 2 yard gain. Racine substituted Magill in the game for George. Two pass attempts went incomplete and the Legion decided to punt. Magill punted the ball into the end zone and the ball was brought out to the 20 yard line for a touchback. Sternaman ran and it resulted in a 5 yard gain. Stinchcomb added 10 more yards on a run and a Chicago first down. Dutch Sternaman ran the ball and it resulted in a 9 yard gain. Stinchcomb was unable to gain any yards on a run attempt and the Legion stopped the Bears. Chicago punted from Racine 45 yard line. The punt rolled and Dalton tried to let the ball roll over the goal line but it stopped on the one yard line. Magill punted the ball for the Legion and it went out to Racine 40 yard line. J. Sternaman carried the ball for a 5 yard gain. Dutch Sternaman gained 2 more yards as the whistle blew to end the game.

FINAL SCORE: HORLICK- RACINE LEGION 0, CHICAGO BEARS 6.

SCORE BY PERIODS:	1st	2nd	3rd	4th	Final
Horlick-Racine Legion	0	0	0	0	0
Chicago Bears	3	0	0	3	6

STARTING ROSTER:

RACINE		CHICAGO
Hayes	Left End	Englund
Woodin	Left Tackle	Garvey
George	Left Guard	Anderson
Schackelton	Center	Larson
Hueller	Right Guard	Smith
Linnan	Right Tackle	Blacklock
Rhenstrom	Right End	Halas
Pearson	Quarterback	J. Sternaman
Elliott	Left Halfback	E. Sternaman
Foster	Right Halfback	Stinchcomb
Gillo	Fullback	LaFleur

SUBSTITUTIONS: RACINE – Gorman for Hueller, Berry for Linnan, Roessler for Rhenstrom, Linnan for Woodin, Langhoff for Foster, Magill for George, Dalton for Pearson. CHICAGO – Scott for Garvey, Garvey for Englund, Walquist for Lanum, Englund for Garvey, Stinchcomb for Walquist, Garvey for Englund, Halas for Hanchie.

FIELD GOALS: E. Sternaman (2).
FIRST DOWNS: Racine (5), Chicago (2).

REFEREE: Downs (Milwaukee)
UMPIRE: Whitlock (Michigan)
HEAD LINESMAN: Penhallegon (Wabash)
TIMER: Fred Maxted (Racine)

HORLICK-RACINE GRIDDERS HOLD BEARS TO 6-0 SCORE

The Legion management was pleased with the crowd that attended the game as well as the fact that none of their players were seriously injured. Although the Horlick-Racine Legion lost their first NFL game, they held the defending World's Champions from scoring a touchdown. In the past two years, no other opponent was able to hold the Bears out of the end zone. This proved to Chicago and the rest of the NFL, the fact that the Legion would be a serious contender in the National Football League. Chicago Bears Owner, Team Manager, and Player, George Halas was quoted as saying; *"The Racine team is one of the strongest the Bears have ever met. We played no stronger team last season, when we won the World's Championship"* This was a great compliment to the Horlick-Racine Legion team and despite the loss, it established Horlick Athletic Field to be known as the home of a tough NFL title contender. The Bears were not expecting such a great battle with the Legion. The following statement was made to the Chicago Bears on that Sunday afternoon in October of 1922;

WELCOME TO HORLICKVILLE!

The Legion would travel to play their next opponent, the Green Bay Packers. Several Racine football teams previously played the Packers in Green Bay, Wisconsin, so this would be a familiar place to the fans as well as a few of the Legion players. Manager Ruetz gave the team a few days off following Sunday's game and the plan was to resume practice on Wednesday. Ruetz told the team that they would practice Wednesday, Thursday and Friday evenings and then they would head to Green Bay, Wisconsin, early Saturday morning.

Plans for the spectators, who wanted to attend the game were made for the game against Packers. Instead of taking the train to Green Bay, arrangements were made to take buses. The Legion management would have to put up a guarantee of $1040 and the fare would come to about $10.50 per person for the fans. Tommy Smader, who was an alderman for the city of Racine and the owner of Tom Smader's Place (A Racine, Wisconsin Tavern) was one of the most active organizers of the buses to Green Bay, Wisconsin. He made plans to have three buses, which were capable of carrying 75 to 100 people to the game. Those buses would leave Smader's headquarters (Smader's Tavern) 333 Main Street in Racine, Wisconsin at 6 am and arrive in Green Bay, Wisconsin at around 11:30 am on game day. The return trip back to Racine would take place after the game, when they fans decided to board the buses. Besides the fans buses, there were many others, who planned to travel to the game via automobile. There were several drivers, who had extra seats to offer to other fans interested in driving with them. Those interested in attending were instructed to call Jack Carls at the J.I. Case T.M. Plant. Legion booster signs were also made available to pick up at Smader's Place for the automobiles making the trip to Green Bay, Wisconsin for the game. Tickets for the game were in big demand, so Legion Team Manager Ruetz made arrangements to have 150 choice seats to be held at Beaumont Hotel in Green Bay until 1 pm on Sunday. The Racine fans would be able to pick them up upon arrival there.

17

In the meantime, while fan travel plans were being made, Manager Ruetz decided to start practicing at Lakeview Park on Tuesday in preparation for the upcoming game against the Packers. A large crowd gathered to watch the team practice. It was decided that practice would be at 4:00 pm for the rest of the week. This would give the team a chance to play in the daylight as well as allow the fans to get a good look at them. The Horlick-Racine Legion was well aware of their next opponent. The Packers had also lost their 1922 NFL home opener but Racine would not take Captain Lambeau's team lightly. Coach Hollenback and George "Babe" Ruetz began focusing on pass defense during their practices. They felt that if they had been able to stop Chicago from completing some of their passes, they would have never had the field position to score their points. The Packers lost to the Rock Island Independents on the prior Sunday by a score of 14-19. Green Bay had scored both their touchdowns on passes and they also had a strong defense. They spent most of the game on their own side of the field but several times, they were able to hold Rock Island from scoring.

Earl "Bud" Gorman, who played guard for the Legion in the game against the Bears was moved to the tackle position for practice. The coaches decided that he would stay at tackle position for the game against the Packers. Under the direction of Coach Hollenback and Captain Gillo, the Racine team practiced defending every pass play possible in order to prepare for the Green Bay Packers.

Team Manager Ruetz announced the starters for team as follows; Norbert Hayes (left end), Whitey Woodin (left tackle), Carl George (left guard), Vincent Shackelton (center), Jack Hueller (right guard), Earl Gorman (right tackle), Elmer Rhenstrom (right end), Dudley Pearson (quarterback), Al Elliott (left halfback), Hank Gillo (fullback) and Bob Foster (right halfback).

C.M. & St. Paul Ry. Station- Racine, Wisc.

The Horlick-Racine Legion team left Racine on Saturday October 7th, 1922 at 9:00 pm via a special Pullman train car on the St. Paul railroad. The arrival time was set for 4:00 am in Green Bay, Wisconsin. The team slept until 6:00 am, at which time, they were awakened by Legion Team Manager George Ruetz. Ruetz had crowded himself into a small upper bunk in the train on the way to Green Bay, so his players could take the larger bunks. He agonized through an uncomfortable night of sleep but he wanted his players to be in good shape for the game against the Packers.

** GAME DAY **

About 200 fans made the trip to watch the Horlick-Racine Legion play the Green Bay Packers. The Packers jumped out to an early lead by scoring a touchdown on a blocked punt but they were unable to get the extra point. The Legion offense would answer that score with a touchdown in the second quarter. On offense, Gillo and Elliott had several runs attempts, which gained big yards. Elliott scored the Legion's only touchdown. Gillo was exceptional in his overall kicking, which included a successful field goal. Elliott played a great game on defense. He was an outstanding player in defending against the many passes of Curly Lambeau. This game was considered an informal "Wisconsin State Championship" playoff game. The trio of Racine, Green Bay and Milwaukee NFL teams would keep track of the best record of head to head games between the teams. This was more than just any NFL League season game, it was the bragging rights of the State of Wisconsin, which was at stake, when these teams played. The Packers outplayed the Legion in the second half and kept the ball in Racine territory for most of the half. With five minutes to play, the Packers started a pass attack in a desperate attempt to win the game. The Legion knocked down several of Lambeau's long passes and held off Green Bay. Player tempers reached a boiling point on the Racine bench when Bob Foster exchanged words with the head linesman about the ball placement. Foster was ejected from the game. Late in the game, Schackleton blew up on a call and threw his head gear onto the bench with a few seconds to go in the game. It was a close, hard fought, emotional game and the Legion team was not pleased with their performance in the second half. Racine made twelve first downs in the first half to six for Green Bay. In the second half, the Packers had eight first downs, while the Legion only had two. The Horlick-Racine Legion defeated the Green Bay Packers by a score of 10 to 6.

PLAY BY PLAY: 1922 NFL SEASON HRL GAME 2
HORLICK-RACINE LEGION VS GREEN BAY PACKERS
Sunday: October 8th, 1922   2:30 pm
Hagemeister Park   Green Bay, Wisconsin

FIRST QUARTER:
  Captain Hank Gillo of the Horlick-Racine Legion kicked off and the ball was received Curly Lambeau of the Green Bay Packers. He ran the ball back to the 25 yard line. Mills gained 2 yards on a run up the middle. The Packers gained two more yards on another run up the middle. Lambeau ran down the line and it resulted in 2 more yards of gain for Green Bay. Cub Buck punted to the Legion and Racine received the ball on the 15 yard line. A run attempt by Elliott was held for no gain. Gillo would gain about a yard and a half on a run up the middle. Pearson gained 3 yards on a run up the middle. Pearson attempted to punt the ball to Green Bay but it was blocked by Wheeler. Lambeau fell on the ball in the back of the end zone and he scored a touchdown for the Packers. Buck was unsuccessful with the place kick for extra point from the 24 yard line. *Score: Racine 0, Green Bay 6.* Gillo kicked off to the Packers with 4 minutes to go. The ball was kicked to the 30 yard line and it was advanced to the 50 yard line by Mathys. Cronin was thrown for a slight loss on an attempted cross tackle play. Buck punted the ball to Racine and it went the Legion goal line. Gillo received the ball and he was tackled after advancing

19

it only two yards. Gillo ran the ball off the line and it resulted in a 2 yard gain. Elliott failed to make a gain with a cross tackle play attempt. Elliott ran the ball and it resulted in a first down for the Legion. Gillo gained 3 yards on a running play, which went through the line. Langhoff gained 2 yards on a cross tackle play. Elliott was thrown for a 2 yard loss after the run attempt. Pearson punted to the Packers. Lambeau received the ball on the 35 yard line and he was stopped in his tracks. Lambeau ran the ball and it resulted in a 3 yard gain with a run around the left end. Lambeau gained 5 yards on a run through the line. Mills gained about a half yard on a run attempt. Buck made a first down and the ball on the 50 yard line. Cronin gained 3 yards with a run around the right end. A completed pass gave the Packers a 6 yard gain. Cronin made a first down with a run around the right end. Mills ran the ball through the line and it resulted in a 5 yard gain. Lambeau gained 1 yard on an off tackle play. Lambeau ran the ball and resulted in a first down with the ball on the 20 yard line. Mills gained 2 yards each on two running plays through the line. A Green Bay completed pass put the ball on the Legion 5 yard line. The Legion pulled Dalton out of the game and substituted Pearson in the game. Lambeau gained 1 yard around the left end. A Mills run attempt was stopped with no gain. A Packers pass went incomplete at the goal line. Langhoff was able to get through the line on an attempted field goal kick by Lambeau. Although it was unsuccessful, he made a beautiful place kick which nearly crossed the bar. The possession of the ball was given back to the Legion on the Racine 20 yard line. Langhoff gained 2 yards on a run as the ended the quarter.

SECOND QUARTER:

Racine had the ball on the Legion 22 yard line. A run up the middle by Gillo resulted in a gain of 7 yards. Racine substituted Hueller in the game for Gorman. The Legion could not get the first down. Langhoff punted to Green Bay. Mathys received the ball on the Packers 10 yard line and advanced it to 35 yard line. Green Bay could not make a first down. Lambeau punted to Racine. Langhoff received the ball on the ten yard line and he advanced it to the 30 yard line. Elliott gained 5 yards on a run off tackle play. On the next play, Elliott gained 10 yards running through the line. Gillo gained 1 yard on a run attempt. Elliott ran the ball and it resulted in a first down. Dalton was stopped with no gain on a run attempt. Elliott gained 20 yards on a run around the end. Elliott added 4 yards with a run through the line. Dalton gained 4 yards on a run. A Racine run resulted in no gain. It was fourth down and goal to go. The ball was on the 2 yard line. Elliott ran the ball over the top of the players and scored a Racine touchdown. Gillo successfully kicked the extra point. _Score: Racine 7, Green Bay 6._ Gillo kicked off to Green Bay and it reached the Packers goal line. The ball was advanced to the 10 yard line, where Dalton tackled the runner. On first down, the Packers fumbled and recovered their fumble. A Lambeau run around the right end resulted in no gain. A Packers attempt to run the ball resulted in no gain. Buck punted to Racine and the ball went down the center of the field. Elliott returned the ball to the Packers 30 yard line. Elliott gained 2 yards with an off tackle run. A Legion pass attempt was incomplete. Gillo set up for a field goal attempt from the 40 yard line but changed his mind. The Legion attempted a pass but it went incomplete. Dalton punted the ball out of the end zone and the Packers took possession of the ball on the 20 yard line. Lambeau attempted a run around the end but was stopped with no gain. Mills gain 2 yards with a run through the line. Cronin gained 7 yards with a run around the end. Buck punted the ball to the 40 yard line and it was received by Langhoff for Racine. He returned the ball to the 20 yard line of the Packers. Gillo gained 8 yards with a run through the line. Langhoff ran the ball for 5 yards and handed it off to Gillo, who was tackled. He was credited for a first down. Elliott ran the ball and it resulted in no gain. Elliott ran the ball and it resulted in a 2 yard gain. A Legion completed pass from Dalton to Langhoff put the ball on the 2 yard line. Gillo kicked a successful field goal from the 15 yard line and scored three more points for Racine. *Score: Racine 10, Green Bay 6.* Gillo kicked off to the Packers and the ball went over the Packers goal line, where it was received by Lambeau. He advanced the ball 10 yards before being tackled. A pass by Buck went incomplete. Another Buck pass was incomplete. A run attempt by the Packers resulted in no gain. The Packers punted the ball and it went out of bounds at the 10 yard line. Racine took possession of the ball. Langhoff gained 1 yard on an off tackle play. A run by Dalton resulted in a gain of 1 yard. A Legion pass from Dalton to Elliott resulted in a 10 yard gain. Gillo gained 1 yard on a run through the line. A Racine run attempt resulted in no gain. Another Legion run attempt resulted in no gain. Green Bay holds the Legion to no gain on fourth down and regained possession of the ball. The Packers attempted a run through the line but they were stopped with no gain. End of the quarter.

THIRD QUARTER:

Captain Hank Gill kicked off to the Packers. Green Bay received the ball on the 10 yard line and the ball was advanced on the kick off to the 32 yard line. Mills lost 1 yard on a run attempt. Lambeau gained 2 yards on a run attempt. The Packers threw an incomplete pass. Buck punted the ball to Racine and Langhoff received the ball on the 20 yard line. On first down, Langhoff was stopped on a run with no gain. Gillo gains 3 yards on a run attempt. Elliott gained 7 yards and a Racine first down. Gillo attempted to run the ball but it resulted in no gain. Dalton gained 7 yards on a short end run. A Legion pass attempt went incomplete. Dalton punted to the 25 yard line. Mathews received the ball for the Packers and he was stopped on the spot. Cronin gained 4 yards on a run around the end. Lambeau gained 10 yards on a run around the right end. Mills gained 6 yards on a run through the line. Lambeau was stopped with no gain by a team effort to advance the ball. Lambeau ran the ball and he gained enough yards for a Packers first down. The ball was on the Legion 45 yard line. Lambeau attempted a run around the left end but it resulted in no gain. A pass attempt by the Packers resulted in a 12 yard gain. Mills ran the ball around the end and he gained 3 yards. A second run around the end by Mills gained 2 yards for the Packers. Lambeau gained 3 yards with a run off left tackle. Cronin gained 2 .yards on a run attempt. Lambeau ran through the line and it resulted in a 1 yard gain. Cronin ran the ball and he made a first down with the ball being on the 10 yard line. Lambeau gained 2 yards on a run around the end. Cronin successfully carried the ball down to the 2 yard line. A run by Lambeau resulted in no gain. The Packers threw an incomplete pass on fourth down and therefore, the ball was turned over to Racine. Dalton gained 1 yard on a run. A Legion run resulted in no gain. Another Racine run attempt resulted in no gain. Gillo punted the ball to the 30 yard line. The ball was received by Lambeau and he was stopped, where he received it. A Lambeau run attempt was unsuccessful as he was thrown for a 2 yard loss. A Packers completed pass gave them a first down with the ball on the 20 yard line. Cronin gained 1 yard and the quarter ended.

<u>*FOURTH QUARTER:*</u>

The Packers had possession of the ball. Green Bay attempted a pass play, which ended up incomplete. Buck punted the ball to Racine, out of bounds on the 30 yard line. Racine took possession of the ball. Langhoff gained 1 yard on a run around the right end. The play was started out of a long snap formation. Gillo ran the ball and it resulted in a 4 yard gain. Elliott attempted to run the ball but it resulted in a 1 yard loss. Langhoff punted the ball to the Packers 30 yard line. The Packers began passing the ball and they were able to gain 5 yards. Racine was penalized 5 yards for being off sides. That penalty gave the Packers a first down. Mills gained 7 yards on a run attempt. Mills attempted a run but it resulted in no gain. Mills gained 5 yards and a Green Bay first down. The ball was located close to mid-field. A Cronin run attempt resulted in no gain. Mathys run the ball to 30 yard line. Racine substituted Gorman in the game for Bauman. Mathys ran the ball four times and he gained a first down for the Packers. The ball was on the 9 yard line. Lambeau gained 1 yard on a run. Davies substituted in the game for Mathys. A Cronin run attempt was thrown for a 1 yard loss. The Packers threw an incomplete pass. Racine took possession of the ball on the Legion 10 yard line. Gillo gained 1 yard with a run through the line. Gillo gained another 3 yards on a run. Racine fumbled the ball but Gillo recovered it. Langhoff punted the ball from the goal line to about mid-field. Davies received the ball for Green Bay and he was stopped in his tracks. Mills attempted to run the ball but it resulted in no gain. Lambeau gained 3 yards on a run. Dalton intercepted a Packers pass attempt. Racine took possession of the ball. Langhoff gained 2 yards on a run around the right end. Elliott fumbled the ball and Buck recovered it on the 30 yard line for Green Bay. Green Bay attempted a run but it resulted in no gain. A Green Bay pass attempt went incomplete. Lambeau gained 2 yards on a run around the left end. The Packers threw a long pass, which ended up incomplete. Racine took possession of the ball on the Legion 28 yard line. Elliott gained 1 yard on a run through the line. Langhoff gained 8 yards on a run attempt. Gillo ran the ball but it resulted in no gain. Langhoff punted the ball out of bounds at the Green Bay 15 yard line. Cronin was thrown for a 2 yard loss. The Packers threw an incomplete pass. Dalton was penalized on the play. The Packers completed a pass for less than 1 yard. Green Bay completed a pass, which resulted in a 9 yard gain. The Packers threw an incomplete pass. A Green Bay run attempt resulted in no gain. Racine took possession of the ball. The Legion completed a 10 yard pass. The ball was located around the 25 yard line. A Legion pass attempt went incomplete. A Racine run resulted in no gain. A Legion run attempt resulted in no gain. The Packers took possession of the ball. Lambeau made a fine run around the end and he advanced the ball to the Legion 15 yard line. A Mills run attempt resulted in no gain. Roessler threw Lambeau for a 10 yard loss resulting in an incomplete pass. The ball was on the 15 yard line. The Packers threw two more passes that both ended up incomplete. Racine took possession of the ball on the Legion 15 yard line. Dalton attempted to run the ball but it resulted in no gain. The game ended.

FINAL SCORE: HORLICK-RACINE LEGION 10, GREEN BAY PACKERS 6.

SCORE BY PERIODS:	1st	2nd	3rd	4th	Final
Horlick-Racine Legion	0	10	0	0	10
Green Bay Packers	6	0	0	0	6

STARTING ROSTER:

RACINE		GREEN BAY
Hayes	Left End	Wheeler
Berry	Left Tackle	Buck
Gorman	Left Guard	Owens
Schackelton	Center	Secord
Magill	Right Guard	Gardner
Baumann	Right Tackle	Murray
Roessler	Right End	Dunnigan
Pearson	Quarterback	Mathys
Langhoff	Left Halfback	Cronin
Elliott	Right Halfback	Lambeau
Gillo	Fullback	Mills

SUBSTITUTIONS: RACINE-Dalton for Pearson, George for Bauman, Hueller for Gorman. GREEN BAY-Regnier for Mathys.

TOUCHDOWNS: Green Bay- Lambeau (1), Racine-Elliott (1)
POINT AFTER TOUCHDOWN: Racine-Gillo (1)
FIELD GOAL: Racine-Gillo (1)

REFEREE: Downer (Milwaukee)
UMPIRE: Davy (Wisconsin)
HEAD LINESMAN: Wiley (Indiana)

   The ride back to Racine was much different than the trip going to Green Bay for George Ruetz. He had a large lower bunk all to himself. He kept the players awake by joyfully humming the tune "All by my Self".
   After the victory, the Racine fans were looking forward to the Legion's next opponent, the Milwaukee Badgers. Like the Legion, the Badgers were new to the NFL but not new to professional football. Milwaukee had played Racine the year before and everyone was anticipating a good rematch.
   The Legion would be the away team but the travel distance to Milwaukee was much shorter than Green Bay. Both teams were expecting a crowd of around 10,000

23

fans with about 2,000 of those fans coming from Racine, Wisconsin. This game would also serve as another unofficial "Wisconsin State Championship" playoff game. The team returned to practice on Wednesday night in preparation for the Badgers. Manager Ruetz and Coach Hollenback were pleased with how their substitutes filled in against the Packers and they planned for some changes to the line-up against the Badgers.

Ruetz and the Legion Team Business Manager Max Zirbes traveled on Wednesday to meet with Milwaukee Badgers team management. They were expecting a large crowd for the game and they wanted all the details worked out ahead of time. They both would return Thursday to meet again with the Milwaukee

C. & N. W. Railway Station- Racine, Wisc.

team management before releasing the details of the game. Ruetz and Zirbes later announced that the entire west side of the Athletic field in Milwaukee had been reserved for Racine fans to occupy during the game. They had completed arrangements, which would accommodate 2,500 to 3,000 Legion fans. Tickets were placed on sale at Rehl's Cigar Stores, Monument Cigar Store and Tom Smader's Place starting on

Friday morning. They would remain on sale until Saturday at 10:30 pm. Any person, who purchased tickets would be guaranteed a seat in the Racine section at the Athletic Park. The Athletic Park was located on the corner of Eighth and Chambers streets in Milwaukee, Wisconsin. The North Shore Line had several trains on the schedule, which frequently traveled to Milwaukee from Racine. Also, this was a short distance to travel in an automobile and many planned to make the trip.

A Legion team practice was held again on Thursday night as well. Prior to their Thursday evening practice, the Legion team headed to Monument Square in downtown Racine. They were honored at a special celebration for the "Made-in-Racine" week. Main Street was roped off from 6th Street to 8th Street to allow for the large crowds to gather during the festivities. The event began at 4:00 pm and the

last event was scheduled to start at 9:00 pm. A "Big Free Dance" was held on Main Street in downtown Racine, Wisconsin and it was again stretching from 6th to 8th Streets with band music being played. Racine products were exhibited in the windows and they drew large crowds of spectators. There was a Ferris wheel and a Merry-go-Round, which were kept full throughout the night despite the chilling lake breezes. The Horlick-Racine Legion football team was announced to the crowd, starting with Team Manager George "Babe" Ruetz.

24

He was announced as the greatest football manager in the country and this brought a wide grin to George's face as he was presented to the crowd. Also, greeted with wild cheers was Legion Trainer Hank Larsen. He would introduce each player from the team. Legion fans seemed to make up a large portion of the audience, since they seemed to know the players before they were introduced.

Preparations for the upcoming game with Milwaukee included techniques to stop their star halfback named Fritz Pollard. He was already considered one of the greatest players of the pro game. He was unique for the fact that he was one of the few black players in the NFL at the time. The Badgers were exceptionally strong in the passing game and they also had a tough defense. Milwaukee had three of Walter Camp's All-American's in their line-up. One of them was Paul Robeson of Rutgers. Walter Camp described him as being one of the greatest defensive ends ever and he said that he was a very powerful player. Robeson was also Black. Camp was quoted as saying, *"There may be Hinkeys, Shevlins, Kilpatricks and Hardwicks but there never was a Robeson and doubt if there ever will be."* Robeson was 6 feet 4 inches. In their game, which was held the week before, he stopped every play that came his way. The Legion was in for a tough battle.

Jack Karls announced that he had left over banners from the supply made for motorists, who attended the Legion-Packers game. He took the banners to Tom Smader's Place on Main Street and Karls said that anyone driving to the game was welcome to pick one up. Racine cheer leaders accompanied the team to Milwaukee. They performed in front of the Racine bleachers. Also, The Racine Legion drum and bugle corps traveled with the football team to Milwaukee, too. Members of the drum corps were asked to call Fred Maxted on Saturday evening or stop down to the Racine Elks club at 10:00 am on Sunday morning. Upon calling Maxted, they would be given information about where to meet at the game or Racine fans with automobiles would provide a ride for drum corps members to Milwaukee. The Racine Legion drum and bugle corps would play outside of the field prior to the game and also inside the Athletic Park during the game.

Manager Ruetz announced, the line-up for the game on Sunday was as follows: Rhenstrom -left end, Woodin-left tackle, Hueller-left guard, Shackelton-center, MaGill-right guard, Linnan-right tackle, Roessler-right end, Dalton-quarterback, Langhoff-left half back, Gillo-fullback, and Elliott-right halfback.

** GAME DAY **

It was estimated the more than 2,500 Racine fans made the trip to Milwaukee for the game. They occupied the entire west section of the grandstand during the game at Athletic Park. Bill Nevin led the cheering of the Racine fans. He was a regular leader of the cheers and yells of the Legion team. He made the crowd so excited and enthusiastic that a Milwaukee fan jumped from their section and tried to emulate Bill.

The Legion drum and bugle corps was there in full force. They made the Racine fans proud as they marched onto the field in their clean white uniforms and played in perfect rhythm on their drums and bugles. They were given a great ovation, when they passed the Milwaukee Badgers seating section, which their fans occupied.

The Milwaukee Badgers outplayed the Horlick-Racine Legion and it resulted in a 20-0 shutout by Milwaukee. The Badgers scored a touchdown within the first seven minutes of the first quarter. They would score a total of three touchdowns and two extra points. Milwaukee Badgers, Fritz Pollard shined in the game. He was able to complete 9 of 16 passes to his targets, Purdy and Doane. The Badgers offense was able to open big holes in the Legion defense and this was how they were successful in the running game. They also had several long passes. Hank Gillo was the only consistent runner for the Legion. On offense, he was the key player that the Legion relied on. He repeatedly gained yards for the team. On defense, he contributed to most of the tackles. He repeatedly stopped plays and made tackles after the Legion defensive line allowed runners to get through the line. "Rowdy" Elliott was unable to get through the Badgers defense until the fourth quarter and then only for short gains. Milwaukee had added two players, Earl Potteiger and George Seasholtz to their roster at the end of the week. Both men made significant contributions to the Badgers team in the game against Racine. Weather conditions were dry and ideal for a football game.

PLAY BY PLAY: 1922 NFL SEASON HRL GAME 3
                HORLICK-RACINE LEGION VS MILWAUKEE BADGERS
                Sunday: October 15th, 1922   2:30 pm
                Athletic Park   Milwaukee, Wisconsin

FIRST QUARTER:
Milwaukee Badgers, Fritz Pollard kicked to Racine and Hank Gillo received the ball on the Legion goal line. He advanced it to the Legion 21 yard line before being tackled. Runs off tackle by Elliott and Langhoff failed to gain any yards on run attempts through the line. Langhoff kicked to Milwaukee, down the center of the field and Pollard received the ball and he ran out of bounds at the 40 yard line on the return. A King run failed to gain any yards. Purdy ran the ball off the right tackle and he gained 4 yards. Doane ran the ball through the line and it resulted in a 1 yard gain. Milwaukee threw an incomplete pass attempt to Robeson. The Badgers were penalized 15 yards for a holding call and that brought the ball back to the 40 yard line. Pollard threw an incomplete pass. Pollard ran through the line and it resulted in a 12 yard gain. He was stopped by Gillo. Robeson threw an incomplete pass. Racine took possession of the ball on the 28 yard line. A run by Dalton failed to gain any yards. Alexander blocked a Gillo pass attempt and he recovered the ball for Milwaukee. He was tackled by Roessler after he took possession of the ball. Pollard ran the ball and it resulted in a 7 yard gain. Purdy ran the ball through the line and he gained 1 yard. A Badgers pass to Robeson advanced the ball to the 3 yard line. Pollard slipped around the left end and it resulted in a Milwaukee touchdown. Gillo was attempting to tackle Pollard but he couldn't stop him from crossing the goal line. Pollard kicked a successful extra point attempt. *Score: Milwaukee 7, Racine 0.* Gillo kicked off the Milwaukee and it was received on the 10 yard line. The ball was advanced on the kick return to the 30 yard line.

The Badgers offense was successful with running the ball around the end as well as through the line. They also passed the ball well. Milwaukee was able to steadily advance the ball down the field to the Racine 30 yard line. The next set of downs resulted in a short gain and incomplete passes. Racine took possession of the ball. A short run be Langhoff and a penalty by Milwaukee gave the Legion a first down on the 35 yard line. Dalton was thrown for a loss but Milwaukee was penalized again and this gave the Racine another first down. Gillo was successful with two running plays through the line and they resulted in gains of 3 and 8 yards. It was a first down for Racine. The Legion attempted two running plays off the tackle and both failed. Racine was penalized for being off sides and the ball was located on the 50 yard line. An incomplete pass by the Legion and Milwaukee took possession of the ball at the 50 yard line as the quarter ended.

SECOND QUARTER:

Pierrotti punted on the first play of the second quarter for the Badgers. Langhoff received the ball on the 15 yard line. It was fumbled by Langhoff and recovered by Milwaukee. Pottieger went in the game at fullback for Milwaukee. An off tackle run by Pollard resulted in no gain. A Milwaukee pass attempt went incomplete. A Badgers pass attempt was completed to the Racine 1 yard line. A field goal attempt by King was blocked but Milwaukee recovered the ball on the 25 yard line. A completed Badgers pass put the ball on the Racine 11 yard line. Pollard ran the ball off tackle and it resulted in a gain. Pollard ran the ball off tackle to score a Badgers touchdown. Purdy drop kick the extra point attempt but it was not successful. *Score: Racine 0, Milwaukee 13.* Gillo kicked off to Milwaukee. Pollard received the ball and he was downed on the 30 yard line. Milwaukee was successful with three running plays through the line and they were able to get the ball to the 41 yard line. The Legion held Milwaukee on downs and regain possession of the ball. Racine substituted Pearson in the game for Dalton. A run around the end by Elliott gained 6 yards for the Legion but the quarter ended.

THIRD QUARTER:

Milwaukee substituted Seasholtz in the game for Pollard. Gillo kicked off to Milwaukee 20 yard line and the Badgers advanced the ball but they were stopped at the 39 yard line. Two off tackle runs by the Badgers put the ball at the 48 yard line. Another run by the Badgers failed to gain and they choose to punt. A Badgers punt was received by Pearson on the Racine 10 yard line. He advanced the ball to the 29 yard line. Milwaukee was penalized for being off sides on first down and the down was replayed. Three attempted running plays around the end by the Legion failed to gain any yards. Pearson punted to Milwaukee and the ball was downed on the 34 yard line. The Badgers gained a total of 4 yards in three downs by running through the line. Milwaukee punted the ball to Racine. The punt was received by Gillo on the 10 yard line and he advanced it to the 25 yard line. A run by Elliott gained 3 yards. Pearson gained a total of 8 yards on two running plays around the end and it was a first down for the Legion. Gillo gained 8 yards on a run through the line. Run attempts by Elliott and Langhoff resulted in no gain. Racine punted to Milwaukee and the ball was downed on Milwaukee 26 yard line. The Badgers gained a total of 18 yards on run attempts by Pottieger and Seasholtz.

Racine held the Badgers without gain on 2nd and 3rd down and Milwaukee punted the ball to the Legion. The Badgers punt was received by Pearson on the five yard line and he was unable to advance the ball. The Legion was unable to gain. Pearson punted to Milwaukee and the ball went out of bounds at the 45 yard line. Racine substituted Dalton in the game for Pearson. A Milwaukee pass attempt went incomplete. Dalton intercepted a Badgers pass attempt on the Racine 14 yard line. A run attempt by Racine resulted in no gain. Langhoff punted to Milwaukee and the ball was downed on the Racine 35 yard line as the quarter ended.

FOURTH QUARTER:

Pollard and Doane went back in the game for Milwaukee. The Badgers advanced the ball down to the 15 yard line with run attempts through the line and around the end by Pollard and Doane. A completed pass from Purdy to Pollard put the ball on the Racine 3 yard line. Doane scored a touchdown and Pollard was successful with the extra point kick. *Score: Racine 0, Milwaukee 20*. Gillo kicked off to the Badgers and Doane received the ball on the 10 yard line. He returned the ball to around the 50 yard line. A holding penalty on Milwaukee brought the ball back to the 20 yard line. Milwaukee turned the ball over to Racine on downs. Racine attempted to pass the ball on all three downs but they were all incomplete. Racine punted the ball and it went into the end zone. Milwaukee took possession of the ball with a first down on the 20 yard line. The Badgers ended up punting the ball to the Legion and the ball was downed around the 50 yard line. Racine gained a total of 3 yards on pass attempts and they decided to punt the ball to the Badgers. Milwaukee could not gain and they punted the ball back to the Legion. Racine took possession of the ball back at the 50 yard line. A Legion pass to Elliott gained 3 yards. A completed Racine pass from Dalton to Gillo gained 8 yards but the game ended.

FINAL SCORE: HORLICK-RACINE LEGION 0, MILWAUKEE BADGERS 20.

SCORE BY PERIODS:

	1st	2nd	3rd	4th	Final
Horlick-Racine Legion	0	0	0	0	0
Milwaukee Badgers	7	6	0	7	20

STARTING ROSTER:

RACINE		MILWAUKEE
Rhenstrom	Left End	Garrett
Woodin	Left Tackle	Webb
Hueller	Left Guard	Fallon
Schackelton	Center	Pierrotti
Magill	Right Guard	Duift
Linnan	Right Tackle	Alexander
Roessler	Right End	Robeson
Dalton	Quarterback	Purdy
Elliott	Left Halfback	King
Langhoff	Right Halfback	Pollard
Gillo	Fullback	Doane

SUBSTITUTIONS: RACINE – Pearson for Dalton, Gorman for McGill, Hayes for Rhenstrom, McGill for Hueller, Baumann for Linnan, Foster for McGill, Heinisch for Roessler. **MILWAUKEE** – Cullenan for Robeson, Robeson for Cullenan, Cochran for Garrett, Garrett for Robeson, Potteiger for Doane, Doane for Potteiger, Seasholtz for Pollard, Pollard for King, Mooney for Purdy, Purdy for Mooney.

    Frank Linnan played half of the game with a broken leg. Frank broke a small bone in his leg during the early part of the game against Milwaukee but never told anyone on the team. He kept playing with the pain until the frequent hits did not allow him to tolerate it, anymore. Linnan was taken to Trinity Hospital in Milwaukee after the game. Due to the injury, he was lost for the season. Linnan was a star player from Marquette University. He played an exceptional college game against Norte Dame in his last year of college football. He was a valuable member of the Legion team and he definitely would be missed.

    Manager Ruetz was only pleased with the play of Hank Gillo in the game against the Badgers. He was not happy with how the rest of the team performed in the Milwaukee game. He was especially displeased with the linemen. He made plans to go to Chicago on Monday to find some new players, so he could replace some of the current members on the Racine roster. Ruetz's plan was to meet with George Halas of the Chicago Bears football club. He returned from Chicago on Monday after having a long conference with Halas and several former university football players. Halas was very accommodating to Ruetz and provided several talented prospects. George Ruetz set it up with the new recruits to be at the next Horlick-Racine Legion practice, which was scheduled for the next day (Tuesday) at Lakeview Park.

    The next game for Racine was against the Toledo Maroons at Horlick Athletic Field on the upcoming Sunday. Toledo was coming off a win over Hammond and they had previously tied Milwaukee. This game was originally scheduled to be played in Ohio but it was changed to Wisconsin. The Legion drum and bugle corps would be performing at halftime and a game ball from the Legion-Packers game would be presented to a fan at the game on that Sunday. They expected the winner to donate the ball to be displayed at the new Memorial Hall in downtown Racine. The reserved tickets for the game

were placed on sale Wednesday at Rehl's Cigar Stores (State and 6th Streets), Monument Cigar Store and Tom Smader's Place.

Captain Gillo addressed the team on Tuesday. He told the players that he was aware that every team has slumps and that the game against Milwaukee was the Legion's time. He reminded them how the team played an exceptionally well game in the Chicago loss and the victory over Green Bay. He stated that he wanted the team to come back strong on Sunday against the visiting Toledo team. He expressed that a win would put the team back in the right direction and they may get another chance at Milwaukee in a post season game. He also mentioned that the Legion was getting wonderful support from the fans and he wanted them to be worthy of this support.

The team practice for Friday was set to take place at 3:00 pm and the fans were encouraged to attend. Ruetz and Gillo were looking over the players and they were going to switch the line-up for the Toledo game. George had added four new players to the team. Ed Miller, who was a player with the Canton Bull Dogs in the prior season. He would contribute to the Legion line at left tackle. Norm Glocksin, who formerly played with the Racine Regulars was brought in. He played with Chicago in the prior season. He stood 6'3" and weighed 230 lbs. Art "Bull" Braman, a former Yale University player, who had experience playing professional football with the Buffalo All-Americans. He played tackle and weighed well over 210 lbs. Braman would replace Linnan at right tackle. "Jab" Murray, who previously played for the Green Bay Packers was also brought in. He was a former Marquette University star lineman, who was over 6 feet tall and weighed around 230 lbs. These experienced players would make immediate contributions to the Legion team. Another change to the line-up would be with Fritz Heinisch, who was local Racine player. Heinisch had played both professional and semi-pro football in Racine, Wisconsin. Fritz was a former player of the Horlick Standards professional football team. The 1921 Horlick Standards played a full schedule, which included games against the Green Bay Packers and the Racine Cardinals of Chicago. Ruetz decided to have Fritz start in the game against Toledo at left end. Heinisch was put into the game in last few minutes against Milwaukee and he was able to close a gap in the line and he also intercepted a long pass. Ruetz decided that Fritz proved himself as a quality player and earned a spot in the line-up.

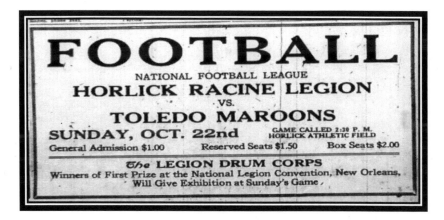

FOOTBALL
NATIONAL FOOTBALL LEAGUE
HORLICK RACINE LEGION
VS.
TOLEDO MAROONS
SUNDAY, OCT. 22nd   GAME CALLED 2:30 P. M. HORLICK ATHLETIC FIELD
General Admission $1.00   Reserved Seats $1.50   Box Seats $2.00

The LEGION DRUM CORPS
Winners of First Prize at the National Legion Convention, New Orleans, Will Give Exhibition at Sunday's Game

THE YELLS

Learn These Yells and Songs

Follow the Cheer Leader

No. 1
SKYROCKET

Siss——
Boom——
Ah——
(WHISTLE)
(name)

No. 2
NINE RAHS

Rah—Rah—Rah
Rah—Rah—Rah
Rah—Rah—Rah
(name) (name) (name)

No. 3
Racine Locomotive
(take it slow)

U—Raaah—Raaah
Ra——cine
U—Raah—Raah
Ra——cine
U—Rah—Rah
Racine
Hurray!

No. 4
(drag it out)

Hit 'em hard
Hit 'em low
Come on, Racine—
LET'S GO

No. 5
THREE RAHS
(take it slow)

Raaaah—
Raaaah—
Raaaah—
(name)

No. 6
(long and short)

Raaah —— Rah
Raaah —— Rah
Raaah —— Rah
Rah, Rah, Rah
RACINE

No. 7

Hold 'em — Racine
Hold 'em — Racine
Hold 'em — Racine

ON WISCONSIN

On Wisconsin! On Wisconsin!
　Plunge right through that line!
Run the ball clear 'round (visiting team)
　A touchdown sure this time—
　　　　Rah! Rah! Rah!
　　　　　(yell them)

On Wisconsin! On Wisconsin!
　Fight on for her fame.
Fight Fellows—
　　　　Fight! Fight! Fight!
　　　　　(yell them)

We'll win this game.

Tickets were selling well for the game and Bill Nevin, Legion lead cheer coordinator had some new cheers to shout out against the Maroons. Hank Gillo took charge of the team practices, all week. He was very knowledgeable of the game and he was developing a new pass attack defense for the Legion. Horlick Athletic Field was in excellent playing condition and this would be the first game, which the Legion played there, since their 1922 NFL home opener against the Chicago Bears.

** GAME DAY **

More than 3,500 fans came out to Horlick Athletic Field to witness the Legion outplay the Maroons during the entire first half of the game but unfortunately they had to witness the Horlick-Racine Legion football team playing poorly in the second half of the game. The Toledo Maroons defeated the Horlick-Racine Legion by a score of 7-0. Costly fumbles took the game from Racine. The Legion kept Toledo on their side of the field during the whole first quarter. They were able to get the ball down to the Toledo 20 yard line on first down during the game but Racine was unable to capitalize on their next three downs. Gillo was unsuccessful in an attempted field goal on fourth down and they lost their opportunity to score.

31

The same scenario would be repeated in the second quarter with the same result. The Legion had the ball on the 20 yard line and once again was held on three downs. Another field goal attempt by Gillo was unsuccessful. After that, Racine would not get another opportunity to score. Toledo would get the only score of the game, a touchdown in the third quarter. The following is a recap of the Maroon's score; they were thrown for a loss on the 50 yard line. On second down, Toledo was penalized 15 yards for holding. The Maroons decided to punt on third down. Elliott was called for clipping on the Racine 33 yard line and that gave Toledo the ball back at the spot of the foul. Annan, Phelan and Falcon successfully ran the ball and moved it down to the Racine 4 yard line. Falcon ran through the middle of the line for a touchdown and Warton added the extra point after touchdown on a place kick.

GAME RECAP/
PLAY BY PLAY: 1922 NFL SEASON HRL GAME 4
HORLICK-RACINE LEGION VS TOLEDO MAROONS
Sunday: October 22nd, 1922   2:30 pm
Horlick Athletic Field   Racine, Wisconsin

FIRST QUARTER:
After the kickoff, the Racine defense was successful in keeping the Toledo offense on their side of the field. The improved line held tough against their opponent. Braman, Gorman and Glocksin couldn't be penetrated in the first half. Fritz Heinisch was quick to help stop any run attack. The Legion was able to get the ball down to the Toledo 20 yard line but they were unable to capitalize on three downs. Gillo was unsuccessful in an attempted field goal on fourth down. The Maroons took possession of the ball. Toledo completed a 20 yard pass from Watson to Myers. This put the ball on Toledo's 40 yard line. Falcon ran the ball through the line and then turned it outside to get to around the 50 yard line. Gillo intercepted a Toledo pass at the Racine 47 yard line. He advanced the ball 4 yards before being tackled. A run by Dalton resulted in a 2 yard loss. A run by Gillo would get the Legion back to the line of scrimmage at the Toledo 49 yard line. End of the first quarter.
SECOND QUARTER:
A Racine pass by Langhoff went incomplete. Another pass attempt by Langhoff was caught by Gorman. He was an ineligible receiver and Toledo took over the ball on the 49 yard line. Elliott intercepted a Toledo pass on the Racine 30 yard line. The Maroons substituted in the game, Kelly for Jones. Two good run attempts by the Legion would get Racine a first down. Another run attempt gained about 5 yards. An off sides penalty by Toledo gave the Legion a first down on the 50 yard line. Langhoff ran the ball through the line and it resulted in 4 yard gain. Elliott ran the ball around the right end and it resulted in a gain of 35 yards. This put the ball on around the 12 yard line. Two run attempts by Elliott gained 2 yards. Racine was penalized 5 yards for being off sides. A Legion pass attempt went incomplete. Toledo committed an off side penalty as Gillo was attempting to drop kick the ball for a field goal from the 20 yard line. The penalty allowed Racine to retain

possession of the ball on the Toledo 15 yard line. Elliott ran the ball and it resulted in a 3 yard gain. An Elliott run attempt resulted in a fumble. Toledo recovered it on the 15 yard line. The Legion line was tough enough to hold the Maroons from getting a first down. Toledo punted the ball to Racine. Langhoff received the punt on the Toledo 45 yard line. He advanced the ball 13 yards before being tackled. The quarter ended with a zero to zero score.

THIRD QUARTER:

Hank Gillo kicked the ball off to the Toledo on the 10 yard line. Phelan received the ball and returned it to the 31 yard line. A Maroon run, by Phelan, was stopped and tackled for a loss of 7 yards by Heinisch. Dalton broke up a pass intended for Watson. Watson ran the ball and it resulted in an 18 yard gain as well as a Toledo first down. He was tackled by Gorman. Watson gained 8 yards on a run play, bringing the ball to the 50 yard line. Phelan was tackled for a loss on a run attempt. The Maroons were penalized 15 yards. The penalty took the ball back to their 35 yard line. Toledo punted the ball to the Legion. There was a penalty against "Rowdy" Elliott for clipping Meyers of Toledo in the back. The penalty was for 15 yards from the Racine 48 yard line. This gave the ball back to Toledo on Racine's 33 yard line. Watson gained 1 yard on a run attempt. A Toledo pass attempt went incomplete. A run attempt around the end by Annan advanced the ball to around the 20 yard line. This was a first down for Toledo. Racine substituted in the game, Hayes for Heinisch. The Legion was penalized 5 yards for Roessler being off sides on the play. Two separate run attempts through the line by Falcon gave Toledo another first down. The ball was on the 10 yard line. Hueller and Woodin substituted in the game for Gorman and Glockskin. Watson gained a total of 5 yards in two run attempts. Falcon took the ball into the end zone for a touchdown. A successful place kick by Watson added the point after touchdown. *Score: Racine 0, Toledo 7.* Annan received the kickoff from Gillo on the 15 yard line. He returned it to the 30 yard line. Annan and Watson combined to gain enough yards for a Toledo first down. Falcon gained 3 yards on a running play. Toledo was penalized 5 yards for being off sides. A Toledo pass to Peabody advanced the ball to their 45 yard line as the quarter ended.

FOURTH QUARTER:

Toledo completed another pass to Annan and he advanced the ball 1 yard after the reception. The Maroons punted to Racine and they took possession of the ball on the Legion 20 yard line. A run attempt by Elliott resulted in a loss of 2 yards. Toledo substituted in the game, White for Myers, at the end position. Racine could not gain any yards. Langhoff punted to the Maroons and Watson received the ball on the Toledo 35 yard line. Watson returned the punted ball to mid-field. Toledo was forced to punt to Racine. Langhoff received the ball and returned it 10 yards to the 30 yard line. Langhoff ran the ball through the line and it resulted in a 4 yard gain. Gillo fumbled the ball and Toledo recovered it on Racine 30 yard line. Watson gained a first down after gaining enough yards on three successful runs. Racine held Toledo from getting another first down. Watson attempted a place kick for a field goal but the kick was blocked by Dalton. Watson recovered the ball on the Racine 35 yard line and Toledo had possession. A run by Phelan resulted in a 2 yard gain.

Watson gained 7 yards on a run attempt. Toledo was penalized 5 yards for being off sides. A pass by Watson was completed to Phelan for an 8 yard gain. He advanced the ball to the 20 yard line. Watson gains 7 yards on a run attempt. Rausch gained 2 yards on a run attempt. Watson attempted a drop kick for field goal but it was blocked. The Maroons recovered the ball, again. They fail to make a first down and possession went to Racine. A 35 yard pass by Gillo went incomplete, after it was knocked down by a Toledo defender. Pearson, Foster and Rhenstrom were substituted into the game for Racine. A pass by Pearson went incomplete. Pearson punted out of bounds on the 42 yard line. Toledo took possession of the ball. Watson ran around the right end and it resulted in a 30 yard gain. This brought the ball to the Racine 12 yard line as the game ended.

FINAL SCORE: HORLICK-RACINE LEGION 0, TOLEDO MAROONS 7

SCORE BY PERIODS:	1st	2nd	3rd	4th	Final
Horlick-Racine Legion	0	0	0	0	0
Toledo Maroons	0	0	7	0	7

STARTING ROSTER:

RACINE		TOLEDO
Heinisch	Left End	Myers
Miller	Left Tackle	Stein
Gorman	Left Guard	Edwards
Murray	Center	Conrad
Glockskin	Right Guard	Jones
Braman	Right Tackle	Horning
Roessler	Right End	Peabody
Dalton	Quarterback	Watson
Langhoff	Left Halfback	Annan
Elliott	Right Halfback	Phelan
Gillo	Fullback	Falcon

SUBSTITUTIONS: RACINE –Hueller for Glockskin, Woodin for Gorman, Hayes for Heinisch, Pearson for Dalton, Foster for Langhoff, Rhenstrom for Roessler. TOLEDO-Kelly for Jones, White for Myers, Gozdowski for Falcon, Rousch for Annan, Petree for Phelan.

TOUCHDOWN: Toledo-Falcon (1)
POINT AFTER TOUCHDOWN: Toledo-Watson (1)

REFEREE: Cahn (Chicago)
UMPIRE: Strothart (Milwaukee Normal)
HEAD LINESMAN: Roe (Notre Dame)
FIELD JUDGE: Penhallegan (Wabash)

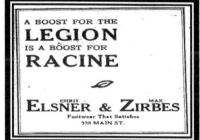

Charlie Dressen

Manager George "Babe" Ruetz announced on Tuesday that he signed two more new players to the Legion roster. Those players were Charlie Dressen, who played the quarterback position and Jack Mintun, who played the center position. Both men were former players of the Chicago (Staleys) Bears. George Halas released the players, so that Ruetz could sign them to a Horlick-Racine Legion player contract.

The Rochester Jeffersons from New York were the Legion's next opponent. They game would be played in Racine. The Jeffs arrived in Kenosha, Wisconsin on Tuesday, October 24, 1922 after the team traveled from Rock Island, Illinois. They played an NFL game on the previous Sunday against the Rock Island Independents. The Rochester management decided to save on travel time and expenses by going directly to Wisconsin and staying the week prior to the game in close proximity. The Rochester team would stay in Kenosha, Wisconsin and practice at Simmons Palace of Sunshine (Simmons Field in Kenosha). The Jeffs started practice on Tuesday afternoon. There were reports about the team from those, who attended their practices. The Rochester Jeffersons team was embraced by the Southport (Kenosha) people and crowds had gathered every day to watch them. Racine was expecting many fans from Kenosha, Wisconsin to attend the game at Horlick Athletic Field. The Kenosha fans planned to occupy the visitors sections and root for the Rochester Jeffs. A number of ticket reservations were made from several Wisconsin cities including Kenosha and Beloit. Members of the Beloit Fairies football team would be coming to support the Belle City (Racine) team. Tickets went on sale Wednesday and they were available at the Monument Cigar Store, Tom Smader's, and Rehl's Cigar Stores on Sixth and State Streets.

Rochester planned a special secret night practice under the lights of Simmons Field on Friday October 27th, 1922. It wasn't long before this information was out to the public. Racine sent scouts down to Kenosha for the Friday night practice in order to gather information about the team. Meanwhile, the Legion team was practicing at Lakeview Park since Tuesday. Captain Hank Gillo designed some new passing plays for the game on Sunday. He was working with new quarterback Charlie Dressen and the rest of the Legion team, all week at practice. Manager Ruetz announced the starting line-up along with their position and jersey number for the game against Rochester. They were as follows: Fritz Heinisch-LE No. 17, Ray Miller-LT No. 14, Earl Gorman-LG No. 11, Jack Mintun-C No. 15, Richard Murray-RG No. 2, Art Braman-RT No. 10, Fritz Roessler-RE No. 16, Charlie Dressen-QB No. 3, Irv Langhoff-RHB No. 8, Al Elliott-LHB No. 5 and Hank Gillo FB No. 1.

** GAME DAY **

JACK MINTIN, Center.

Jack Mintun

Hank Gillo proved on that Sunday that he was a one of the great players of the game. Gillo also showed why he was such a valuable player to the Horlick-Racine Legion Football team. He was successful in scoring three field goals and gave Racine a 9-0 victory over the Jeffs. It was agreed by all that Hank was easily the star of that game. He had several successful run attempts including one for a fourteen yard gain. Gillo played an all-around exceptional game with the support of his team. The leadership of new quarterback Dressen and the strength of Mintun, who played center showed that they were quality additions to the Legion team. Mintun opened big holes in the line for Gillo to run through and he also made several tackles on defense. Langhoff and Elliott contributed on offense in both the running and passing attack of Racine. "Rowdy" Elliott made some great cork screw drives through the middle of the line. "Candy" Miller and "Buddy" Braman solidified the defensive line and stopped Rochester from scoring. There were 3,000 plus fans, who attended the game at Horlick Athletic Field.

The Legion had two opportunities, with the ball on the 5 yard line, to score in the first half. The Jeffersons held them without a score. Gillo successfully gained yards, ranging from eight to fourteen yards on his running plays. He received a standing ovation, when he was taken out of the game with under a minute to go.

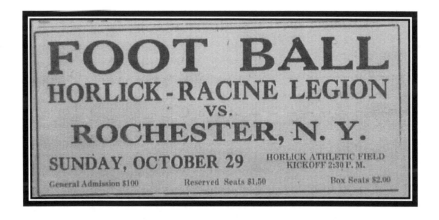

FOOT BALL
HORLICK-RACINE LEGION
vs.
ROCHESTER, N. Y.
SUNDAY, OCTOBER 29   HORLICK ATHLETIC FIELD
                       KICKOFF 2:30 P. M.
General Admission $1.00   Reserved Seats $1.50   Box Seats $2.00

PLAY BY PLAY: 1922 NFL SEASON HRL GAME 5
                 HORLICK-RACINE LEGION VS
                 ROCHESTER (NY) JEFFERSONS
                 Sunday: October 29th, 1922   2:30 pm
                 Horlick Athletic Field   Racine, Wisconsin

FIRST QUARTER:

Gillo kicked off to Rochester and the ball was received on the 2 yard line. The Jeff's advanced the ball to the 22 yard line and Langhoff made the tackle. Rochester's Miller attempted two runs, which were unsuccessful. Rochester fumbled the ball but they recovered it with a 10 yard gain and a first down. Two run attempts by the Jeff's failed to gain any yards. Lowery punted the ball to Racine and it went out of bounds on the Rochester 47 yard line. Langhoff gained 6 yards on a run attempt. Elliott gained 3 yards on a run attempt. Gillo ran the ball and it resulted in a gain of 5 yards and a Racine first down. Elliott gained 2 yards on a run play. Elliott ran the ball for another gain of 3 yards but he fumbled it on the 30 yard line. The ball was recovered by Rochester's Thompson. A run around the end by Argus gained 10 yards and a Jeff's first down. Roessler tackled Wynne for a 10 yard loss. Wynne gained 3 yards on a run play. Rochester punted the ball to the Racine 20 yard line. Dressen received the ball and advanced it to the 35 yard line. Rochester was penalized 5 yards for being off sides. A run by Elliott gained 7 yards. Langhoff ran the ball for 3 yard gain and a Racine first down. A run by Gillo gained 2 yards. Elliott threw a perfect pass to Langhoff. The pass resulted in a gain of 11 yards and the ball was on the 35 yard line. Gillo made a spectacular run, gaining 14 yards. The ball was on about the Rochester 20 yard line. Elliott gained 5 yards on a run play. A quarterback run play by Dressen gained 2 yards for the Legion. Elliott gained 5 yards on a run play. Gillo ran the ball and he gained about 1 yard. Elliott gained 2 yards on a run play. A run by Elliott was stopped with the ball on the 5 yard line. Elliott completed a pass to Roessler for a gain of 3 yards on fourth down. The ball was turned over on downs to Rochester. Rochester punted the ball to Racine from their end zone. The ball was received by Langhoff on the 40 yard line. He advanced the punt return 22 yards. Gillo gained 1 yard on a run. Gillo gained another 3 yards on a run. Dressen advanced the ball for a 2 yard gain. Racine gained close to 4 more yards but it was not enough for a first down and they lost the ball on downs. Rochester punted the ball. Dressen received the ball at the 35 yard line. He advanced the ball Rochester 24 yard line. A pass from Elliott to Langhoff gained 8 yards. A run around the end by Dressen gained 4 yards. The ball was on Rochester's 12 yard line and this ended the quarter. There was no score in the game.

SECOND QUARTER:

Racine had the ball on the Rochester 12 yard line. A Langhoff run attempt resulted in no gain. A Dressen run attempt resulted in no gain. Rochester was penalized 5 yards for holding. This gave Racine a first down. Langhoff failed to gain any yards on a run play. Run attempts by Gillo and Elliott gained a total of 3 yards. A run by Elliott was unsuccessful. Rochester took possession of the ball on the 4 yard line. Wynne and Argus combined with two run attempts through the line and one run around the end for a total of 10 yards. This gave the Jeff's a first down. Wilson attempted a run, which resulted in no gain and he was tackled by Roessler of Racine. Roessler tackled Wynne for a loss on a run attempt. Racine held Rochester to a gain of 4 yards in three downs. The Jeff's punted to the Legion and Dressen received the ball on the 20 yard line. He advanced the ball to the 29 yard line before being tackled. Elliott gained 6 yards on a run off tackle. Langhoff gained 6 yards and a first down on a run through the line. Dressen ran the ball and it resulted in a 4 yard gain. Gillo run gained 4 more yards on a run play. A Racine pass from Elliott to Langhoff put the ball on the 50 yard line. A Legion pass went incomplete. A Legion pass down the middle was intercepted by Smith. Argus gained 1 yard for Rochester. An off tackle run, by Wynne, gained 3 yards. Wynne gained another 7 yards with a run around the end. Braman was injured and Foster went in the game to play right tackle for the Legion. Mintun stopped Wynne on the Racine 40 yard line. Mintun tackled King for a loss. A Rochester pass went incomplete. The Jeff's punted the ball to the Legion. Wynne kicked the ball out of bounds on the Racine 1 yard line. Racine decided to punt to Rochester. Langhoff punted from the Legion end zone to the Racine 39 yard line. Murray stopped the Rochester quarterback on the 40 yard line. Rochester gained a total of 2 yards on two run attempts through the line. A Rochester run attempt resulted in a fumble. The ball was recovered by Roessler for Racine on the 35 yard line. A Legion pass attempt went incomplete. Rochester was penalized 5 yards. Langhoff gained 3 yards on a short run around the end. Elliott gain about 2 yards on a run off the left tackle but not enough for the first down. Langhoff punted the ball to the Jeffs and it went to 20 yard line. Roessler tackled the Rochester player after the reception and he fumbled the ball. Gillo recovered the fumble on the Racine 20 yard line. The quarter ended with no score in the game.

THIRD QUARTER:

Paul Meyers, a former University of Wisconsin star, substituted at the left end position for Rochester. Gillo kicked off to the Jeffs and the ball went to the Rochester 1 yard line. The Jeff's received the ball and returned it to the Rochester 27 yard line. Rochester ran the ball and they had gains of 7 yards, 2 yards and 3 yards. This gave the Jeff's a first down. Gillo tackled Argus for a loss on a run play. Wynne gained 3 yards on a run play for Rochester. The Jeff's attempted a punt but Racine blocked it. Miller recovered the ball for the Legion on the Rochester 33 yard line. A Dressen run resulted in no gain. A Racine run attempt resulted in no gain. A Racine pass attempt by Gillo was intercepted by Wynne on the 28 yard line. Rochester gained 2 yards on a run around the end. The Jeff's could not gain any more yards. They punted to the Legion and the ball went out of bounds at the 35 yard line. Langhoff gained 2 yards on a run around the end. Elliott gained 4 yards on an off tackle run. Gillo gained 2 yards with a run through the center of the line. Gillo set up at the 37 yard line for a place kick for field goal. A perfect snap from Mintun to Dressen, who set the hold and Gillo kicked the ball over the cross bar. This gave the Legion, their first points of the game. *Score: Racine 3, Rochester 0.* Gillo kicked off to the Jeff's. Wynne received the ball at the Rochester 1 yard line.

Wynne advanced the ball to the 20 yard line. A Rochester run resulted in no gain. A completed pass to Myers gained 6 yards and he was tackled by Hayes. Rochester gained 2 more yards on a run play. They punted on fourth down. Dressen received the punt on the 37 yard line. Elliott gained 9 yards on an off tackle run. Gillo gained 4 yards with a run through the center of the line. This was a first down for the Legion. Elliott gained 8 yards on a run play. Langhoff gained 8 yards with a run along the side lines. Langhoff ran off tackle and it resulted in a 2 yard gain. An incomplete pass was thrown by Racine. Elliott gained 5 yards on a run. A punt attempt by Racine's Gillo was blocked but it was recovered by the Hayes for the Legion. An Elliott run attempt resulted in no gain. Langhoff gained 5 yards on a run. A run by Dressen resulted in no gain. Gillo was successful with a place kick for field goal from the 20 yard line. *Score: Racine 6, Rochester 0.* Gillo kicked off to the Jeffs and it went to the Rochester 1 yard line. Lehrer received the ball and returned it for the Jeff's to the 20 yard line. Rochester completed a pass to Wynne. He received the ball and advanced it to the 50 yard line. The quarter ended.

FOURTH QUARTER:

Rochester had possession of the ball on the 50 yard line. On a run attempt, Wilson fumbled the ball but he was able to recover it. Foster tackled him for a 6 yard loss. Rochester started a passing attack and they were able to move the ball down to the Racine 32 yard line. Elliott intercepted a Rochester pass on the Racine 20 yard line. Langhoff gained 3 yards on a run play. Elliott gained 4 yards on a run through the line. Gillo punted to Rochester and Meyers received the ball on the 45 yard line. He advanced the ball to the 50 yard line and then he was tackled by Foster. Argus was stopped by Foster with no gain. A Jeff's pass went incomplete, broken up by Racine. Wynne gained 11 yards on a pass. Wynne gained another 3 yards on a pass. Mintun intercepted a Rochester pass on the 30 yard line. Langhoff gained 4 yards on a run play. Elliott gained 1 yard on a run play. Racine punted the ball to Rochester and Wynne received it on the 45 yard line. Rochester threw an incomplete pass. A pass attempt by the Jeff's was intercepted by Elliott on the 44 yard line. Gillo ran that ball and it resulted in a gain of 2 yards. Elliott and Langhoff, each ran for 2 yard gains. Gillo ran through the line and it resulted in a spectacular 14 yard gain. After being held with no gains for two downs, Langhoff was able to gain 3 yards on a play. On fourth down, Gillo place kicked another field goal from the 32 yard line. *Score: Racine 9, Rochester 0.* Gillo kicked off to the Rochester and the ball went to the Jeffs 5 yard line. Lehrer received the ball and advanced it to the 25 yard line. Rochester threw two incomplete passes. They punted the ball to the Racine 45 yard line. Langhoff received the ball for the Legion and advanced it to the 50 yard line. Gillo gained 6 yards on a running play through the line. Langhoff gained 6 yards on a run. Gillo made a sensational 17 yard gain with a run through the line of Rochester. Dalton came in the game to replace Gillo. Gillo received a standing ovation, when he left the field. Langhoff advanced the ball to the 20 yard line. Dressen was thrown for a loss and the whistle blew. The game ended.

FINAL SCORE:
HORLICK-RACINE LEGION 9, ROCHESTER, NY JEFFERSONS 0

SCORE BY PERIODS:	1st	2nd	3rd	4th	Final
Horlick-Racine Legion	0	0	6	3	9
Rochester, NY. Jeff's	0	0	0	0	0

STARTING ROSTER:

RACINE		ROCHESTER
Hayes	Left End	Benton
Miller	Left Tackle	Mattee
Gorman	Left Guard	Dooley
Mintun	Center	Alexander
Murray	Right Guard	Thompson
Braman	Right Tackle	Smith
Roessler	Right End	Anderson
Dressen	Quarterback	Wilson
Langhoff	Left Halfback	Wynne
Elliott	Right Halfback	Argus
Gillo	Fullback	King

SUBSTITUTIONS: RACINE –Foster for Braman, Dalton for Gillo. ROCHESTER-Bachmaier for Smith, Smith for Bachmaier, Lowery for Mattee.

FIELD GOALS: GILLO (3)

The Racine fans were excited about the Legion victory and the great play of Gillo as well as both Dressen and Mintun. Dressen's leadership also played a big part in the victory. The hard work of Mintun at the center position added to the many yards gained by the Racine players. It was stated that every man on the team played great football on that Sunday. The fans believed that if the Racine athletes kept the pace, which they set on Sunday, they would go through the rest of the season without a defeat. The Horlick-Racine Legion football team wasted no time, they started practice on Monday at Lakeview Park for the upcoming game. They would take on the Louisville Colonels on the following Sunday at Horlick Athletic Field.

Team Manager George "Babe" Ruetz of the Horlick-Racine Legion football team was in Chicago on that Monday. He was attending a National Football League meeting. Ruetz mentioned that all in attendance were elated at the success of the season, so far. They scoffed at the theory that the pro game was not as popular as the college game. Those at the meeting agreed that large attendance numbers proved that the pro game was popular with the football fans. Information was released on the controversial Taylorville-Carlinville football game. It was believed that some of the paid players, who were involved in that game were current college players. It was stated that players covered their faces in order to disguise their identity. Charlie Dressen, quarterback for the Horlick-Racine Legion football team played quarterback in the Taylorville-Carlinville game. The discussion of this topic at the NFL meeting in Chicago brought up the fact that a League Code of Ethics would help to legitimize the pro game. An NFL Code of Ethics document was drafted. It was as follows:

Charlie Dressen

NATIONAL FOOTBALL LEAGUE: CODE OF ETHICS   1922

Members of this League are expected to conduct themselves as gentlemen and sportsmen. Any flagrant violation of this principle may subject the offending member to suspension or expulsion.

No member shall knowingly make false representation through advertising as to the personnel of his or a competitive team in an effort to deceive the public for his own financial betterment. The confidence of the public is to be desired above all else.

No member shall have a player on his team under an assumed name.

Tampering with players on college teams shall not be tolerated by this league. The same creates much unfavorable public sentiment against professional football and is deplored and discouraged by this league. An adequate supply of football players who have completed their academic status exist and by confining ourselves to these men, much favorable sentiment shall be ours.

While attending the meeting, George Ruetz was able to complete the rest of the Legion 1922 NFL schedule. It was set to make for an interesting end of the season. Racine would get another game with both the Green Bay Packers and the Milwaukee Badgers at Horlick Athletic Field. The Legion team would get another chance at the Milwaukee team on Thanksgiving Day. Racine was defeated by Milwaukee 20-0 early in the season but Manager Ruetz and Hank Gillo claimed it would be a different in the Thanksgiving Day game. A win by Racine would get them back in the race for the "State Title" or the state bragging rights as they had already defeated the Packers during the season. Racine and Green Bay were rivals ever since, the Legion fielded a football team and the Packers wanted to avenge the earlier season loss to Racine. They were expecting that a special train would be coming down from Green Bay to carry the Packer fans to Racine, Wisconsin for the match up.

Ruetz announced, the players that he used in the previous week would be on the roster for the rest of the season. Shortly after making this announcement, Ruetz heard that Knute Hansen had just returned home from his trip through South America. Hansen played for the Racine Legion Post No. 76 football team in 1921. George searched for Knute and tried to entice him to join the Legion team, once again. He knew his experience would be a valuable addition to the team. Hansen would only be around for a couple of weeks but Ruetz wanted him to play the guard position, while he was back in Racine.

Manager Ruetz had the team out several times during the week at both Lakeview Park and Horlick Athletic Field to prepare for their upcoming opponent, the Louisville, KY. Colonels. The team went through some grueling practices. A win over the Colonels would put the Legion at a .500 winning percentage. They especially worked on the passing game with "Rowdy" Elliott and Irv Langhoff. These players were outstanding in the running game but Ruetz wanted their passing skills perfected. Two special promotions for the Legion/Colonels game were announced. First, the football from the previous game, which Hank Gillo kicked the three field goals to give the 9-0 victory against Rochester was going to be displayed in the trophy room of the new Memorial Hall building. A certificate was printed in the newspaper and fans were instructed to fill out the form and present it Sunday at Horlick Athletic Field with their game ticket. A form from those received at the field would be drawn at halftime and one fan would be selected. Their name would be placed on the football, which would be presented to the trophy room. Second, the Legion management had invited 200 young ladies, who have been active in phoning, etc. to attend the Racine/Louisville game as their guests. This was to show that Racine, Wisconsin is really entitled to the name, Belle City. It was expected that this galaxy of beauty would wreak havoc on the impressionable Kentucky gentlemen and allow the home boys to pile up a big score against them.

Manager Hertzman of the Louisville Colonels contacted Manager Ruetz to announce his line-up for the game Sunday. Hertzman also told Ruetz that he was adding Richard Gibson, a tackle from Centre College, who left school to take a business position in Louisville, Kentucky. Hertzman immediately signed him up before anyone else in pro football. He had added several former college stars including Red Mac Cullom, also from Centre College as well as Hubert Wiggs, an All-Southern player from Vanderbilt.

The Legion had been working hard on developing a new offense for Louisville. The Ruetzman (Horlick-Racine Legion players) displayed an exceptional defense in the previous game and they were expected to stop all the plays that the Colonels hurled at them. Racine was expecting the largest crowd of the season. Tickets

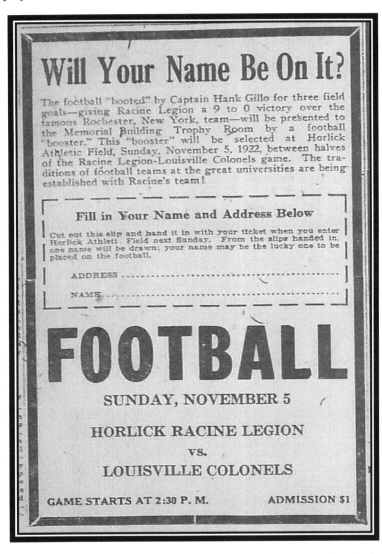

would be on sale until noon Sunday at the Monument Cigar Store, Tom Smader's and Rehl's Cigar Stores on Sixth Street and State Street.

** GAME DAY **

Slipping, sliding and plunging, the Horlick-Racine Legion football team established a new National Football League record for scoring. The Legion scored 9 touchdowns and 3 extra points to give them a 57-0 victory over the Colonels on Sunday afternoon at Horlick Athletic Field. Racine broke the record previously held by the Canton Bulldogs, who defeated the same team by a score of 38-0. The Legion made 31 first downs in the game. The Colonels were held to only one first down. It was in the first quarter. The conditions were wet and muddy and this contributed to a slippery football and several fumbles by both teams. The kicking game was greatly affected by these conditions. Punts and kicks feel short. The bad weather was also related to less than expected attendance. There was under 1,000 fans at the game. The Gillobirds (Legion team) played the kind of game, which one didn't often get to watch because of all the scoring. They were able to take chances, which they would not be able to do in a tight scoring game. Racine ran successfully through the Kentucky line with gains of 10 and 20 yards. There was a trick pass play that resulted in a 40 yard gain by Langhoff. Charlie Dressen returned a Louisville punt 60 yards in the second quarter. Manager Ruetz was able to give the second string players, a chance to see some action after Gillo, Elliott, Langhoff and Dressen scored a combined 5 touchdowns and a total of 31 points in the first half. The second string substitutes played as well as the first string players. Wally Sieb (1921 Horlick Standards), who was a Racine high school star, played an exceptional game. His running resulted in many large gains for the Legion. Hayes, who usually played at the end position, filled in for Gillo at fullback. He almost duplicated the great plays of the former Colgate All-American. Bob Foster, who had been playing tackle during the previous few weeks, also played a brilliant game at his old halfback position. It took just 7 plays from the start of the game for the Ruetzmen to score the first touchdown.

PLAY BY PLAY: 1922 NFL SEASON HRL GAME 6
HORLICK-RACINE LEGION VS LOUISVILLE COLONELS
Sunday: November 5th, 1922   2:30 pm
Horlick Athletic Field   Racine, Wisconsin

FIRST QUARTER:

Racine maintained possession of the ball for most of the first quarter as well as the entire game. Louisville was never able to get the ball into Racine territory. Racine started the game with a big play and the Legion was able control the ball throughout the game. Elliott ran off the left tackle and it resulted in a 40 yard gain on a special pass triple pass play by Racine. Gillo ran the ball and it resulted in a 10 yard gain. Gillo ran the ball and it resulted in a 2 yard gain. Gillo scored a touchdown on a run play. Gillo kicked a successful extra point after touchdown. *Score: Racine 7, Louisville 0.* Louisville took of the ball possession. Padan ran through the line and it resulted in an 8 yard gain. Boldt ran the ball and it resulted in a 3 yard gain as well as a first down for the Colonels. Racine was able to stop Louisville from gaining any more yards. Dressen gained yards with several runs off tackle and around the ends. Gillo ran 12 yards and it resulted in another Legion touchdown. A Gillo kick for the extra point was unsuccessful. *Score: Racine 13, Louisville 0.* The first quarter ended.

SECOND QUARTER:

Racine took possession of the ball. A trick play was executed by Dressen and he ran 10 yards around the left end to score a touchdown for the Legion. Gillo kicked the ball for the point after touchdown but it was blocked by the Colonels. *Score: Racine 19, Louisville 0.* Captain Gillo was retired from the game and "Butts" Hayes substituted in the game for him. Miller went into the game at left end and Hueller substituted in the game at the guard position. "Jab" Murray kicked off to the Colonels. Boldt received the ball and he was downed on the Louisville 5 yard line. The Colonels punted the ball to the Legion and it went out of bounds on the Louisville 20 yard line. Langhoff gained 5 yards on a run play. Dressen gained 5 yards on a run play. Elliott gained 10 yards and a touchdown for Racine. Murray's kick for the point after touchdown was blocked. *Score: Racine 25, Louisville 0.* Racine sent Sieb to substitute in the game for Elliott. The Legion sent Foster to substitute in the game for Langhoff. The new legion backfield began functioning as well as the starters. Racine kicked off to Louisville. The ball was received by Meeks and he was tackled by Sieb of the Legion. The Legion team was able to hold the Colonels from making a first down and they were forced to punt. Louisville punted to Racine. Dressen received the ball and he was tackle on the Legion 40 yard line. A run by Sieb gained 6 yards. Hayes ran the ball and it resulted in a 6 yard gain. This resulted in a first down for Racine. Foster battled his way for a 20 yard gain. This resulted in another first down for Racine. The Colonels held the Legion from getting another first down. An attempted place kick for a field goal by the Legion was unsuccessful because the ball was wet and it was difficult to handle for kicking. The ball was turned over to the Colonels. Louisville attempted three plays and they all resulted in tackles for losses. The Colonels punted to the Legion. Dressen received the ball. He made a spectacular return of 60 yards. He received the ball on the Racine 30 yard line and he advanced the ball to the Louisville 10 yard line. Dressen was tackled by Padan. Racine was unable to score a touchdown. The ball was turned over to Louisville on downs. Louisville punted to Racine in order to move the ball away from deep in their own territory. A run by Sieb and a run by Hayes advanced the ball enough to get a first down for Racine. Foster ran for a 20 yard gain and a touchdown for the Legion. This was the fifth touchdown for Racine. Murray missed the kick for the point after touchdown. *Score: Racine 31, Louisville 0.* Murray kicked off to Louisville but he was unable to get any distance because of the slippery ball. The quarter ended.

THIRD QUARTER:

When Racine took possession early in the third quarter. Foster carried the ball three times. Foster was able to gain 7 yards on each of his three carries. Sieb ran around the right end and it resulted in an 11 yard gain. He crossed the goal line. Wallie (Sieb) scored the sixth touchdown for the Legion. Langhoff, who replaced Dressen at quarterback, kicked a successful point after touchdown. *Score: Racine 38, Louisville 0.* On the next possession for Racine, they were advancing the ball down the field. It looked as though they were going to score another touchdown. Racine fumbled the ball and lost possession to Louisville. The third quarter ended.

FOURTH QUARTER:

Racine regained possession of the ball. Foster and Sieb were consistently gaining 5 yards on each run. Likewise, Langhoff and Hayes were successful on their run plays. Racine advanced the ball to Louisville's 5 yard line. Langhoff ran around the end and it resulted in a 5 yard gain. He scored the Legion's seventh touchdown. A fumbled snap prevented Murray from successfully scoring a point after touchdown. *Score: Racine 44, Louisville 0.* Hayes kicked off to the Colonels and the ball went to the Louisville 30 yard line. Louisville punted to Racine. Langhoff received the ball. He returned it to the Louisville 30 yard line. Irv (Langhoff) ran the ball twice for gains of 9 yards each. Hayes ran the ball and it resulted in a 4 yard gain. Sieb carried the ball and gained 8 yards, which resulted in a touchdown for the Legion. A pass from Langhoff to Sieb gave Racine one point for a successful point after touchdown play. *Score: Racine 51, Louisville 0.* Gorman received the kickoff on the Racine 40 yard line. A Langhoff run attempt gained 20 yards. The Legion was on the Louisville 40 yard line. Racine lost the ball on a fumble. The Colonels took possession of the ball. The Colonels could not gain and they were forced to punt on fourth down. Louisville punted to Racine. Heinisch received the ball and he advanced it to the 45 yard line. The Racine backs continued to gain yards through the Louisville defensive line. A pass from Langhoff to Sieb resulted in a 22 yard gain. Hayes gained 5 yards on a run through the line. Foster ran the ball and gained 7 yards, which resulted in a touchdown for Racine. Murray missed the kick for the point after touchdown. *Score: Racine 57, Louisville 0.* Sieb gained 3 yards on a run. Foster and Hayes combined for a total of a 10 yard gain for the Legion. The ball was on the Louisville 40 yard line. The game ended.

FINAL SCORE: HORLICK-RACINE LEGION 57, LOUISVILLE COLONELS 0.

SCORE BY PERIODS:	1st	2nd	3rd	4th	Final
Horlick-Racine Legion	13	18	7	19	57
Louisville Colonels	0	0	0	0	0

STARTING ROSTER:

RACINE		LOUISVILLE
Hayes	Left End	Gruber
Miller	Left Tackle	Card
Gorman	Left Guard	Megrath
Mintun	Center	Higgins
Murray	Right Guard	Otto
Braman	Right Tackle	Gibson
Roessler	Right End	McCollum
Dressen	Quarterback	Boldt
Elliott	Left Halfback	Padan
Langhoff	Right Halfback	Meeks
Gillo	Fullback	Irwin

SUBSTITUTIONS: RACINE –Hueller, Foster, Sieb, Heinisch, Baumann. LOUISVILLE- Ford, Englehard, Olmstead, Brucklacker.

TOUCHDOWN: Racine-Gillo (2) Sieb (2) Elliott (1) Langhoff (1) Dressen (1)

POINT AFTER TOUCHDOWN: Racine-Gillo, place kick (1) Langhoff, place kick (1) Langhoff to Sieb-pass to end zone (1)

FIRST DOWNS BY PERIODS:	1st	2nd	3rd	4th	Total
Horlick-Racine Legion	8	9	5	7	29
Louisville Colonels	1	0	0	0	1

REFEREE: Downer
UMPIRE: Strothart
HEAD LINESMAN: Larson

George G. Ruetz was pleased with the victory against Louisville but he was not going to allow his team to get over confident. Wallie Sieb played a fine game at the halfback position and Ruetz was considering the idea of making Sieb a starter for the next game. The Legion started their first practice of the week at 2:30 pm and they didn't leave Lakeview Park until 6:00 pm. Ruetz had plans to put the Legion team through some strenuous practices for the remainder of the week in order to prepare for their next game on Saturday. Racine would be playing at home against the Columbus, OH. Panhandles. The Panhandles were headed by Joe Carr, who was president of the National Football League. Columbus had a reputation of being a good football team. They were four-time World Champions and they had been in second place, three times. The Panhandles featured Frank Nessler, who weighed 240lbs. He was the last of the three famous Nessler brothers to play the game. The

47

Nessler brothers contributed to the past success of the Columbus team. Frank was known as a triple threat man. He had excelled in the kicking, running and passing aspects of the game of football. One of his favorite targets to throw his long passes was Columbus end, Homer Ruh. Homer once caught an 87 yard pass from Frank, which became a new football record.

Manager Ruetz wanted this Armistice Day game to further prove that he had developed a team, which could stack up against any team in the league. The next game would be considered extra special because of the annual Armistice Day celebration. It would be played on Saturday instead of Sunday. The celebration included a special automobile parade. The parade was headed by the American Legion post No. 76 drum and bugle corps under the direction of Irv Hanson. Car owners were asked to decorate their automobiles with flags and other appropriate items. Those who were not able to attend the game were asked to at least attend the parade. The city of Racine had been divided into four sections. The drivers were told to meet at one of the following locations before 1:00 pm; <u>Section one</u>, under the direction of Art Anderson would meet at the Junction. <u>Section two</u>, under the direction of Jack Carls would meet at the Flat Iron Square. <u>Section three</u>, under direction of Ernie Mrkvicka would meet at the Lincoln School. <u>Section four</u>, under the direction of William Abrahamson would meet at the H&M Works. All of the Racine automobile drivers were asked leave from the nearest most convenient point at 1:10 pm. All sections gathered at Monument Square in downtown Racine at 1:30 pm. The parade left from Monument Square. This is where the automobiles combined with the American Legion Post No. 76 drum and bugle corps. The parade would proceed through the local business streets of the city. After leaving the business streets, it proceeded north on Main Street then turned west on High Street to Horlick Athletic Field. There was a special program given at the field. All Racine factories closed at 11:00 am Saturday, so that their employees could attend the game and celebration. The local Racine stores remained open. Later that Saturday evening, the 32nd Division Association held their annual Armistice Ball.

Horlick-Racine Legion football team, Business Manager Max Zirbes announced that in the future only Horlick Athletic Field sections A, B, C, D and E would be held for reservations. All the other seats (2,500), which were previously held for reservation would be open for those having general admission tickets. Also, there was a price drop for kids (youth) tickets. Any youngster (child) under the age of 12 years would be admitted for two bits (50 cents) for the remaining games. The ducats (tickets) were available for sale until noon Saturday at the Monument Cigar Store, Tom Smader's, and Rehl's Cigar Sixth Street and State Street Stores. The halftime entertainment of the Racine/Columbus game featured an American Legion Post No. 76 drum and bugle corps performance. This was the first performance of the corps, since they received a special honor from the National department of Veterans.

** GAME DAY **

The crowds began to arrive early for the game but the total count was not up to expectations. They needed the fans to give better support in the remaining home games in order for the team to profit at the end of the season. Racine and Columbus both reported to their dressing rooms on time and stated that their respective players were in good condition to play the game. The teams were evenly matched as to the player weight totals. A good competitive game was expected.

The Legion team outfought and outplayed the Columbus Panhandles from the kick off to the final whistle. The Horlick-Racine Legion grid (football) squad piled up another victory on Armistice Day. The Legion team won by a score of 34-0. The Columbus Panhandles showed up to Racine as being highly respected as the "Grandfathers of Professional Football". The Racine team was able to make veteran player Frank Nesser and the rest of the Panhandles squad look like their day had past. Columbus was only able to make several big gains on offense in the first two minutes of the game but the Legion defensive line held the Columbus team like a proverbial stone wall for the rest of the game. The Panhandles tried to find a weakness in the Racine defense but attempts to run the ball through the line, around the ends and pass plays were mostly unsuccessful. The Racine offense made twenty six first downs in comparison to six by Columbus. The Legion team scored a total of five touchdowns and four points after touchdown. They scored two touchdowns in the first quarter, one touchdown in the third quarter and two more touchdowns in the fourth quarter. Gillo, Elliott, Langhoff and Dressen were all able to make repeated gains around the ends, off tackle and through the line for the Racine offense. Every player on the Racine offense played well. Dressen played exceptionally well in his performance at quarterback. He was undoubtedly one of the greatest additions that the Racine team made for the season. Time after time, Charlie brought the fans to their feet with his long end runs and sneaks through the line, which resulted in big gains for the Legion. The second string players (Sieb, Heinisch, Hueller and Foster) were sent in the game and played just as well as the first string players. The Ruetzmen outclassed the visitors for an easy victory.

PLAY BY PLAY: 1922 NFL SEASON GAME HRL 7
HORLICK-RACINE LEGION VS COLUMBUS PANHANDLES
Saturday: November 11th, 1922   2:30 pm
Horlick Athletic Field   Racine, Wisconsin

FIRST QUARTER:

Gillo kicked off to the Columbus 10 yard line. Rapp received the ball and he returned it to the 30 yard line. He was tackled by Elliott. On the first play for Columbus, Rapp ran around Roessler's end of the Legion line for a large gain. The ball was on the Racine 40 yard line. Racine was penalized for being off sides. Snoots attempted a run but he was tackled for a 1 yard loss. Rodgers ran the ball through the line and it resulted in a 6 yard gain. A Columbus pass attempt was blocked and it went incomplete. Rodgers dropped back to 40 yard line in order to attempt a place kick for a field goal. The ball went short and wide. Racine took possession of the ball on the Legion 20 yard line. Gillo ran the ball through the line and it resulted in a 7 yard gain. Elliott ran the ball, which gained 5 more yards and a Racine first down. Langhoff ran the ball and it resulted in a 1 yard gain. Elliott ran the ball and he gained 3 more yards. A Legion pass attempt went incomplete. Langhoff punted the ball out of bounds on the Columbus 15 yard line. Columbus ran the ball twice through the line for a total of a 3 yard gain. Nesser punted to Langhoff on the Racine 30 yard line and he returned the ball 4 yards. Langhoff ran the ball and it resulted in a gain of 5 yards. Gillo ran the ball and it resulted in a gain of 3 yards. Dressen ran the ball and it resulted in a gain of 4 yards as well as a Racine first down. Elliott gained 2 yards on a run. Racine went into a spread formation, Mintun passed to Langhoff and he turned the completed pass into a 40 yard gain. The ball was on the Columbus 18 yard line. Gillo gained 3 yards on a run attempt. Dressen gained 15 yards on a double pass and the first touchdown of the game for the Legion. Gillo place kicked for the point after touchdown. *Score: Racine 7, Columbus 0.* The Panhandles kicked off to Racine. Langhoff received the ball on the 5 yard line and returned it to the 34 yard line. A Legion pass went incomplete. Elliott gained 1 yard on a run. Langhoff punted to Columbus. Snoots received the ball on the 49 yard line and he was tackled, where he caught the ball. Rodgers ran the ball off tackle and it resulted in a 3 yard gain. No gain on second down for Columbus. An incomplete pass was thrown by the Panhandles. Nesser attempted to punt and it was blocked by Racine. Roessler recovered the blocked kick on the Racine 46 yard line. Two runs by Gillo and Langhoff combined for a 9 yard gain. Dressen advanced the ball 1 yard and it resulted in a Racine first down. Langhoff ran the ball for about a 30 yard gain, to the Columbus 15 yard line. Elliott could not gain any yards. Gillo ran the ball through the middle of the line and it resulted in a Legion touchdown. Gillo missed the kick for the point after touchdown. *Score: Racine 13, Columbus 0.* Gillo kicked off to the Panhandles. Rapp returned the ball from the 10 to the 25 yard line. Rapp ran the ball and it resulted in a 10 yard gain. Rodgers ran the ball through the line and it resulted in a 10 yard gain. The ball was on the Columbus 45 yard line as the first quarter ended.

SECOND QUARTER:
Columbus gained 2 yards on a run attempt. A Nesser pass attempt went incomplete. Murray intercepted a Panhandles pass and he was tackled on the Racine 40 yard line. Gillo ran the ball through the line and it resulted in an 11 yard gain. Langhoff and Elliott ran the ball for a combined total gain of a 15 yard gain and a Legion first down. The ball was on the Columbus 34 yard line. Gillo and Elliott ran the ball for a combined total gain of 5 yards. Racine was penalized 5 yards for being off sides. Dressen was hurried on a pass and Rapp intercepted it on the Columbus 26 yard line. Columbus was unable to gain any yards. They punted on third down. Dressen received the ball on the 35 yard line and returned it 18 yards to the 47 yard line of Columbus. Racine sent Foster in the game to substitute

50

for Elliott. Langhoff punted the ball to the 10 yard line. Nesser gained 3 yards with a run through the right tackle. The Racine defense did not allow any more yards to be gained and Columbus punted the ball. Langhoff received the ball on the 40 yard line. A Racine pass attempt was intercepted by H. Rue on the 36 yard line. Columbus threw incomplete passes and they could not gain any yards by running the ball. Nesser punted the ball and it went out of bounds on the Racine 45 yard line. Gillo and Foster ran the ball for a combined total of 11 yards. It was a first down for Racine. Foster, Dressen and Gillo ran the ball for a combined total of 13 yards. This was another first down for Racine. Foster gained 7 yards on a run attempt. Gillo gained enough yards to get another first down for Racine. A Langhoff run attempt resulted in a fumble, which was recovered by the Panhandles on the 5 yard line of Columbus. Columbus elected to punt the ball in order to get it out of their own territory. Langhoff received the ball and he was tackled on the Columbus 30 yard line. Dressen was penalized 15 yards for clipping on the punt return. Columbus regained possession of the ball on the 50 yard line. A Columbus pass attempt went incomplete as the quarter ended.

THIRD QUARTER:

Columbus kicked off to open up the second half of the game. They were penalized for being off sides on the kick and Nesser had to kick off again but this time from the 35 yard line. Gillo received the ball at the Racine 15 yard line. He advanced it to the 39 yard line. Columbus substituted Mulbarger for Gumps at the tackle position. Gillo and Langhoff ran the ball for a combined total of 4 yards. Elliott completed a pass to Hayes on the Columbus 45 yard line. Racine sent Foster to substitute in the game for Elliott. Langhoff fumbled the snap on the punt but he successfully kicked the ball to the Columbus 30 yard line. Gaulke gained 8 yards on a short end run. Snoots gained 3 yards on a run. Columbus made a first down. Gaulke and Rapp ran the ball for a combined total of 9 yards. The ball was on the 50 yard line. Columbus gained another 17 yards and two more first downs. The ball was on the Racine 33 yard line. In two run attempts, the Panhandles gained a total of 5 yards. A Columbus pass went incomplete. Nesser dropped back to place kick for a field goal but it was blocked by Racine. Murray recovered the ball on Racine 28 yard line. The Legion punted to Columbus on the Panhandles 15 yard line. Nesser punted the ball to Racine and it was received by Dressen on the 50 yard line. Dressen returned the ball 22 yards. Elliott gained 16 yards on a run around the end. The ball was on the Columbus 12 yard line. Gillo ran the ball and it resulted in a gain of 9 yards. Elliott ran the ball and it resulted in a gain as well as a Racine first down. Gillo ran the ball over the goal line and scored a Legion touchdown. A pass from Gillo to Langhoff scored the point after touchdown. _Score: Racine 20, Columbus 0._ The Panhandles kicked off to Racine and the ball went into the Legion end zone. Racine took possession of the ball on the Legion 20 yard line. Elliott gained just under 10 yards with a run around the end. Langhoff gained 3 yards with a run through the right guard position. It was a first down for the Legion as the quarter ended.

FOURTH QUARTER:

The Legion substituted Hueller in the game for Braman. Gillo ran the ball and it resulted in a 10 yard gain as well as another Racine first down. The ball was on the 43 yard line of Racine. Elliott fumbled but Roessler recovered the ball and it resulted in a 2 yard gain. Langhoff gained 5 yards on a run. A pass from Dressen to Elliott advanced the ball to the Columbus 45 yard line. This was another Racine first down. Langhoff ran the ball and it resulted in a 10 yard gain. Dressen ran the ball and it resulted in a 10 yard gain. The ball was on the Columbus 28 yard line. The Legion substituted Foster in the game for Elliott. Roessler gained 23 yards on a run around the end. The ball was on the Panhandles 5 yard line. Gillo ran the ball in the end zone and scored a Racine touchdown. Gillo successfully place kicked for a point after touchdown. *Score: Racine 27, Columbus 0.* The Legion substituted Sieb in the game for Langhoff. Columbus kicked off to the Legion. Elliott received the ball on the 5 yard line and he advanced it to the 40 yard line. Hayes ran the ball and it resulted in a 4 yard gain. Foster gained 3 yards on a run. Dressen gained 43 yards, moving the ball to the 12 yard line of Columbus. Foster ran the ball and it resulted in a 9 yard gain. Hayes advanced the ball for a Racine first down. It was first and goal to go on the 2 yard line. Foster ran the ball in the end zone and scored a Legion touchdown. Murray successfully kicked the point after touchdown. *Score: Racine 34, Columbus 0.* Columbus kicked off to Racine and the ball went into the end zone. Racine took possession of the ball on the Legion 20 yard line. Several gains by Sieb, Dressen, Foster and Roessler took the ball to the Columbus 44 yard line. Murray gained 4 yards on a run attempt. Columbus stopped Racine from getting a first down and the Legion punted the ball. Foster punted the ball to the Panhandles 20 yard line. The punt was recovered by Gorman as the game ended.

FINAL SCORE: HORLICK-RACINE LEGION 34, COLUMBUS PANHANDLES 0.

SCORE BY PERIODS:

	1st	2nd	3rd	4th	Final
Horlick-Racine Legion	13	0	7	14	34
Columbus Panhandles	0	0	0	0	0

STARTING ROSTER:

RACINE		COLUMBUS
Hayes	Left End	Ziegler
Miller	Left Tackle	Conley
Gorman	Left Guard	Stevenson
Mintun	Center	Woolford
Murray	Right Guard	Nesser
Braman	Right Tackle	Mulbarger
Roessler	Right End	H. Ruh
Dressen	Quarterback	Gualke
Elliott	Left Halfback	Rapp
Langhoff	Right Halfback	Snoots
Gillo	Fullback	Rodgers

SUBSTITUTIONS: RACINE– Foster for Elliott, Hueller for Braman, Heinisch for Hayes, Hayes for Gillo, Sieb for Langhoff. **COLUMBUS–** Karsh for Conley, Gump for Stevenson, Hopkins for Ziegler, Carroll for Mulbarger, Glassman for H. Ruh, E. Ruh for Rapp.

TOUCHDOWN: Racine- Gillo (3), Dressen (1), Foster (1)

POINT AFTER TOUCHDOWN: Racine- Gillo, place kick (2), Murray, place kick (1), Gillo to Langhoff-pass to end zone (1)

FIRST DOWNS BY PERIODS:	1st	2nd	3rd	4th	Total
Horlick-Racine Legion	6	6	4	10	26
Columbus Panhandles	3	0	3	0	6

Since the game was on Saturday, other NFL teams were not playing. The great pro football player Jim Thorpe was in attendance to witness the game at Horlick Athletic Field against the Columbus Panhandles. Thorpe said that the Legion had one of the smoothest working machines that he had seen in the pro game. After the game, Joe Carr had nothing but praise for the Legion team. Carr was manager of the Columbus team as well as president of the National Football League. He told Horlick-Racine Legion Manager Ruetz that outside of the backfield, which the Canton team once had consisting of Jim Thorpe, Pete Calac and Francis Dunn, he had never seen a better backfield than Racine has right now.

The Legion team barely had time to celebrate because they had to focus on their next opponent. The Legion would play their bitterest rival, the Green Bay Packers. They two cities had a history of playing each other in the game of football. This was another home game for Racine at Horlick Athletic Field. They had defeated Green Bay by a score of 10 to 6 in the first game that they played against each other in the 1922 NFL season. The Legion needed to win this state rivalry game to stay in the battle, not only for NFL league standings but also the "State Championship". The "State Championship" was a Wisconsin battle between the NFL teams from Milwaukee, Racine and Green Bay. The team with the most wins of head to head games between those three teams would be considered the champion.

Green Bay had strengthened their line and polished their passing attack. They had one of the strongest passing games in the NFL. Their passing attack consisted of Curly Lambeau, at quarterback, hurling the ball to Lyle Wheeler and Lynn Howard on the receiving end. The Packers were expecting a win against Racine on Sunday. The Legion started practice Tuesday evening at Lakeview Park and continued throughout the week. Gillo and Ruetz had the Legion team out for some strenuous practices focusing on the pass attack of the Packers offense as well as the strength of their defense in order to prepare for the Green Bay.

The ducats (tickets) for the Legion/Packers game went on sale at Monument Cigar Store, Tom Smader's, and Rehl's Cigar Stores on Sixth Street and State Street. Several hundred fans made plans to travel by train and automobile to support the Packers at Horlick Athletic Field. The Green Bay Packers organization at first

53

reserved 200 tickets but they later contacted the Legion management to increase the reserved number to 400 tickets. The Green Bay management also made arrangements for a telephone to be installed on Saturday morning at the playing field of Horlick Athletic Field. The Packers arranged for a play by play service to communicate each play back to Green Bay, Wisconsin. This was done, so that those fans who could not make the trip could get a complete account of the game. The game start time was set back to 2:15 pm to allow the Packer fans, who drove by automobile to get a head start back to Green Bay after the game. Those supporting the Packers were to be seated on the east side of the Horlick Athletic Field seating. The Packers also were planning to bring their own cheer leader. Since Racine had one of their own, everyone was expecting a loud and exciting atmosphere. Plans were made to have the Legion drum and bugle corps perform at halftime.

The Legion and the Packers, both had different starting line ups, since the last time the two teams met in Green Bay, Wisconsin. Whitey Woodin, who played for Racine was now in a Packers uniform. Manager Ruetz announced that he was able to sign another player to the Racine roster. Don Murry, a tackle, who played for University of Wisconsin. He was barred from playing college football because of a complaint from the University of Illinois. They accused Murry of playing in the famous Taylorville game on the last Thanksgiving Day. Don admitted that he played in the game but he was not enrolled as a student and he did not accept any money for playing. He was teaching at a country school near his home town of Taylorville, Illinois. Murry reported to practice on Friday and he would probably see playing time at left tackle and "Candy" Miller would move to left end. Racine made many changes, since the last time that they met the Packers. They added, tackles, Ed "Candy" Miller, Art "Bull" Braman as well as Charlie Dressen, who played quarterback and Jack Mintun, at the center position, to the their roster. The Packer additions, since the last meeting of these two teams were Romanus "Peaches" Madolny, a guard from Notre Dame, Walter Nieman, a center from Michigan, F.L."Jug" Earp, a tackle from Monmouth, Lynn Howard, a right end from Indiana and Eddie Usher, a left halfback from Michigan. Every player that Green Bay had in their starting line-up was a former college star but the Ruetzman were ready for them as they were playing exceptional football, lately. The Legion had scored 100 points in the last three games.

The Green Bay Packers had a weight advantage on the Horlick-Racine Legion squad. The Racine players made up in speed, what they lacked in weight. The following is a chart of the reported weight of each player for both teams.

<u>Roster information- player name, weight, position and college (GBP players)</u>

RACINE		GREEN BAY	College
Hayes-175 lbs.	Left End	Wheeler-180 lbs.	Ripon
Miller-202 lbs.	Left Tackle	Buck-245 lbs.	Wisconsin
Gorman-224 lbs.	Left Guard	Madonly-230 lbs.	Notre Dame
Mintun-190 lbs.	Center	Neiman-208 lbs.	Michigan
Murry-211 lbs.	Right Guard	Gardner-208 lbs.	Wisconsin
Braman-210 lbs.	Right Tackle	Earps-210 lbs.	Monmouth
Roessler-190 lbs.	Right End	Howard-210 lbs.	Indiana
Dressen-145 lbs.	Quarterback	Mathys-160 lbs.	Indiana
Langhoff-155 lbs.	Left Halfback	Usher-200 lbs.	Michigan
Elliott-178 lbs.	Right Halfback	Lambeau-195 lbs.	Notre Dame
Gillo-188 lbs.	Fullback	Mills-175 lbs.	Penn State

The Horlick-Racine Legion team was playing their best brand of football but they were lacking in attendance at the games. The rainy weather played a factor in lower than expected numbers and the temperature was dropping in Racine, Wisconsin. To date, the average attendance was at 2,200, while they needed it to be 3,000 in order to break even. The team management was not concerned about profit but it also did not want to be in debt. The low numbers brought the need for the average attendance of 4,000 in the final three games of the season, which were at home, in order to break even for the year. The management expected large crowds for those games because there outcome was important to the team. The Legion played Green Bay followed by Hammond, Ind. and then on Thanksgiving Day, they would have a rematch with Milwaukee.

The following business communication was sent out by Max Zirbes, who was the business manager of the Racine Legion Athletic Association.

Zirbes Statement
Racine, Wisconsin   November 15, 1922

To All the Football Fans of Racine:

The management of the Horlick-Racine Legion Football team wishes at this time to express its thorough appreciation of the wonderful support given by the citizens of Racine and vicinity and also of the newspapers for their splendid co-operation.

Racine Post No. 76 American Legion believes in Racine and will give unreservedly of its efforts to any movement for the good of our city. The Racine Legion Athletic association in its football program this year is bringing to Racine the major league of football, the National Football League, composed of the strongest teams in the United States.

The personnel of these teams is made up of the greatest football stars developed in recent years on the famous college football teams. Naturally, our competition is of the strongest, and while we cannot guarantee to win at our pleasure, we can promise good football to the fans.

We have given every effort toward building a winning team. All will agree that Team Manager "Babe" Ruetz has built up a wonderful machine.

It has cost more to do this than we expected, and we are now placed in a position where we must appeal to the loyalty of every football fan to help boost the attendance at every game. We feel that our team is a great asset to the city of Racine. We feel that Racine is big enough and live enough to support a team of this caliber.

Football is not a commercial proposition with us, but it is purely a civic enterprise, and our fondest hopes are to break even financially, for the season.

The three remaining games will demonstrate in attendance whether or not National Football League will be successful in Racine.

Again I appeal to all football fans to attend every game and to help boost attendance by encouraging prospective fans to see the games.

"May we expect you all at the Green Bay Packers game next Sunday, November 19th?"

(Signed)
Racine Legion Athletic Association
Max J. Zirbes
Business Manager

Line Up

No.	HORLICK-LEGION
6	L. E.—Hayes
10	L. T.—Bramon
11	L. G.—Gorman
15	C.—Mintin
2	R. G.—Jab Murray
9	R. T.—Dan Murray
16	R. E.—Roessler
3	Q. B.—Dressen
8	L. H.—Langhoff
5	R. H.—Elliott
1	F. B.—Gillo

Subs—Heinisch, 17, end; Hueller, 12, guard; Sieb, 17, end; Foster, 4, half; Miller, 14, tackle.

No.	GREEN BAY PACKERS
6	L. E.—Wheeler
15	L. T.—Buck
10	L. G.—Madolny
19	C.—Nieman
14	R. G.—Gardner
11	R. T.—Earps
17	R. E.—Howard
5	Q. B.—Mathys
1	L. H.—Usher
22	R. H.—Lambeau
21	F. B.—Mills

Subs—Hayes, 9; Woodin, 8; Davis, 2; Cronin, 3; Gardella, 4; Glick, 12.

Side 1   Horlick-Racine Legion vs. Green Bay Packers game program sheet

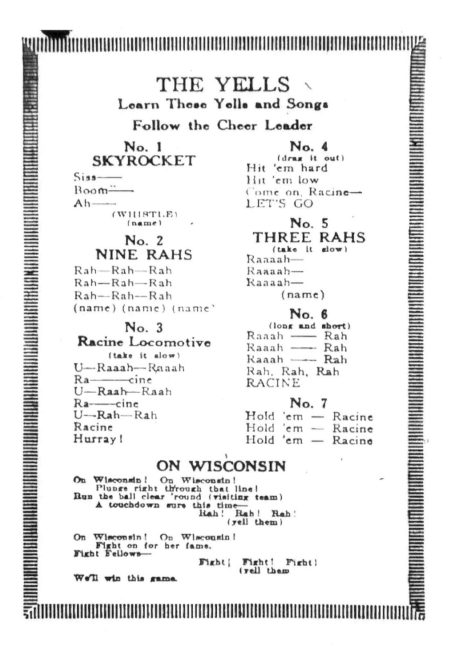

THE YELLS
Learn These Yells and Songs
Follow the Cheer Leader

No. 1
SKYROCKET
Siss——
Boom——
Ah——
(WHISTLE)
(name)

No. 2
NINE RAHS
Rah—Rah—Rah
Rah—Rah—Rah
Rah—Rah—Rah
(name) (name) (name)

No. 3
Racine Locomotive
(take it slow)
U—Raaah—Raaah
Ra——cine
U—Raah—Raah
Ra——cine
U—Rah—Rah
Racine
Hurray!

No. 4
(drag it out)
Hit 'em hard
Hit 'em low
Come on, Racine—
LET'S GO

No. 5
THREE RAHS
(take it slow)
Raaaah—
Raaaah—
Raaaah—
(name)

No. 6
(long and short)
Raaah —— Rah
Raaah —— Rah
Raaah —— Rah
Rah, Rah, Rah
RACINE

No. 7
Hold 'em — Racine
Hold 'em — Racine
Hold 'em — Racine

ON WISCONSIN
On Wisconsin! On Wisconsin!
Plunge right through that line!
Run the ball clear 'round (visiting team)
A touchdown sure this time—
Rah! Rah! Rah!
(yell them)

On Wisconsin! On Wisconsin!
Fight on for her fame.
Fight Fellows—
Fight! Fight! Fight!
(yell them)
We'll win this game.

Side 2   Horlick-Racine Legion vs. Green Bay Packers game program sheet

To alleviate any doubt, Manager Ruetz announced that the game between **Racine** and **Green Bay** would be played. He stated that rain, hail, sleet or snow would not stop this game from being played.

** GAME DAY **

The Horlick-Racine Legion and the Green Bay Packers played a hard fought game. Each team was penalized 15 yards for slugging (fighting). The end result was a 3 to 3 tie. Lambeau and Gillo, each kicked a field goal in the fourth quarter to score the only points of the game. Lambeau kicked a 15 yard field goal, early in the fourth quarter.

The first quarter was filled with a back and forth game in which neither team was able to consistently gain. Both teams frequently exchanged punts. Each team was

Richard Murray

able to get one first down in both the first and second quarter. Racine was outplayed by Green Bay in the third quarter. They were successful with the running attempts around the end. The Packers, with the wind at their backs, were able to punt much more successfully than the Legion. The Legion successfully moved the ball in the fourth quarter. Dressen excelled on the offensive side of the ball for Racine. He had several short run attempts around the end as well as two long running plays, which brought the fans to their feet. Jack Mintun and Richard "Jab" Murray consistently opened holes in the center of the line for the Legion backs to run through. Gillo added big yardage gains with several run attempts through the line. Foster was equally impressive. They kept the ball consistently on the Green Bay end of the field by making big gains from both running and passing plays on offense.

In the final quarter, Racine made four first downs and the Legion defense held the Packers to none. The Legion defense successfully shut down the Packers passing attack. Gillo had a great game defensively. Mintun and Murray also contributed big defensively for the Legion. They were able to get through the Packer line, time after time, to stop plays before they were able to get started. The Packers were only able to complete one pass in five attempts. On the other hand, Racine completed five passes on seven attempts. For the game, Racine had a total of seven first downs to Green Bay's four. Early in the fourth quarter, Racine moved the ball into field goal range. Captain Gillo attempted a place kick for field goal. One of the Green Bay lineman was able to get his hand on the ball and it rolled over the goal line. Charlie Dressen recovered the ball in the end zone for a touchdown. However, Referee Moore failed to see the ball get touched and he would not allow the score.

59

Racine definitely ended this game with an exciting finish. Late in the fourth quarter, a series of runs by Gillo, Elliott and Langhoff moved the ball for the Legion down to the Packers 20 yard line. Gillo attempted a kick for a field goal but it was blocked by Mills. The Packers recovered the ball on around the 30 yard line. Green Bay was penalized 15 yards for roughness and the ball was placed on about the 10 yard line. Buck punted the ball to the Packers 40 yard line. Dressen received the ball and he was tackled. Heinisch substituted in for Hayes, who was badly beat up in the previous plays. A Legion pass went incomplete. There was only 15 seconds left to play. This is when Chuck Dressen called Roessler to the side and detailed the plans to knock the Packers from the "State Championship". Dressen was quoted as saying; *"As soon as I get the ball. I am going to criss-cross the backfield. You stand on the 35 yard line at the edge of the field. Hold up your hand when you get there and never mind, where I am. I'll get the ball to you. It's our only chance. When you get it, fall outside, if you can't get away for a touchdown and we'll let Hank Gillo kick us into a tie"* The play worked as planned. Dressen was being chased in his own backfield. He threw a perfectly straight 28 yard pass to Roessler on the 35 yard line. Roessler could not get to the end zone, so he headed out of

HEINISH
Half Back—No. 20

Fritz Heinisch

bounds at the Packers 20 yard line. By rule, the ball was brought out to the center of the field. With 5 seconds remaining in the game, Gillo successfully kicked the ball through the uprights as the whistle blew. The game ended in a tie at 3 points each. Horlick Athletic Field erupted; the Legion fans went wild and rushed the field to congratulate the hero of the play, the valiant Hank Gillo. Everyone was paying attention to Gillo but none was being paid to Fritz Heinisch. Heinisch was only in the game for the last 15 seconds but in that short time, he made a large contribution to the outcome of the game. Fritz successfully handled two Green Bay tacklers, who were trying to stop Roessler from getting down field to receive the pass from Dressen. He also was part of the great blocking that did not allow any Packers through the line on the field goal kick by Gillo. Fritz was laid out on the field after the kick, trying to catch his breathe. He was kicked in the jaw, while blocking for the field goal attempt. Heinisch fractured his jaw bone and the team would later announce that he was out for the remainder of the season. Hank had not forgotten the hard work of Heinisch, who contributed to making that kick successful. He worked his way through the large crowd of fans on the field to get to Fritz. With the assistance of some of his teammates, Hank cleared a space, so that Fritz would not be trampled and he could regain his wind. The kick by Gillo was an amazing ending that somewhat mirrored a December 4[th,] 1921 game between the Green Bay Packers and Racine Legion (sponsored only by the American Legion Post No. 76 in 1921). More than 8,000 people witnessed that game, which also ended in a 3 to 3 tie.

Gillo kicked a field goal, which tied the score at the end of that game, too.

PLAY BY PLAY: 1922 NFL SEASON HRL GAME 8
              HORLICK-RACINE LEGION VS GREEN BAY PACKERS
              Sunday: November 19th, 1922   2:15 pm
              Horlick Athletic Field   Racine, Wisconsin

FIRST QUARTER:
   Gillo kicked the ball off to Green Bay on the 15 yard line. They advanced the ball
to the 28 yard line. The Packers failed to gain in two run attempts through the line.
Buck punted out of bounds on Racine 35 yard line. The Legion gained a total of 8
yards in three downs. On fourth down, the Legion attempted to make a first down
but they were unsuccessful. Green Bay took possession of the ball on the Racine 43
yard line. The Packers gained a total of 10 yards on running plays. This was a first
down for Green Bay. The Packers were unsuccessful in gaining any yards on three
plays. Buck attempted a place kick for field goal. The kick was unsuccessful and
Racine took possession of the ball at the 20 yard line. Gillo gained a total of 9 yards
in three downs. On fourth down, Langhoff punted the ball out of bounds at the 50
yard line. Green Bay made 7 yards on off tackle runs in three downs. On fourth
down, buck punted out of bounds at the Racine 18 yard line. Dressen failed to gain
any yards on a quarterback sneak through the line. Dressen gained 11 yards on a
run around the end. This was a first down for the Legion. Elliott gained 3 yards on
an off tackle run. Gillo gained 1 yard on a run through the line. Langhoff punted to
the Packers. Mathys received the ball and he was tackled immediately on the 30
yard line. The quarter ended.

SECOND QUARTER:
   Green Bay gained 6 yards on two off tackle runs. The Packers fumbled the ball
and Gillo recovered it on the Green Bay 37 yard line. The Packers were penalized 5
yards for being off sides. Langhoff gained 2 yards with a run around the end. Elliott
gained 4 yards on a run attempt. Gillo attempted a place kick for a field goal but it
was unsuccessful. Green Bay took possession of the ball on the 20 yard line. Buck
punted the ball to Racine. Dressen received the ball on the Racine 40 yard line and
he was immediately tackled. A 15 yard penalty for roughing was called on Racine
during a Legion pass play and the ball was placed on the Racine 25 yard line.
Langhoff punted out of bounds at the Green Bay 35 yard line. Lambeau gained 10
yards with a run around the left end. The Packers attempted a pass but it was
intercepted by Langhoff on the 50 yard line. Racine was only able to gain 9 yards in
four downs. Green Bay took possession of the ball on the Packers 41 yard line.
Usher ran the ball and it resulted in a gain of 20 yards but the Packers were
penalized for holding. Buck punted the ball to the Legion and it went out of bounds
at the Racine 44 yard line. Racine substituted Foster in the game for Elliott. Racine
was penalized 15 yards for holding. Langhoff punted to the Packers and it went to
the Green Bay 35 yard line. Mathys received the ball and he was immediately
tackled. Green Bay failed to gain in two downs. A Packer pass attempt went
incomplete. Buck punted the ball to the Legion and Dressen received the ball on the

61

Racine 20 yard line. Dressen signaled for a fair catch but he was hit by a Green Bay player. The Packers were penalized and the ball was moved to the Legion 40 yard line. Foster gained 2 yards on a run through the line. A Legion pass from Dressen to Roessler gave Racine a 15 yard gain. Foster and Gillo combined runs attempts gained a total of 4 yards for Racine. Langhoff punted the ball out of bounds at the Packers 10 yard line as the quarter ended.

THIRD QUARTER:

   Gillo kicked off to the Green Bay 10 yard line and they returned it to the 30 yard line. An exchange of punts gave the Packers the ball on the Racine 39 yard line. Green Bay fumbled the ball and Braman recovered the ball for the Legion on the Racine 35 yard line. Gillo gained 1 yard on a run attempt. Elliott gained 3 yards on a run attempt. A pass from Dressen to Roessler gave the Legion a 13 yard gain. Racine attempted another pass but it was intercepted by the Packers on the Green Bay 40 yard line. The Legion sent Murray to substitute in the game for Miller. There was another exchange of punts, which gave Green Bay possession of the ball on the Racine 30 yard line. Green Bay gained 10 yards in two off tackle run attempts. Four more run off tackle plays by the Packers gave them a first down on the 7 yard line. The Packers gained 4 yards on a short run around the end. Green Bay attempted a run through the line but they were unsuccessful as the quarter ended.

FOURTH QUARTER:

   The fourth quarter opened with the Packers having possession of the ball on the Legion 3 yard line. It was third down and goal to go for the Packers. Another Green Bay run attempt through the line failed to gain. Lambeau went back and booted a successful place kick for field goal through the uprights. _Score: Racine 0, Green Bay 3_. Mintun kicked off to the Green Bay goal line and the ball was downed on the 15 yard line. The Packers gained 7 yards in three downs. Buck punted the ball to the Racine 40 yard line. Dressen caught the ball and he made a great run advancing the ball to the 20 yard line. Langhoff gained 7 yards on a run around the end. Two run attempts by Foster and Dressen failed to gain any yards. Gillo attempted a place kick. During the kick, the ball was touched by a Packers player and it rolled over the goal line. Dressen recovered the ball and it resulted in a Racine touchdown. The referee ruled that it was not a touchdown for Racine. Green Bay was given possession of the ball on the Packers 20 yard line. The Packers attempted two run plays through the line but they resulted in no gain. Buck punted to the 50 yard line. Dressen received the ball and he was immediately tackled. Gillo gained 2 yards with a run through the line. Foster gained 7 yards on a run attempt. Dressen gained 3 yards with a run around the end. This was a first down for Racine. Foster ran off tackle and it resulted in a four yard gain. Gillo gained 3 yards on a run through the line. Langhoff gained 2 yards on a run attempt. Racine fumbled the ball and the Packers recovered it on the Legion 25 yard line. Green Bay lost 5 yards in two downs. Buck punted the ball to Racine on the 50 yard line. Dressen received the ball and he was immediately tackled. Foster ran the ball and it resulted in an 8 yard gain. Gillo gained 1 yard on a run. A pass from Dressen to Roessler gained 7 yards for Racine. This was another first down for the Legion. Foster ran the ball and it resulted in a 2 yard gain. Dressen gained 5 yards on a run around the end. A Legion run attempt through the line failed to gain any yards. Gillo attempted a place kick for a field goal but the kick was blocked by Green Bay. The Packers recovered the ball on the 30 yard line. Green Bay was penalized for holding on the first play. Buck punted the ball to Racine at the Packers 40 yard line. Dressen received the ball and he was immediately tackled. Racine sent Heinisch to substitute in the game for Hayes. A Racine pass attempt was incomplete. Dressen completed a pass attempt to Roessler. He advanced the ball to the 20 yard line. Gillo successfully made a perfect place kick for field goal as the game ended.

FINAL SCORE: HORLICK-RACINE LEGION 3, GREEN BAY PACKERS 3.

SCORE BY PERIODS:

	1st	2nd	3rd	4th	Final
Horlick-Racine Legion	0	0	0	3	3
Green Bay Packers	0	0	0	3	3

STARTING ROSTER:

RACINE		GREEN BAY
Hayes	Left End	Hayes
Miller	Left Tackle	Buck
Gorman	Left Guard	Woodin
Mintun	Center	Nieman
J. Murray	Right Guard	Gardner
Braman	Right Tackle	Earps
Roessler	Right End	Howard
Dressen	Quarterback	Mathys
Langhoff	Left Halfback	Usher
Elliott	Right Halfback	Mills
Gillo	Fullback	Gardella

SUBSTITUTIONS: RACINE– Foster for Elliott, Elliott for Foster, Foster for Elliott, Don Murry for Miller, Heinisch for Hayes. GREEN BAY- Lambeau for Mills, Mills for Gardella, Nadolny for Nieman, Wheeler for Howard, Gardella for Usher.

FIELD GOAL: Racine-Gillo, place kick (1) Green Bay- Lambeau, place kick (1)

FIRST DOWNS BY PERIODS:

	1st	2nd	3rd	4th	Total
Horlick-Racine Legion	1	1	1	4	7
Green Bay Packers	1	1	2	0	4

REFEREE: Moore (Boston Tech)
UMPIRE: Larson (Milwaukee)
HEAD LINESMAN: Osthof (Wisconsin)

Standings for the Wisconsin State Title (as of November 20th, 1922)

	W	L	T
Milwaukee Badgers	1	0	1
Horlick-Racine Legion	1	1	1
Green Bay Packers	0	1	2

Negotiations began between Racine Manager Ruetz and Manager Calhoun of the Green Bay Packers to play again for a post season game on December 3rd. The two discussed playing a game at a neutral site in Milwaukee. It was expected that completed arrangements for that game would need to be finished in only few days after the discussion. A contract would need to be signed later in that the week.

Practice began, once again, on Tuesday at Lakeview Park. The following Sunday, the Horlick-Racine Legion would play the Hammond, Ind. Pros at Horlick Athletic Field. Hammond had strengthened their line-up in hopes of defeating Racine. This would be the seventh home game of the 1922 NFL season for the Legion. The Legion would play without Fritz Heinisch, who broke his jaw bone and "Jab" Murray, who suffered a leg injury in the Packers game. His Physician had ordered him to rest the injured leg for one week. Jack Hueller would replace Murray at right guard for the Hammond game.

The fact that even near capacity crowds could not keep the Legion balance sheet from showing red, the team management was evaluating whether or not, it would be too financially risky with hosting another home game after the team played Hammond in Racine. The team already had a small deficit. Racine was scheduled to play Milwaukee in Racine on Thanksgiving Day. A decision was reached on Wednesday afternoon after a two hour meeting of the Racine Legion Athletic Association; the game scheduled on Thanksgiving against the Milwaukee Badgers would be transferred from Horlick Athletic Field to the Athletic Park in Milwaukee, Wisconsin. Also, it will be played at 10:00 am, instead of the afternoon. A transportation committee began to make plans to allow anyone, who wished to attend the game, to be able to return home in time for a 1 o'clock Thanksgiving dinner. All advance tickets would be redeemable at the game on Sunday against Hammond. Any reserved seats could be exchanged at the usual ticket outlets for other reserved seats at Sunday's game.

As soon as the word spread that there were plans to move the game on Thanksgiving Day to Milwaukee, there was a remarkable and unexpected uprising of the fans. Telephone calls swamped the Legion officials. In several factories, mass meetings of football fans were held to protest against the decision of the board. Business men pleaded for the Legion officials to stay with the original schedule. It was declared that in hundreds of homes, the Thanksgiving festivities were being planned around the football game. Everyone had admitted that the Legion management was being fair in offering 7 out of 10 game at Home in Racine but they wanted this game against Milwaukee to also be played in Racine. So, the Team management decided to grant the wish of the fans and take a chance of either financial success or failure with a home game against Milwaukee. The Legion

64

management in turn, asked the people of Racine to attend the game on Sunday and Thursday in full force by bringing as many friends with them as possible. Team Manager Ruetz and Business Manager Max Zirbes supported the game being played in Racine. They both wanted to maintain the team's following of fans, averaging 2,700 for the 1922 NFL season. Manager Ruetz said that the game on Sunday was going to cost the Horlick-Racine Legion a total of $2,600. Of this total, $500 will go for players insurance, $150 for rain insurance, $100 to pay for the officials, $700 for minor expenses and the remainder for the Hammond "Guarantee". Also, there were the salaries of the Racine players to be taken care of. The team needed Horlick Athletic Field packed on Sunday, the following Thursday and about 3,000 fans to attend a probable post season game between the Legion and the Packers in Milwaukee on December 3rd for them to take care of their financial deficit. The team had given the fans good wholesome entertainment, all season long. They also lived up to the predictions of being a very competitive team.

Ruetz announced that he had acquired a new tackle and halfback, who would be at Racine in time for Sunday's game. They would take the place of the injured veteran players (Richard "Jab" Murray and Fritz Heinisch) and he added that both players were stars of national prominence as well as each fitting in well with the team. He would announce their names upon their arrival, which was planned for the Saturday before the game with Hammond.

A short statement was released by the Horlick-Racine Legion to the fans:

"Let's pack the park and prove that Racine will stand by the fastest, strongest, grittiest football team ever assembled in the state"
(Signed)
W.L. Haight, Commander- American Legion
L.A. McDowell, Athletic Officer- Post 76
Max J. Zirbes, Business Manager
Raymond Weins, Chairman,-Finance Committee
William Wadewitz, Chairman-Ticket Committee
George G. Ruetz, Team Manager
Arthur J. Morrissey, Assistant Manager
Lester F. Bowman, Chairman-Grounds Committee

The Milwaukee game was quite a distraction but now the focus was now back on the Hammond Pros. The Legion management adjusted the kickoff time to 2:15 pm for this game, too. The adjustment of the game time was because of the earlier approach of darkness. Tickets were available at the usual outlets, Monument Cigar Store, Tom Smader's, and Rehl's Cigar Stores on Sixth Street and State Street.

The Hammond Pros held the Milwaukee Badgers to 0-0 tie, a couple of weeks earlier. Racine was expecting a good battle. Hammond featured several college football stars, which included Jay "Inky" Williams, who played at the end position and he was a former Brown University All-American, playing center was Frank Rydzeski, a former Notre Dame Captain and starting at right halfback,

65

John Shelbourne.

Manager Ruetz announced that two players would be joining the Horlick-Racine Legion for the game on Sunday against Hammond. They were Jerry Johnson and Ed Healey, who were both formerly with the Rock Island Independents. Rock Island was finished with their 1922 NFL season schedule and they agreed to loan Racine those players. Johnson was rated as one of the greatest halfbacks in professional football. The previous Sunday, he ran for big gains in their game against the Chicago Bears. Healey was a powerful lineman and he was considered better than the great "Duke" Slater. If they both reported to the team in time, each player was expected to see playing time in the Hammond game.

Ruetz made a few switches to the starting line-up for the upcoming Hammond game. Ed Miller was going to be moved to left tackle, Don Murry would be at right tackle and "Bull" Braman was going to be moved to the right guard position. He had plans to use two sets of backs in the game. Elliott, Gillo and Langhoff would be one set in the backfield. The second set in the backfield was Hayes at fullback with Foster and Johnson at the halfback positions. In an attempt to rest up some of the starters for the Thanksgiving game in three days, Ruetz was planning to start the second set in the backfield for the Hammond game. Dressen was going play the quarterback position for the entire game.

"ED" MILLER, Tackle.

Ed Miller

** GAME DAY **

The Horlick-Racine Legion did not show their best brand of football but they defeated the Hammond Pros by a score of 6-0 at Horlick Athletic Field on Sunday November 26th, 1922. A touchdown in the first five minutes of the game gave the Legion team, the victory. They received a punt from Hammond on the pros 47 yard line. A Racine series of gains fueled by both running plays and pass completions, allowed them to get the ball down to the 3 yard line. A pass from Dressen to Roessler in the end zone gave the Legion a touchdown, which was the only score of the game. Johnson missed the point after touchdown kick. He ran the ball well but Johnson was not familiar with the team signals and it affected his play throughout the game. Racine outplayed Hammond during the entire game. Don Murry started at right tackle for Racine and time after time, he broke through the Hammond offensive line to stop plays in the backfield. The Legion made thirteen first downs to the Pros three. The Ruetzman kept the ball consistently in Hammond's territory with their successful passing game. Dressen was suffering from a sore leg and he did not attempt to run the ball as much as he usually would have. The two sets of backs were utilized by Racine. They were equally successful in making gains.

66

However, the Pros seemed to tighten their defensive line, when the Legion moved close to their goal line. Steve Sullivan, the Hammond quarterback was able to gain consistently for their offense. He had one of the most exciting runs of the game. Sullivan took the opening kick of the third quarter and returned it fifty yards from the Hammond twenty five yard line to the Racine twenty five yard line.

PLAY BY PLAY: **1922 NFL SEASON HRL GAME 9**
HORLICK-RACINE LEGION VS HAMMOND PROS
Sunday: November 26th, 1922   2:15 pm
Horlick Athletic Field   Racine, Wisconsin

FIRST QUARTER:
Mintun kicked off to the Hammond goal line to start the game. The ball was returned to the 21 yard line. Hammond lost 10 yards in two downs. Sullivan punted to Racine. Dressen received the ball and he was tackled on the Pros 47 yard line. Johnson ran the ball through the line and it resulted in a 5 yard gain. Foster ran the ball off tackle and it resulted in a 5 yard gain. Hayes gained 1 yard on a run through the center of the line. Foster ran the ball through the line and it resulted in a 2 yard gain. A pass from Dressen to Johnson gained 5 yards. Foster ran the ball through the line and it resulted in a 5 yard gain. Foster gained another 3 yards on a run attempt. Johnson lost 4 yards on an attempt to run around the end. Johnson gained 4 yards on a run through the line. A pass from Dressen to Roessler put the ball on the 3 yard line of Hammond. Another pass from Dressen to Roessler in the end zone scored a touchdown for Racine. Johnson attempted a place kick for the point after touchdown. It was blocked. *Score: Racine 6, Hammond 0.* Mintun kicked off to Hammond with the ball going to the 10 yard line and the Pros advanced it to the 21 yard line. Hammond failed to gain in two downs. Sullivan punted the ball to the Legion. Dressen received the ball on the Racine 35 yard line and he advanced the ball 10 yards. Racine was penalized for being off sides on first down. The Legion fumbled the ball on second down. Williams recovered the ball for Hammond on the 40 yard line. The Pros gained 1 yard on a run through the center of the line. Hammond attempted a pass but it was intercepted by Hayes on the Racine 25 yard line. Foster gained 5 yards on a run through the line. Hayes gained 1 yard. Johnson punted to Hammond. Sullivan received the ball and he was immediately tackled on the Hammond 45 yard line. The Pros lost 17 yards in three downs. Sullivan punted to Racine and the ball went out of bounds on the 43 yard line. Foster gained 6 yards on an off tackle run. Johnson failed to gain any yards on a run around the end. Johnson attempted a place kick for field goal from the 47 yard line. It was blocked and Hammond recovered the ball on the Pros 27 yard line. Sullivan gained 7 yards on a run around the end as the quarter ended.

67

SECOND QUARTER:

Hammond attempted a pass but it was intercepted by Hayes at the 50 yard line. Racine gained a total of 5 yards in three downs. Johnson punted the ball to the 20 yard line. The ball was received by Sullivan and he was tackled by Don Murry. Rhenstrom was substituted in the game by Racine at right end for Roessler. Hammond was penalized for holding. Sullivan punted to the Legion. Foster received the ball on the 30 yard line and advanced it to the 15 yard line. Johnson gained 3 yards on an off tackle run. Dressen was tackled for a 5 yard loss on attempted run around the end. Johnson attempted a place kick for field goal but the ball went out of bounds on the 10 yard line. Sullivan punted to Racine. Dressen received the ball and he was tackled on the Hammond 40 yard line. Johnson gained 11 yards in two run attempts through the line. Foster gained 3 yards with a run through the line. Hayes gained 3 yards on a run attempt. Hayes gained 2 more yards with a run through the center of the line. On fourth down, a run by Foster resulted in no gain. Hammond was given possession of the ball on the Pros 15 yard line. Sullivan punted to Dressen on the 30 yard line. Dressen received the ball but failed to gain any yards. Hayes gained 1 yard on a run through the center of the line. A Legion pass attempt went incomplete. Johnson punted out of bounds at the Hammond 25 yard line. The Pros lost 2 yards in two downs. Sullivan punted to Racine. Foster received the ball and he was tackled on the Racine 25 yard line. Johnson punted to Sullivan and he was tackled on the 50 yard line. Hammond completed a pass and it resulted in a 6 yard gain. A Pros pass attempt went incomplete. Another Hammond pass attempt was intercepted by Mintun on the Racine 45 yard line and he advanced it to Hammond 35 yard line. A Racine pass from Dressen to Johnson gained 11 yards as the half ended.

THIRD QUARTER:

To start the second half, Elliott substituted in the game for Foster by Racine and Hueller substituted in the game for Gorman by the Legion. Mintun kicked off to Sullivan, who received the ball on the Hammond 25 yard line. He returned the kickoff back 50 yards to the Racine 25 yard line. The Pros gained 14 yards in four run attempts through the line. A Hammond pass attempt went incomplete. Another Hammond pass attempt was intercepted by Elliott on the Racine 12 yard line. Elliott gained 26 yards on a run around the end. The ball was on the Racine 38 yard line. The Legion fumbled the ball on a run through the line. Hammond recovered the fumble on the Legion 35 yard line. Hammond attempted two passes but they both were incomplete. Another Hammond pass attempt was intercepted by Don Murry on the 25 yard line. Two run attempts through the line gained 3 yards for the Legion. Johnson punted to the Pros. Sullivan received the ball and he was tackled on the 40 yard line. Hammond was penalized 15 yards for holding. Sullivan punted to the Legion. Dressen received the ball and he was tackled on the 50 yard line. Elliott, Dressen and Johnson each carried the ball for a total gain of 14 yards on run attempts through the line and around the end. Johnson punted out of bounds at the Hammond 35 yard line. Sullivan punted on first down and the ball went out of bounds at the Racine 35 yard line. Langhoff substituted in the game for Johnson by Racine. Gillo substituted in the game for Hayes by the Legion. Gillo gained 4 yards

68

on a run through the center of the line. Elliott gained 2 yards on a run off the tackle. The Legion punted to the Pros. The Pros punted back to the Legion. The Legion received the punt on the 50 yard line but the Racine was penalized for roughing the kicker and the ball was given back to Hammond on the Pros 45 yard line. Hammond gained a total of 10 yards on four attempts. Roessler substituted in the game for Rhenstrom by Racine. A Hammond pass went incomplete. Sullivan punted out of bounds on the Legion 3 yard line. Langhoff, Gillo, Dressen and Elliott each carried the ball for a total gain of 14 yards in four downs. A pass from Dressen to Roessler gave Racine a 4 yard gain. An exchange of punts gave Racine possession of the ball on the Hammond 48 yard line. Gillo gained 2 yards on a run through the center of the line. Elliott gained 2 yards on a run off the tackle as the quarter ended.

FOURTH QUARTER:

Langhoff punted to the Pros on the 20 yard line. Sullivan punted to the Legion and they received the ball on the 45 yard line. Racine completed a pass with no yards gained. A Dressen pass was intercepted by Hammond on the 45 yard line. Hammond gained 11 yards in four downs with Shelbourne making a first down for the Pros. The Pros failed to gain any yards in two attempts. A Hammond pass attempt was broken up by Roessler and it went incomplete. Another Pros pass attempt was intercepted by Gillo. The Legion took possession of the ball on the Hammond 25 yard line. Langhoff gained 7 yards on a run through the line. Gillo made the first down with a 3 yard run for Racine. Langhoff ran through the line and it resulted in a 4 yard gain. Gillo gained 3 yards on a run. Dressen made a First down for the Legion. Langhoff gained 7 yards on a run around the end. Gillo gained 4 yards and a first down for the Legion. Elliott ran through the line and it resulted in a 4 yard gain. Dressen gained 6 yards and a Legion first down. Gillo gained 3 yards on a run. Elliott gained 3 more yards on a run. Langhoff gained 3 yards and a Legion first down. Elliott ran the ball and it resulted in no gain. A completed pass from Dressen to Roessler gained 5 yards. A Legion pass attempt went incomplete. The Legion could not gain and the possession of the ball was turned over to Hammond on the 20 yard line. A Hammond pass attempt went incomplete. Two more pass attempts by the Pros were each broken up by Roessler. Hammond punted the ball to the 43 yard line. Gillo ran through the line and it resulted in a 3 yard gain. Elliott gained 3 more yards on a run. Dressen gained 4 yards and a Legion first down. Langhoff gained 3 yards. Langhoff gained 4 yards on a run. The game ended.

FINAL SCORE: HORLICK-RACINE LEGION 6, HAMMOND PROS 0.

SCORE BY PERIODS:	1st	2nd	3rd	4th	Final
Horlick-Racine Legion	6	0	0	0	6
Hammond Pros	0	0	0	0	0

TOUCHDOWN: Racine- Roessler (1)

69

STARTING ROSTER:

RACINE		HAMMOND
Miller	Left End	Williams
Braman	Left Tackle	Tallant
Gorman	Left Guard	Barry
Mintun	Center	Rydzeski
J. Murray	Right Guard	Tierney
D. Murry	Right Tackle	Cerman
Roessler	Right End	Hanke
Dressen	Quarterback	Sullivan
Foster	Left Halfback	Cering
Johnson	Right Halfback	Besta
Hayes	Fullback	Shelbourne

SUBSTITUTIONS: RACINE– Rhenstrom for Roessler, Elliott for Foster, Hueller for Gorman, Roessler for Rhenstrom, Langhoff for Johnson, Gillo for Hayes, Foster for D. Murry. HAMMOND- Hess for Cering, Knopp for Shelbourne, Govier for Besta, Kohl for Hanke.

FIRST DOWNS BY PERIODS:

	1st	2nd	3rd	4th	Final
Horlick-Racine Legion	3	2	2	6	13
Hammond Pros	0	0	2	1	3

REFEREE: Williams
UMPIRE: Larson
TIME KEEPER: Maxted

  The attendance at Sunday's grid (football) game between the Horlick-Racine Legion and the Hammond Pros was one of the lowest attendance that the Legion team had all season. Only 1,084 paying fans passed through the turnstiles according to Manager Ruetz. The Legion management had been looking for a packed park after they had changed their minds and agreed with the fans about playing the Thanksgiving game in Racine. They agreed with the fans that it was the right to play the Milwaukee Badgers on the Thanksgiving Day at Horlick Athletic Field instead of in Milwaukee, where a much larger crowd would most likely have attended the game. It was expected that the fans would show their appreciation on that Sunday by turning out in large numbers but they didn't.
  Early in the previous week, unknown to Manager Ruetz, the upper management of the Horlick-Racine Legion team met to discuss the financial condition of the Racine Legion Athletic Association. As a result of smaller than needed crowds that attended the 1922 NFL games in Racine, the management drew up a contract in which each player on the team signed, agreeing to play the game against Hammond for 25 percent of their salary. The money each player was paid for that game barley covered their expenses. Local supporters of the football team took great pride in the

fact that the players on the team were some of the best around. They were not only selected with regard to their playing ability but also with regard to their character and personality. The opponents of professional football had repeatedly attacked the professional game on the basis that the players were in it only for the money and not the spirit of the game. However, local supporters knew that this had no basis to the truth for such criticism. In the case of the Legion, in spite of the small attendance at that last game, the players had continued to put forth their best efforts at all times. Those players expressed such loyalty even though the Legion management had not been able to meet the payroll regularly.

Information about the 1922 Horlick-Racine Legion squad was released about some of the players:

Ed "Candy" Miller
He played tackle and end for the past three years on the Purdue University football team. Miller earned a degree in engineering during 1921 from Purdue. He was a player with the Canton Bull Dogs for the 1922 NFL season until he was released to play for Racine by Mr. Hay, who was the Canton Bull Dogs manager.

Art "Bull" Braman
He was captain of the famous Exeter team and he also played on the Yale team, while attending school there. In 1921, Braman played for the professional football team, the Buffalo All-Americans. In 1922, he was a Chicago representative of a large Lumber Company.

Earl "Bud" Gorman
He was well known by the Racine fans. Gorman played football several years with Racine teams. During the war, he played on the Camp McArthur team, which was the Champion of the Southwest in 1917.

Jack Mintun
He played with the Chicago Staleys (1922 Bears) for the past two seasons. Mintun was a member of the Staleys, when they won the Professional Football Championship in 1921. After the Racine season, he would return to Decatur, Illinois. Jack holds a responsible position at the Staley Factory.

Richard "Jab" Murray
He was an Attorney in Marinette, Wisconsin. Murray had been playing professional football for the past two years. He played football at Marquette University and he was one of the greatest stars, who had played there.

Don Murry
He was still a student attending the University of Wisconsin. Don played on the university football team but he was declared ineligible to play because of an alleged accusation that he participated in the famous Taylorville-Carlinville game in the prior year.

Fritz Roessler
He was a star end playing for Marquette University in 1921. Roessler had been a sensational player for the Legion, getting better and better each game.

Charlie "Dynamite" Dressen
He was a member of the Chicago Staleys (1922 Bears) in 1921. He was not in college, so he played in the famous Taylorville-Carlinville Game. Dressen played on the Taylorville team and he scored the only touchdown in the game. During the summer, he played baseball with the St. Paul American Association team.

Irv Langhoff
He was captain of the 1920 Marquette University football team. Langhoff played football in Racine for the past two seasons. He works in the clothing business in Milwaukee, Wisconsin.

Al "Rowdy" Elliott
He played for the University of Wisconsin team, the past three years. Elliott was a unanimous choice for the All-Western team and received honorable mention for the All-American team.

Henry "Hank" Gillo
He was an All-American fullback from Colgate University. Gillo was well-known to every football fan in the city of Racine.

Jerry Johnson
He was a star with Morningside College, a few years prior and Johnson was picked as an All-Iowa halfback. In 1919, Jerry played for the Municipal Pier team of Chicago, who were the Champion Service team of the Country. That same year, Johnson was picked by Walter Eckersall as the All-Service halfback. He was enlisted in the service until a few months early. He played for the Rock Island Independents team, who had completed their NFL schedule. They loaned Jerry to the Legion team for the remainder of the season.

The following players were also members of the Horlick-Racine Legion team but these players were from the local Racine area and they were more known to the people of Racine;

Bob Foster, Jack Hueller, Norbert "Butts" Hayes, Elmer "Swede" Rhenstrom, Fritz Heinisch, Wallie Sieb and Carl "Buddy" Bauman.

THE LINEUP

LEGION TEAM

No. 14—MILLER .... left end
No. 10—BRAMAN .... left tackle
No. 11—GORMAN .... left guard
No. 15—MINTUM .... center
No. 9—JAB MURRAY .... right guard
No. 25—DON MURRAY .... right tackle
No. 16—ROESSLER .... right end
No. 3—DRESSEN .... quarterback
No. 8—LANGHOFF .... left half
No. 5—ELLIOTT .... right half
No. 1—GILLO .... fullback

Line Substitutes—No. 12, Hueller; No. 17, Heinish; No. 19, Braman! No. 18, Rhenstrom.
Backfield Substitutes—No. 4, Foster; No. 2, Johnson; No. 6, Hayes; No. 7, Scib.

MILWAUKEE BADGERS

No. 18—ALEXANDER .... left end
No. 19—WEBB .... left tackle
No. 16—TOMLIN .... left guard
No. 15—PIERRETTI .... center
No. 20—DUFFT .... right guard
No. 6—COPLEY .... right tackle
No. 17—ROBESON .... right end
No. 10—McMILLIN .... quarterback
No. 1—POLLARD .... left halfback
No. 12—GREEN .... right halfback
No. 9—DEANE .... fullback

Substitutes: No. 5—Fallen, No. 8; Mooney, No. 2; Weltman, No. 14; Purdy.

A JOLLY GOOD TIME
SEE THE LEGION
TRIM MILWAUKEE
THANKSGIVING DAY
Last Game
Price $1.00   Kick-off 2:15 P. M.

73

The Horlick-Racine Legion was set to play their last home game in Racine for the 1922 NFL season on Thursday against the Milwaukee Badgers. The much anticipated rematch between these two teams was finally upon them. The team went through two hard practices on Tuesday and Wednesday at Lakeview Park in preparation for the Thanksgiving showdown. They developed a better defense, which they believed would be able to stop the Badgers as well as some new offensive plays. Racine was focused on Fritz Pollard of the Milwaukee team. He consistently gained with long runs and pass receptions, when they played the Badgers earlier in the season.

Manager Ruetz was planning to use the same two sets in the backfield for the game against Milwaukee. Although, this game, he would feature Gillo at fullback, Langhoff and Elliott at halfbacks, to start. The Milwaukee team sent scouts to watch the game of Racine playing against Hammond, so they could prepare for the Legion. Tickets were available for sale at Monument Cigar Store, Tom Smader's, and Rehl's Cigar Stores on Sixth and State Streets. The game was schedule to start at 2:15 pm on Thanksgiving Day.

** GAME DAY **

More than 3,500 fans braved the wet and blistering cold weather to witness the Horlick-Racine Legion defeat the Milwaukee Badgers by a score of 3-0 in an NFL Thanksgiving Day Game. The fans topped off their Thanksgiving dinner with a victory of the "Wisconsin Championship" by Racine defeating Milwaukee. Play after play, Gillo, Dressen and Johnson were able to break through the defensive line of the Badgers for gains ranging from 1 to 35 yards. The Legionnaires (Racine team) out played Milwaukee team in the first half. The Badgers made adjustments to their offense by moving one of their star players, Jimmy Conzelman into the quarterback position. Racine had three opportunities to score a touchdown but they made mistakes, which did not allow them to score. Racine would get their only score on a field goal by Hank Gillo from the 35 yard line in the second quarter. Gillo attempted two other field goals but a strong wind did not allow him to get the ball across the uprights, again. Everyone on the Racine team contributed to the team effort to win the game. The defense was able to contain Fritz Pollard and did not allow him the big gains, which he was able to get during in the last meeting, when they played each other.

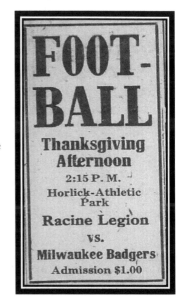

FOOT-
BALL

Thanksgiving
Afternoon
2:15 P. M.
Horlick-Athletic
Park
Racine Legion
vs.
Milwaukee Badgers
Admission $1.00

74

PLAY BY PLAY: **1922 NFL SEASON HRL GAME 10**
HORLICK-RACINE LEGION VS MILWAUKEE BADGERS
Thursday: November 30th, 1922   2:15 pm
Horlick Athletic Field   Racine, Wisconsin

FIRST QUARTER:

Mintun kicked off to Milwaukee. The ball was received by Conzelman on the 10 yard line and he advanced it to the 20 yard line, where he was tackled by "Jab" Murray. Purdy ran the ball and it resulted in a 3 yard gain. The Badgers could not gain any more yards. Pierotti punted to Racine. Dressen received the ball on the Racine 28 yard line. He advanced the ball on the kick return 8 yards to the 36 yard line of Racine. Gillo ran the ball and it resulted in a 2 yard gain. Langhoff failed to gain any yards on a run around the end. Langhoff punted to Milwaukee and they received it on the Badgers 45 yard line. Conzelman ran the ball and it resulted in a 1 yard gain. Conzelman attempted to run but it resulted in no gain. On third down, Milwaukee could not gain any yards and they were penalized 15 yards for holding. The ball was moved back to about the Badgers 30 yard line after the penalty. Pierrotti punted to the Legion. Dressen received the ball and he was tackled by Slater on the Racine 30 yard line. Elliott gained 2 yards on a run. Gillo gained 1 yard on a run. Langhoff punted to the Badgers. Purdy received the ball and he was tackled at the 40 yard line by Don Murry. A run by Conzelman resulted in 5 yard loss, when he was tackled behind the line by Braman. Milwaukee punted to Racine. Dressen received the ball on the 35 yard line. A 10 yard penalty put the ball on the 45 yard line. A run attempt by Pollard was stopped with no gain. A run attempt by Purdy was stopped with no gain. Milwaukee punted the ball to the Legion. Dressen received the ball on the 10 yard line and he advanced it to the Racine 20 yard line. Langhoff gained 2 yards on a run through the line. Dressen gained 10 yards on a run attempt. Gillo gained 15 yards on a run attempt. Elliott gained 3 yards on a run attempt. Dressen gained another 10 yards and the ball was on the Milwaukee 40 yard line. Gillo ran for 3 yards on a run attempt. Elliott gained 8 yards on a run attempt. Gillo attempted a run and it resulted in no gain. A pass attempt to Elliott went incomplete. Gillo dropped back to attempt a place kick for field goal. The Legion faked the attempt and Gillo threw a pass but it went incomplete. Milwaukee received possession of the ball on the Badgers 28 yard line. Doane ran the ball for a 6 yard gain. Purdy gained 2 yards on a run attempt. Pollard gained 1 yard on a run attempt. Conzelman punted to Racine. Dressen received the ball on the Racine 10 yard line and he advanced the ball to the Racine 47 yard line. Gillo gained 2 yards on a run attempt. Elliott gained 5 yards on a run attempt. Gillo gained 1 yard on a run attempt. Langhoff fumbled the snap on a punt attempt. He was able to recover the ball and kick it to the Badgers 10 yard line. The quarter ended.

SECOND QUARTER:

Milwaukee had possession of the ball on the Badgers 10 yard line. Pollard gained 4 yards on a run through the line. Purdy attempted a run and it resulted in no gain after he stumbled over Pollard and lost his footing. Conzelman punted to Racine. Langhoff received the ball and he was tackled by Slater and Purdy on the Racine

40 yard line. Dressen gained 4 yards on a run attempt. Elliott gained 1 yard on a run attempt. Langhoff was tackled for a 4 yard loss. Gillo punted the ball in the backfield from the Racine 45 yard line to the Milwaukee 20 yard line. Doane gained 3 yards on a run attempt. The Badgers were penalized 5 yards for being off sides. Conzelman attempted to run but it resulted in no gain. Pollard gained 5 yards on a run attempt. Milwaukee punted the ball to Racine. Dressen received the ball on the 50 yard line and he advanced it to the Badgers 42 yard line. Dressen gained 14 yards on a run attempt. Langhoff ran the ball and it resulted in a gain of 3 yards. Dressen gained 3 yards on a run attempt. Gillo prepared to place kick for field goal from the 30 yard line but there was a bad snap. Milwaukee took possession of the ball on the Badgers 30 yard line. Pollard gained 1 yard on a run attempt. Conzelman gained 3 yards on a run attempt. Milwaukee punted to the Legion. Dressen received the ball on the Badgers 41 yard line. Elliott gained 12 yards on a run through the line. A Racine pass went incomplete. Elliott completed a pass to Langhoff and it resulted in a 20 yard gain. This completed pass put the ball on the Milwaukee 27 yard line. Langhoff attempted a run and it resulted in no gain. Elliott gained 1 yard on a run attempt. A Racine pass attempt went incomplete. Gillo kicked a successful field goal from the 35 yard line. *Score: Racine 3. Milwaukee 0.* Foster was substituted in the game for Elliott by Racine. Johnson was substituted in the game for Langhoff by the Legion. Mintun kicked off the ball to Milwaukee. Conzelman received the ball on the 10 yard line and he advanced the ball to the 35 yard line, where he was tackled by Miller. Pollard gained 1 yard on a run. A Badgers pass attempt went incomplete. A punt attempt by Pierrotti was blocked by Racine but it was recovered by Milwaukee's right tackle #6 Copley on the Badgers 45 yard line. Pollard attempted a run around the end but he was tackled by Don Murry and it resulted in no gain. A Milwaukee pass attempt was knocked down by Foster. A second pass attempt by the Badgers went incomplete. Pierrotti punted the ball to the Racine 39 yard line. Dressen gained 1 yard on a run through the line. Johnson ran off tackle for a 23 yard gain as the quarter ended.

THIRD QUARTER:

Milwaukee substituted Collins in the game for Coplin at the end position. Also, they substituted Dufft in the game for Keefe. Racine did not make any substitutions at the beginning of the third quarter. Slater kicked off to Racine. Dressen received the ball on the 15 yard line and he was tackled by Purdy after he advanced the ball to the 45 yard line. Gillo gained 5 yards on a run through the center of the line. Gillo broke away on a run and advanced the ball 20 yards to the Milwaukee 30 yard line. Racine fumbled the ball and Robeson of Milwaukee recovered the ball on the Badgers 15 yard line. Robeson attempted a run but it resulted in no gain. Mooney gained 2 yards on a run. Pierrotti attempted to punt the ball to the Legion and it was blocked Racine. Foster received the blocked punt on the Milwaukee 30 yard line. The Badgers were penalized 10 yards and Racine took possession of the ball on the Milwaukee 20 yard line. Dressen gained 2 yards on a run attempt. Gillo gained 1 yard on a run attempt. A Racine pass from Dressen to Johnson gained 5 yards for the Legion. Dressen gained 3 yards with a run through the center of the line and it was a Legion first down. The ball was on the Milwaukee 8 yard line. Johnson gained

5 yards with a run off tackle. Johnson gained 1 yard with a run through the line. Johnson attempted a run but he was tackled for a 2 yard loss. Gillo attempted a place kick for field goal from the 12 yard line but the wind took the ball wide of the goal posts. Milwaukee took possession of the ball on the Badgers 20 yard line. Mooney gained 2 yards on a run attempt. The Badgers could not gain any yards in two attempts. Milwaukee punted the ball to the Legion. Dressen received the ball on the Racine 45 yard line. Johnson attempted a run but it resulted in no gain. Dressen was tackled for a 5 yard loss when Purdy broke through the Racine defensive line. Racine punted to Milwaukee. Conzelman carried the ball around the left end from the Badgers 20 yard line to the Legion 45 yard line. Milwaukee tried a fake formation and they were penalized 5 yards for being off sides. Conzelman completed a pass to Robeson and it resulted in a 5 yard gain. Conzelman gained 8 yards on a run around the end. Conzelman gained 2 more yards with another run around the end. It was a first down for the Badgers. Purdy attempted a run but he was tackled by Mintun and it resulted in no gain. Conzelman was tackled for a 5 yard loss by both Gorman and Braman. A Milwaukee pass was blocked and it fell incomplete. Pierrotti punted to the Legion. Dressen received the ball and he was tackled, where he received the ball on the 30 yard line. Racine completed a pass to Johnson and it resulted in a 4 yard gain. Johnson attempted a run but it resulted in no gain. Racine was penalized 5 yards. Johnson punted to Milwaukee and the ball went to the 20 yard line. Gillo broke up a Badgers pass attempt. Purdy fumbled the ball and Gorman recovered the ball on the Milwaukee 25 yard line for Racine. Johnson, Gillo and Dressen combined for a total gain, advancing the ball down to the Milwaukee 12 yard line. Johnson gained 2 yards on an off tackle run. Racine substituted Hayes in the game for Miller. Milwaukee intercepted a Racine pass on the Badgers 5 yard line. Pollard gained 5 yards on an off tackle run. Conzelman was tackled for a 1 yard loss. Pierrotti attempted a punt but it was blocked by the Legion. "Jab" Murray recovered the blocked punt on the Milwaukee 5 yard line as the quarter ended.

FOURTH QUARTER:

The Legion had possession of the ball at the Milwaukee 5 yard line as the quarter began. They attempted three running plays but they could not gain. Gillo attempted a place kick for field goal but the ball went wide. The Badgers took possession of the ball on the Milwaukee 20 yard line. Milwaukee attempted three running plays, which resulted in no gain. They punted the ball to Racine. Racine punted the ball back to Milwaukee and the ball was on the Badgers 32 yard line. Conzelman made several short gains, while running around the ends from the long snap formation. Milwaukee was penalized for being off sides. The Badgers punted to the Legion. Racine punted back to Milwaukee and they received the ball on the Badgers 20 yard line. A Milwaukee pass resulted in a 6 yard gain. Milwaukee gained 5 yards on a run through the line. Conzelman gained 23 yards on a run around the end from the long snap formation. A Milwaukee pass completion gained 10 yards and the ball was on the Racine 36 yard line. Racine substituted Elliott in the game for Foster. Conzelman gained 5 yards in three short runs around the ends. Conzelman attempted a drop kick for field goal but he fumbled the ball. Racine took possession of the ball on the Legion 25 yard line. Racine was penalized 5 yards for being off sides. Gillo gained 5 yards on a run through the center of the line. Johnson punted to Conzelman and he was tackled at the 50 yard line. Milwaukee was penalized 5 yards for being off sides. Conzelman gained 12 yards on a run around the end. Milwaukee attempted two passes and both were incomplete. With 5 seconds to play, Conzelman attempted a drop kick for field goal but it was not successful and the game ended.

GILLO'S EDUCATED TOE HELPS LICK MILWAUKEE

FINAL SCORE: HORLICK-RACINE LEGION 3, MILWAUKEE BADGERS 0.

SCORE BY PERIODS:

	1st	2nd	3rd	4th	Final
Horlick-Racine Legion	0	3	0	0	3
Milwaukee Badgers	0	0	0	0	0

FIELD GOALS: Racine-Gillo, place kick (1)

STARTING ROSTER:

RACINE		MILWAUKEE
Miller	Left End	Copley
Braman	Left Tackle	Webb
Gorman	Left Guard	Tomlin
Mintun	Center	Perriotti
J. Murray	Right Guard	Keefe
D. Murry	Right Tackle	Slater
Roessler	Right End	Robeson
Dressen	Quarterback	Purdy
Elliott	Left Halfback	Conzelman
Langhoff	Right Halfback	Pollard
Gillo	Fullback	Doane

SUBSTITUTIONS: RACINE– Foster for Langhoff, Johnson for Elliott, Hayes for Miller, Elliott for Johnson. MILWAUKEE- Collins for Copley, Dufft for Keefe, Fallon for Robeson, Mooney for Pollard, Conzelman for Purdy, Purdy for Conzelman.

FIRST DOWNS BY PERIODS:

	1st	2nd	3rd	4th	Total
Horlick-Racine Legion	4	4	3	0	11
Milwaukee Badgers	0	0	1	4	5

The Horlick-Racine Legion defeated the Milwaukee Badgers, but they would play their final game of the season in just two more days on Sunday December 3rd, 1922. This only allowed them two practices in order to prepare for the rival Packers. Tickets were on sale starting on Friday and ending on Saturday at 11:00 pm because the tickets needed to be returned to Milwaukee. The Racine-Green Bay game would be played in Milwaukee in order to attract a larger crowd as they had in the past. Red Nevin would be there to lead the cheering and all sorts of pep stunts to get the team going for the Racine side. There was a reserved Racine section on the west side of the Athletic Field in Milwaukee. The reserved section seats were being sold at $1.65 each. General admission seats were sold for a $1.10 each. They were available at the Monument Cigar Store, Tom Smader's, and Rehl's Cigar stores on Sixth and State Street locations. The Horlick-Racine Legion football players were planning to leave for the game Sunday at 11:00 am from Tom Smader's Place on Main Street. All players were asked to report at that time. The old Armistice hour of 11 played another important part in the Legion history as the ticket sale at the local outlets closed at 11:00 o'clock, the night before. Armistice Day was November 11th. The 11th hour on the 11th day in the 11th month was significant to the history of the Armistice Day remembrance. Also, plans were made to have buses leave for the fans from Tom Smader's on Sunday, too. These buses would take the fans right to the Park and return from the Park after the game.

Joe F. Carr, president of the National Football League named Bobbie Cahn of Chicago and Jim Holloway of Northwestern to handle the Horlick-Racine Legion-Green Bay Packers "State Championship" professional football game. This pair of arbitrators were considered to be the best in post graduate (professional) football. Larsen would be the head linesman.

The Gillomen (Legion team) went through a short signal drill on Saturday afternoon in preparation for their battle on Sunday with the Green Bay Packers. The Legion gridders (football players) had developed a number of new and bewildering plays to hurl at Green Bay. They also developed a strong defense for the Packers and the Ruetzmen (Horlick-Racine Legion team) were confident that they could halt the Green Bay assaults at the line, around the ends and overhead.

As the 1922 season was ending, arrangements were being organized for a season ending banquet.

The "State Professional Championship" was on the line, once again and Racine intended to clinch the title for the 1922 season with a victory in the rematch against the Packers on Sunday December 3rd, 1922.

** GAME DAY **

More than 2,000 fans attended the game at Athletic Field in Milwaukee, Wisconsin. Unable to stop the brilliant passing attack and the sweeping end runs by the Packers, the Horlick-Racine Legion fell to defeat that Sunday by a score of 14-0. The Legion players were outclassed and outplayed at nearly every stage of the game. Green Bay kept the ball in Racine territory, most of the game as well as the Ruetzman on defense. It was obvious that Racine schedule of games had finally caught up to them. They had played Hammond, Milwaukee and Green Bay in the short span of eight days. Also, Racine was playing with several injured players. Gillo played the game with a small bone broken in his right leg, which had occurred back in the Hammond game and it affected his play against the Packers. Also, "Rowdy" Elliott broke a rib in the game against Milwaukee. The entire Legion team was bruised and banged up. It showed in their performance. Curly Lambeau and Charlie Mathys, former Notre Dame University stars connected on three long passes and allowed them the two touchdowns that the Packers scored. Racine was able to effectively stop Green Bay from scoring anymore points by consistently blocking their field goal attempts. The Packers scored on their first possession in the second quarter. Lambeau threw a 25 yard pass to Mathys. He ran the ball another 40 yards. Dressen barley missed tackling Mathys before he reached the end zone and scored a touchdown. After the Green Bay touchdown, it seemed as though Racine was playing to up to their potential. They were able to get the ball down close to the Packers end zone but they could not score. It was a disappointing way to end the inaugural NFL season for the Horlick-Racine Legion football team.

PLAY BY PLAY: **1922 NFL SEASON HRL GAME 11**
                    HORLICK-RACINE LEGION VS GREEN BAY PACKERS
                    Sunday: December 3rd, 1922   2:15 pm
                    Athletic Park   Milwaukee, Wisconsin

FIRST QUARTER:
   Gillo kicked off to the Packers. "Curly" Lambeau received the ball on the 5 yard line and he advanced it to the Green Bay 32 yard line. The Packers gained 2 yards on two run attempts through the line. Buck punted to Racine. Dressen received the ball and he was tackled on the Racine 5 yard line. Johnson punted to Green Bay. Mathys received the ball and he was tackled on the Racine 35 yard line. In three attempts, the Packers were tackled for a loss of 10 yards. Buck punted to the Legion. Dressen received the ball and he was tackled on the 10 yard line. Gillo gained 5 yards on a run through the center of the line. Langhoff gained 1 yard on a run off tackle. Johnson punted to the Packers. Mathys received the ball and he tackled on the 45 yard line. Racine was penalized 5 yards for being off sides. Green Bay gained 2 yards, on a run through the line. The Packers gained 3 yards on a run around the end. Green Bay lost 1 yard on a double pass. Lambeau attempted a place kick for field goal but the ball was blocked. Dressen recovered the ball on the Racine 27 yard line. Johnson gained a total of 4 yards on two off tackle run attempts. Johnson punted the ball to the Packers and the ball went out of bounds on the Green Bay 30 yard line. The Packers attempted to run the ball through the center of the line but it resulted in no gain. Green Bay gained 2 yards on a run through the center of the line. Lambeau gained 8 yards on a run around the left end. This was a first down, for Green Bay. Lauer gained 7 yards on a run through the line. Lauer gained 7 yards on a run off tackle. This was another first down for Green Bay. The Packers ran the ball three times for a total gain of 11 yards and a first down. A Packers run

attempt into the line resulted in no gain. Green Bay attempted two passes and both passes went incomplete. Buck attempted a place kick for field goal from the Packers 47 yard line but it fell short. Dressen caught the field goal attempt at the 5 yard line and he returned it to the 19 yard line. Gillo gained 3 yards on a run through the line. Gillo gained 4 yards on a run through the line. The Legion could not gain and the Packers took possession of the ball. Green Bay gained a total of 4 yards in two downs with run attempts through the line. Lambeau gained 15 yards on a run around the left end. Green Bay attempted a run through the line but they were tackled for a 2 yard loss. The Packers gained 1 yard on a run through the center of the line. Usher gained 2 yards on a run off the tackle as the quarter ended.

SECOND QUARTER:

Green Bay had possession of the ball on the 34 yard line at the opening of the second quarter. Lambeau attempted a drop kick for field goal but the ball was blocked and it ended up going wide of the goal post. Racine received possession of the ball on the 20 yard line. Dressen gained 5 yards on a run through the center of the line. Gillo ran through the center of the line and it resulted in a 3 yard gain. Gillo gained 2 yards and a Racine first down. Green Bay was penalized 5 yards for being off sides on first down. The Legion gained a total of 4 yards on a two run attempts through the line by Johnson and a run around the end by Dressen. Johnson punted to the Packers. Mathys received the ball and he was tackled on the 39 yard line. Green Bay gained 1 yard on a run through the center of the line. A pass from Lambeau to Lauer gave the Packers a 15 yard gain. Green Bay gained 1 yard on a run through the center of the line. The Packers attempted a run around the right end but they were tackled for a 2 yard loss. Lambeau completed a pass to Mathys on the 20 yard line and he ran the ball over the goal for the Packers touchdown. Buck successfully place kicked for the point after touchdown. _Score: Racine 0, Green Bay 7_. Lambeau kicked off to Racine. Johnson received the ball on the 10 yard line and he advanced the ball to the 25 yard line. Johnson attempted a run around the end but it resulted in a 1 yard loss. A Legion pass went incomplete. Dressen gained 1 yard on a run around the end. Gillo gained 20 yards on a run through the center of the line. Johnson gained 5 yards on a run off tackle. Langhoff gained 6 yards on short run around the end. A Racine pass attempt was intercepted by Usher on the Green Bay 10 yard line. Green Bay attempted a run through the line but they fumbled the ball. Racine recovered the ball on the Packers 10 yard line. Langhoff gained 5 yards on a short run around the end. Gillo gained 1 yard on a run through the center of the line. Langhoff gained 3 yards on a run around the end. Johnson failed to gain on fourth down with the ball on the Packers 2 yard line. Green bay took possession of the ball. Bucked punted the ball from the Green Bay end zone. Dressen received the ball and he was tackled on the 32 yard line. A Legion pass attempt was intercepted by Usher on the Packers 10 yard line. Racine substituted in the game Foster for Langhoff and Hayes for Miller. Green Bay gained 1 yard on a run through the center of the line. The Packers attempted another run through the line and it resulted in no gain as whistle blew for the end of the quarter.

THIRD QUARTER:

Gillo kicked off to Green Bay at the start of the third quarter. They received the ball on the 20 yard line and advanced it to the 29 yard line. The Packers failed to gain any yards on two downs. Buck punted the ball to the Legion. Langhoff received the ball and he was tackled on the 22 yard line. Gillo gained 5 yards in three run attempts at the center of the line. Racine punted to Green Bay. The Packers punted to the Legion. They received the ball on the Racine 15 yard line. Langhoff and Johnson each attempted a run off tackle, which resulted in no gain. Johnson punted to the Packers and they were stopped on the Green Bay 40 yard line. The Packers gained 3 yards in two plays. Buck punted to Racine. Dressen received the ball and he was tackled on the Racine 21 yard line. Langhoff gained 3 yards on a run off tackle. Johnson gained 3 yards on a run off tackle. Dressen gained 6 yards on a run around the right end. Gillo gained 2 yards on a run through the center of the line. Dressen attempted a center sneak but it resulted in no gain. Johnson gained 3 yards on a run through the line. Johnson punted the ball to the Packers. Green Bay was penalized for holding on the punt and Racine was given the ball back on the Packers 45 yard line. Langhoff attempted a run around the end but it resulted in a 2 yard loss. Racine fumbled the ball and Green Bay recovered it on the 50 yard line. The Packers gained 5 yards in three downs. Buck punted to the Legion. Johnson received the ball and he was tackled on the 12 yard line. Johnson gained 6 yards on a run through the line. Gillo gained 3 yards in two runs through the center of the line. Johnson punted to Mathys and he was tackled on the Packers 46 yard line. Green Bay gained 3 yards on a run the right tackle. The Packers gained 1 yard on a run around the left end. A pass from Lambeau to Mathys gained 20 yards for Green Bay. The Packers gained 3 yards in two a runs through the line. A Green Bay pass attempt went incomplete. Buck attempted a place kick for field goal but it was unsuccessful as the ball went wide of the goal post. Racine took possession of the ball on the Legion 20 yard line. Elliott substituted in the game for Langhoff by the Legion. Johnson gained 1 yard on a run through the line. Racine fumbled the ball but they recovered it on the Legion 24 yard line as the quarter ended.

FOURTH QUARTER:

Elliott attempted a run around the end, which resulted in no gain. Johnson punted the ball out of bounds on the Green Bay 45 yard line. The Packers gained 4 yards in three runs through the line. Buck punted the ball to Racine. Dressen received the ball and he was tackled on the 16 yard line. Racine fumbled the ball and Green Bay recovered it on the Legion 18 yard line. The Packers were unable to gain in two attempts to run through the line. Buck attempted a place kick for field goal from the Legion 25 yard line but it was blocked by Elliott. The Packers regained possession of the ball. The Packers completed a pass from Lambeau to Mathys and he was tackled by Miller on the Legion 20 yard line. Green Bay successfully attempted short runs around the end and runs through the line, which gained a total of 17 yards. The ball was on the Racine 3 yard line. Gardella attempted to run and it resulted in no gain. Usher gained 2 yards on a run through the line. Usher ran through the line for the Packers second touchdown. Buck successfully kicked the point after touchdown and the game ended shortly afterwards.

Score: Racine 0, Green Bay 14.

FINAL SCORE: HORLICK-RACINE LEGION 0, GREEN BAY PACKERS 14.

SCORE BY PERIODS:

	1st	2nd	3rd	4th	Final
Horlick-Racine Legion	0	0	0	0	0
Green Bay Packers	0	7	0	7	14

TOUCHDOWNS: Green Bay- Mathys (1) Usher (1)
POINT AFTER TOUCHDOWN: Green Bay-Buck, place kick (2)

STARTING ROSTER:

RACINE		GREEN BAY
Miller	Left End	Wheeler
Braman	Left Tackle	Buck
Gorman	Left Guard	Woodin
Mintun	Center	Nieman
J. Murray	Right Guard	Lyle
D. Murry	Right Tackle	Earps
Roessler	Right End	Hayes
Dressen	Quarterback	Mathys
Langhoff	Left Halfback	Usher
Johnson	Right Halfback	Lauer
Gillo	Fullback	Lambeau

SUBSTITUTIONS: RACINE– Hayes for Miller, Foster for Langhoff, Langhoff for Foster, Elliott for Langhoff, Foster for D. Murry. GREEN BAY- Howard for Wheeler, Gardella for Lauer, Gardner for Howard.

FIRST DOWNS BY PERIODS:

	1st	2nd	3rd	4th	Total
Horlick-Racine Legion	0	3	1	0	4
Green Bay Packers	4	1	1	1	7

   The season ended on a low note but now it was time to celebrate all the accomplishments of the Horlick-Racine Legion football team for the 1922 NFL season. Another announcement was made that the members of the team would be the guests at a banquet to be given in their honor on Tuesday December 5th, 1922 at the Elks Club. The Elks Club was located in downtown Racine. All fans, who wanted to make reservations to attend the banquet were instructed to telephone No. 7950 on Monday night. Tuesday Morning would be the last opportunity to make reservations. The banquet was arranged by American Legion Post No. 76 Athletic Director La Mont A. McDowell and Commander Walter Haight. There were plans made for speeches by several players and team management, which included Team Manager George "Babe" Ruetz, Legion Business Manager Max Zirbes and Team Captain Hank Gillo.

The players, who were to be the guests of honor were the following: Ray "Candy" Miller (left end), Art "Bull" Braman (left tackle), Earl "Bud" Gorman (left guard), Jack Mintun (center), Richard "Jab" Murray (right guard), Don Murry (right tackle), Fritz Roessler (right end), Irv Langhoff (left half), Jerry Johnson (right half), Al "Rowdy" Elliott (right half), Hank Gillo (fullback), Charlie "Dynamite" Dressen (quarterback) as well as substitutes Norbert "Butts" Hayes, Bob Foster, Wallie Sieb, Elmer "Swede" Rhenstrom and Fritz Heinisch. Among the players, who spoke that night were Jack Mintun, Irv Langhoff, "Rowdy" Elliott, Bob Foster, Fritz Roessler, "Bud" Gorman, Wallie Sieb, Fritz Heinisch, "Bull" Braman, Jack Hueller, Carl George, "Swede" Rhenstrom, Charlie Dressen as well as Hank Gillo. There were also speeches made by George "Babe" Ruetz, Ray Weinz, Max Zirbes, L.A. McDowell, Charles Younggreen, Walter Haight, Billy Sawyer, Jack Helm, James Allen, Arthur Simpson and a special speech by A.J. Horlick. All of those men complimented the team on an outstanding season. Music was provided an Orchestra and Jack Koening sang several selections during the evening. The gathering was scheduled to start at 7:00 pm. The banquet was put together on short notice in order to allow the players to return to their jobs and the cities, where they lived.

Over 200 people attended the banquet as well as the Legion team management and players. In order to make the night enjoyable, a game was played. The "conversational" game, as it was called, consisted of two teams. One of the teams was called the "Horlick-Legion squad" and it was consisted of the players and the other team was called the "All-American boosters" and it was made up of the Legion management. They game was played and they kept score similar to a real football game. Every member was called upon to speak by (conversational game referee) Vilas Whaley, who was the toastmaster of the banquet. Each time someone was called upon to speak, it was considered "carrying the ball" and this was how they kept score between the teams. "Referee" Whaley would announce their performance as to how much ground they gained or lost based on their speech. Before introducing the speakers, Mr. Whaley said that professional football was as clean as college football now. He added that the Horlick-Racine Legion would field a team for the 1923 NFL season and they will be a contender for the NFL title. Most of the players said that they were delighted to play with such a fine team that had been assembled by the Legion management. They also had nothing but kind words for the Legion organization and each hoped to play in Racine for the next season. The players offered to give their best performances for the 1923 season towards winning a pennant (NFL championship). The players expressed that the Legion management was doing more to put the professional game of football on a "High plane" than any other organization. They liked the fact that playing for the Horlick Eleven (Horlick-Racine Legion team) was similar to playing for their college teams-which meant they thought of the Legion team as a quality run organization. Commander Walter Haight of the American Legion Post No. 76 scored the only touchdown for his team, when he made the announcement that the Legion would field a team in the NFL for next season and they were in pro football to stay. He said that the past season had been a successful one despite the fact that they lost the title for "State Championship" in the last game of the year and the Athletic association was still in a financial hole. Commander Haight suggested that business organizations of the city of Racine like the Chamber of Commerce, etc. should financially back the Legion team in the future. He explained that the athletic association had been incorporated separately and it could have declared bankruptcy thus escaping payment of its debts. He stated that the Legion team had no intention of doing this and they were going to back up everything in which it started. They planned to pay their debts and keep their record clean. He contended that the city of Racine received valuable advertising through the team participating in the National Football League and therefore, the business men of Racine should be interested enough to see that the team had enough financial backing. Chuck Dressen, popular Legion quarterback said that most of the pro teams had cliques made up of players, who represented certain colleges. He said that for example, the Illinois players on the same team would insist that only Illinois players be allowed to score the points for the team. He added that this caused much "Ill Feeling" on those teams and this type of behavior did not happen with the Legion team. Dressen said that the Racine team did not have as many star players as some of the other teams but it did have better spirit and this was how they defeated teams, who should have outclassed (defeated) the Legion. Captain Hank Gillo was praised by the organization for helping to win most of their games in the 1922 season. Gillo said, he was proud to play for the Horlick-Racine Legion and also to be associated with the members of the squad. Hank spoke of the season being a successful one. He also boasted that the Legion team played the best elevens (teams) in the country and won most of the games. Gillo then playfully spoke to the fact that the Legion management should not have scheduled the post season game with the Green Bay Packers. It costs the Legion a "State Championship". He scored a perfect place kick for field goal worth 3 points, breaking a 7-7 tie. It gave the players a 10-7 victory in the "Conversational football game" Gillo had pleaded with the team management not to play Green Bay for the post season game. The team was not in good enough shape to handle a third game in the eight day span. He didn't want to give the Packers a chance at the title, after they had just played each other in a game, which ended in a tie. Hank told Ruetz after the loss to Green Bay that a well-rested team would defeat the Packers in the future. Ruetz spoke up and he explained that the game was scheduled because the Athletic Association needed the money. He also admitted that the game was played against the advice of Captain Gillo.

Referee Whaley presented Fritz Heinisch, who was recently married, with a beautiful silver cream and sugar set on behalf of the team. Fritz thanked the players for the gift and he said that he would always cherish it.

Athletic Director McDowell, who was very involved in American Legion being involved in the game of football, gave his praise for the great work of Ray Weins in promoting the Legion football team ticket sales, Sig Rudd for keeping the team books and finances, Max Zirbes for his all-around promotion of the team and also George "Babe" Ruetz, who sacrificed his personal business to manage the team. McDowell said, these men and their assistants worked hard with no thought of reward. In regard to their efforts, he said, this was the reason that the Legion had a successful team on the field and nearly ended the season in a successful manner as far as finances were concerned. Mr. McDowell urged the fans attending the banquet to talk football all winter long. He said, the Legion had 2,000 fans in which it could depend on and if it could get 2,000 more football fans, the team would be financially successful.

Ray Weins said, the Legion team had aimed high that year and they had nearly hit the mark. He praised the members of the squad for their excellent play and the Legion football management for assembling a high class gridiron outfit (a great team). The success of the early ticket sale drive helped carry the team for part of the season. The fans began to drop out after using up their tickets. He said that next season, more effort would be placed on the opening ticket sale drive.

Manager George Ruetz said that Legion had accomplished their goal of fielding a successful team that year. Ruetz thanked everyone for the support that they gave to the team throughout the season. George also complimented the members of the squad on their spirit that they showed during the season and said that all the men would be asked to report next year. Again, he spoke of reason for and the outcome of the final game against Green Bay as well as the status of players, Miller and Murry. Ruetz explained, *"Both men were sick and unable to show their best brand of the grid game. The state of the treasury compelled us to play the game. We were behind financially and had to meet Green Bay again for financial reasons."* Ruetz added, once the Racine people become educated to professional football, five or six thousand people will attend the games. He said that much of the team's success was largely due to the work of men, who never received any pay or praise such as Hank Larsen, who took care of the uniforms, Billie Kautz, who was always on the job to do anything that you asked of him. He also mentioned Ralph Hogaboam, who was the team trainer, Bill Wadewitz and his assistant ticket sellers, Allie Zirbes, Marshal and others. George went on to say, *"I knew we were taking a chance at losing when we went into the Green Bay game last Sunday. They had more first string than we did and several of our best players were sick. I am not offering this as an alibi. "Candy" Miller was in bed most of last week. "Rowdy" Elliott ought to not have been there, Don Murry was not well and we had more sick men on the field. With an even break, we could have knocked them off. A college team plays a seven or eight game schedule. We play eleven, three of them in the last eight days of the season. There are only three teams topping us in the National Pro League, the Chicago Bears, the Cardinals and the Canton Bulldogs. Next year, we will be on top at the finish."*

Business Manager Max Zirbes, who served on many civic committees in the past, said that the Legion football committee was the best and most active of any organization of any similar group in which he had worked with. The committee was plugging (promoting) all the time. He also praised the unsung heroes, who raked the field, carried the dunnage (equipment), patrolled the fences, etc. saying that they helped put the team in a high place at the end of the season. Jim Allan, president of the Belle Baseball Association was an honored guest at the banquet. He said that Racine was big enough to support professional football and baseball. He suggested that the Racine business men get behind both teams and help support them. He complimented those, who operated the football team and he said, the team had much to do with advertising of the city of Racine.

Charles (C.C.) Younggreen, who was the publicity man for the team, paid a glowing tribute to the members of the squad and the management of the team. He predicted that Racine would have another great eleven next fall and they will receive the support of the Racine people. Younggreen, who was director of the Association of Commerce in Racine, added that he was going try to get the organization to help out next season. He also added that Racine is known from coast to coast because of the drum corps as well as the football team, which was fielded by the Legion and it deserves support.

William Sawyer commented, the Legion had a wonderful team and that Racine would support it.

Arthur Simpson, who was an exalter ruler for the Elks club, said that he hoped the team would make this banquet an annual event and always holds it at the Elks club. They would always be welcome there, he proclaimed that the Elks supported the Legion in whatever they start. He added, they proved this in their past support and they will continue it in the future.

Racine Alderman Tom Smader had to leave the gathering early because of a City Council meeting. Before he left, Smader said, it was his first year as a football booster but he was one for life now. He considered the past season a successful one and complimented the Legion management on assembling a winning team consisting of high class men.

Jack Helm of the Racine Times-Call newspaper was asked to speak for both Racine newspapers (Racine Times-Call and Racine Journal News) and he said, he had done all they could do to boost the team in Racine.

William Horlick, Sr.

The last man to speak was Mr. A.J. Horlick, son of William Horlick, Sr. He said that his father, William Horlick, Sr. was not able to attend the banquet but he extended his best greetings to the team and the management as well as complimenting on the great brand of football being played that season. He added that his father attended every home game, enjoyed them thoroughly and even chose to not attend University of Wisconsin football games, so that he would be in town for the Legion games. Horlick explained that clean sports do a great deal to breed contentment in a city and he was looking forward to a great season next year. Mr. Horlick stated that the Racine newspapers were responsible for helping make this football season a successful one. He recalled that the sport editors promised at the beginning of the season to give their support and they kept their promise. He assured everyone that the Horlick family would continue to support the team.

Bill Nevin, official cheer leader that season, led the cheers for the evening. Following the end of the banquet, Jack Koening led the men in singing "On Wisconsin"

Mr. Whaley, named an Honor All-American team, which consisted of men, who had taken the lead in promoting professional in Racine.

The line-up was as follows:

Horlick-Legion		All-Americans
Miller	Left End	Morrissey
Braman	Left Tackle	Rudd
Gorman	Left Guard	Wratten
Mintun	Center	Younggreen
Hueller	Right Guard	Wadewitz
Foster	Right Tackle	Haight
Roessler	Right End	Maxted
Langhoff	Quarterback	McDowell
Elliott	Left Halfback	Bowman
Dressen	Right Halfback	Zirbes
Gillo	Fullback	Ruetz

LEGION RESERVES- George, Heinisch and Sieb.
TRAINERS- Hank Larsen, Ralph Hogaboam and Billie Kautz.
COACH- Harry Leonard (Zuppke)

"Conversational" game results
SCORE- Legion 10, All-Americans 7.
TOUCHDOWNS- Dressen (1) and Haight (1).
PLACE KICK- Gillo (1)

With the close of the 1922 NFL grid (football) season, the squad and team management dispersed for the off season. They went back to their other occupations. The following is a list describing their occupations outside of professional football for most of those involved with the 1922 Horlick-Racine Legion football team:

- Captain Henry "Hank" Gillo (fullback) was an instructor a Bayview High school, Milwaukee, Wisconsin.

- Al "Rowdy Elliott (right halfback) moved to Racine, Wisconsin and he was seeking employment.

- Irving Langhoff (left halfback) was a manager for a family owned clothing store, Stumpf & Langhoff Stores in Milwaukee, Wisconsin.

- Bob Foster (halfback) was managing a tire store in Milwaukee, Wisconsin.

- Don Murry (right tackle) returned to Madison, Wisconsin. -to resume his studies at University of Wisconsin.

- Richard "Jab" Murray (right guard) was a prominent attorney. He returned to his law practice located in Marinette, Wisconsin.

- Earl "Bud" Gorman (left guard) moved to Racine, Wisconsin and continued to train at the Elks gym for his well-known boxing career.

- Jack Mintun (left end) returned to his position as foreman at the Staley Manufacturing Company in Decatur, Illinois.

- Charlie Dressen (quarterback) returned to Decatur, Illinois, so he could spend time with his wife's family. He was playing professional baseball during the summer as a member of the St. Paul Club but his contract was sold to the Washington, D.C. Club.

- Fritz Roessler (right end) returned to his job as an architect in Milwaukee, Wisconsin.

- Ed "Candy" Miller (end) returned to Canton, Ohio to play basketball with the Canton Team.

- Art "Bull" Braman (left tackle) returned to his job as a broker on the Chicago Board of Trade.

➢ Jerry Johnson (halfback) formerly of Rock Island, Illinois stayed in Racine, Wisconsin and he was looking for a job.

➢ Norbert "Butts" Hayes (left end) returned to his position as a Walworth County Road commissioner, located in Elkhorn Wisconsin.

➢ Jack Hueller (substitute guard) worked for the Klitzen Radio Company in Racine, Wisconsin.

➢ Fritz Heinisch (substitute halfback) was employed at the H&M Body Plant in Racine, Wisconsin.

➢ Wallie Sieb (substitute end) was employed by Case, Inc.-T.M. South Works in Racine, Wisconsin.

➢ Ralph Hogaboam (trainer) was a foreman employed by the Webster Electric Company.

➢ George "Babe" Ruetz (team manager) was owner of a grocery store in Racine Wisconsin.

➢ Max Zirbes (team business manager) was part owner of a shoe store in Racine, Wisconsin.

HORLICK - RACINE - LEGION
FOOTBALL TEAM
1922

L. A. McDowell
Post No. 76 Comm.

George G. Ruetz
Team Manager

William Horlick,
Sr. Owner

Dr. Morrissey
Asst. Mgr.

Max Zirbes
Business Mgr.

Billie Kautz
Trainer

Ralph Hogaboam
Trainer

Hank Larson
Trainer

Hank Gillo
No. 1 Fullback

Charlie Dressen
No. 3 Quarterback

Al Elliott
No. 5 Halfback

Jack Mintun
No. 15 Center

Irving Langhoff
No. 8 Halfback

Fritz Roessler
No. 16 End

91

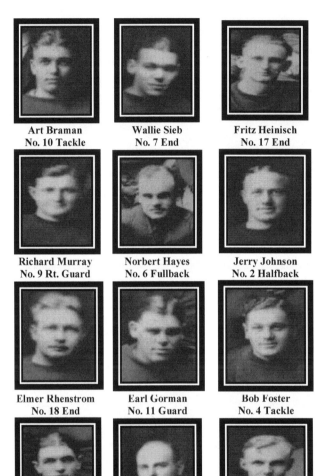

Art Braman No. 10 Tackle	**Wallie Sieb** No. 7 End	**Fritz Heinisch** No. 17 End
Richard Murray No. 9 Rt. Guard	**Norbert Hayes** No. 6 Fullback	**Jerry Johnson** No. 2 Halfback
Elmer Rhenstrom No. 18 End	**Earl Gorman** No. 11 Guard	**Bob Foster** No. 4 Tackle
Don Murry No. 9 Rt. Tackle	**Jack Hueller** No. 12 Rt. Guard	**Ed Miller** No. 14 End

Elks Club in Racine, Wisconsin.
The 1922 Horlick-Racine Legion team banquet was held there.

The Canton Bulldogs were 1922 NFL Champions. The Bulldogs finished with the best record 10-0-2. The Chicago Bears took 2nd place and the Chicago Cardinals finished in 3rd place. The difference between the two Chicago teams was the fact that the Bears played and won one more game. Green Bay finished tied for 7th place finish with Dayton and Racine held the 6th position in the final 1922 NFL standings with a 6-4-1 (.600 winning percentage) record. Five teams finished the season without a win.

93

HORLICK - RACINE - LEGION
FOOTBALL TEAM
1922

1922 Horlick-Racine Legion

No. 1 Wallie Sieb No. 2 Elmer Rhenstrom No. 3 Fritz Roessler No. 4 Ed Miller No. 5 Jack Mintun
No. 6 Art Braman No. 7 Jerry Johnson No. 8 Jack Hueller No. 9 Earl Gorman No. 10 Don Murry
No. 11 Al Elliott No. 12 Hank Gillo-Captain No. 13 Irv Langhoff No. 14 Bob Foster
No. 15 Richard Murray No. 16 Ralph Hogaboam-Trainer No. 17 Dr. Arthur J. Morrissey-Asst. MGR
No. 18 Norbert Hayes No. 19 Charlie Dressen No. 20 Fritz Heinisch No. 21 Hank Larson-Trainer
No. 22 Billie Kautz-Trainer No. 23 Max Zirbes-Business MGR No. 24 George Ruetz-Team MGR
No. 25 L.A. McDowell-Commander of Racine Post No. 76
No. 26 William Horlick, Sr.- Owner

95

Chapter 2:
Horlick-Racine Legion
1923 NFL season

   The National Football League President, Joe F. Carr announced that the NFL scheduled a two-day League meeting for Saturday July 28, 1923 and Sunday July 29, 1923. The weekend meetings were held to complete the 1923 NFL schedule, appoint officers and approve three additional franchises. Cleveland, Ohio, Duluth, Minnesota and St. Louis, Missouri, each had teams that applied for the league.
   The Following teams were represented at the meetings:
Rochester (New York) Jeffersons, Buffalo (New York) All-Americans, Cleveland (Ohio) Indians, Canton (Ohio) Bulldogs, Akron (Ohio) Pros, Dayton (Ohio) Triangles, Toledo (Ohio) Maroons, Columbus (Ohio) Tigers, Marion (Ohio) Oorang Indians, Louisville (Kentucky) Brecks, Evansville (Indiana) Crimson Giants, Hammond (Indiana) Pros, Chicago (Illinois) Cardinals, Chicago (Illinois) Bears, Rock Island (Illinois) Independents, Milwaukee (Wisconsin) Badgers, Racine (Wisconsin) Horlick-Racine Legion, Green Bay (Wisconsin) Packers, Minneapolis (Minnesota) Marines.
   George "Babe" Ruetz, manager of the Horlick-Racine Legion had been busy since May preparing for the upcoming 1923 NFL season. Ruetz was working on securing players in order to compliment his 1922 team. George announced that he received a signed contract for the 1923 season from Hank Gillo, who was captain and fullback of the 1922 Horlick-Racine Legion. Gillo reported that he was in great shape, weighing 210 pounds. He spent the summer away from his teaching job, working as a structural steel worker.

The local Racine football fans were focused on baseball. They attended a St. Paul vs Milwaukee Brewers game on September 16, 1923 in Milwaukee, Wisconsin and their intention was to honor a Legion football player. Charlie Dressen, Horlick-Racine Legion quarterback and St. Paul baseball player was the person, who they were focusing on. A fine gold watch, as it was described, was to be presented to Dressen at the baseball game in order to honor his 1922 NFL season with the Horlick-Racine Legion. Prior to the game, an announcement was made; anyone who wished to make a donation towards the purchase of the watch, could stop by Smader's Place in Racine, Wisconsin. They could view the watch at Tommy Smader's Place and have their name added to the list with a contribution.

Manager Ruetz announced the 1923 NFL schedule for the Horlick-Racine Legion. Their schedule consisted of 12 games, 6 home and 6 away. Ruetz was chairman of the National Football League schedule committee and he selected home games on Armistice Day as well as Thanksgiving Day, as he had done for the previous season. The Green Bay Packers and the Milwaukee Badgers would take on Racine for those two special days. Those two teams were the Legion's biggest rivals.

1923 NFL Schedule: Horlick-Racine Legion

Sept 30	Toledo Maroons	Horlick Athletic Field (Racine, Wisconsin)
Oct 7	Chicago Bears	Horlick Athletic Field (Racine, Wisconsin)
Oct 14	Milwaukee Badgers	Milwaukee, Wisconsin
Oct 21	Akron Pros	Horlick Athletic Field (Racine, Wisconsin)
Oct 28	Green Bay Packers	Green Bay, Wisconsin
Nov 4	Minneapolis Marines	Minneapolis, Minnesota
Nov 11	Green Bay Packers	Horlick Athletic Field (Armistice Day)
Nov 18	Toledo Maroons	Toledo, Ohio
Nov 25	Hammond Pros	Hammond, Indiana
Nov 30	Milwaukee Badgers	Horlick Athletic Field (Thanksgiving Day)
Dec 2	Minneapolis Marines	Horlick Athletic Field (Racine, Wisconsin)
Dec 9	Akron Pros	Akron, Ohio

George was looking to make a few changes in the Legion line up for 1923. He brought in Jack Milton, who was a former Big Ten captain and All-American player. He would play either quarterback or halfback. Milton could punt the ball up to 70 yards. Punting was a weak point for the Racine squad last season, so they were looking for help from Jack. Another player, who Ruetz brought in to look at, was Leonard M. Smith, who played for the University of Wisconsin football team in 1922. He received an honorable mention by Walter Camp on his All-American team selections. Smith was fast and weighed 200 lbs. with a height of 5'11". He would be a tackle for the Horlick-Racine Legion team. In addition, George Hartong, a lineman from Chicago University was going to be in Racine to participate in the first work out of the season. He was 6'0" tall and weighed 210 lbs. Hartong would make a valuable addition to the team because he played the center, guard and tackle positions, very well. Wallace "Shorty" Barr played quarterback for the University of Wisconsin in 1922 and he would also be joining the Legion team. NFL Teams from Chicago, Green Bay and Columbus, Ohio, all were seeking to make Barr, a member of their teams. He was a good friend of Hank Gillo and he promised Hank that if he played professional football, he would wear a Racine uniform. In addition, there was Bill McCaw, who played end for Indiana University. He was a high school football head coach in Kenosha, Wisconsin. A look was given to Les Lunde, a quarterback and halfback from Ripon, Fred Grover, a halfback from Lawrence University, William Hulbert, who was a halfback from University of Chicago as well as other players, who were brought in to get a tryout with Racine. Don Murry was not going to return to the team because he found a position as an athletic director for a school in Hudson River, New York.

Hank Gillo was returning to the team but he was stepping down as captain. He could not devote enough time to the duties because of his teaching career. Gillo was a mathematics teacher at Bay View High School in Milwaukee, Wisconsin. Hank did not intend on playing for the 1923 season but he changed his mind in the summer months. His teaching job did not allow him to attend early afternoon practices. Irv Langhoff would fill that role for the team and Gillo would coach the players. Other returning members under contract were Ed "Candy" Miller-Purdue (end), Art "Bull" Braman-Yale (tackle), Earl "Bud" Gorman-Army (guard), Jack Mintun-(center), Richard "Jab" Murray-Marquette University (right guard), Fritz Roessler-Marquette University (right end), Charlie Dressen-(quarterback), Al "Rowdy" Elliott-University of Wisconsin (halfback), Jack Hueller-(right guard) and Fritz Heinisch-(end).

The team scheduled their first practice of the 1923 NFL season for Saturday September 15th, 1923 2:00 pm at Lakeview Park in Racine, Wisconsin.

A large delegation of Horlick-Racine Legion football fans traveled to Milwaukee, Wisconsin via automobile. They attended the St. Paul Saints vs Milwaukee Brewers baseball game. The fans (known as "Friends of Dressen") were there to attend a special presentation for Charlie Dressen, who was the 1922 quarterback for the Horlick-Racine Legion and third baseman for the Saints. A special collection was taken up by Tom Smader, president of the Racine City Council, for the purchase of a gold watch to present to Dressen. They wanted to send Charlie a message, which was they had not forgotten how well he played for the Legion in 1922 and express their excitement of Charlie signing a 1923 contract to play for Racine. Charlie was one of the favorite players of the 1922 Horlick-Racine Legion NFL team. In the third inning of the game, when Dressen went to bat, the Racine fans swarmed the field. Charlie was presented with the gold watch and a gold football fob. A presentation was made by Racine Mayor Armstrong on behalf of the Legion fans. Dressen promised to report to Manager Ruetz as soon as the baseball season was over. After the game, Dressen was brought back to Racine and a banquet was served in his honor. It was held at Tommy Smader's camp above the Rapids (Racine, Wisconsin). Many Racine officials were present on Tommy's invitation.

The Horlick-Racine Legion held their first practice of the season on Saturday and followed it with a second on Sunday. A Large crowd of fans gathered at Lakeview Park to look the team over and give them a welcome reception. Most of the players appeared to be in good physical condition. Captain Irv Langhoff put the players through some limbering up exercises. Coach Hank Gillo introduced some of the new plays that he would be using for the 1923 season. They were preparing for their first game of the 1923 NFL season on September 30th against the Toledo Maroons. Horlick-Racine Legion Manager George Ruetz said that all early indications were that the team would be even more successful than last season. He also announced, the team would be wearing new Olive Drab uniforms including the socks for the 1923 season. The old uniforms would be used only in practice. Jim Allan, president of the Racine Baseball Association rescheduled to take his team on the road in order to allow the Horlick-Racine Legion to be able to host their game at Horlick Athletic Field. There was a mix up in dates because of the fact that the Midwest baseball season was extended mid-way through the season. Manager Ruetz did not know this in advance and therefore, he booked a game for September 30th.

In preparation for the 1923 NFL season, a large amount of work had to be done to get Horlick Athletic Field transformed from baseball to football. All the bleachers were swung in line with the grandstand and much of the football playing field had to be covered with sod in order to fill in the baseball infield.

The team made plans to play a scrimmage game against former Legion player Chief Angus LookAround and his team down in Antioch, Illinois.

The Wagoner Agency, Inc. gave away 5,000-1923 Legion schedules during a Horlick professional baseball game at Horlick Athletic Field. This would mark the start of the community support for the 1923 Racine professional football season.

A meeting was set by the Legion Football Boosters for Thursday September 20th, 1923 at the Association of Commerce Hall. It would be presided over by Ray Weins, who had been active in American Legion

Memorial Hall- Racine, Wisconsin

projects. The purpose of the meeting was to organize ticket selling drive from September 21st -29th, 1923 for the sale of Horlick-Racine Legion game tickets. The city of Racine mayor and city council donated a silver cup, which was to be awarded to the team selling the most season tickets during the drive. A silver cup was won last year by H&M Boosters and displayed at Memorial Hall. A silver and bronze loving cup was presented to the ticket selling Captain William Abrahamsom (H&M Boosters) at the meeting for his team to display, elsewhere. The cup was engraved with the following:

Horlick-Racine Legion Football
Team
Presented to
H. & M. Boosters
1922 Champion Football Booster
Team
William Abrahamson, captain:
Fred Atherton, Carl Boernke, Alex Derse, Charles Hayek, Riley Hosier,
E. F. Jones, Edward Kleiner,
Orval Lawson, M. J. Miller, Jacob L. Snyder
Representative Racine Boosters
W.J. Higgins, Jr., Sadie E. Jensen, S. Knudson

The Presentation speech at the ticket seller drive was given by Vilas Whaley, commander of the American Legion in Wisconsin. Speeches were given by Ray Weins, Max Zirbes, Medora Roskilly, George "Babe" Ruetz and Charles Younggreen. Several players of the Legion football team including Coach Hank Gillo and Captain Irv Langhoff were present to meet the ticket sellers. This stirred up enthusiasm at the meeting. The ticket sellers were arranged into 15 teams. It was voted that the teams for the ticket campaign that year were not restricted to any certain territory in the sale of the tickets. The ticket drive was divided into quarters, the same as a real football game. Credits were counted on a point system. There was 6 points (touchdown) given for each sale of a season reserved seat ticket sold. There was 3 points (field goal) given for every general admission season ticket sold. The ticket selling quarters were "played" on the following 1923 dates:

First Quarter: September 21st – 22nd
Second Quarter: September 24th – 25th
Third Quarter: September 26th – 27th
Fourth Quarter: September 28th – 29th

A score was maintained at the Monument Square Cigar Store in downtown Racine for all too see the progress of each team. There was great success in the advance sale of tickets in the prior year and therefore, the Legion Athletic Association decided to repeat it again in 1923. The Officers of the Association were L.A. McDowell, president, Raymond Weins, vice President, Sig M. Ruud, secretary and treasurer, George G. Ruetz, Dr. A. J. Morrissey and Max Zirbes were team managers.
The following letter was sent out to each player, who was placed on the 15 ticket selling teams:

101

"The American Legion football booster game, unique in football history, and intimately associated with the splendid record of our football team, has been established as one of the valued traditions of our City."

"The players on the 1923 booster teams have been selected with the same care that Hank Gillo and Irv Langhoff have used in building the 1923 Horlick-Racine-Legion football team."

"This letter is to commemorate your selection as a player in the American Legion football booster game, Sept 21-29, 1923, and to pledge to you and your team the enthusiastic interest and active support of the citizens of Racine and the members of our organization."

"Win in the biggest football game ever played."

"Let the enthusiasm and energy of our team be an inspiration to our football team and spur them on to victories."

Signed- William H. Armstrong , Mayor; A.C. Mehder, President-Association of Commerce; Harry Vandergrind, President-Kiwanis Club; Frank H. Miller, President-Rotary Club; J. Allan Simpson, President-Lions Club; T.H. Vanhorn, President-AD Club and Raymond Weins, Chairman-American Legion Booster Committee.

The members/team position of the 1923 Ticket selling teams were as follows:

"Gridettes" – Captain and Fullback, Bessie Jandl; Left halfback, Katherine Foley; Right halfback, Harriet burns; Quarterback, Mrs. John Reid, Jr. ; Left end, Eva Larsen; Left tackle, Mrs. Nate Silver; Left guard, Virginia Pell; Center, Mildred Kristerius; Right guard, Lulu Hochguertel; Right tackle, Mrs. Raymond Weins; Right end, Emily Ruston.

"Bullock Bear Cats" – Captain and Fullback, R.L. Bullock; Left halfback, Tom Dickenson; Right halfback, H.F. Moers; Quarterback, J.A. Lawrence; Left end, Earl Trauger; Left tackle, Frank H. Miller; Left guard, Arthur Stoffel; Center, Carl Anderson; Right guard, Emil Rasmussen; Right tackle, W.L. Haight; Right end, Grover Miller.

"Case Eagles" – Captain and Fullback, George W. Smith; Coach, E.E. Russell; Left halfback, Stephen Bull; Right halfback, Hugh Williams; Quarterback, John Carls; Left end, A.F. Bowman; Left Tackle, Herbert Morgan; Left guard, William Albright; Center, George Jorgenson; Right guard, S.J. Sorenson; Right tackle, Earl Larke; Right end, Ralph Smith.

"Clover Leafs" – Captain and Fullback, George Pendell; Left halfback, Griff Roberts; Right halfback, George Nelson; Quarterback, William Abrahamson; Left end, James Brehm; Left tackle, Art Hansen; Left guard, Leo Scheuss; Center, Joe Young, Jr. ; Right guard, Fred Schulz; Right tackle, Randall Laycock; Right end, Al Lee.

"Gillo Birds" – Captain and Fullback, Charles Wiegrand; Left halfback, D.R. Healy; Right halfback, George Danek; Quarterback, Conrad Lahr; Left end, Ed Zahn; Left tackle, Tom Smader; Left guard, J. Klesges; Center, Louis Shaw; Right guard, C.B. Cook; Right tackle, J. Leuker; Right end, L. Bronenkant.

"H. & M. Boosters" – Captain and Fullback, Riley Hosier; Left halfback, Albert Statz; Right halfback, D.J. Miller; Quarterback, Jacob L. Snyder; Left end, Tony Sorenson; Left tackle, Larry Quirk; Left guard, W.H. Rode; Center, A.A. Derse ; Right guard, Charles Hayek; Right tackle, Phil J. Dahlberg; Right end, E.F. Jones.

"Junction All-Stars"- Captain and Fullback, J.A. Christensen; Left halfback, Alfred Christensen; Right halfback, C. Olsen; Quarterback, J. Huber; Left end, George Nelsen; Left tackle, William Larsen; Left guard, H.E. Hinners; Center, C.A. Jillson; Right guard, Ben Silver; Right tackle, Nick Flore; Right end, O. Frings.

"Lake Fronts"- Captain and Fullback, M.O. Lawson; Left halfback, Charles Brose; Right halfback, Larry Lowe; Quarterback, L.E. Hegen; Left end, William Cook; Left tackle, H.C. Freeman; Left guard, Harold Spencer; Center, Art Stindle; Right guard, Art Johnson; Right tackle, Ted Seith; Right end, Jack Haney.

"North Ends"-Captain and Fullback, Joe Mura; Left halfback, Charles Bloom; Right halfback, William Gersonde; Quarterback, Art Kwapil; Left end, _____ ; Left tackle, Jack Schievensky; Left guard, A.O. Wendt; Center, Bernard Healy; Right guard, Russell Gallagher; Right tackle, Charles Prudent; Right end, Albert Galser.

"Self Starters" – Captain and Fullback, F. Dederich; Left halfback, Art Naleid; Right halfback, Abe Silver; Quarterback, Henry Hilgers; Left end, Dave Semmes; Left tackle, George Rybacek; Left guard, Herb Brown; Center, Fred Tegtmeyer; Right guard, Bill Higgins; Right tackle, Wallace Kelley; Right end, Henry Thompson.

"Speed Boys" –Captain and Fullback, Ernest Mrvicka; Left halfback, Charles Kannenberg; Right halfback, Ralph Kehl; Quarterback, Irving Hansen; Left end, Harry Anderson; Left tackle, Ollie Ritter; Left guard, Victor Holm; Center, James Swartout; Right guard, Howard Manchester; Right tackle, Ed Foley; Right end, L.C. Smith.

"State Street Boosters" –Captain and Fullback, Fred DeMarals; Left halfback, H. Christensen; Right halfback, A.G. Duckmann; Quarterback, A.E. Wilkins; Left end, Ed Christensen; Left tackle, L.A. Derse; Left guard, Ben Pederson; Center, George Hanson; Right guard, Dan Casterton; Right tackle, Marvin Lloyd; Right end _____ .

"Industrial Go-Getters" –Captain and Fullback, Louis Monk. Other names not reported.
"Un-named group" –Captain and Fullback, Miss Medora Roskilly. Other names not reported.

An announcement was made that the Horlick-Racine Legion tickets outlets would be the same as last season-Monument Cigar Store, Tom Smader's Place, and Rehl's Cigar Stores (Sixth and State Streets). The tickets for the first game on September 30th, 1923 were made available on Sept 27th at the ticket outlets. Sideline boxes for the season were made available at the cost of $85. This included 6 home games and each box was able to seat 8 people. Those interested were told to contact Max Zirbes.

The Racine team continued to practice in front of large crowds at Lakeview Park on Friday evening, Saturday afternoon and Sunday morning. Among the players, who were reporting to practice was the following: Halfback Al "Rowdy" Elliott, one of the stars of the 1922 Legion team and a fan favorite; Jack Milton of Chicago, an All-American halfback; Les Lunde, Wallace "Shorty" Barr, Bill McCaw, Ed Miller, Fritz Roessler, Art Braham, Len Smith, Richard "Jab" Murray, Earl "Bud" Gorman, George Hartong and Jack Mintun were all present at practice. Charlie Dressen was expected to report after the baseball season and he would play at the quarterback position. In his absence, "Shorty" Barr was handling the quarterback position and Mintun played center with McCaw and Roessler taking positions in the line. Gillo was practicing at fullback along with Langhoff and Elliott, who were at halfback positions.

The first game of the 1923 NFL season was a week away (Sunday September 30th, 1923) and field preparations were in order. The Legion had a large crew of men out at Horlick's Athletic Field in order to prepare for the game against the Toledo Maroons. New bleachers were being built and the old bleachers needed to be turned around in order to transform the baseball field into a football field. Horlick's crew was busy.

The grid (football field) was laid out in an east-west direction for the 1923 NFL season, so that the new $17,000 grandstand could be utilized in the best possible way for the spectators. The playing field was set up to run as close as possible to the grandstand. Two covered bleachers and one open bleacher were placed at the end of the grandstand. The grandstand seats were reserved and sold for $1.50 each. The grandstand box seats sold for $2.00 each. The bleacher seats sold for $1.00. Eight person premium boxes were again placed in front of the bleachers at Horlickville. Those tickets sold for $2.00 each.

The south side of the field was set up with covered and open bleachers. The covered bleachers were centered with the field and sold for $1.50 each. The open bleachers were placed on the end of each side of the covered bleachers and these seats sold for $1.00 each. Premium boxes were placed in front of those bleachers, too. Those sold for $2.00 each seat. A new feature was added for the 1923 Season. It was a "Knot Hole Section" for Children under 16 years old. They would be admitted to the Horlick-Racine Legion games for 25 cents.

The Legion football tickets were valued as cash and could be applied to the purchase of higher valued seats. Spectators were allowed to reserve tickets in advance at the discretion of the ticket station. The reservations were honored on the first and second day of the ticket sale. If the person reserving the tickets did not pay for the tickets by the end of the second day, the tickets would be again placed on sale to the public. Horlick Athletic Field total football spectator seating was 3,500 seats for the 1923 NFL season. There were 1,907 General Admission seats, 1,337 reserved seats and 256 Premium box seats. The ducats (tickets) were on sale at Smader's Place, Monument Cigar Store, and Rehl's Cigar Store at both the Sixth and State Street locations.

Horlick's Malted Milk Co. - Racine, Wisc.

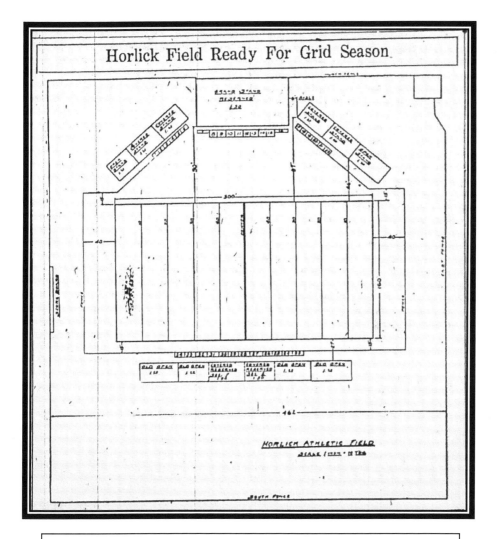

1923 Horlick Athletic Field "Home of the NFL Horlick-Racine Legion" Football Field and spectator stands layout.

The Toledo Maroons arrived in town on Saturday evening. The Maroons defeated the Legion by a score of 7-0 in a 1922 NFL season game. They won most of their games in the prior season, while holding the League Champion Canton Bulldogs to two tie score games. This game was set to be a tough challenge for the Legion. Gil Falcon, Toledo coach and captain was familiar to the people of Racine as he played professional football at the fullback position in the area for several years. The Maroons had acquired Dutch Lauer (University of Detroit) from the Green Bay Packers. "Red" Watson returned as quarterback for Toledo. He was from Texas (A&M) and played an exceptional game against Racine in 1922. Gillo's former college teammate, Colgate All-American tackle Clarence "Steamer" Horning was in the starting line-up for Toledo. Also starting for the Maroons was Dutch Strauss, an All-Southwestern fullback from Phillips University as well as Walter "Tillie" Voss, who was an All-America from Detroit University. These two teams had equally matched talent and both were expecting a hard fought battle.

Horlick-Racine Legion 1923 ROSTER:

	Name	Position	College/Pro
1.	Hank Gillo	Fullback	Colgate
2.	Art Braman	Tackle	Yale
3.	Jack Mintun	Center	Chicago Staleys
4.	Charlie Dressen	Quarterback	Chicago Staleys
5.	Les Lunde	Halfback	Ripon
6.	Bill McCaw	End	Indiana
7.	Irv Langhoff	Halfback	Marquette
8.	John Milton	Halfback	Idaho
9.	Wallace Barr	Quarterback	Wisconsin
10.	Fritz Heinisch	End	Independent
11.	Al Elliott	Halfback	Wisconsin
12.	Fritz Roessler	End	Marquette
13.	George Hartong	Guard	Purdue
14.	Jack Hueller	Guard	Independent
15.	Ed Miller	End	Purdue
16.	Bob Foster	Tackle	Independent
17.	Len Smith	Tackle	Wisconsin
18.	Earl Gorman	Guard	Independent

FOOTBALL TOMORROW

Horlick-Racine Legion vs. Minneapolis Marines
Kick-Off 2:15 Sharp   Horlick Athletic Field

THE last home game, can you imagine it? Doesn't seem possible that the football season is nearly over, does it? Dope claims that the season is going to be closed here with one of the best games of the year. It will be remembered that the Marines handed Racine a neat trimming on their own grounds a few weeks ago. Then they played Rock Island to a tie. With Williams behind the line Sunday it should be some game to watch.

Of course the grounds will be crowded for this last game of the season; that's understood. But it certainly would be fine if the record crowd of the year would hearten the boys on to victory.

** GAME DAY **

An exciting finish to an evenly matched game, which was scoreless for three quarters resulted in a 7 to 7 tie. Beginning ceremonies were presented by Racine Mayor William Armstrong. He awarded a trophy cup to George Smith for his winning ticket selling team; the "Case Eagles" A big basket of flowers was presented to the Legion team by the Racine Baseball Club. Mayor Armstrong performed the honorary "First Kick" to start the 1923 NFL season. The ball went three yards and the 1923 season officially began for the Horlick-Racine Legion. The Maroons made eight first downs and the Legion had seven. Racine's Jack Mintun played an exceptional game at center, battling a fierce Toledo line. Al Elliott and Hank Gillo had their usual outstanding showing on both offense and defense. Both teams missed an opportunity to score in the second quarter with failed field goal attempts. The Legion attempted a field goal early in the second quarter from the Toledo twelve yard line but it was blocked. Toledo missed a field goal attempt from the Racine ten yard line as time expired in the half. The Maroons scored early in the fourth quarter on a thirty yard pass from Hill to Voss. They added an extra point and led the game 7-0. A brilliant forward passing attack staged by the Horlick-Racine Legion in the last five minutes of the game, allowed them to tie the powerful Toledo Maroons 7-7. A fifty yard pass from Wallace "Shorty" Barr to Fritz Roessler put the ball on the Legion two yard line. It was one of the longest forward passes ever registered in the National Football League at the time and it brought the entire 3,500 fans attending the game to their feet. Three unsuccessful run attempts at the end zone and a final pass from Barr to Roessler scored the touchdown, which set up the tie. Gillo successfully booted the place kick for the extra point and the game was tied.

PLAY BY PLAY: 1923 NFL SEASON HRL GAME 1
                  HORLICK-RACINE LEGION VS TOLEDO MAROONS
                  Sunday: September 30th, 1923   2:30 pm
                  Horlick Athletic Field   Racine, Wisconsin

FIRST QUARTER:

   Conrad kicked to Racine and the ball went out of bounds at the Racine 33 yard. Conrad had to kick off again. On a second attempt by Conrad, he kicked the ball to the Racine 10 yard line. Barr received the ball and advanced it to the Legion 30 yard line. The Legion gained 1 yard on a run through the line. Langhoff attempted a run, which resulted in a 1 yard loss. Racine punted to Toledo and the ball was received on the Maroon 48 yard line. Strauss ran the ball and it resulted in a gain of 8 yards. Racine held Toledo for no gain on the next two downs. The Maroons ran the ball, off tackle and it resulted in a 2 yard gain as well as a first down. Toledo gained 7 yards on a run through the line. The Maroons ran the ball and it resulted in a gain as well as a first down. Toledo ran the ball and it resulted in a 1 yard gain. Toledo ran the ball through the line and it resulted in a 2 yard gain. A Strauss run attempt on third down resulted in no gain. Conrad punted the ball to the Racine goal line. Barr received the ball and advanced it 10 yards before being tackled. Milton gained 2 yards on a run through the line. Racine could not gain a first down. Langhoff punted the ball to the 30 yard line. McNamara received the ball and fumbled it. Braman recovered the ball for Racine. Barr attempted to advance the ball but it resulted in no gain. The ball was on the 30 yard line. A Milton run attempt was stopped and it resulted in no gain. Langhoff punted the ball to the 50 yard line. The Maroons received the ball. Two Toledo run attempts through the line, each resulted in a 1 yard gain. A Watson pass attempt to Voss resulted in an incomplete pass. Conrad punted to the Legion. Barr received the ball on the Racine 25 yard line. A Langhoff run attempt resulted in no gain. The Legion was unable to advance the ball in two downs. Barr punted to the Maroon 48 yard line as the quarter ended.

SECOND QUARTER:

   A Lauer run attempt resulted in a 1 yard loss with a tackle by Milton. A Watson pass attempt to Voss went incomplete. "Rat" Watson gained 9 yards on run around the end. Toledo made a first down on a run through the line. Lauer gained 2 yards on a run attempt. A Maroon pass attempt went incomplete. A Watson run attempt resulted in no gain. Lauer punted the ball and it went out of bounds. Racine took possession of the ball on the 21 yard line. Gillo ran the ball through the line and it resulted in a 1 yard gain. Racine substituted Roessler in the game for McCaw at the end position. Gillo ran the ball and it resulted in a 9 yard gain as well as a Legion first down. Langhoff ran the ball and it resulted in a 10 yard gain and another

Racine first down. Gillo ran the ball and it resulted in a 9 yard gain. It was just short of another first down. Racine substituted "Rowdy" Elliott in the game for Langhoff at the left halfback position. Langhoff ran the ball through the line and it resulted in a gain of 2 yards. It was a Legion first down. Elliott ran the ball and it resulted in a gain of 4 yards. Milton ran the ball through the line and it resulted in a gain of 4 yards. A completed forward pass from Barr to Elliott resulted in a 20 yard gain for Racine. A Legion run attempt resulted in no gain. The ball was on the Toledo 15 yard line. Elliott ran the ball through the line and it resulted in a gain of 3 yards. A Racine pass attempt went incomplete. Gillo attempted a place kick from the 20 yard line but it was blocked by the Maroons. Barr recovered the ball for the Legion and it was on the 19 yard line of Toledo. Elliott gained 4 yards on a run. Toledo was penalized 5 yards for holding. An Elliott run attempt resulted in no gain. A Racine pass attempt went incomplete. Gillo punted the ball to the Maroons. Toledo was penalized for holding. A Racine run attempt resulted in a fumble on the Maroon 10 yard line. Toledo kicked the ball to Racine. Barr received the ball on the 45 yard line and advanced it to the 31 yard line. A Legion pass was intercepted by Hill, on the Maroon 20 yard line. Lauer gained 3 yards on a run through the line. Lauer was tackled for a 1 yard loss by Milton. Conrad punted to the Legion and the ball went to the Racine 29 yard line. The Toledo defense tackled Barr for a 10 yard loss. Barr kicked to Toledo and they received the ball on the 49 yard line. Racine substituted Foster in the game for Braman. Horning kicked to the Legion. Barr received the ball on the Racine 10 yard line. Barr advanced the ball to the 20 yard line. He was tackled as the quarter ended.

THIRD QUARTER:

Gillo kicked the ball to Toledo and it went to the Maroon 10 yard line. Voss received the ball for Toledo and advanced it to the 25 yard line. He was tackled by Milton. Lauer ran the ball and it resulted in a 3 yard gain with the ball being on the 28 yard line. Conrad punted the ball to Racine. Barr received the ball on the 40 yard line. He advanced the ball 5 yards. A Langhoff run attempt resulted in no gain. Racine was penalized 5 yards for being off sides on the play. Milton gained 3 yards on a run attempt. A Gillo run attempt resulted in no gain. Milton kicked the ball to Toledo. Lauer received the ball on the 25 yard line. He was tackled by Mintun. A Lauer run attempt was stopped by Gillo with no gain. Toledo punted the ball to Racine and it went to the 40 yard line. Barr received the ball and advanced it 7 yards. A Langhoff run attempt resulted in no gain. Barr passed the ball to Langhoff and it resulted in a 33 yard gain as well as a Racine first down. The ball was on the Maroon 20 yard line. Gillo ran the ball and it resulted in a 12 yard gain as well as a Racine first down. A Langhoff run attempt resulted in no gain. Another Langhoff run attempt resulted in no gain. Gillo ran the ball and it resulted in a 2 yard gain. A Racine pass attempt went incomplete. The Legion turned over the ball on downs. Toledo took possession of the ball on the Maroon 20 yard line. The Maroons gained 4 yards on a run through the line. Toledo gained 7 yards on another run through the line. Lauer attempted two running plays through the line and both resulted in no gain. Toledo punted to Racine and the ball went to the Legion 20 yard line. Racine attempted two running plays and both resulted in no gain. Barr punted to the 50 yard line. Horning ran the ball through the line and it resulted in a 3 yard gain. The Maroons punted to the Racine 37 yard line. The Legion advanced the ball 2 yards to the 39 yard line. The quarter ended.

FOURTH QUARTER:

Langhoff ran the ball and it resulted in no gain. Gillo ran the ball through the line and it resulted in a 3 yard gain. Gillo punted to Toledo. The Maroons received the ball and advanced it on the Racine 41 yard line. A Toledo pass attempt went incomplete. Racine was penalized for holding. The ball was on the 36 yard line. Toledo substituted Watson in the game for Lauer. Watson was tackled for a loss by Braman. The ball was on the 38 yard line. Hill completed a pass to Voss. He advanced the ball to the Racine 15 yard line. Voss ran the ball around the end and scored a touchdown. Voss successfully kicked the extra point. *Score: Racine 0, Toledo 7.* Racine substituted into the game Elliott and Roessler for McCaw and Milton. Gillo kicked the ball off to the Toledo goal line. Watson received the ball and advanced it to the 20 yard line. Watson ran the ball and it resulted in a 3 yard gain. Hill ran the ball and it resulted in a 6 yard gain. Jones ran the ball and made a first down for the Maroons. Watson ran the ball and he gained 2 yards. Racine substituted in the game Hueller for Gorman. A Toledo run attempt resulted in no gain. The Maroons were penalized 5 yards for delay of game. Toledo punted to Racine and the ball was received at the 50 yard line. A pass from Barr to Elliott went incomplete. "Shorty" Barr dropped back to the 41 yard line and hurled a pass 55 yards, which was received by "Fritz" Roessler at the Toledo 4 yard line. He was stopped there. Elliott ran the ball through the line and it resulted in a 1 yard gain. Barr was stopped with no gain. A short pass from Barr to Elliott resulted in a touchdown. Gillo kicked a successful extra point attempt. *Score: Racine 7, Toledo 7.* Racine substituted Foster in the game for Braman. Gillo kicked off to Toledo and the ball went out of bounds. Gillo kicked again and the ball was received at the Toledo 15 yard line. The Maroons advanced the ball to the 50 yard line. A Toledo pass went incomplete. Watson passed the ball to Hill and it resulted in an 11 yard gain. It was a first down for Toledo. The Legion substituted Heinisch in the game for Miller. Hill gained 20 yards on a run around the end. A Toledo pass was intercepted by Barr on the 19 yard line. He advanced the ball to the 25 yard line. Langhoff ran the ball through the line and it resulted in a gain of 3 yards. Barr ran the ball through the line and it resulted in a gain of 2 yards. Elliott ran the ball through the line and it resulted in a gain of 3 yards. Barr punted to Maroons. Watson received the ball on the Toledo 25 yard line. Watson gained 14 yards on a run play but Toledo was penalized 10 yards for holding. Horning attempted a run but he was tackled for a 1 yard loss. Toledo punted to Racine. Barr received the ball and he was tackled. The game ended.

FINAL SCORE: HORLICK-RACINE LEGION 7, TOLEDO MAROONS 7.

SCORE BY PERIODS:	1st	2nd	3rd	4th	Final
Horlick-Racine Legion	0	0	0	7	7
Toledo Maroons	0	0	0	7	7

TOUCHDOWNS: Racine- Roessler (1) Toledo- Voss (1)
POINT AFTER TOUCHDOWN: Racine- Gillo (1) Toledo- Voss (1)

STARTING ROSTER:

RACINE		TOLEDO
Miller	Left End	Voss
Braman	Left Tackle	Batchelor
Gorman	Left Guard	Jones
Mintun	Center	Conrad
Hartong	Right Guard	McNamara
Smith	Right Tackle	Horning
McCaw	Right End	Seyfrit
Barr	Quarterback	Watson
Langhoff	Left Halfback	Hill
Milton	Right Halfback	Lauer
Gillo	Fullback	Strauss

SUBSTITUTIONS: RACINE –Elliott for Langhoff, Langhoff for Elliott, Elliott for Milton, Roessler for McCaw, Heinisch for Miller, Foster for Braman, Hueller for Gorman. TOLEDO-Gillis for Jones, Hunt for Batchelor, White for Seyfrit, Fitzgerald for Watson.

FIRST DOWNS BY PERIODS:	1st	2nd	3rd	4th	Total
Horlick-Racine Legion	0	2	2	1	5
Toledo Maroons	2	1	1	4	8

REFEREE: Jim Holloway (Chicago)
UMPIRE: Stothart (Milwaukee Normal)
HEAD LINESMAN: Thomas (Chicago)
TIME KEEPER: Fred Maxted (Racine)

The Racine fans were excited about the home opener. The Legion played a solid game and proved that they could compete with one of the best in the NFL. A thrilling long pass from Barr to Roessler demonstrated that they possessed the skills necessary to be a winning franchise. The next opponent would also test the ability of Racine to compete with the top teams in the League. The Chicago Bears would be coming to Horlick Athletic Field in Racine on the following Sunday. The Legion team was looking to avenge a hard fought 6-0 loss, which they received at home in the 1922 NFL season home opener. This was the only meeting between the two teams scheduled for the 1923 season. It was anticipated to be strong showdown, which was expected to draw a record crowd.

A few changes were made to develop the organization. Jack Melvin of the American Legion Post No. 76 was added as assistant business manager. He would report to Business Manager Max Zirbes. Together, they would handle the financial details of the Horlick-Racine Legion Football Team. Team Manager George Ruetz also hired Bill Hynd (Simmons trainer) to be in charge of the conditioning of the Horlick-Racine Legion players for the 1923 season. Hynd would begin to develop more speed and resistance in the Legion squad. Starting on Tuesday, Ruetz scheduled practice every evening of the week at Lakeview Park in order to prepare the team for the Bears. The Chicago Bears were led by Star Right End George Halas and Halfback Dutch Sternaman. (Sternaman kicked both field goals that added up to the 6-0 defeat in 1922) The Bears lost to the Rock Island Independents 3-0 in their season opener. Both squads made changes to their rosters. The Bears added six players for the upcoming game and Racine was anticipating the return of Charlie Dressen from the St. Paul Baseball team. Ruetz planned to add R. J. Halliday to his roster. Richard "Death" Halliday was a former University of Chicago player. He would play right end for the Legion. Halliday would sign his contract to play for Racine on October 7th, 1923. Roessler and Elliott were expected to start for the game against the Chicago Bears. Milton strained a ligament in his foot and therefore, he would not play in the game.

A new grandstand was built to increase the seating at Horlick Athletic Field to 5,000. William Horlick, Sr. commissioned the construction of the permanent grandstand as well as several movable stands at a total cost of $25,000.

Team Photographer G. A. Malme was scheduled to take motion pictures of the Legion/Bears game. He was planning to be stationed for the filming on top of the new grandstand. From there, he would have a clear view of the entire football field. Efforts were being made to have a press box built on the roof, which would allow him as well as the sports writers, an easier way to view the entire field at Horlickville.

The Legion and Bears teams averaged about the same player weight. The Horlick-Racine Legion team average was 196 lbs., while the Chicago Bears averaged 198 lbs. prior to their matchup. The Racine line from end to end averaged 202 lbs. The Chicago line from end to end averaged 204 lbs. The Legion backfield averaged 185 lbs., while the Bears backfield averaged 182 lbs.

The line-ups were as follows:

Horlick-Racine Legion 1923 Roster

Starters:

No.	Name	Position	Wt.	College
15	Ed Miller	Left End	195 lbs.	Purdue
2	Art Braman	Left Tackle	210 lbs.	Yale
6	Bill McCaw	Left Guard	195 lbs.	Indiana
3	Jack Mintun	Center	190 lbs.	Chicago Staleys
13	George Hartong	Right Guard	220 lbs.	Purdue
17	Pat Smith	Right Tackle	195 lbs.	Wisconsin
12	Fritz Roessler	Right End	190 lbs.	Marquette
9	Wallace Barr	Quarterback	200 lbs.	Wisconsin
11	Al Elliott	Left Halfback	165 lbs.	Wisconsin
7	Irv Langhoff	Right Halfback	160 lbs.	Marquette
1	Hank Gillo	Fullback	210 lbs.	Colgate

Substitutes:

No.	Name	Position	Wt.	College
8	John Milton	Halfback	170 lbs.	Chicago
10	Fritz Heinisch	End	165 lbs.	Independent
14	Jack Hueller	Guard	205 lbs.	Independent
16	Bob Foster	Tackle	125 lbs.	Independent
18	Earl Gorman	Guard	210 lbs.	Indiana

115

Chicago Bears 1923 Roster

Starters:

No.	Name	Position	Wt.	College
19	F. Hanny	Left End	200 lbs.	Indiana
16	Ed Healy	Left Tackle	190 lbs.	Dartmouth
18	H. Anderson	Left Guard	194 lbs.	Notre Dame*
13	George Trafton	Center	220 lbs.	Notre Dame*
2	Joe LaFluer	Right Guard	222 lbs.	Marquette
12	Hugh Blacklock	Right Tackle	221 lbs.	Michigan Aggies*
7	George Halas	Right End	180 lbs.	Illinois*
8	Red Bryan	Quarterback	170 lbs.	Chicago
3	D. Sternaman	Left Halfback	185 lbs.	Illinois
9	Jake Lanum	Right Halfback	186 lbs.	Illinois
5	George Bolan	Fullback	205 lbs.	Purdue

Substitutes:

No.	Name	Position	Wt.	College
17	Ralph Scott	Tackle	224 lbs.	Wisconsin*
15	P. Flaherty	End	204 lbs.	Washington
10	Gus Fetz	Halfback	145 lbs.	Chicago
6	Art Garvey	Guard	230 lbs.	Notre Dame

*Denotes All-American Selection

** GAME DAY **

"Dutch" Sternaman kicked a field goal to score the only points of the game for either team. The Chicago Bears defeated the Horlick-Racine Legion by a score of 3-0 in one of the hardest fought and most spectacular battles ever played on the Racine Gridiron (Horlick Athletic Field football field in Racine, Wisconsin), up to that point. The only score of the game came in the second quarter, when the Bears were stopped on the Racine 10 yard line. Sternaman dropped back to the 35 yard line and kicked the ball through the goal post for 3 points. It was the second time in two years that Sternaman had kicked a field goal to defeat the Legion. In the prior season, Sternaman kicked two field goals to defeat Racine 6-0 at Horlick Athletic Field. The Bears were able to keep the ball in Legion territory for three quarters but the Ruetzmen (Horlick-Racine Legion team) fired back in the fourth quarter. They had two opportunities to score in the fourth period but they were unable to capitalize. Racine was able to move the ball to the Chicago 20 yard line. Gillo dropped back for the place kick for field goal but the snap from Mintun to Langhoff was juggled and then he dropped the ball.

116

This gave the Bears defense enough time to penetrate the Legion line and Gillo was forced to kick the ball off the ground without a tee. The kick was blocked but Fritz Heinisch recovered the ball on the 36 yard line for Racine. Barr threw a 30 yard pass to Miller, who had an open field ahead of him but he dropped the ball. The pass went incomplete. The game ended on a last pass attempt to score for the Legion. It was a battle to the end.

Hank Gillo was one of the Racine stars of the game. He played exceptionally well on both offense and defense. On defense, he was able to stop the Bears offense, play after play, whether they ran through the line or around the end. Offensively, Gillo was able to gain many yards on the ground. Elliott, Barr and Meyers also played well in the game for Racine.

More than 4,000 fans witnessed this sensational and bitterly fought battle between Chicago and Racine, which lasted to the final whistle.

PLAY BY PLAY: 1923 NFL SEASON HRL GAME 2
HORLICK-RACINE LEGION VS CHICAGO BEARS
Sunday: October 7th, 1923   2:30 pm
Horlick Athletic Field   Racine, Wisconsin

FIRST QUARTER:

Gillo kicked off the ball for Racine. Chicago's Dutch Sternaman received the ball on the Bears 20 yard line and advanced it to the 30 yard line. One the first play of the series, Chicago fumbled the ball and lost 10 yards on the recovery. Bolan ran the ball and it resulted in a 3 yard gain. The Bears punted the ball to the Legion. Barr received the ball and he was stopped on the 35 yard line. Langhoff gained 5 yards on a run around the right end. Gillo ran the ball and it resulted in a 1 yard gain. Gillo ran the ball and it resulted in a 4 yard gain as well as a Legion first down.

Elliott ran the ball through the line and it resulted in a 1 yard gain. Langhoff gained 5 yards on a run through the line. A Racine pass attempt went incomplete. Barr punted the ball to the 29 yard line. Chicago took possession. A Lanum run attempt resulted in no gain. Dutch Sternaman ran the ball around the end and it resulted in a 10 yard gain. It was a first down for Chicago. Lanum gained 4 yards on a run through the line. Bolan gained 5 yards on a run attempt. Racine substituted Hueller in the game for Braman. Bolan gained 3 yards on a run attempt and it was a first down. Bolan ran through ball but it resulted in no gain. Lanum ran the ball through the left end and it resulted in a four yard gain. Sternaman attempted a place kick for field goal from the 30 yard line but he was unsuccessful. Racine took possession, of the ball on the Legion 30 yard line. Elliott ran the ball through the line and it resulted in a 1 yard gain. Gillo ran the ball through the line and it resulted in a 5 yard gain. Barr punted the ball to the Chicago 30 yard line and the receiver was immediately tackled by Tong (Hartong). Sternaman ran the ball and it resulted in a 3 yard gain. Bolan ran the ball and it resulted in a 7 yard gain as well as a Bears first down. Byron ran the ball and it resulted in a 4 yard gain. Bolan ran the ball and it resulted in a gain of 3 yards. Byron threw a pass to Halas and it resulted in a 20 yard gain as well as another first down. The ball was on the Racine 30 yard line. Bolan ran the ball twice for a total of an 8 yard gain. Halas ran the ball around the right end and it resulted in a 6 yard gain as well as another Chicago first down. Bolan ran the ball through the line and it resulted in a 5 yard gain. Chicago had the ball on the Racine 12 yard line as the first quarter ended.

SECOND QUARTER:

Bolan ran the ball and it resulted in a gain of 3 yards as well as a first down for the Bears. The ball was on the 9 yard line. Sternaman ran the ball through the line and it resulted in a 1 yard gain. The Bears fumbled the ball and Langhoff recovered the ball on the 7 yard line for Racine. Gillo attempted a run through the line but it resulted in no gain. Barr ran the ball through the line and it resulted in a 9 yard gain. Langhoff ran the ball and it resulted in a 1 yard gain as well as a Legion first down. A run attempt by Elliott resulted in a 5 yard loss after being tackled by Halas. Gillo attempted a run, which resulted in no gain. Gillo punted the ball to the 50 yard. Chicago received it and advanced it to the Racine 45 yard line. Chicago was penalized for clipping on the return and the ball went back to Racine. Gillo ran the ball through the line and it resulted in a 3 yard gain. Elliott attempted to run but it resulted in no gain. Halas intercepted a Racine pass on the 45 yard line and ran it back to the 40 yard line. Sternaman ran the ball through the line and it resulted in a 6 yard gain. Lanum was tackled by Gillo after a 3 yard gain. Byron ran the ball through the line and it resulted in a Chicago first down. Lanum ran the ball around the right tackle and it resulted in a 3 yard gain. A pass from Byron to Sternaman gained 10 yards for the Bears. Bolan ran the ball through the line and it resulted in a 2 yard gain. Sternaman ran the ball and it resulted in a gain of 1 yard. Bolan ran the ball and it resulted in a gain of 1 yard. Sternaman attempted a place kick for field goal from the Racine 15 yard line. The ball went soaring over the goal post and the Bears scored 3 points. *Score: Racine 0, Chicago 3*. Racine sent Foster in the game for Elliott. Gillo kicked off the ball into the Bears end zone.

118

Chicago started with the ball on the 20 yard line. Sternaman gained 7 yards on a run through the line. Sternaman gained another 15 yards on a run around the right end. It was a first down for Chicago. Byron gained 25 yards on a run around the left end and another first down. The quarter ended.

THIRD QUARTER:

Gillo kicked off to Chicago. Bolan received the ball on the 2 yard line. He advanced the ball to the 38 yard line. Lanum ran the ball and it resulted in a 6 yard gain. Bolan ran the ball and it resulted in a 1 yard gain. Sternaman lost 2 yards on a pitch back. Lanum punted to Racine. Langhoff received the ball on the 27 yard line. Elliott attempted a pass but he was tackled for a 10 yard loss. Barr punted the ball to the Bears. Sternaman received the ball on the 50 yard line. He advanced the ball and Sternaman was tackled by "Candy" Miller at the Racine 40 yard line. Lanum lost 1 yard on a run attempt. Sternaman ran the ball and it resulted in a gain of 2 yards. Byron attempted a pass but it was intercepted by Mintun at the 20 yard line. Gillo punted to the Bears. Fetz received the ball on the 40 yard line and he was tackled by Elliott. Fetz gained 11 yards on a run around the end and he was tackled by Langhoff. Bolan ran the ball and it resulted in a 1 yard gain. A Chicago pass attempt went incomplete. Byron attempted another pass, it was intercepted by Elliott. He advanced the ball from the 30 yard line to the 45 yard line. Racine substituted Gorman in the game for Tong (Hartong). Gillo ran with the ball but it resulted in no gain. A Racine pass attempt went incomplete. Another pass attempt from Barr to Roessler went incomplete. Barr punted to Chicago. Fetz received the ball on the 20 yard and he advanced it to the 22 yard line. Sternaman gained 2 yards on a run through the line. Lanum ran the ball and it resulted in a gain of 3 yards. Roessler tackled Fetz for a 2 yard loss. Fetz punted to the Legion. Langhoff received the ball on the Racine 40 yard line. Langhoff advanced the ball to the Bears 31 yard line. Gillo ran the ball through the center of the line and it resulted in a 6 yard gain. Langhoff ran the ball and it resulted in a 2 yard gain. Chicago substituted Sternaman in the game for Fetz. Gillo ran with ball but it resulted in no gain. Gillo gained 1 yard on a run attempt. The Bears took possession of the ball on the Chicago 26 yard line. Lanum gained 9 yards on a run through the line. Byron ran the ball for a 10 yard gain and a Chicago first down. Byron gained 5 yards on a run around the right end. Sternaman ran the ball and it resulted in a 3 yard gain. Bolan ran the ball but it resulted in no gain. The ball was on the Racine 49 yard line, when the quarter ended.

FOURTH QUARTER:

Lanum punted to the Legion. Barr received the ball and he was tackled on the Legion 18 yard line. Langhoff gained 11 yards on a run around the right end. It was a Legion first down. Gillo ran the ball and it resulted in a 2 yard gain. Langhoff ran the ball and it resulted in a 6 yard gain. A Gillo run attempt was stopped by Sternaman without gain. Barr punted the ball to the Bears and the ball went to the 30 yard line. A Byron run attempt was stopped without gain. A Sternaman run attempt around the end was stopped by Gillo without gain. A Chicago pass attempt went incomplete. Racine substituted Miller in the game for Meyers. The Bears punted the ball to Racine and it went to the Legion 30 yard line.

119

Langhoff received the punt and he advanced it to the 35 yard line. Langhoff gained 3 yards on a run through the line. A Racine pass attempt went incomplete. Racine punted the ball to the Bears and it went to the 50 yard line. Halas received the ball and advanced it 2 yards. Lanum gained 7 yards on a run attempt. A Bolan run attempt resulted in no gain. A Sternaman run attempt resulted in no gain. Byron punted the ball into the Racine end zone. The Legion took possession on the Legion 20 yard line. Barr gained 8 yards on a run attempt. Gillo gained 20 yards on a run through the line. Barr completed a pass to Langhoff and it resulted in a 25 yard gain. The ball was on Bears 35 yard line. A Legion pass attempt went incomplete. Barr ran the ball 9 yards to the Chicago 26 yard line. Gillo ran the ball and it resulted in a 1 yard gain as well as a Racine first down. An Elliott run attempt resulted in no gain. Barr passed the ball to Miller and it resulted in a 6 yard gain. The ball was on the Chicago 20 yard line. Gillo signaled for a place kick for field goal. Langhoff could not immediately get the ball set for the kick and Gillo had to kick the ball without a tee as well as off the ground. The Bears defense penetrated the line and blocked Gillo's kick. The ball bounced back to the Racine 36 yard before it was recovered by Legion player, Fritz Heinisch. A pass attempt from Barr to Heinisch went incomplete. A Barr pass attempt was intercepted by Byron on the 4 yard line and he returned it to the 35 yard line as time expired in the game. The game ended.

FINAL SCORE: HORLICK-RACINE LEGION 0, CHICAGO BEARS 3.

SCORE BY PERIODS:	1st	2nd	3rd	4th	Final
Horlick-Racine Legion	0	0	0	0	0
Chicago Bears	0	3	0	0	3

FIELD GOAL: Chicago-Sternaman (1)

STARTING ROSTER:

RACINE		CHICAGO
Miller	Left End	Hanney
Braman	Left Tackle	Scott
Gorman	Left Guard	Healey
Mintun	Center	Trafton
Hartong	Right Guard	Garvey
Smith	Right Tackle	Blackburn
McCaw	Right End	Halas
Barr	Quarterback	Byron
Langhoff	Left Halfback	Sternaman
Milton	Right Halfback	Lanum
Gillo	Fullback	Bolan

SUBSTITUTIONS: RACINE –Hueller for Braman, Foster for Elliott, Gorman for Tong, Miller for Meyers. CHICAGO-Sternaman for Fetz.

FIRST DOWNS BY PERIODS:	1st	2nd	3rd	4th	Totals
Horlick-Racine Legion	0	0	0	0	0
Chicago Bears	0	3	0	0	3

REFEREE: Stothart
UMPIRE: Joyce
HEAD LINESMAN: Whyte
TIME KEEPER: Fred Maxted

Although Racine did not defeat Chicago, they played equally with one of the best in the NFL. Before leaving Racine on Sunday, Chicago Bears Manager George Halas asked Horlick-Racine Legion Manager George Ruetz, if they could schedule a game in Chicago on November 25th, 1923. This game would undoubtedly draw a large crowd and Ruetz was anxious to schedule it. The Legion had a game scheduled with the Hammond Pros on November 25th. Manager Ruetz immediately wrote NFL President Joe Carr, asking if that game could be cancelled. He explained that a large number of local fans would accompany a trip to Chicago but very few could get as far as Hammond. A special train for those, who wanted to attend the game in Chicago was scheduled in anticipation of a rematch with the Bears.

The Legion began practice on Tuesday in preparation for their next game against the Milwaukee Badgers at Milwaukee. Coach Gillo and Captain Langhoff began to focus on the play of the offensive and defensive line. The Bears were able to get long gains and they wanted to tighten the line, so they could stop other teams from getting long runs against the Legion. The offensive line needed to give Barr more time in order for him to have a better opportunity to pass the ball.

Charlie Dressen announced that he would report to Racine. The "Rabbit" (Dressen), who played third baseman for the St. Paul Baseball American Baseball Association Club wired Manager Ruetz to let him know that he would be available to practice with the team prior to the game on Sunday against Milwaukee. With the combination of Dressen and Barr, Racine would have the best two quarterbacks playing in the NFL. Both men were also exceptional substitutes at the halfback position.

John Milton, who was out of the previous Sunday's game because of a torn ligament was practicing and ready to return for the game against the Milwaukee Badgers. Every player was ready for the upcoming game and there were no injuries to report.

There was a lot of interest in this game between Legion and Badgers because it was the first game between any of the NFL Wisconsin teams for the season. The Green Bay Packers had the best record in 1922 of the three teams- Milwaukee Badgers, Horlick-Racine Legion and Green Bay Packers. Therefore, they won the 1922 "Wisconsin Title". Many fans were planning to attend the game in Milwaukee on that Sunday and Legion Manager George Ruetz made special arrangements to have extra train cars on the North Shore Line, which would carry fans to the game.

Charlie Dressen had not reported to the team yet, so Manager Ruetz sent him a wire message. He told Dressen to report as soon as possible. Chuck was under contract with the St. Paul American Association Club until Oct. 15th but he was now expected to report to the Horlick-Racine Legion in time for the Akron game, which was scheduled for a week from Sunday.

A Large numbers of fans were expected to travel by automobile to attend the Horlick-Racine Legion vs. Milwaukee Badgers NFL game in Milwaukee, Wisconsin. Tickets for the game were on sale in Racine, Wisconsin at Oscar Fring's Drug Store on Junction Ave, Rehl's Cigar Stores on State Street and Sixth Ave as well as Tom Smader's Place and the Monument Cigar Store starting on the Thursday morning prior to the game. Those tickets were all reserved in the section on the west side, which was set aside for the Racine fans. Those tickets would not be available for sale at the game and fans were encouraged to get their ducats (tickets) early. The game was scheduled to take place at the Borcherts Park on Eight and Chambers Streets in Milwaukee. The American Association Baseball Park was the same park at which, they played each other in the prior season. The tickets sold for $1.50 each plus an extra 15 cent war tax. Only the $1.65 tickets were on sale in Racine. General admission tickets would be available for $1.00 at the field gate in Milwaukee on the day of the game. The Horlick-Racine Legion team did not have to pay a war tax on their home games.

Jack Melvin handled the business affairs of the club as Max Zirbes accompanied the Legion drum corps to San Francisco, CA. Jack was known as progressive business man, who knew football. For several years, Melvin was connected to the Horlick Standards professional football team as well as managing other football, baseball and basketball teams.

The Milwaukee Badgers had an entirely new team for 1923 with the exception of their star 1922 fullback, Dinger Doane. The Badgers played Jim Thorpe's team on the previous week and played the St. Louis Browns to a scoreless tie in their first game of the season. Jimmy Conzelman, Milwaukee manager and quarterback, would be the player that the Racine team would have to watch out for. He was an excellent passer, who also ran the ball well. Conzelman also kicked for the Badgers. Jimmy was a constant threat on the gridiron to the opposing team.

Milwaukee Badgers 1923 Roster

Starters:

No.	Name	Position	Wt.	College/Pro
11	Sacks	Left End	175 lbs.	Chicago Cardinals
19	Blalock	Left Tackle	210 lbs.	Baylor
18	Smith	Left Guard	220 lbs.	Chicago Bears
15	Madolney	Left Guard	220 lbs.	Green Bay Packers
16	Larson	Center	185 lbs.	Notre Dame
20	Underwood	Right Guard	265 lbs.	Rice Institute
4	Wenke	Right Tackle	205 lbs.	Nebraska
13	Winkleman	Right End	175 lbs.	Arkansas
1	Conzelman	Quarterback	175 lbs.	Washington
5	Turner	Left Halfback	165 lbs.	Lombard
3	Erickson	Right Halfback	180 lbs.	W. & J.
14	Doane	Fullback	200 lbs.	Tufts

Substitutes:

No.	Name	Position	Wt.	College/Pro
17	G. Strickland	Guard	190 lbs.	Lombard
2	Mooney	Halfback	165 lbs.	Georgetown
12	McGinnes	Tackle	210 lbs.	Marquette

Horlick-Racine Legion 1923 Roster

Starters:

No.	Name	Position	Wt.	College
5	Paul Meyers	Left End	170 lbs.	Wisconsin
15	Ed Miller	Left Tackle	195 lbs.	Purdue
18	Earl Gorman	Left Guard	210 lbs.	Independent
3	Jack Mintun	Center	190 lbs.	Chicago Staleys
13	George Hartong	Right Guard	214 lbs.	Purdue
17	Pat Smith	Right Tackle	192 lbs.	Wisconsin
12	Fritz Roessler	Right End	185 lbs.	Marquette
9	Wallace Barr	Quarterback	194 lbs.	Wisconsin
11	Al Elliott	Left Halfback	175 lbs.	Wisconsin
7	Irv Langhoff	Right Halfback	158 lbs.	Marquette
1	Hank Gillo	Fullback	195 lbs.	Colgate

Substitutes:

No.	Name	Position	Wt.	College
2	Art Braman	Left Tackle	210 lbs.	Yale
6	Bill McCaw	Guard	195 lbs.	Indiana
8	Jack Milton	Halfback	168 lbs.	Chicago
10	Fritz Heinisch	End	165 lbs.	Independent
14	Jack Hueller	Guard	205 lbs.	Indiana
16	Bob Foster	Tackle	195 lbs.	Indiana

** <u>GAME DAY</u> **

   Paul Meyers, former University of Wisconsin star end received a pass from Legion
quarterback, Wallace "Shorty" Barr to score the touchdown, which led to a tie
game. Barr, in the last 3 minutes of the game, passed the ball from the Racine 25
yard line to the Milwaukee 25 yard line, where Meyers received the ball and he ran
it in for a Racine touchdown. The Horlick-Racine Legion football team tied the
Milwaukee Badgers by a score of 7-7 in an NFL season game, which was sizzling
with excitement. The Badgers scored their only touchdown on a fluke Legion punt
play. Barr punted the ball for Racine and it sailed high but short. The ball bounced
back behind the Racine goal line. There was a pile up in the end zone for the ball.
After the referee pulled all the players off the ball, he awarded Milwaukee's Turner
possession of the ball, which gave them a touchdown. The game was played evenly
throughout. Milwaukee had ten first downs and Racine had twelve.

PLAY BY PLAY: **1923 NFL SEASON HRL GAME 3**
                  HORLICK-RACINE LEGION VS MILWAUKEE BADGERS
                  Sunday: October 14th, 1922   2:30 pm
                  American Association Baseball Park
                  Milwaukee, Wisconsin

FIRST QUARTER:
   Gillo kicked off the ball for Racine. The ball was received by Sachs on the 30 yard
line and he returned the ball 5 yards. In Milwaukee's first series, they were unable
to advance the ball for a first down. The ball was turned over to the Legion after an
unsuccessful fourth down attempt. Langhoff and Gillo made large gains to give
Racine two first downs. Racine advanced the ball to the 50 yard but turned it was
over to the Badgers after they were unsuccessful in attempting to get a first down on
fourth down. The Badgers were successful on several run attempts by Conzelman
through the line. The ball was advanced down to the Racine 20 yard line. After
getting the ball far into Legion territory, Milwaukee turned the ball over to Racine.
After an unsuccessful three downs attempted by Racine, they punted to Milwaukee.
Milwaukee was unsuccessful in three downs and the Badgers punted to the Legion.
Racine was unsuccessful in three down attempts and they punted to the Badgers.
Milwaukee was unable to get a first down and they punted to the Legion. Racine
could not gain for a first down and they punted to Milwaukee. Milwaukee was able
to get four first downs. Conzelman and Doane were each successful with consistent
long run attempts through the line and around the end. Together, they advanced the
ball down to the Racine 7 yard line. Racine was able to hold the Badgers for four
downs and they turned the ball over to the Legion on the Racine 2 yard line. Racine
decided to punt the ball in order to get it out of Legion territory. Barr punted the
ball into the air but a strong wind took the ball and it flew back to the Racine 8 yard
line. The ball bounced from the 8 yard line back into the end zone. Milwaukee's

Turner jumped on the ball and the referee signaled for a Badgers touchdown. A long argument followed the play but the referee stood his ground on the touchdown call. Conzelman successfully kicked for the extra point. *Score: Racine 0, Milwaukee 7.* After a kick off and exchange on downs, Racine had the ball on the 50 yard line as the quarter ended.

SECOND QUARTER:

Racine turned the ball over on downs to Milwaukee. The Badgers ran the ball and it resulted in a gain of 20 yards. It was a first down for the Badgers. Milwaukee ran the ball and it resulted in a gain of 15 yards. Milwaukee gained another first down. The Badgers were unsuccessful in three downs and punted to the Legion. Conzelman punted the ball from the 50 yard line and it went out of bound on the Racine 5 yard line. Racine decided to punt the ball to get it out of the Legion territory. Barr punted the ball from the Racine end zone. The punt sailed 40 yards. Conzelman received the ball and returned the ball, up field. He fumbled the ball as he was being tackled by Langhoff. Langhoff recovered the ball but he also fumbled the ball. The ball was recovered by Racine Center Mintun. He was able to advance the ball with his marvelous pivots, while side stepping and shaking off several Badgers. Mintun advance the ball 75 yards to the Milwaukee 10 yard line. He was tackled by a racing Badgers end Winkleman. As Mintun was being tackled by Winkleman, he fumbled the ball. Sachs recovered the fumble for Milwaukee. The Milwaukee Badgers took possession of the ball. Conzelman gained 8 yards on a run attempt. Sachs was called for holding and the Badgers were penalized 15 yards. Conzelman punted the ball for Milwaukee and Racine received the ball on the 50 yard line. Racine was able to gain two first downs.

THIRD QUARTER:

Racine still had possession of the ball. They were able to gain four first downs. The Legion turned the ball over to the Badgers. Milwaukee was able to gain one first down.

FOURTH QUARTER:

Racine took possession of the ball. They were able to get 4 first downs. The Legion completed several passes. Racine was able to advance the ball with several run attempts through the line. The ball was on the Badger 15 yard line. Barr set up a fake formation. He was able to complete a pass over the corner to Meyer. Meyer received the ball in the end zone and scored a Racine touchdown. Gillo successfully kicked the extra point and the Racine fans went wild. The game was tied. *Score: Racine 7, Milwaukee 7.* Milwaukee received the ball. They began to advance the ball down field. They were able to get four first downs. Conzelman, Doane and Erickson carried the ball with fast and furious run attempts. The ball was within kicking distance of the field goal post. Conzelman attempted a place kick for field goal. The ball was blocked by Mintun. The Badgers were given possession of the ball after the blocked kick because of a holding penalty. Conzelman attempted another kick. The Legion players rushed through the line and hurried Conzelman on the kick. He was unable to complete the kick. The game ended.

FINAL SCORE: HORLICK-RACINE LEGION 7, MILWAUKEE BADGERS 7.

SCORE BY PERIODS:

	1st	2nd	3rd	4th	Final
Horlick-Racine Legion	0	0	0	7	7
Milwaukee Badgers	7	0	0	0	7

TOUCHDOWNS: Racine- Meyers (1) Milwaukee- Turner (1)
EXTRA POINT: Racine- Gillo (1) Milwaukee- Conzelman (1)

STARTING ROSTER:

RACINE		MILWAUKEE
Meyers	Left End	Sachs
Miller	Left Tackle	Blailock
Gorman	Left Guard	Smith
Mintun	Center	Larson
Hartong	Right Guard	Underwood
Smith	Right Tackle	Wenke
Roessler	Right End	Winkleman
Barr	Quarterback	Conzelman
Langhoff	Left Halfback	Erickson
Elliott	Right Halfback	Turner
Gillo	Fullback	Doane

SUBSTITUTIONS: RACINE– Heinisch for Roessler, Roessler for Heinisch, Romney for Gillo, Gillo for Romney, Foster for Elliott, Elliott for Foster, Braman for Miller, Miller for Braman, McCaw for Gorman, Hueller for McCaw. MILWAUKEE- Strickland for Smith

FIRST DOWNS BY PERIODS:

	1st	2nd	3rd	4th	Total
Horlick-Racine Legion	2	2	4	4	12
Milwaukee Badgers	4	1	1	4	10

REFEREE: Moore
UMPIRE: Downer
HEAD LINESMAN: Hanley

126

Over 4,000 fans attended the game in Milwaukee. The crowd was electric. Racine fans cheered loudly to the "Racine Locomotive" cheer, as it was one of their favorites. Russell Smith, Milwaukee left guard and former Navy player fractured his left shoulder, while trying to stop Jack Mintun's 65 yard run. Racine escaped the game with no injuries.

The Legion would practice four nights at Lakeview Park- Racine, Wisconsin in order to prepare for their upcoming game against Akron, Ohio. Pros.

Akron Pros team owner, Frank Neld added a few key players to prepare his team for Racine. Dutch Hendrian would serve as both quarterback and coach for the Pros. Several key players were former Ohio State University players.

FOOTBALL

SUNDAY, OCT. 21st
AKRON, OHIO
vs.
HORLICK RACINE LEGION
HORLICK ATHLETIC FIELD
KICKOFF 2:30 P. M.   ADMISSION $1.00

An announcement was made that Charlie Dressen would not report to the Horlick-Racine Legion football team. Several Major League Baseball teams were interested in buying out his baseball contract from the St. Paul Baseball Club and Dressen did not want to risk playing football and possibly getting injured. The Major League Baseball Washington team was expected to sign Charlie for the 1924 season.

** GAME DAY **

Three long place kicks by Hank Gillo gave the Horlick-Racine Legion team a victory over the Akron Pros. The Legion won the game by a score of 9-7 at Horlick Athletic Field in Racine, Wisconsin. Gillo had successfully kicked field goals with the distances of 50, 49 and 30 yards. The 50 yard kick set an NFL record. Hank kicked the winning field goal with Akron leading 7-6 at the end of the game. The Pros only points were scored on an interception by Frank Nesser. He returned the interception from the 40 yard line to score a defensive touchdown for Akron. The Legion threatened to score in the first quarter but was unable to get the ball across the goal line. Gillo and Richard "Death" Halliday (new Legion player, former University of Chicago player) were the stars for this game. Gillo's consistent running gave Racine, many of its first downs. He played a great game on defense as well as a spectacular game at the kicking position. Halliday played strong defensively and he was on the receiving end of several long Legion passes. Racine had 13 first downs and Akron had 4 first downs for the game.

127

PLAY BY PLAY: 1923 NFL SEASON HRL GAME 4
HORLICK-RACINE LEGION VS AKRON PROS
Sunday: October 21st, 1923   2:30 pm
Horlick Athletic Field   Racine, Wisconsin

FIRST QUARTER:
   Gillo kicked off to Akron at the start the game. The ball was received on the Akron 34 yard line. The Pros were unable to gain any yards in two downs. They decided to punt to Racine. Langhoff received the ball on the 30 yard line of the Legion and he was tackled. Elliott ran the ball off tackle and it resulted in a 1 yard gain. Gillo plunged (ran) through the center of the line and it resulted in a 21 yard gain. It was a first down for Racine. A combination of run attempts through the line along with consistent gains, advanced the ball for the Legion to the Akron 20 yard line. Racine was unable to advance the ball in three attempts. Gillo attempted a field goal from the 35 yard line for the Legion. The kick went wild and Akron was given the ball on the Pros 20 yard line. Three run attempts were unsuccessful for Akron. They chose to punt the ball. Barr received the ball for Racine at the 50 yard line. Racine was unable to advance the ball. They punted to Akron. The Pros were unable to advance the ball and they punted to the Legion. A Racine pass from Barr to Langhoff put the ball on the Akron 40 yard line. Gillo ran the ball three times and it resulted in a 4 yard gain. Racine chose to attempt a field goal. Hank attempted a field goal from the Pros 45 yard line. The ball fell short of the cross bar and rolled over the goal line. Akron took possession of the ball on the Pros 20 yard line. Akron lost 3 yards in three attempts to run the ball. They punted the ball and it was received by Langhoff. He was tackled at the Pros 46 yard line. Elliott gained 3 yards on a run off tackle. Gillo ran the ball through the center of the line and it resulted in a 3 yard gain. The quarter ended.
SECOND QUARTER:
   Racine had possession of the ball on the Akron 35 yard line. Gillo dropped back to the 48 yard line and successfully kicked a place kick for field goal over the cross bar. *Score: Racine 3, Akron 0.* Gillo kicked off to Akron. Nesser received the ball and he was downed on the Pros 20 yard line. Akron attempted a run around the left end, which resulted in a 10 yard loss. Akron punted to Racine. Langhoff received the ball on the 50 yard line. He advanced it to the Akron 39 yard line. Two pass attempts by Racine went incomplete. A Legion run gained 1 yard. Gillo dropped back to the 50 yard line in order to kick a field goal attempt. He booted the ball between the goal posts, which was another three points for Racine. *Score: Racine 6, Akron 0.* Akron kicked off to Racine. The ball was received on the 50 yard line. Racine attempted three plays, which resulted in no gain. They punted the ball to the Pros. The Pros attempted three plays, which resulted in no gain. Akron punted the ball to the

128

Legion. Racine attempted three passes and all were incomplete. Akron was able to break through the Legion line and hurry Barr on his pass attempts. With the ball on the Racine 48 yard line, Barr attempted a long pass, which was intercepted by Nesser. He sprinted 60 yards down the field and scored a touchdown for Akron. Racine lined up off sides on the Akron extra point attempt. The extra point attempt was good and the penalty was declined. *Score: Racine 6, Akron 7.* Gillo kicked off to the Pros and the ball was downed on the Akron 35 yard line. The Pros gained a total of 7 yards on three off tackle run attempts. Akron punted to the Racine 28 yard line. Langhoff received the ball and he was immediately tackled. The Legion punted the ball to the Pros. Akron punted the ball to Racine. They took possession of the ball at the 50 yard line. Gillo gained 2 yards on a run through the line. Langhoff ran the ball off tackle and it resulted in a 7 yard gain. Racine substituted Milton in the game for Langhoff. Milton ran the ball off tackle and it resulted in a 4 yard gain. It was a Racine first down. The quarter ended.

THIRD QUARTER:

Akron kicked off to Racine. Elliott ran the ball through the line and it resulted in a 10 yard gain. Langhoff ran the ball through the line and it resulted in a 10 yard gain as well as another Legion first down. Gillo attempted a place kick for a field goal but it missed the goal post by inches. Akron took possession of the ball. The Pros were penalized for holding. They were able to run the ball with many successful yardage gains. Akron attempted a criss-cross run play, which resulted in a loss of yardage. The Pros moved the ball to the Racine 40 yard line. Hendrian attempted a drop kick for field goal. The kick was unsuccessful. It fell short of the goal post. Racine took possession of the ball. A Racine pass attempts went incomplete. The Legion could not gain and Akron regained possession of the ball. The Pros were penalized 15 yards for holding. Hendrian attempted another drop kick for field goal. It was also unsuccessful. Racine took possession of the ball. They were stopped after advancing the ball and Akron took possession at the 48 yard line. The quarter ended.

FOURTH QUARTER:

Akron punted the ball to Racine. Barr received the ball on the 25 yard line. He advanced it to 35 yard line before being dragged down by the Pros. A pass from Barr to Halliday gained 15 yards for Racine. The ball was on the 50 yard line. Gillo bucked (ran) through the center of the line and it resulted in a 3 yard gain. A Racine pass attempt went incomplete. Akron was penalized another 15 yards for holding. Elliott gained 2 yards on a run through the line. Barr gained another 2 yards on a run through the line. Gillo attempted another field goal from back at the 42 yard line. Again, it missed by inches. Akron was given possession of the ball on the 20 yard line. Racine held them with no gain. Akron attempted a punt to Racine. It was partially blocked. Barr fell on the ball at the Akron 48 yard line. Gillo plowed (ran) through the line and it resulted in a 5 yard gain. Barr passed the ball to Halliday and it resulted in a 20 yard gain. The ball was once again in close enough distance for a field goal attempt. Gillo stepped back to the 30 yard line and booted a successful field goal kick for Racine. *Score: Racine 9, Akron 7.* Racine was able to take control of the ball for the rest of the game. They gain yardage on run attempts through the line and around the ends. They punted on third down. Akron attempted several unsuccessful passes. Barr intercepted a Pros pass on the Akron 41 yard line as the game ended.

FINAL SCORE: HORLICK-RACINE LEGION 9, AKRON PROS 7.

SCORE BY PERIODS:	1st	2nd	3rd	4th	Final
Horlick-Racine Legion	0	6	0	3	9
Akron Pros	0	7	0	0	7

TOUCHDOWNS: Akron- Nesser (1)
EXTRA POINT: Akron- Hendrian (1)
FIELD GOAL: Racine- Gillo, place kicks (3)

STARTING ROSTER:

RACINE		MILWAUKEE
Meyers	Left End	Malone
Miller	Left Tackle	Scott
Gorman	Left Guard	Stewart
Mintun	Center	Mills
Hartong	Right Guard	Hardy
Smith	Right Tackle	Folwers
Roessler	Right End	Nesser
Barr	Quarterback	Hendrian
Langhoff	Left Halfback	Haley
Elliott	Right Halfback	Cramer
Gillo	Fullback	Michaels

SUBSTITUTIONS: Racine– Heinisch for Miller, Foster for Langhoff, Milton for Hueller, Gorman for Hueller, Milton for Elliott.

FIRST DOWNS BY PERIODS:	1st	2nd	3rd	4th	Final
Horlick-Racine Legion	6	1	2	4	13
Milwaukee Badgers	0	0	2	2	4

REFEREE: St. John
UMPIRE: White
HEAD LINESMAN: Hanley

Attendance for the game was low. Racine had to pay Akron their "Guaranteed Money" to play the game and therefore, they lost out financially on the game. However, The Legion was able to get the game victory, thanks to Hank Gillo and his kicking game. The addition of Richard "Death" Halliday had really paid off for Racine. He had sure hands with each pass that was thrown to him and he was able to gain yards after the catch. Several of the Ruetzmen suffered injuries in the game. Both Miller and Roessler had foot injuries. Milton's leg was still hurting from the injury, which he received in the game against Chicago. Captain Irv Langhoff was tackled from behind in the game and sustained a severe leg fracture. He had to be carried off the field. This was a season ending injury for Langhoff as an x-ray later showed a fracture near the ankle.

Charlie Dressen finally reported to the team. He began practice on Wednesday night (October 24, 1923). This was good news for the Legion as Charlie would be needed more than ever with the loss of Irv Langhoff. The addition of Dressen gave Racine two great players at quarterback. Both Dressen and Barr could play either quarterback or halfback. Dressen was an excellent field general, who was a speedy open field runner and also excelled in the forward pass. Charlie was a favorite with the Racine fans in the 1922 season and the followers of the grid game were pleased that he would be wearing a Legion uniform, again in 1923. Manager Ruetz was expected to use Dressen at the quarterback position and move Barr into a halfback or end position.

Irving Langhoff	***	Charlie Dressen

The Horlick-Racine Legion squad would face one of their toughest opponents on the following Sunday. They were scheduled to play the Green Bay Packers at Green Bay, Wisconsin. The team would finish out the week with practice on Thursday and Friday. Several new plays were added on offense. The team was drilled on the defense of the passing game as Green Bay had a good aerial attack. Hank Gillo was once again captain of the Horlick-Legion football team. He turned down the honor at the beginning of the season but now that Langhoff was out, he agreed to take charge.

The Legion organization expected a large number of fans to travel the estimated 150 miles to the game via automobile. There were plans for several automobile parties to start out Saturday afternoon and travel to Oshkosh, Wisconsin and spend the night. They would head to Green Bay on that Sunday morning. The rest of the fan automobiles, the "main gang", would start out Sunday morning for the game. The Legion team traveled on a midnight train over the Northwestern track at 10:33 pm. They spent the night in sleeper cars, so that they would be fresh for the game on

Sunday. The plan was to go to the Beaumont Hotel in Green Bay, Wisconsin at 8:30 am for breakfast on Sunday. Following breakfast, the team would attend a light practice and then rest until the kickoff of the game. Several fans were planning on riding the same train as the team. The Elks were planning on having a special Pullman car on that train for their members and friends.

Green Bay had been one of the main rivals of the Horlick-Legion grid squad for the past three seasons. The Legion would not play at home (Horlick Athletic Field) again until November 11th. The Green Bay Packers would be coming to Racine, Wisconsin to play on Armistice Day.

Tickets were on sale in Racine on Thursday night at the usual places. Manager Ruetz had a section of seats reserved, so that the Racine fans could sit together. Advance reservations were heavy and 150 seats were expected to be set aside. Proceeds from the game would go towards purchasing blankets for the needy.

The Racine Journal News was planning to cover the game in their usual big league style. They would be sending reports back to Racine at the end of each quarter. Those, who were planning to make the trip in the Journal-News car were; Jack Roberts, sports editor along with Harry LePoidevin, Hank Larsen, George Westrich, Emanuel Paulsen and Arnold Klein. They were planning to appropriately decorate the car with Journal News signs.

** GAME DAY **

Racine went to the top of the list in the race for the professional football honors in Wisconsin, when they defeated their old arch enemy, the Green Bay Packers by a score of 24 to 3 on the Packer gridiron by the clever use of the forward pass. Outclassing the Green Bay at their specialty, the forward pass. The Legion uncorked the aerial attack, which swept the Packers off their feet. The Ruetzman scored in three periods. Green Bay proved to be dangerous at all stages of the game but Racine held them several times within the Legion five yard line. Racine was the first to score. Hank Gillo kicked a successful field goal at the beginning of the second quarter to give Racine three points. Later in that period, Barr passed the ball to Milton, who ran the ball in for a touchdown. Early in the third quarter, Barr completed another pass to Halliday, which resulted in a second Legion touchdown. The Packers would not be denied. Cub Buck kicked a field goal in the third quarter, which gave Green Bay their only points of the game. In the fourth quarter, Racine would solidify the victory with another touchdown pass, which was received by Elliott. The Ruetz Machine (HR Legion) hit stride, thanks to "Shorty" Barr, "Death" Halliday, "Rowdy" Elliott, Jack Milton and of course, Hank Gillo.

PLAY BY PLAY: **1923 NFL SEASON HRL GAME 5**
HORLICK-RACINE LEGION VS GREEN BAY PACKERS
Sunday: October 25th, 1923   2:30 pm
Bellevue Park   Green Bay, Wisconsin

FIRST QUARTER:
Gillo kicked off to Green Bay, to start the game. Mathias received the ball on the 10 yard line and he returned the ball to the 20 yard line. The Packers opened the game with an aerial attack. They were able to complete a series of passes, which advanced the ball to the Racine 20 yard line. The Legion was able to hold the Packers on three downs and Green Bay attempted a field goal on fourth down. Buck kicked the ball but it went wild, to the outside of the goal post. Racine took possession of the ball at the 20 yard line. Gillo ran the ball through the center of the line and it resulted in a 13 yard gain. Milton ran the ball and it resulted in a 3 yard gain. Elliott ran the ball off tackle and it resulted in a 2 yard gain. Elliott ran the ball through the line but he fumbled it. Green Bay recovered the ball on the Racine 40 yard line. The Packers were unable to gain yards, attempting to run the ball. Lambeau tried a drop kick for field goal but it went low. Barr caught the ball on the 20 yard line, where he was tackled. Racine was able to gain yards with run attempts through the line and around the ends. They gained 15 yards. Barr punted the ball to the Packers. Mathias received the ball and he was tackled on the Packers 10 yard line. Green Bay was able to gain 20 yards with four run attempts through the line. The quarter ended.

SECOND QUARTER:
Green Bay had possession of the ball on the Packer 39 yard line. The Packers failed to gain any yards on a run through the line. A Packers pass attempt went incomplete. Buck punted the ball and it went out of bounds on the Green Bay 45 yard line. Racine attempted a run through the line but it resulted in no gain. Barr passed the ball to Elliott and it resulted in a 12 yard gain. Gillo ran the ball through the center of the line and it resulted in a 1 yard gain. Barr gained 2 yards on a run around the end. Milton ran the ball and it resulted in a 1 yard gain. Gillo dropped back to the 30 yard line and booted a successful place kick between the uprights and it gained 3 points for Racine. *Score: Racine 3, Green Bay 0.* Gillo kicked off the ball to the Packers and the ball was received by Lambeau on the 10 yard line. He advanced the ball to the 25 yard line. The Packers failed to gain on a run attempt. Green Bay lost 2 yards on a pass attempt. Buck punted the ball to the 50 yard line. Barr received the ball and he was tackled. Gillo gained 1 yard on a run through the line. Elliott gained 1 yard on a run through the line. A Legion pass attempt went incomplete. Barr punted the ball out of bounds on the Packers 3 yard line. Buck passed to Mathys and it resulted in a 10 yard gain. A Packers pass attempt went incomplete. Hartong intercepted a Green Bay pass attempt on the 20 yard line and he ran it back to the Green Bay 2 yard line. Gillo ran the ball and it resulted in a 1 yard gain. Milton attempted to run the ball but it resulted in no gain. Barr lost 2 yards on a run attempt. The Legion turned the ball over to Green Bay on the 3 yard line. The Packers were able to gain 3 yards in two run attempts through the line.

134

Elliott intercepted a Green Bay pass on the 40 yard line and returned it to the 30 yard line. Barr was tackled behind the line of scrimmage for a 10 yard loss. A Barr pass completion to Elliott put the ball on the 20 yard line. The Legion attempted two run attempts through the line that gained a total of 1 yard. Gillo attempted a place kick for field goal but the ball went out of bounds at the Green Bay 2 yard line. Racine substituted in the game Miller for Meyers, Foster for Milton and Hueller for Gorman. Green Bay took possession of the ball. A Green Bay pass was intercepted by Elliott at the 40 yard line. He ran the ball back to the 30 yard line. A Legion pass attempt went incomplete. Another pass from Barr to Halliday put the ball on the 10 yard line. Barr threw a pass to Romney and he scored a Racine touchdown. Gillo kicked a successful extra point attempt. The quarter ended. *Score: Racine 10, Green Bay 0.*

THIRD QUARTER:

Mathys kicked off to Racine. Elliott received the ball on the 10 yard line. He advanced it to the 22 yard line. Racine was unable to advance the ball. "Shorty" Barr punted the ball to the Green Bay 30 yard line. Mathys received the ball and he advanced it to the 25 yard line, where he fumbled it. Halliday recovered the ball for Racine. Gillo gained 1 yard on a run through the line. Barr gained 3 yards on a run attempt. A pass from Barr to Elliott gained 10 yards for the Legion. The ball was on the Green Bay 12 yard line. Racine attempted a run but it resulted in no gain. A short pass from Barr to Halliday scored a touchdown for Racine. Gillo kicked a successful extra point. *Score: Racine 17, Green Bay 0.* Mathys kicked off the ball to Racine. Barr received the ball on the 10 yard line and he advanced it to the 15 yard line. Barr punted to the Packers on the Green Bay 10 yard line. A Green Bay pass attempt went incomplete. Another Packers pass attempt went incomplete. A pass from Lambeau to Mathys was completed for a 10 yard gain. Green Bay completed another pass. Racine was penalized for being off sides. This put the ball on the 50 yard line for the Packers. Buck ran the ball through the line and it resulted in a 3 yard gain. Buck completed a pass for the Packers. Another pass from Buck to Mathys was completed for a 10 yard gain. Green Bay completed a pass. The Packers completed another pass and the ball was on the Racine 20 yard line. A Green Bay pass attempt was intercepted by Halliday on the 15 yard line. A run attempt by Elliott resulted in a 3 yard loss. Barr ran the ball and it resulted in a 3 yard gain. Barr punted the ball to the 50 yard line. Buck ran the ball twice and gained a first down for Green Bay. The Packers attempted a pass but it was broken up by Racine and resulted in an incomplete pass. Another pass attempt was broken up by the Legion and resulted in an incomplete pass. Buck dropped back to the 30 yard line and kicked the ball for a successful field goal attempt. *Score: Racine 17, Green Bay 3.* Racine kicked off to Green Bay. The Legion gained possession of the ball. They were able to advance the ball down to the Green Bay 9 yard line. Racine was unable to get a first down. They turned the ball over to the Packers on downs. Green Bay had the ball on the Packers 10 yard line. The ball was on the Packers 8 yard line and the Legion had possession as the quarter ended.

FOURTH QUARTER:

Racine was unable to get a first down and they turned the ball over to the Packers. Buck punted to the Legion 40 yard line. Barr received the ball and he was immediately tackled. Milton ran the ball and it resulted in a 2 yard gain. Gill gained 1 yard on a run attempt. Barr ran the ball and it resulted in a 6 yard gain. Barr punted the ball to the Green Bay 5 yard line. A Green Bay pass resulted in a 15 yard gain. Another Packers pass attempt went incomplete. Green Bay attempted another pass but it was intercepted by Hartong on the Packers 20 yard line. He advanced the ball to the 3 yard line. Racine was unable to score a touchdown. Gillo attempted a place kick for field goal but the ball went wide of the upright. Green Bay took possession of the ball on the 20 yard line. The Packers attempted a pass but it was intercepted by Elliott. He advanced the ball to the 30 yard line. Barr attempted a run around the end but it resulted in a 10 yard loss. Barr passed the ball to Elliott and it resulted in a 10 yard gain. Another Legion pass attempt went incomplete. Gillo attempted another place kick for field goal, which was unsuccessful. The ball went out of bounds on the Green Bay 2 yard line. The Packers took possession of the ball. Mathias attempted a pass but it was intercepted by Elliott on the 40 yard line. He advanced the ball 10 yards. A Legion attempt to run through the line resulted in no gain. Barr completed a pass to Halliday and the ball was on the Green Bay 10 yard line. Barr heaved a pass to Elliott over the goal line, which resulted in another Racine touchdown. Gillo kicked the ball for a successful extra point. *Score: Racine 24, Green Bay 3*. Racine kicked the ball off to Green Bay. The Packers attempted several passes but the Legion defense did not allow them to complete another pass. Dressen substituted in the game for Barr. The Legion took possession of the ball but they made no more efforts to score. Racine had possession of the ball as the game ended.

FINAL SCORE: HORLICK-RACINE LEGION 24, GREEN BAY PACKERS 3.

SCORE BY PERIODS:	1st	2nd	3rd	4th	Final
Horlick-Racine Legion	0	10	7	7	24
Green Bay Packers	0	0	3	0	3

TOUCHDOWNS: Racine- Milton (1) Halliday (1) Elliott (1)
EXTRA POINT: Racine- Gillo (3)
FIELD GOAL: Racine- Gillo (1) Green Bay- Buck (1)

STARTING ROSTER:

RACINE		GREEN BAY
Meyers	Left End	Gray
Braman	Left Tackle	Buck
Gorman	Left Guard	Woodin
Mintun	Center	Niemann
Hartong	Right Guard	Gardner
Smith	Right Tackle	Earps
Halliday	Right End	Wheeler
Barr	Quarterback	Mathys
Elliott	Left Halfback	Basing
Milton	Right Halfback	Lambeau
Gillo	Fullback	Gavin

SUBSTITUTIONS: RACINE– Miller for Meyers, Foster for Milton, Hueller for Gorman, Dressen for Barr.

REFEREE: Whyte (Milwaukee)
UMPIRE: White (Green Bay)
HEAD LINESMAN: Coffeen (Beloit)

Pass Attempts By Periods

Horlick-Racine Legion	1st	2nd	3rd	4th	Total
Completed	0	4	3	4	11
Incomplete	0	2	1	1	4
Combined Total					15
Green Bay Packers					
Completed	6	2	4	4	14
Incomplete	2	6	6	14	28
Combined Total					42

The Green Bay Gazette Newspaper gave the Horlick-Racine Legion full credit for their victory over the Packers. They had printed that this was the worst beating that the Packers ever had, to date. G. W. Calhoun, sports editor of the Gazette was quoted as saying; *"Well, it won't make any difference one hundred years from now"*. He also was a member of the management for the Green Bay Packers.

Total attendance for the game was approximately 3,800. There were about 350 Racine fans, who attended the game against Green Bay. They all occupied the east stands and Red Nevin was back as main leader of the Racine cheers. Most of the fans traveled to the game via automobile and they found the roads leading to Green Bay in good condition. The Racine Legion Athletic Association officers were pleased in the way that the Racine women had been supporting the team. More than 100 women made the trip to the game against Green Bay. Women had also been turning out in large numbers for the home games at Horlick Athletic Field in Racine, Wisconsin.

Racine would meet Green Bay again on Armistice Day at the Legion's home field. Tickets for their next home game against the Packers were set to go on sale Thursday (November 1, 1923) in order to give fans time to pick up good seats for the rematch.

The next game for the Legion was against the Minneapolis Marines in Minnesota. The Horlick-Racine Legion football team made plans to take a special Pullman train car to Minnesota for the game against the Marines. A total of about five to six extra train cars were expected to be added on the route going to Minneapolis. Fans were told to contact Max Zirbes in order to make reservations on one of the Pullman cars.

The Legion team wasted no time by celebrating the victory. They started to practice again at Lakeview Park despite the cold and snow. Captain Gillo kept his men on their toes at all times and he was making sure that none of them would be out of condition, when they traveled to Minnesota. Manager Ruetz was planning to take a full squad to Minneapolis for the game. He made plans to stay at the Andrews Hotel, while they were in Minneapolis. The Legion organization received $650 from the Marines organization in order to cover expenses.

The Marines were made up of a heavy (weight total) line and fast full/half backs. They had been in existence for four years and also were experienced in the professional grid (football) game. They were the only team in their area until the Duluth, MN. Kelleys came along. Ed Walker, sports editor for the Minneapolis Journal was secured to cover Sunday's game between the Horlick-Racine Legion and the Minneapolis Marines for the Racine Journal News. There were also plans to have bulletins sent to the Journal News office in Racine, Wisconsin after each period (quarter). Walker was going to send a long telegram after the game, too. Besides this arrangement, a messenger boy had been arranged for the afternoon. He was going to have a place on the Racine bench at Nicolet Park next to George "Babe" Ruetz, manager of the Legion team. He was secured to send telegrams over the Western Union wire at the end of each quarter.

NFL President Joseph F. Carr made arrangements to have Walker officiate the game along with Halsey Hall, sports editor of the St. Paul Pioneer Press. The head linesman was set to be Art Von of Duluth, Minnesota.

138

** GAME DAY **

Racine did not cross the Minneapolis goal line and fell to the Marines by a score of 13 to 6. The six points came from field goals kicked by Hank Gillo. Minneapolis gained more running and passing yards than the Racine. Racine did outplay Minneapolis in the first half of the game but the Marines came back in the second half, to give their best showing of the year. Pahl's punting was the feature of the game. The Marines kept Racine on defense for much of the second half.

PLAY BY PLAY: 1923 NFL SEASON HRL GAME 6
                  HORLICK-RACINE LEGION VS MINNEAPOLIS MARINES
                  Sunday: November 4th, 1923   2:30 pm
                  Nicolet Park   Minneapolis, Minnesota

FIRST QUARTER:
Racine was able to move the ball down the field to the Minneapolis 5 yard line. A Racine pass was knocked down by the Minneapolis. The Marines were able to hold the Legion at the goal line without scoring. The quarter ended.
SECOND QUARTER:
Racine moved the ball into position for a field goal attempt. Hank Gillo kicked a successful field goal. *Score: Racine 6, Minneapolis 0.* The Legion kicked off to the Marines. Kaplan received the ball on the Marines 15 yard line. He returned the ball 15 yards to the Minneapolis 40 yard line. A Kaplan pass was completed to Paul Flinn and it resulted in a 15 yard gain. The Marines had the ball on the Legion 45 yard line. Louis Pahl ran the ball through the line, twice. He gained a first down for the Marines. The ball was on the Racine 33 yard line. Kaplan ran the ball off tackle and it resulted in a 7 yard gain. Racine was penalized for being off sides on the play. Sampson ran the ball through the line and it resulted in a 3 yard gain. Kaplan passed the ball to Mohr. He leaped high into the air in the back of the end zone and caught the ball, which scored a Marines touchdown. A Legion defending back was attempting to intercept the pass and he drove Mohr into a fence. He was knocked unconscious for several minutes. After Mohr recovered, Kaplan attempted a drop kick for the extra point but it was unsuccessful. The quarter ended. *Score: Racine 6, Minneapolis 6.*
THIRD QUARTER:
Racine had possession the ball for most of the quarter. Barr attempted and completed several passes for the Legion. However, the Legion receivers were unable to break the loose from the Marine tacklers. Several times, Racine was in scoring distance but they were unable to get into the end zone. Minneapolis also moved the ball down the field but they were stopped by Racine without scoring. The quarter ended.

FOURTH QUARTER:

The Legion and Marines each continued to move the ball down the field towards each other goal lines. The Legion had possession of the ball. They attempted a pass, but it was intercepted by Mohr. He advanced the ball for 15 yards, before being tackled at the Racine 35 yard line. The very next play was one of the greatest and most exciting of the game. Kaplan passed the ball into a group of Marines and Legion players. The ball was received by Cleve, out of the group and he advanced the ball 10 yards across the goal line. Kaplan drop kicked the ball for a successful field goal for Minneapolis. *Score: Racine 6, Minneapolis 13.* The game ended.

FINAL SCORE: HORLICK-RACINE LEGION 6, MINNEAPOLIS MARINES 13

SCORE BY PERIODS:

	1st	2nd	3rd	4th	Final
Horlick-Racine Legion	3	3	0	0	6
Minneapolis Marines	0	6	0	7	13

TOUCHDOWNS: Minneapolis- Cleve (1) Mohr (1)
EXTRA POINT: Minneapolis- Kaplan, drop kick (1)
FIELD GOAL: Racine- Gillo, place kick (2)

STARTING ROSTER:

RACINE		MINNEAPOLIS
Meyers	Left End	Mohr
Braman	Left Tackle	Tersch
Gorman	Left Guard	Tierney
Mintun	Center	Mehre
Hueller	Right Guard	Gaustad
Smith	Right Tackle	Baril
Halliday	Right End	Flynn
Barr	Quarterback	Kaylan
Romney	Left Halfback	Hudson
Elliott	Right Halfback	Cleve
Gillo	Fullback	Pahl

SUBSTITUTIONS: RACINE– Foster for Elliott, Elliott for Foster, Foster for Braman. MINNEAPOLIS– Sampson for Hudson, Christianson for Mohr, Mohr for Christianson, Cramer for Gaustad,

REFEREE: Art Von
UMPIRE: Ed Walker
HEAD LINESMAN: Halsey Hall

The Horlick-Racine Legion football team arrived at the train station in Racine, Wisconsin at 9:00 am on Monday November 5, 1923. The team was feeling down about the loss and expressed that they should have easily beat Minneapolis. Despite the loss, they did mention the fact of which, they were treated well during their stay in Minnesota. The football field was dry and there was no rain that day. Attendance was low, so the Minneapolis Marines lost money on the game because they had to pay the Legion their "Guaranteed Money" for playing the game. The game only drew 1,200 fans.

The Legion started practice again to take on their bitter rival, the Green Bay Packers at Horlick Athletic Field in Racine, Wisconsin. Captain Gillo made sure that his men would be in top condition for the game. He knew what the Packers were capable of despite the one-sided victory of the last meeting between the teams. Racine was developing a fast and bewildering attack to hurl at the Packers. The Legion worked on new passing plays as well as a number of new formations, so as to develop end running plays and off tackle smashes. They believed that these new plays would give them another victory over Green Bay. The Legion had a long practice on Friday at Lakeview Park and a shorter practice on Saturday with a focus on running through their plays. The Packers viewed Gillo as a dangerous threat to their team.

Tickets had been on sale since, the prior Thursday in order to allow for the fans to get their tickets early. They were available at the usual places, Smader's, Monument Cigar Store, and Rehl's Cigar Stores located on Sixth Street and State Street.

Curley Lambeau had scheduled practice twice a day, morning and evening, since the Racine defeated them by such a large margin, the last time. He concentrated on the pass defense. George DeLair of Green Bay, Wisconsin was appointed to the task of organizing the Packers entertainment for their fans. He gathered musicians to put together a Jazz band, which would open the eyes of the fans at Horlickville (Horlick Athletic Field). DeLair was also looking to find someone to lead the cheers of the Packer fans. Anyone, who was qualified for the task was urged to phone 120, immediately. On Friday afternoon prior to the game on Sunday, the Packers played a scrimmage game in order to prepare themselves for the rematch at Racine. Following the scrimmage, the team met at the assembly room of the Green Bay Courthouse for a chalkboard discussion. The Packers made arrangements to have extra train cars available for their fans, who wanted to make the trip. They also asked the Legion organization for a large block of 200 reserved seat tickets in anticipation of demand for the ducats (tickets). These seats were located behind the Green Bay bench. The Packers team stayed at St. George Hotel, while they were in Racine, Wisconsin for the game.

Manager Ruetz was anticipating Charlie Dressen, who just returned to the team last week, to leave in order to play baseball in Cuba. Dressen received an offer from the American Association Baseball team to play a barnstorming tour in Cuba. He said that this would provide employment for him during the winter months. The following baseball season, Dressen would be playing third base for the Major League baseball team in Washington, D.C. of the American League. Charlie told

141

Manager Ruetz, he would let him know on Thursday (October 1, 1923), whether he would accept that offer or not.

Racine was leading the race for the "State Title" with a victory over Green Bay and a tie against Milwaukee. In 1922, the Packers and Legion tied for the state honors at the end of the regular season. A post season game was arranged on December of 1922, up in Milwaukee, Wisconsin to play for the "Wisconsin Championship". Green Bay won the game by a score of 14-6.

The Green Bay Packers set up an open wire at Horlick Athletic Field in Racine, Wisconsin in order to send a play by play account of the game that would be played between the Packers and Legion. Green Bay fans, who could not travel to Racine would be able to follow the game at Turner Hall in Green Bay, Wisconsin.

Green Bay had three former 1922 Racine players, Whitey Woodin, Norbert "Butts" Hayes and Don Murry on their roster. The Packers team arrived in Racine, Wisconsin on Sunday morning and spent the morning on their special Pullman train car. The famous Racine Legion drum corps, which won first prize in their competition in San Francisco, California earlier in the year, paraded the Racine city streets during the early afternoon. The drum corps gathered at H&M Body plant and marched out to Horlick Athletic Field, where Director Oliver put them through their paces.

A special halftime attraction was arranged by Joe Oliver's Misfits and the Topaz Tigers. The Topaz Tigers Misfit football team challenged Joe Oliver's Misfit Army to game at halftime. Captain and quarterback "Siki" Barst dusted off his old costumes and brought a new bag of tricks to spring on the unsuspecting fans and entertain the crowd. The entertainers planned to parade out to Horlick Athletic Field from Monument Square in downtown Racine, Wisconsin, prior to game time. They were known for their comedy stunts and their act was a big hit two years ago, when they performed at halftime of the Racine Legion vs Chicago Blues professional football game at Horlick Athletic Field. Those who wished to communicate with the entertainers were directed to contact Head Coach Bill Dolan, Topaz Arcade 232 Main Street Racine, Wisconsin or phone Prospect 978.

The Legion organization planned to bring the Horlick-Racine Legion players to Horlick Athletic Field in a special group of automobiles. They announced that needed another 12 automobiles to participate in the special transportation group. This was all part of the Armistice Day celebration presented by the Horlick-Racine Legion organization.

Manager George "Babe" Ruetz announced on Saturday that he had signed a new player, A. C. Bauer. He played college football for the Illinois Fighting Illini. He planned to alternate Bauer with "Candy" Miller at the left tackle position. Bauer was 6'2" in his socks and tipped the scales at 210 lbs. Braman was injured during the game at Minneapolis and he would not suit up for the game against the Packers. Fritz Roessler, who had been out of the game for two weeks was healed and ready to play again. He would wear the #12 Jersey. Jimmy Baxter, a star baseball pitcher for the Horlick's baseball team was promised a chance to play as a back for the Legion. Ruetz told Baxter, he would possibly get a chance in the second half of the game. Baxter was a grid (football) star, a few years back in Toledo, OH. The Racine baseball fans were anxious to see what he could do on the football field. Foster, Hueller and Heinisch, all would be in uniform and they could except to see action in the game.

Manager Ruetz reported both the Chicago Cardinals and the Chicago Bears expressed interest in playing against the Horlick-Racine Legion on November 25, 1923 in Chicago, Illinois. Both teams realized, the Legion team was one of the strongest eleven (team) in the National Football League and that they would be a big draw in Chicago. They were anxious to call off their own home games to get this match up. NFL President Joe Carr was contacted and he had yet to make a decision.

The Green Bay Packers fan automobiles left Green Bay, Wisconsin at noon on Saturday November 10, 1923 and they were headed to Milwaukee, Wisconsin. They planned to spend the night at the Medford Hotel before heading to Racine, Wisconsin on Sunday. The Green Bay Packers team left for Racine, Wisconsin via train and they arrived at the 11:00 am on Sunday. A jazz band from Green Bay, Wisconsin accompanied the team. They planned to have lunch at their hotel prior to heading to Horlick Athletic Field for the game.

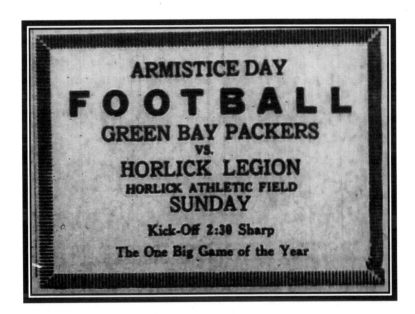

Green Bay Packers 1923 Roster

Starters:

No.	Name	Position	Wt.	College
11	Wheeler	Left End	180 lbs.	Ripon
17	Leaper	Left End	175 lbs.	Wisconsin
10	Buck	Left Tackle	225 lbs.	Wisconsin
6	Woodin	Left Guard	210 lbs.	Marquette
12	Niemann	Center	175 lbs.	Michigan
7	Lyle	Right Guard	180 lbs.	Minnesota
8	Gardner	Right Guard	210 lbs.	Wisconsin
9	Earps	Right Tackle	225 lbs.	Montana
16	Murray	Right Tackle	200 lbs.	Marquette
5	Gray	Right End	175 lbs.	Princeton
14	Hayes	Right End	170 lbs.	Marquette
4	Mathys	Quarterback	170 lbs.	Indiana
15	Basing	Left Halfback	180 lbs.	Lawrence
1	Lambeau	Right Halfback	185 lbs.	North Dakota
3	Mills	Fullback	180 lbs.	Pennsylvania

Horlick-Racine Legion 1923 Roster

Starters:

No.	Name	Position	Wt.	College
5	Meyers	Left End	170 lbs.	Wisconsin
10	Heinisch	Left End	165 lbs.	Independent
15	Miller	Left Tackle	195 lbs.	Purdue
18	Gorman	Left Guard	205 lbs.	Independent
3	Mintun	Center	185 lbs.	Wisconsin
13	Hartong	Right Guard	214 lbs.	Purdue
14	Hueller	Guard	200 lbs.	Indiana
7	Smith	Right Tackle	190 lbs.	Wisconsin
16	Foster	Right Tackle	195 lbs.	Indiana
6	Halliday	Right End	175 lbs.	Chicago
2	Braman	Left Tackle	210 lbs.	Yale
9	Barr	Quarterback	195 lbs.	Wisconsin
11	Elliott	Left Halfback	175 lbs.	Wisconsin
8	Milton	Right Halfback	165 lbs.	Chicago
1	Gillo	Fullback	195 lbs.	Colgate

FOOTBALL TOMORROW

Horlick-Racine Legion vs. Green Bay Packers
Kick-Off 2:30 Sharp   Horlick Athletic Field

THERE isn't much left to say about this game... Pretty near everything has been said! Everybody knows its the biggest game of the year.

Everybody knows it will be a tooth and nail proposition from the first toot to the last. Everybody knows that the State Championship is at stake... Nope! there's nothing left to say or do except to be there and see one of the greatest grid battles of the season, barring none.

Standing room will be at a premium. Better snap out of it early tomorrow.

AN EDITORIAL

"All for one and one for all" is a great slogan. It's a thought that is well worth considering when individuals are looking 'round for a watchword to guide them in their civic attitude. Folks who want to catch the spirit of co-operation, should attend the football game at Horlick Athletic field tomorrow. There will be a lesson worth the learning.

Observant folks will notice the confidence, the good cheer, the encouragement that is tendered to the players on the field. They will notice how this spirit helps these players carry on, how it gives them the courage to come back strong when things have gone all wrong.

Wouldn't it be a great and glorious day when that same attitude was one hundred per cent among residents for their city? Of course there are a great many who are enthusiastic now. Perhaps more of them in Racine than in most towns. But just think how much more productive for good would be the efforts of civic workers if this spirit was one hundred per cent instead of say fifty or sixty.

In every community there are a certain number who take the burden of the obligations that should rightly be shouldered by all. These are the folks who always stand ready and willing to help in anything that goes for the betterment of their town. Boosters we call them. They are good people to know and to deal with. Some of them are represented on this page today. If you'll read the names of the business men on this page who co-operated in making this publicity possible for the Legion you will come to know a number of real boosters.

West Side Laundry Co.

Sunshine Wet Wash Laundry

** GAME DAY **

The Green Bay Packers attacked and smothered the Horlick-Racine Legion football team on Sunday November 12th, 1923 at Horlick Athletic Field in Racine, Wisconsin. The Packers scored 16 points and the Legion was unable to record any points. Green Bay definitely outplayed Racine in every quarter of the game. They ran around the ends, off tackle and completed passes for large gains. The Legion defense was only effective in stopping the Packers, when they ran up the middle of the line. Mintun, Hartong and Gorman stopped every play coming through the middle with the support of Gillo, who played a great game defensively. Green Bay displayed a strong offensive line and a fighting backfield. The attack by the Packers was led by Lambeau, Mills and Mathys. They had big gains through the tackles and around the ends. Racine made only three first downs and they were only able to gain through pass completions. Racine was affected by the loss of two players. Paul Meyers did not play in that game on Sunday; he had to return home because of the sudden death of his Father. "Rowdy" Elliott was lost early in the game because of a leg injury. The largest crowd of the season, more than 4,000 fans witnessed the game.

PLAY BY PLAY: 1923 NFL SEASON HRL GAME 7
       HORLICK-RACINE LEGION VS GREEN BAY PACKERS
       Sunday: November 11th, 1923   2:30 pm
       Horlick Athletic Field   Racine, Wisconsin

FIRST QUARTER:
The Green Bay Packers kicked off to the Horlick-Racine Legion for the start of the game. Barr received the ball on the 20 yard line and he advanced it 1 yard. Racine had possession of the ball on the 21 yard line. Romney attempted a run, which resulted in a 1 yard loss. The Legion gained a total of 2 yards in two more downs. They opted to punt. Barr punted to the Packers and Mathys received the ball on the Green Bay 43 yard line. He was immediately tackled. Green Bay attempted a run but it resulted in no gain. The Packers gained 15 yards on a run through the left tackle. Mathys gain 3 yards on a run through the right tackle. A pass from Lambeau to Mills gained 15 yards for the Packers. The ball was on the Racine 29 yard line. Green Bay fumbled the ball. Mathys recovered the ball for the Packers and advanced it to around the Racine 10 yard line. Mills advanced the ball around the end and he scored a Packers touchdown. A penalty on the play, off sides by Green Bay, took away the touchdown and brought the ball back to the 19 yard line. Green Bay lost 3 yards on a run attempt. Mathys attempted a run, which resulted in no gain. A pass attempt from Lambeau to Mills went incomplete. Buck tried a place kick for field goal at the Racine 20 yard line. The ball went wild and they did not score. The Legion took possession of the ball on the Racine 20 yard line. Barr punted the ball to Green Bay and it went out of bounds on the 40 yard line. A run attempt by the Packers resulted in no gain. Lambeau gained 15 yards on a run

146

attempt. Lambeau gained 4 yards on a run off the tackle. He gained another yard on a run through the center of the line. A Green Bay pass attempt was broken up by Racine. Buck punted the ball to the Legion. It was received by the Legion on the Racine 10 yard line. Racine chose to punt to the Packers. Barr punted the ball to the Green Bay 48 yard line. Mathys received the ball and he returned it to the Racine 48 yard line. He was tackled by Mintun. Mills ran the ball and it resulted in a 1 yard gain. Lambeau fumbled the ball. He was able to recover his own fumble but he lost 5 yards. Mills ran the ball and it resulted in a 2 yard loss. Buck punted the ball to Racine. Barr received the ball on the Racine 10 yard line. Barr fumbled the ball. The ball was recovered by Gardner. The Packers had possession of the ball. Mathys gained 3 yards on a run through the line. Mills gained 3 yards on a run off the right tackle. Lambeau ran the ball. He cut across the field and after a long run, he was able to gain the 1 yard needed to cross the goal line and scored a touchdown. Buck attempted a place kick for point after touchdown but it was unsuccessful. *Score: Racine 0, Green Bay 6.* Only a few minutes remained in the first quarter. Gillo kicked off to the Packers 5 yard line. Green Bay returned the ball 20 yards. The Packers gained 6 yards on a run around the end. A Green Bay pass attempt went incomplete. Buck punted the ball to Racine. Barr received the ball on the 38 yard line, where he was immediately tackled. Racine attempted a pass but it went incomplete as the quarter ended.

SECOND QUARTER:

Barr punted the ball to Green Bay. Buck received the ball for the Packers. Green Bay punted the ball to Racine. Barr received the ball for the Legion. A punting duel took place between Barr and Buck. Both the Packers and the Legion team were unable to score and the ball remained in Racine territory for most of the quarter. Racine attempted several pass attempts but they were only able to complete one.

"Rowdy" Elliott re-injured his left knee and he was taken out for the rest of the game. The Legion substituted Roessler in the game for Elliott. They also substituted Wheeler in the game for Hayes. Racine had possession of the ball on the 39 yard line as the quarter ended.

THIRD QUARTER:

Gillo kicked off to the Packers and the ball went to the 10 yard line. Mills received the ball and returned it to the 33 yard line. The Packers were able to advance the ball with several passes off tackle and end run attempts. A Green Bay pass from Lambeau to Mathys resulted in a gain of 20 yards and the Packers had the ball on the Legion 25 yard line. Racine held Green Bay for three downs without gaining any yards. Buck dropped back to the 38 yard line and he successfully kicked a place kick for field goal. *Score: Racine 0, Green Bay 9.* Racine took possession of the ball and they were able to advance it. The Packers gained possession of the ball and they moved successfully down the field. Green Bay ran the ball through the line and around the ends. The Packers were able to advance the ball to the Racine 5 yard line. The Legion held the Packers from scoring a touchdown. Green Bay lost yardage. The Packers had possession of the ball on the Legion 12 yard line as the quarter ended.

FOURTH QUARTER:

Lambeau ran the ball through the line and it resulted in a 4 yard gain. Mills ran the ball but it resulted in no gain. Racine substituted Foster in the game for Miller. Gavin ran the ball through the center of the line and it resulted in a 2 yard gain. Mills quickly ran the ball around the right end. He scored a touchdown for Green Bay. Buck kicked a successful extra point. *Score: Racine 0, Green Bay 16.* Racine took possession of the ball. The Legion had several pass attempts. The Packers intercepted a Racine pass. Green Bay had possession of the ball in Racine territory but they could not advance the ball. Racine regained possession of the ball. Again, the Legion had several pass attempts. Green Bay intercepted another Racine pass. The Packers were able to advance the ball down the Racine side of the field. Green Bay had possession of the ball on the 1 yard line as the game ended.

FINAL SCORE: HORLICK-RACINE LEGION 0, GREEN BAY PACKERS 16.

SCORE BY PERIODS:

	1st	2nd	3rd	4th	Final
Horlick-Racine Legion	0	0	0	0	0
Green Bay Packers	6	0	3	7	16

TOUCHDOWNS: Green Bay- Lambeau (1) Mills (1)
EXTRA POINT: Green Bay- Buck (1)
FIELD GOAL: Green Bay- Buck (1)

STARTING ROSTER:

RACINE		GREEN BAY
Miller	Left End	Hayes
Bauer	Left Tackle	Buck
Gorman	Left Guard	Woodin
Mintun	Center	Niemann
Hartong	Right Guard	Gardner
Smith	Right Tackle	Earps
Halliday	Right End	Basing
Barr	Quarterback	Mathys
Elliott	Left Halfback	Mills
Romney	Right Halfback	Lambeau
Gillo	Fullback	Gavin

SUBSTITUTIONS: RACINE– Roessler for Halliday, Halliday for Elliott, Elliott for Halliday, Foster for Bauer. GREEN BAY- Wheeler for Hayes, Lyle for Earps, Murray for Gardner.

REFEREE: Cahn (Chicago University)
UMPIRE: Whyte (University of Wisconsin)
HEAD LINESMAN: Coffeen (Beloit College)

148

It was a disappointing loss for Racine. They were hoping to defeat Green Bay and take the "State Title" for the 1923 NFL season. After the loss, Green Bay was 2-1-0, Racine was 1-1-1 and Milwaukee was 0-1-1 in competition between the NFL Wisconsin teams.

Manager Ruetz made an announcement on Wednesday November 13th, 1923 regarding their next opponent. He stated that NFL Toledo Maroons needed to cancel their game against the Horlick-Racine Legion for the following Sunday or play the game in Racine, Wisconsin. Toledo management told Ruetz, their team was short of funds because of amount of fans that they had been drawing. Ruetz announced that team would not play again until the following Sunday. Team practices were cancelled until Friday afternoon.

NFL President Joe Carr decided to allow Racine to cancel their game with the Hammond, Ind. Pros on Sunday November 25, 1923. Horlick-Racine Legion Business Manager Max Zirbes and Team Manager George Ruetz made a special trip to Chicago, Illinois with the intention of scheduling a game against the Chicago Cardinals for that Sunday at Comiskey Park in Illinois. It was announced that tickets for the game against the Chicago Cardinals would go on sale starting Wednesday morning November 20, 1923. A limited number of tickets would be available at Smader's 331 Main Street in Racine, Wisconsin. The tickets were provided by the Cardinals and they were box seats available at $2.20 each, which included the war tax. All the seats provided would be under cover at the field in Chicago. There was a special section reserved for Racine fans and it was located directly behind the Legion team bench. Grandstand seats were going for a $1.65 each and they were only available at the gate in Chicago. Tickets for a special train to the game could also be purchased with game tickets.

The Racine Legion Post No. 76 drum corps was planning to travel on the 9:45 am train to Chicago on game day and arrive before noon. Racine provided a 60 piece drum corps. They would return to Racine on the 11:15 pm train from the Adams Street station in Chicago. Fans who purchased tickets at Smader's before 8:00 pm on Friday would be accommodated on the train, which would also carry the drum corps. The fare was $1.60 each way. Chicago Cardinals Manager Chris O'Brien announced that The Knights of Columbus along with the American Legion in Chicago would also provide entertainment to the fans attending the game, which included special guests, the Wounded War Veterans of Chicago. Football fans from the state of Wisconsin were going to travel to Chicago on Saturday to watch the college football game between Wisconsin and Illinois. After that, the plan was to stay overnight and attend the Legion-Cardinals game on the next day. Many current and former University of Chicago students were going to be at the game to cheer on former Chicago college players; Romney, Hartong and Halliday, who would be in uniform for the Horlick-Racine Legion football team.

Three players were released from the Racine roster. They were Ed "Candy" Miller (End-Purdue), Art "Bull" Braman (Tackle-Yale) and A.C. Bauer (Tackle-Illinois). Manager Ruetz began searching for players at the tackle, end and halfback positions. Ruetz added to his roster, Rollie Williams, a former All-Conference halfback and Howard Stark, who was a right tackle. Both formerly played for the

University of Wisconsin. Williams was offered a contract with Racine at the beginning of the season but he turned it down to take the athletic director position at Millikin University in Decatur, IL. Richard "Jab" Murray was recalled back from the Green Bay Packers. He was under contract with the Legion but loaned to the Packers for the part of season. He was brought back because they needed him again to play with Racine for the remainder of the year. Earl "Bud" Gorman would not be in uniform for the game against Chicago. He was scheduled to battle a boxing match against Homer Smith in Kalamazoo, Michigan on Monday November 26, 1923.

Practice resumed again on Tuesday November 20th, 1923 at Lakeview Park in Racine, Wisconsin. The Legion also practiced on Wednesday and Friday of that week in preparation for their game against Paddy Driscoll and the Chicago Cardinals at White Sox Park in Chicago, IL. The team practiced Friday in the drizzling rain. The Cardinals had a record of 6-1 for the seven NFL games, which they had played prior to their game against Racine. Their only loss was from the undefeated Canton Bulldogs.

** GAME DAY **

The Horlick-Racine Legion squad was able to outwit and outplay the Chicago Cardinals on their own field. The Horlick-Racine Legion defeated the Chicago Cardinals by a score of 10-4 on Sunday November 25th, 1923 before a very large crowd. It was estimated that 7,000 people attended the game. There were 750 Racine fans, who were in attendance and 500 of those fans traveled to the game via train and automobile on that day. The rest stayed over from the Wisconsin-Illinois College game on Saturday.

Chicago was the first to score with a safety before the end of the first quarter. Racine spent much of the first quarter trying to run the ball against Chicago but Racine was unable to capitalize and they were more successful passing against the Cardinals. Hank Gillo booted a place kick for field goal and it resulted in 3 points for Racine. This was in the third quarter of the game and it gave the Legion a one point lead. Meyers was advancing the ball after a Racine pass reception, late in the second quarter but he fumbled as he was crossing the Cardinals goal line. "Shorty" Barr scored a touchdown for the Legion with 3 minutes to go in the final quarter and it was the only one from either team. Hank Gillo kicked a successful extra point for Racine. He also played an exceptional game at fullback with several long run attempts including a 40 yard run to get the ball down to the Cardinals 20 yard line. Chicago attempted several passes late in the fourth quarter and they were able to move the ball down close to the Racine end zone. Anderson, who played end for the Cardinals received a pass but he fumbled the ball with one minute to go in the fourth quarter. Racine recovered the ball. Barr ran the ball, while attempting to run out the clock. He intentionally ran back into the Legion end zone during his stall tactic. Barr was tackled in the Legion end zone as the game ended and Chicago scored a second safety, which gave them two more points. Racine had a total of eight first downs and Chicago had six.

PLAY BY PLAY: **1923 NFL SEASON HRL GAME 8**
                HORLICK-RACINE LEGION VS CHICAGO CARDINALS
                Sunday: November 25th, 1923   2:15 pm
                Comiskey Park   Chicago, Illinois

FIRST QUARTER:

Gillo kicked off for Racine and the ball was received by Chicago at the Cardinals 15 yard line. Chicago advanced the ball 15 yards to the 30 yard line. The Cardinals were unable to gain any yards. Driscoll punted the ball for Chicago and Barr received it on the Legion 30 yard line. Gillo gained 2 yards on a run through the center of the line. Williams gained 3 yards on a run off the tackle. Racine was penalized for 5 yards for being off sides. Barr punted the ball to the Chicago 30 yard line. Mohardt received the ball for the Cardinals and returned it to the 50 yard line. Chicago gained 4 yards on a run. Driscoll ran through the line and it resulted in a 1 yard gain. Chicago was held with no gain. Driscoll punted the ball out of bounds at the Racine 15 yard line. Barr gained 2 yards on a run through the line. Barr punted the ball to the Cardinals 45 yard line. Driscoll received the ball and he was immediately tackled. Mohardt gained 2 yards on a run. Chicago was held with no gain on second down. Driscoll ran the ball through the line and it resulted in a 6 yard gain. Williams stopped a run attempt by Mohardt and it resulted in no gain. Racine took possession of the ball. On first down, Halliday attempted a run, which resulted in a loss of yardage. A Legion pass attempt was incomplete. A Racine run attempt resulted in no gain. Chicago took possession of the ball. Driscoll attempted a place kick for field goal from the 40 yard line. The kick was short and therefore, it resulted in no points. The Legion took possession of the ball on the 20 yard line. Barr punted out of bounds at the Cardinals 45 yard line. Mohardt ran the ball through the line and it resulted in a 6 yard gain. Driscoll attempted a run but he was tackled for loss by Mintun. A Cardinals pass attempt was intercepted by Barr on the 28 yard line. Racine was held with no gain. Chicago was penalized for 5 yards for being off sides. The Legion advanced the ball and it resulted in a first down. A run attempted by Elliott was stopped with no gain. A pass from Barr to Elliott resulted in a 20 yard gain. A run by Barr resulted in no gain. A Legion pass from Barr to Elliott resulted in a 7 yard gain. A run attempt by Elliott resulted in no gain. Barr punted the ball to the Chicago 10 yard line. Paddy Driscoll received the ball and he was immediately tackled by Mintun. Mohardt ran the ball through the line and it resulted in a 9 yard gain for Chicago. The Cardinals advanced the ball 2 yards. Chicago gained another 3 yards. Paddy Driscoll punted the ball to the Racine 35 yard line. Gillo received the ball and he was immediately tackled. Elliott ran the ball through the line and it resulted in a 4 yard gain. Barr completed a pass to Elliott and it resulted in a 15 yard gain. Racine advanced the ball with a run through the line. It resulted in a 2 yard gain. A Legion pass attempt went incomplete. Another Racine pass attempt went incomplete. Barr punted the ball to the 25 yard line. Chicago received the ball and advanced it to the 28 yard line. The tackle was made by Hueller for Racine. The Cardinals ran the ball, which resulted

151

in a 1 yard gain. Chicago punted to Racine from the 16 yard line. Barr received the ball on the Racine 35 yard line. He fumbled the ball but it was recovered by Mintun, for the Legion.

SECOND QUARTER:

Williams gained 4 yards on a run around the end. Elliott ran the ball and it resulted in a 1 yard gain. Chicago intercepted a Racine pass on the 50 yard line. Driscoll ran the ball through the line and it resulted in a 5 yard gain. King advanced the ball and it resulted in a 4 yard gain before he was tackled by Meyers. Chicago advanced the ball for 6 yards and a Cardinals first down. The Cardinals advanced the ball for a 1 yard gain. Chicago ran the ball through the line and it resulted in another 4 yard gain. A Cardinals pass attempt was broken up by Halliday and it went incomplete. Driscoll attempted a drop kick for field goal from the 28 yard line. The kick was short and he did not score. Elliott recovered the ball for the Legion, on the Racine 10 yard line. He advanced the ball to the 12 yard line. Johnny Mohardt was injured on the play. Chicago substituted C. McMahon in the game for Mohardt. Barr punted the ball to the 45 yard line. The Cardinals lost ground on a fumble. Crangle gained 2 yards on a run around the left end. A pass from Driscoll to Anderson resulted in an 11 yard gain for Chicago. Crangle advanced the ball and it resulted in a 2 yard gain. A Cardinals attempt to advance the ball was stopped by Mintun with no gain. Driscoll attempted a kick for field goal from the 35 yard line but again it resulted in no score. Racine took possession of the ball on the Legion 20 yard line. Racine attempted a run, which resulted in no gain. The Legion attempted another run, which resulted in no gain for Racine. Barr punted the ball to the Chicago 43 yard line. The Legion substituted Perrotti in the game for Jack Hueller. Chicago ran the ball through the line and it resulted in an 8 yard gain. Driscoll attempted to advance the ball but he was stopped by Stark. A Cardinals pass attempt in the back of the Racine end zone went incomplete. Chicago punted the ball to Racine on the 5 yard line. Barr received the ball and he was immediately tackled. Elliott ran the ball and it resulted in a 1 yard gain. Elliott attempted to run the ball but it resulted in no gain. Barr punted the ball and it hit Elliott and bounced back. Barr fell on the ball in the back of Racine end zone. Chicago was awarded a safety, which was worth 2 points as the quarter ended. *Score: Racine 0, Chicago 2.*

THIRD QUARTER:

Gillo kicked off the ball to the Cardinal's 25 yard line. Anderson received the ball and he advanced it to the 30 yard line. Chicago advanced the ball and it resulted in a 3 yard gain. The Cardinals advanced the ball and it resulted in a 2 yard gain. Chicago advanced the ball and it resulted in a first down. Driscoll ran the ball and it resulted in a 7 yard gain. He advanced the ball again for a 2 yard gain. Driscoll advanced the ball for another Chicago first down. The Cardinals were held with no gain. Chicago was held again with no gain. Driscoll attempted to punt the ball but it was blocked by Racine. Hueller recovered the blocked punt on the Legion 30 yard line and he advanced it to the 46 yard line. Gillo ran the ball and it resulted in a 2 yard gain. A Legion pass from Barr to Elliott resulted in an 11 yard gain with the ball advancing to the 35 yard line. A Racine pass from Barr to Meyers resulted in a 3 yard gain. Another Legion pass from Barr to Elliott advanced the ball to the 25 yard line. Chicago took a time out. Barr ran the ball around the right end and it resulted in a 9 yard gain. Gillo advanced the ball but it wasn't enough for a Racine first down. Elliott advanced the ball for a Legion first down. Chicago took another time out. Barr attempted to advance the ball but it resulted in no gain. Barr ran the ball through the line and it resulted in a 3 yard gain. The ball was on the Cardinals 2 yard line. Chicago held Racine from scoring a touchdown. Gillo dropped back to the 15 yard line and successfully place kicked a field goal. *Score: Racine 3, Chicago 2*. Gillo kicked off the ball to the Chicago 25 yard line. The Cardinals received the ball and they advanced it to the 37 yard line. McInerney ran the ball to the 45 yard line. Chicago was held with no gain. The Cardinals attempted a pass, which was intercepted by Halliday on the Chicago 35 yard line. The quarter ended.

FOURTH QUARTER:

The Legion substituted Al Perrotti in the game for Jack Hueller. Gillo ran the ball and it resulted in a 1 yard gain. Elliott attempted to advance the ball but it resulted in no gain. Elliott gained 5 yards on a run around the end. Barr punted the ball to the 50 yard line. Chicago took possession of the ball. Driscoll ran the ball and it resulted in a 1 yard gain. Chicago attempted a pass but it went incomplete. The Cardinals attempted another pass but it went incomplete. Driscoll punted the ball to the 35 yard line. Halliday received the ball for Racine and he advanced it to the 42 yard line. Barr ran the ball through the line and it resulted in a 5 yard gain. Gillo broke through the Cardinals line and ran the ball for a 38 yard gain. Elliott attempted a run around the left end but it resulted in no gain. Barr passed the ball to Elliott on the 10 yard line. He advanced the ball to the Chicago 2 yard line. Barr gained 1 yard on a run through the center of the line. Williams attempted to advance the ball but it resulted in no gain. Barr ran the ball around the left end and he scored a touchdown for Racine. Gillo successfully place kicked for the extra point. There was about 3:00 left to go in the game. *Score: Racine 10, Chicago 2*. Gillo kicked off to the Cardinals. Driscoll received the ball and he was tackled at the Chicago 20 yard line. Chicago attempted a run off tackle and it resulted in a short gain. The Cardinals attempted a run around the end, which resulted in a short gain. Chicago attempted another run off tackle but they were unable to get a first down. The Cardinals punted to the Legion. Racine attempted a run around the end, which resulted in a short gain. The Legion attempted a run off tackle, which resulted in a short gain. Racine attempted another run around the end, which resulted in a short gain, but they were unable to get a first down. The Legion punted to Chicago. The Cardinals attempted a pass, which was intercepted by Elliott on the Racine 40 yard line. Gillo gained 2 yards on a run through the center of the line. Barr attempted to advance the ball and it resulted in no gain. Barr attempted to punt the ball to the Cardinals. The ball hit Elliott and it was given to Chicago on the Racine 45 yard line. Crangle attempted a pass to Anderson on the Legion 1 yard line. Anderson received the ball and he was hit by Elliott. He fumbled the ball and it was recovered by Elliott for Racine. Barr dropped back into punt formation. The Cardinals rushed in on the punt and Barr elected to take a safety rather than allow Chicago to block the punt and possibly score a touchdown. *Score: Racine 10, Chicago 4*. Racine was given the ball on the 20 yard line with one minute to go in the game. Barr tucked the

153

ball in securely and he allowed Chicago to tackle him twice for a loss, so that he could run out the clock. The game ended.

FINAL SCORE: HORLICK-RACINE LEGION 10, CHICAGO CARDINALS 4.

SCORE BY PERIODS:

	1st	2nd	3rd	4th	Final
Horlick-Racine Legion	0	3	0	7	10
Chicago Cardinals	2	0	0	2	4

TOUCHDOWNS: Racine- Barr (1)
EXTRA POINT: Racine- Gillo, place kick (1)

FIELD GOAL: Racine- Gillo, place kick (1)
SAFETY POINTS: Chicago- (2)

STARTING ROSTER:

RACINE		CHICAGO
Meyers	Left End	Kiley
Stark	Left Tackle	Montgomery
Hueller	Left Guard	Brennan
Mintun	Center	McInerney
Hartong	Right Guard	Buckeye
Smith	Right Tackle	R. Smith
Halliday	Right End	Anderson
Barr	Quarterback	Driscoll
Williams	Left Halfback	B. McMahon
Elliott	Right Halfback	Mohardt
Gillo	Fullback	Koehler

SUBSTITUTIONS: RACINE– Perrotti for Hueller, Hueller for Perrotti, Perrotti for Hueller. CHICAGO– Zola for Brennan, King for Mohardt, Crangle for B. McMahon.

REFEREE: Moore
UMPIRE: Borren
HEAD LINESMAN: Malloy

FIRST DOWNS BY PERIODS:

	1st	2nd	3rd	4th	Total
Horlick-Racine Legion	3	0	3	2	8
Chicago Cardinals	2	2	2	0	6

—Courtesy Chicago Tribune
Here you see Shorty Barr giving Chicago and Racine fans the thrill of their lives. He aviates over the goal and a flock of Cardinal stars for the only touchdown of the game.

Horlick-Racine Legion @ Chicago Cardinals   Sunday November 25th, 1923

Racine had successfully defeated the Chicago Cardinals in front of a large crowd. The game was the matchup, which everyone had expected and it once again proved the Horlick-Racine Legion could play with the best teams in the NFL. During the third quarter, George Westrich, who was a member of the Racine Journal-News staff jumped up from his seat and led the Racine section in cheering. This was after the Cardinals had called their second time out in an attempt to stop Racine's momentum.

The Legion was scheduled to play their next two games at home. The next game was scheduled for Thanksgiving Day against the Milwaukee Badgers at Horlick Athletic Field in Racine, Wisconsin. The following Sunday, Racine would play the Minneapolis Marines at Horlick Athletic Field. Their final game on December 9th, 1923 against the Akron Pros was expected to be cancelled because of poor finances of the Akron team.

Tickets went on sale Monday November 26th, 1923 for the game against Milwaukee. The attendance was expected to be large because the last game that these teams played against one another, ended in a tie. The Badgers were in second place in the NFL until their loss against Green Bay, a few weeks earlier.

The Legion held practice on Tuesday night November 27th, 1923 at Lakeview Park. Manager George Ruetz announced that Rollie Williams would not be playing in the game on Thursday because he would be coaching for the Milliken University team in their final game of the season. George was pleased with the game Stark played against Chicago and he signed him to a contract.

Racine had a busy schedule to round out the 1923 season. They would play the Milwaukee Badgers on Thursday and Minneapolis Marines on Sunday. Both games would be played at Horlick Athletic Field. There was also still the possibility of a last game of the season at Akron, Ohio on December 9th. Ruetz also received offers from several teams for post season games. Offers were received from the Chicago Bears, Canton Bulldogs and the Chicago Cardinals.

FOOTBALL TOMORROW

Horlick-Racine Legion vs. Milwaukee Badgers
Kick-Off 2:30 Sharp　　Horlick Athletic Field

EVER since football was born the best game of the season was always saved for Thanksgiving Day. This year is no exception. Every football fan in this territory knows the power of the Milwaukee Badgers; and the speed.

There is as much rivalry between the two teams as there is in a stiff game of galloping dominoes for beau coup Francs.

You'll see the team that took the Cardinals into camp last Sunday at Chicago. The team that all Racine is proud of, Yes, - there will be plenty of action tomorrow. From the first "toot" to the last you'll breath fast and furious with excitement.

The park will be jammed but there will be plenty of room for you... if you come early.

AN EDITORIAL

Everybody loves a winner and that's one reason why the Horlick-Racine Football team is so popular. There is another reason why football is popular in Racine. A very vital reason, too. It is the loyal support of Racine business men and fans. Take, for instance, the business men who have made this page possible. They are boosters for their city. It's because we have men like these in Racine that practically all the things worth while are made possible. There is not a knocker or cold water artist in the bunch. Read them over, one by one. You've seen their names before. You'll see them again. Always connected with some civic project that would do good, deader'n a door knob if Racine didn't have men like them to push it through. If you don't know them go in and meet them. You'll meet up with some real he-men boosters that you'll be proud to know.

** <u>GAME DAY</u> **

The Horlick-Racine Legion did not play up to their capabilities and they were defeated by a score of 16-0. The Milwaukee Badgers were able to consistently stop the Racine running and passing attempts. They hurried the quarterback and therefore, the Badgers were able to intercept the ball three times. The Legion receivers dropped several passes and the defense was unable to stop Milwaukee. Elliott was a bright spot in an off day for the Legion team. He played a consistent game at halfback and an exceptional game on defense.

The Badgers played a great football game. Milwaukee took advantage of every opportunity in the game and they were unstoppable on offense and defense. Hal Erickson played an exceptional game for the Badgers. He ran 55 yards after receiving a punt in the first quarter. This set up Milwaukee's first touchdown. He also had a 25 yard run in the 4th quarter, which moved the ball far into Racine territory.

<u>*PLAY BY PLAY:*</u> 1923 NFL SEASON GAME 9
HORLICK-RACINE LEGION VS MILWAUKEE BADGERS
Thursday: November 28th, 1923   2:15 pm
Horlick Athletic Field   Racine, Wisconsin

<u>*FIRST QUARTER:*</u>
Winkleman kicked off to Racine. The ball was received by Elliott on the 10 yard line. He advanced the ball to the 20 yard line, where he was tackled. On the first play, Elliott ran the ball through the end and it resulted in a 15 yard gain. It was a first down for Racine. Barr advanced the ball and it resulted in a 25 yard gain as well as another Legion first down. The ball was on the Milwaukee 40 yard line. Gillo ran the ball through the line and it resulted in a 1 yard gain. Romney ran the ball through the line for another 1 yard gain. A Racine pass attempt went incomplete. Gillo attempted a place kick for field goal but it was not successful. The ball was downed on the Badger 10 yard line. Milwaukee punted the ball to Racine. Conzelman kicked the ball and it was received by Barr at the 50 yard line. He was immediately tackled. A Racine pass from Barr to Halliday resulted in a 20 yard gain for the Legion. The ball was on the Milwaukee 30 yard line. The Legion was able to advance the ball down to the Badger 12 yard line with run attempts by Elliott and Romney. Gillo attempted another kick for field goal but it was unsuccessful. Milwaukee took possession of the ball. Racine regained possession of the ball. The Legion lost 4 yards in three attempts to advance the ball. Racine had the ball on the Legion 22 yard line. Barr punted to Milwaukee. Erickson received the ball on the 40 yard line and he advanced it to Racine 4 yard line, where he was tackled. Milwaukee ran the ball twice. The Badgers ran the ball twice. Doane advanced the ball over the goal line for a Badgers touchdown. Winkle kicked the ball for a successful extra point. <u>*Score:*</u> *Racine 0, Milwaukee 7.* Gillo kicked off to Milwaukee. The ball was received by the Badgers at the Milwaukee 24 yard line. A run attempt by the Badgers resulted in a 1 yard gain. Conzelman punted to Racine.

The ball was received by Barr on the Legion 30 yard and he was immediately tackled. Romney advanced the ball around the end and it resulted in a 2 yard gain. Barr attempted a pass. The ball was intercepted by the Badgers. Milwaukee advanced the ball to the Racine 20 yard line.

SECOND QUARTER:

Milwaukee was able to gain 11 yards in two attempts and it resulted in a first down. The Badgers lost 2 yards in two attempts. Winkle dropped back to the 20 yard line and he place kicked the ball for a successful field goal. *Score: Racine 0, Milwaukee 10.* Racine was able to get possession of the ball. Barr ran the ball around the end and it resulted in an 11 yard gain as well as a Legion first down. A pass from Barr to Halliday resulted in a 15 yard gain. The ball was on the Milwaukee 23 yard line. Barr heaved a pass over the goal line to Halliday. Halliday fumbled the ball and it was given to Milwaukee on the Badger 20 yard line.

THIRD QUARTER:

Milwaukee was able to advance the ball but they were unable to score. Racine was able to advance the ball but they were unable to score. Both teams exchanged possession of the ball throughout the quarter.

FOURTH QUARTER:

Racine was able to get possession of the ball. A Legion pass attempt was intercepted on the Racine 20 yard line. Milwaukee took possession of the ball. A Badger pass resulted in a 9 yard gain. Milwaukee gained 4 more yards on two off tackle run attempts. Winkle dropped back to the 19 yard line and he was successful with his place kick for field goal. *Score: Racine 0, Milwaukee 13.* Racine kicked the ball to Milwaukee. Conzelman received the ball and he advanced it to the Badgers 35 yard line. In two attempts, Milwaukee was able to gain 7 yards. Conzelman punted the ball to Racine. Barr was there to receive the ball but it went over his head. The ball was downed on the Racine 1 yard line. Racine punted the ball to the Badgers. Barr was punting from the Legion end zone. He was able to get the ball to the 20 yard line of Racine. Milwaukee gained 5 yards in three attempts. Winkle dropped back to the 22 yard line on fourth down. He was successful with another place kick for field goal. *Score: Racine 0, Milwaukee 16.* The game ended.

FINAL SCORE: HORLICK-RACINE LEGION 0, MILWAUKEE BADGERS 16.

SCORE BY PERIODS:	1st	2nd	3rd	4th	Final
Horlick-Racine Legion	0	0	0	0	0
Milwaukee Badgers	7	3	0	6	16

TOUCHDOWNS: Milwaukee- Doane (1)
EXTRA POINT: Milwaukee- Winkleman (1)
FIELD GOALS: Milwaukee- Winkleman (3)

158

STARTING ROSTER:

RACINE		MILWAUKEE
Meyers	Left End	Sachs
Stark	Left Tackle	Blailock
Hueller	Left Guard	Smith
Mintun	Center	Larson
Hartong	Right Guard	Underwood
Smith	Right Tackle	Wenke
Halliday	Right End	Reichie
Barr	Quarterback	Conzelman
Elliott	Left Halfback	Winkleman
Romney	Right Halfback	Erickson
Gillo	Fullback	Doane

SUBSTITUTIONS: RACINE– Gorman for Hueller, Heinisch for Barr.
MILWAUKEE- Mooney for Reichie, McGinnis for Reichie, Maltax for Underwood.

REFEREE: Amee
UMPIRE: Whyte
HEAD LINESMAN: Downer

Legion quarterback "Shorty" Barr came out of the game, late in the fourth quarter, due to injury and it was determined that he had broken a rib. This news was probably as heart breaking as the loss to Milwaukee. He would be out for the remainder of the season.

Racine would resume practice on Friday in preparation for their game on Sunday. Ruetz announced that Milt Romney would replace Barr at quarterback and Williams would return for the game against the Minneapolis Marines. This would be the final home game of the 1923 NFL season for the Horlick-Racine Legion. The Marines defeated the Legion in their last meeting, earlier in the season. The ducats (game tickets) were on sale at Tom Smader's, the Monument Cigar Store and Rehl's Cigar Stores on both Sixth Street and State Street Stores.

Rollie Williams

159

MINNEAPOLIS AT RACINE, SUNDAY, DEC. 2nd

GAME CALLED AT 2:15

Referee: Holloway, Chicago
Umpire: Bohrn, Evanston
Head Linesman: White, Milwaukee

Horlick-Racine Legion　　Minneapolis Marines

Myers	L. E.	Moha (1), St. Thomas
Stark	L. T.	Tersch (5), Independent
Mueller	L. G.	Tierney (17), Minnesota
Minton	C.	Mehre (16), Capt., Notre Dame
Tong	R. G.	Guasted (14), Independent
Smith	R. T.	Baril (4), St. Thomas
Halliday	R. E.	Flynn (15), Minnesota
Romney	Q. B.	Kaplan (3), Hamline
Elliott	L. H. B.	Cleve (18), St. Olaf
Williams (4)	R. H. B.	Pahl (6), Independent
Gillo	F. B.	Hudson (2), Creighton

Reserves

Gorman (16)	Christianson (9), North Dakota
Zinnan (15)	Kraemer (19), South Dakota
Roessler (12)	Hanson (7), South Dakota
Foster (18)	Sampson (12), Independent
Baxter (7)	Irgens (10), Independent
Heinish (10)	

FOOTBALL TOMORROW

Horlick-Racine Legion　vs.　Minneapolis Marines
Kick-Off 2:15 Sharp　　　　Horlick Athletic Field

THE last home game, can you imagine it? Doesn't seem possible that the football season is nearly over, does it? Dope claims that the season is going to be closed here with one of the best games of the year. It will be remembered that the Marines handed Racine a neat trimming on their own grounds a few weeks ago. Then they played Rock Island to a tie. With Williams behind the line Sunday it should be some game to watch.

Of course the grounds will be crowded for this last game of the season; that's understood. But it certainly would be fine if the record crowd of the year would hearten the boys on to victory.

160

** <u>GAME DAY</u> **

The Horlick-Racine Legion squad trounced the Minneapolis Marines on Sunday December 2nd, 1923 by a score 23-0. Captain Hank Gillo and Rollie Williams scored all the points in the game but Milt Romney played an exceptional game at quarterback and on defense. He intercepted six passes. Every member of the starting line-up was able to contribute to this victory. Jimmy Baxter, member of the Horlick Co. professional baseball team saw some playing action at the end of the game, which was to the delight of the crowd.

PLAY BY PLAY:　1923 NFL SEASON HRL GAME 9
　　　　　　　　　HORLICK-RACINE LEGION VS MINNEAPOLIS MARINES
　　　　　　　　　Sunday: December 2nd, 1923　2:15 pm
　　　　　　　　　Horlick Athletic Field　Racine, Wisconsin

FIRST QUARTER:

Gillo kicked off to the Minneapolis 35 yard line. Kaylan received the ball and advanced it back to the 30 yard line. The Marines gained 3 yards on a run through the right tackle. Minneapolis gained another 3 yards on a run through the center of the line. Minneapolis punted the ball to Racine. Williams received the ball on the Legion 40 yard line and advanced it to the Marines 40 yard line, where he was tackled. Gillo plunged through the line and it resulted in a 1 yard gain. A run attempt by Romney resulted in no gain. Williams ran the ball through the right end and it resulted in a 7 yard gain. Gillo attempted a place kick for field goal but it fell short, resulting in no points. The ball was downed on the 18 yard line. The Marines took possession of the ball. Hudson ran the ball and he advanced it to the 30 yard line. Minneapolis attempted to run the ball through the center of the line but they were stopped by Racine. The ball was fumbled on the play and the Marines lost 5 yards on the recovery. Pahl gained 7 yards on a run through the center of the line. The Marines punted to the Legion from the Racine 30 yard line. Williams received the ball and returned to the 50 yard line. Gillo ran the ball and it resulted in a 1 yard gain. A Romney run attempt resulted in no gain. Romney gained 5 yards on a run through the left end. Minneapolis was penalized 15 yards for roughing. Williams ran the ball through the line and it resulted in a 4 yard gain. The ball was on the 30 yard line. A run by Gillo gained 2 yards for Racine. A run attempt by Romney resulted in a 2 yard loss. Gillo attempted a place kick for field goal from the 40 yard line but it was unsuccessful. Minneapolis took possession of the ball on the Marines 20 yard line. A Marines run attempt through the center of the line resulted in no gain. A Minneapolis run attempt resulted in a 1 yard gain. The Marines punted the ball to the Legion and it went to the Racine 42 yard line. A Racine run attempt through the line resulted in no gain. Romney ran the ball through the line and it resulted in a 2 yard gain. A Romney run attempt around the left end resulted in no gain. Romney punted the ball to Minneapolis. They received the ball on the Marines 35 yard line. A Marines attempt to run the ball through the center of the line was stopped by Mintun and resulted in no gain. The ball was fumbled but Minneapolis recovered it. A Marines pass attempt went incomplete. Minneapolis punted the ball to Racine. Williams received the ball on the 40 yard line and he advanced it to the 45 yard line. Gillo ran the ball and it resulted in a 2 yard gain. Heinisch ran the ball around the left end and it resulted in a 2 yard gain. Williams ran the ball and it resulted in a 1 yard gain as the quarter ended.

SECOND QUARTER:

Romney punted the ball to the Marines 30 yard line. Minneapolis plunged the ball through the line and it resulted in a 1 yard gain. A run attempt by the Marines resulted in no gain. A Minneapolis fumble on the next play resulted in a 2 yard loss. The Marines punted the ball to the Legion. Williams received the ball on the Racine 10 yard line. He sprinted down the field before being stopped at the Minneapolis 40 yard line. A run attempt around the left end by Heinisch resulted in no gain. Romney gained 5 yards on a run around the left end. A Legion pass went incomplete. Gillo attempted a place kick for field goal from the 45 yard line but it was not successful. Minneapolis took possession of the ball on the Marines 20 yard line. A Marines run attempt was stopped by Stark and it resulted in no gain. Minneapolis gained 1 yard on a run through the line. Kaylan punted the ball to Racine from the Marines 10 yard line. Williams received the ball on the 50 yard line and he advanced it to the 40 yard line. Elliott substituted in the game for Heinisch by Racine. A Racine pass went incomplete. Elliott ran the ball through left tackle and it resulted in a 9 yard gain. Gillo made a successful place kick for field goal from the 39 yard line. *Score: Racine 3, Minneapolis 0.* Gillo kicked off the ball to the Marines. The ball was received by Minneapolis on the Marines 10 yard line by Pahl and he advanced it to the 24 yard line. Minneapolis gained 3 yards on a run attempt. The Marines gained 3 yards on a run attempt. A Minneapolis pass went incomplete. The Marines punted to the Legion. Williams received the punted on the 39 yard line and he was immediately tackled. Racine gained 1 yard on a plunge through the line. A run attempt through the line by Gillo resulted in no gain. Romney punted the ball to the Marines and they received it on the 25 yard line. Minneapolis gained 2 yards on a run through the center of the line. The Marines were penalized 15 yards for roughing, once again. A tackle by Halliday resulted in a 3 yard loss for the Marines. Minneapolis punted the ball to Racine from the Marines 10 yard line. Halliday received the ball on the 30 yard line and he made a "Fair Catch". Gillo attempted a place kick for field goal from the 35 yard line but it was not successful. Minneapolis took possession of the ball on the 20 yard line. The Marines gained 3 yards on a run through the line. Minneapolis gained 2 yards on a run through the line. A Marines pass resulted in a 12 yard gain. The Marines substituted Kraemes in the game for Tersch. A Minneapolis pass went incomplete. A Marines pass attempt was intercepted by Elliott on the 50 yard line. He advanced the ball to the Minneapolis 30 yard line. Racine substituted Barr in the game for Romney. A Legion pass from Barr to Halliday resulted in a 20 yard gain. A Racine pass attempt to the end zone went incomplete. Minneapolis took possession of the ball on the Marines 20 yard line. A completed pass by the Marines resulted in a 10 yard gain. Racine was penalized 5 yards for being off sides on the play. A Minneapolis pass from Kaylan to Moe resulted in a 30 yard gain. A Marine pass attempt was intercepted by

Halliday on the Racine 35 yard line. He advanced it to the Minneapolis 30 yard line as the half ended.

THIRD QUARTER:

  Hudson kicked off the ball to Racine. Romney received the ball on the Legion 15 yard line and he advanced it to the 50 yard line. Gillo ran the ball through the line and it resulted in a 1 yard gain. Elliott ran the ball through the line and it resulted in a 1 yard gain. Romney ran the ball through the line and it resulted in a 1 yard gain. Romney punted the ball to the Minneapolis and the ball went out of bounds at the 11 yard line. The Marines gained 7 yards on a run around the right end. A Minneapolis run attempt was stopped by the Racine line and it resulted in no gain. A Marines run attempt around the right end resulted in a 5 yard loss. Minneapolis gained 3 yards on a run around the left end. The Marines punted the ball to the Legion. Elliott received the ball on the 30 yard line and he advanced it to the 45 yard line. Williams broke through the line and he advanced the ball from the 45 yard line to the 30 yard line. Romney ran the ball through the left end and it resulted in an 8 yard gain. Elliott plunged through the line and it resulted in a 10 yard gain. The ball was on the Minneapolis 7 yard line. Gillo ran the ball through the line and it resulted in a 6 yard gain. Gillo ran the ball through the line and it resulted in a 1 yard as well as a Legion touchdown. Gillo kicked the ball for a successful point after touchdown. *Score: Racine 10, Minneapolis 0.* Racine substituted Foster in the game for Stark. Gillo kicked off the ball to the Marines. They received the ball on the Marines 5 yard line and it was advanced to the 15 yard line, where he was tackled. A Minneapolis run attempt resulted in a 3 yard gain. The Marines gained 2 yards on a run attempt. The Legion was penalized for being off sides. This gave the Marines a first down. A Minneapolis pass attempt was intercepted by Romney on the 40 yard line. He advanced it to the 32 yard line. Williams made a sensational run for 32 yards and it resulted in a touchdown for Racine. Gillo kicked a successful extra point. *Score: Racine 17, Minneapolis 0.* Racine substituted Linnan in the game for Hartong. Gillo kicked off the ball and the ball flew so far that it went over the goal post. The Marines took possession of the ball on the 20 yard line. Minneapolis ran the ball through the center of the line but it resulted in no gain. A Marine run attempt around the left end resulted in a 2 yard loss. Minneapolis punted the ball to the 49 yard line. Racine received the ball and fumbled it. The Marines regained possession of the ball. Minneapolis ran the ball through the line and it resulted in a 1 yard gain. A Minneapolis pass attempt went incomplete. Another Minneapolis pass attempt went incomplete. The Marines punted out of bounds on the Racine 39 yard line. Romney ran the ball and it resulted in a 5 yard gain. Gillo ran the ball through the center of the field from the Marine 45 yard line and he scored a touchdown, while dodging eight opposing players. Gillo's kick for the extra point was not successful. *Score: Racine 23, Minneapolis 0.* Gillo kicked off the ball to the Minneapolis 10 yard line. The Marines received the ball and they advanced it to the 20 yard line. A Minneapolis run attempt resulted in no gain. Another Minneapolis run attempt resulted in no gain. The Marines completed a pass, which resulted in an 8 yard gain. Minneapolis punted the ball to the Legion. Elliott received the ball on the 35 yard line. He fumbled the ball and lost possession of it. The Marines recovered the ball. The Legion was penalized for roughing and the ball was moved to the 25 yard line. A Marines run attempt around the right end resulted in a 6 yard loss. A Minneapolis pass resulted in a 6 yard gain. The ball was on the Legion 25 yard line as the quarter ended.

FOURTH QUARTER:

A Marines pass was intercepted by Romney on the 20 yard line and he advanced it to the 25 yard line. Elliott gain 1 yard on a run around the right end. Gillo plunged through the left tackle and it resulted in a 15 yard gain. Williams ran the ball and it resulted in a 4 yard gain. A Legion pass was intercepted by Minneapolis on the 30 yard line. A Marines pass from Kaylan to Kraemer resulted in a 7 yard gain. Another Marines pass went incomplete. A Minneapolis run attempt resulted in a 1 yard gain. Minneapolis punted the ball to Racine. Elliott received the ball on the 25 yard line. He fumbled the ball and lost possession of it. The Marines recovered the ball. A Marines pass attempt went incomplete. Another Marines pass attempt went incomplete. Minneapolis could not advance the ball and Racine took possession of the ball on the 20 yard line. A Legion run attempt resulted in no gain. Romney fumbled the ball on a Racine trick play. He recovered the ball on the 15 yard line. Romney punted the ball to Minneapolis. The ball was grounded on the 40 yard line. A Marines pass was intercepted by Romney on the 50 yard line and he advanced it to the 45 yard line. A Racine pass to Linnan was completed. The ball was advanced to the Minneapolis 42 yard line. Williams attempted a run, which resulted in no gain. Gillo ran the ball through the line and it resulted in a 2 yard gain. The Legion substituted Baxter in the game for Elliott. A Legion pass attempt went incomplete. Romney punted the ball to the Minneapolis 20 yard line. The Marines gained 2 yards on a run attempt. Minneapolis gained 1 yard on a run attempt. Hudson ran the ball through the line and it resulted in a 10 yard gain. Minneapolis ran the ball and it resulted in a 4 yard gain. The Marines ran the ball and it resulted in a 2 yard gain. A run attempt by the Marines resulted in no gain with a tackle by Mintun. A Minneapolis pass attempt went incomplete. Racine took possession of the ball on the 40 yard line. A Legion run attempt resulted in a 2 yard gain. Gillo ran the ball and it resulted in a 1 yard gain. A pass from Romney to Foster advanced the ball to the 30 yard line. A Racine pass attempt went incomplete. Minneapolis took possession of the ball. The Marines could not advance the ball. They punted the ball to Racine. Williams received the ball on the Legion 20 yard line and he advanced it to the 40 yard line. Baxter ran the ball through the line and it resulted in an 8 yard gain. Baxter ran the ball and it resulted in a 3 yard gain. The ball was around the 50 yard line as the whistle sounded and the game ended.

FINAL SCORE: HORLICK-RACINE LEGION 23, MINNEAPOLIS MARINES 0

SCORE BY PERIODS:	1st	2nd	3rd	4th	Final
Horlick-Racine Legion	0	3	20	0	23
Minneapolis Marines	0	0	0	0	0

TOUCHDOWNS: Racine- Gillo (2) Williams (1)
EXTRA POINT: Racine- Gillo, place kick (2)
FIELD GOAL: Racine- Gillo, place kick (1)

STARTING ROSTER:

RACINE		MINNEAPOLIS
Halliday	Left End	Mohr
Stark	Left Tackle	Tersch
Hueller	Left Guard	Tierney
Mintun	Center	Mehre
Hartong	Right Guard	Gaustad
Smith	Right Tackle	Baril
Meyers	Right End	Flynn
Romney	Quarterback	Kaylan
Williams	Left Halfback	Cleve
Heinisch	Right Halfback	Pahl
Gillo	Fullback	Hudson

SUBSTITUTIONS: RACINE– Roessler for Halliday, Foster for Stark, Gorman for Hueller, Hueller for Gorman, Barr for Romney, Romney for Barr, Elliott for Heinisch, Baxter for Elliott. MINNEAPOLIS– Kraemer for Tersch, Tersch for Kraemer.

REFEREE: Jim Holloway (Chicago)
UMPIRE: Bohr (Evanston)
HEAD LINESMAN: Whyte (Milwaukee)

    The Horlick-Racine Legion football team closed the 1923 NFL season with a splendid victory over the Minneapolis Marines. They defeated the Marines by a score of 23-0. Williams and Gillo, both played brilliant football for Racine behind a line that opened up big holes on offense. The Legion defense was able to consistently stop the attack of the Marines and held them from scoring. They game featured two spectacular touchdown plays by Racine. Rollie Williams raced 32 yards down the field through the entire Minneapolis team in the third quarter for a Legion touchdown. Hank Gillo plunged through the center of the line and he ran 60 yards for a touchdown, which was also in the same quarter as the William's touchdown. Milt Romney added several gains around each end on offense but he even shined more on Defense. He was able to intercept the ball 6 times from Minneapolis in the game. Williams also had an exceptional game of punting as well as returning Minneapolis punts. The Legion played a solid shut out and ended their 1923 Home game schedule with great success.

The Horlick-Racine Legion announced that their final game of the season against Akron, Ohio was definitely cancelled. The Akron management called off the game because they were experiencing the same financial difficulties as Racine.

On Monday December 2, 1923, Horlick-Racine Legion Team Manager George "Babe" Ruetz handed in his resignation. He stated that the reason that he was stepping down from the team was that he was unable to continue to give the great amount of time that the sport demanded as well as his health. Ruetz stated that he would aid the organization in any way possible with the Racine NFL franchise. He offered to take the new manager to Chicago for the next NFL meeting, so that they could be properly introduced. Several rumors were started as to who would replace George as the Legion football team manager. L.A. McDowell, Legion commander and president of the Racine Legion Athletic Association was out of the city and unavailable to comment on the resignation of Ruetz. The future of the team was uncertain at that point. It was believed that the management of the Legion football team would be taken over by Jack Melvin or Dr. Morrissey, who both assisted George in the operation of the team during the 1923 season. The National Football League had their next meeting scheduled for January 10th, 1924 in Chicago, Illinois.

The Racine American Legion Post No. 76 would continue to support NFL football in Racine, Wisconsin, if the new board members took the recommendations of the outgoing board. The board met on Monday December 10th, 1923 at the Elks Club in Racine for their last meeting of the year. Sig Ruud presented a report from the Racine Legion Athletic Association favoring the continuation of the NFL franchise. Sig's presentation gave a comprehensive report covering team receipts, disbursements and average attendance at both home and away games as well as other important information. The total 1923 attendance at all the games that the Horlick-Racine Legion was involved in, totaled 29,709. This was a 33 percent increase over the 1922 season. The average attendance at the home games was 2,600. It was 3,526 for the away games. The gate receipts showed a 13 percent increase over the previous year but the payroll had a 15 ½ percent increase. All of the Post No. 76 directors were pleased with the financial report of the team despite the deficit.

A meeting was scheduled for Thursday December 13th, 1923 in order to select new members to the board for the Racine Post No. 76 of the American Legion. A Dinner for Post No. 76 officers was scheduled for 6:00 pm and it would be followed by showing, the film of the American Legion drum corps trip to San Francisco, CA.

Collyer's News Bureau (Chicago, IL.) announced their 1923 National Football League All Star player selections. It was known as the "Collyer's All Star Pro Elevens" There was a first team and second team comprised of one selected player for each offensive position. Hank Gillo was selected for the 1923 Collyer's All Star Pro Eleven- first team fullback position.

On Saturday December 15th, 1923, a banquet was held to honor the 1923 Horlick-Racine Legion Football Team at the Racine Country Club. More than a 150 people attended the event. Attorney Mortimer Walker was the toastmaster and Grover Miller led the group in singing. The speakers for the evening included Dr. J.S.

Sidley, L.A. McDowell, retiring commander of the Racine Legion Post No. 76, Vilas Whaley, state commander of the Racine Legion Post No. 76, Thorwald Beck, city of Racine district attorney, Arthur Loeb, director of the Racine Legion Post No. 76, Max Zirbes, new commander of the Racine Legion Post No. 76, Frank Miller, Harold Pugh, Henry Rogers, George Smith and C. C. Younggreen of Milwaukee, Wisconsin. Players from the Horlick-Racine Legion football team, who spoke were Hank Gillo, George Hartong, Len Smith, Art Braman, and Irving Langhoff. George "Babe" Ruetz, resigning team manager also gave a speech.

Toastmaster Walker presented a fine gold watch and chain from the Racine Legion Post No. 76 to outgoing Manager George "Babe" Ruetz. Ruetz, who was taken by surprise as he did not expected any reward for his long and faithful service to the team. Ruetz followed his presentation with a speech in which he defended professional football *"as it's played today"*.

The main topic of the evening was about raising money to continue the Legion NFL franchise for the 1924 season. Plans of financing a team for the 1924 season was submitted by Attorney Milton J. Knoblock. The "Knoblock plan" was introduced and explained by Attorney Knoblock as follows:

"I am interested in football because I enjoy the entertainment of watching a good football game, but more than that, because I believe that it is the cleanest, healthiest, manliest sports on the list. I have great admiration for the qualities of sportsmanship, manliness and persistence which is unquestionably developed by the game of football, as it is now played. I have great admiration for the physical courage and physical fitness and also for the mental courage and the spirit of fairness which it creates, not only in the players, but in the spectators."

"I believe that the football that has been promoted by the Racine Legion for the last three years in this city has been a valuable thing for this community from several standpoints. It has given to the people of Racine and particularly to the young people and especially to the young men and boys, a clean, healthy, wholesome outdoor entertainment. It has created, particularly among the young people of the community, a strong spirit of civic pride having our football team, if possible, and a spirit of cooperation in doing everything possible for the success of the team and of the community and of the organization, the Racine Legion, which is represented by the team."

"I feel that it would be a pity for the city of Racine to lose this organization and this spirit, after it has been developed to the degree that it now has and I believe that if the Racine Legion is properly supported and receives proper encouragement financially and otherwise from the football fans and the people of Racine, that it can unquestionably produce for the 1924 season, a football team, which will take the Championship of the State and of the League. It is unfortunate, however, that in each successive year for the past three years, the Legion has sustained a substantial deficit in the operation its team and that this deficit has consistently grown until for the 1923 season, it amounts to a very substantial sum of money."

"I believe, it is impossible to conduct a football team along the proper sportsmanlike lines and make any money on it. And I believe, it is worth any actual loss, which is taken to the city of Racine and to the football fans to have a team here. I do not believe,

however, that the Racine or any other organization can be expected to give all of the time and effort and services of its members, which it has given freely for the past three years, without any compensation and then at the end of the season have the added burden of, in some way making up the deficit amounting to thousands of dollars."

"I presume everyone knows that the Racine Legion has conducted the football team, has furnished it's drum corps for entertainment, it's members for officials, ushers, ticket salesmen, solicitors, and for every other purpose, at absolutely not cost to the football team or the people of Racine and that all the money received from the sale of tickets or from any other source of income, which the football team had has gone solely to the payment of salaries of the players and their traveling and other necessary expenses."

"I am reliably informed that unless the Legion is assured of some sort of support, both financial and otherwise, greater than they have received during the past three years, the board of directors does not feel that it can assume the responsibility of again supporting a football team and the responsibility of making up any deficit that will occur in the year 1924 and subsequent years."

"I believe that men, who supported the football team in the past years were assured in the near future of some substantial financial support for the coming season, they would unquestionably be able to produce for you a better football team at a great less expense, and I fully believe if the football fans of Racine will get behind the Legion at this time with the assurance of some money for the purpose of securing the best players and of developing them and the added assurance of support during the season which the present contribution of funds will assure them, that there is no question but what Racine can produce the championship team of the league for the year 1924."

"I need hardly tell you what this would mean, not only to the Legion and to the football fans, but to the city of Racine in the way of favorable publicity."

"For that reason, I have devise a very simple plan for the raising of the funds, which I desire to submit to you. I believe that there are in Racine not less than 1,000 individuals, who are sufficiently interested in football as a sport, in football as an advantage to the city, and in football as an advantage to the Racine Legion, to contribute now in money the sum of $10.00 each toward a fund for the purpose of helping produce a championship Legion football team for the year 1924. I may be on the wrong about this, but I believe it is worth trying, so that the Legion or anyone else who plans on supporting a football team for future years, may find out now whether or not the community is behind them. If there are 1,000 people, who are willing to support a football team to that extent, there can be raised a fund of $10,000 to be turned over to the Legion for use for that purpose: that is, not for the purpose of covering any past deficits, but for the purpose of producing a championship team for next year and future years. If there are not 1,000, there may be 500 or more, who will support this sport to that extent. If there are not more than 500 people in this city, right now, who will contribute at this time, $10.00 a piece in cash for the football team, then I believe the Legion and the backers of the team should know it now, because without that minimum support, in this community, it is obvious they will never successfully conduct a football team and they might as well get the information at this time as any other and cease efforts along these lines."

168

"Therefore, I have prepared a little plan and proposal that I will submit to you for the purpose of raising $10,000. If possible, and not less than $5,500 to be used for the expenses of the Racine Legion Championship football team for the year 1924, in the following form: "Whereas, the Racine Post of the American Legion has for three seasons past promoted, supported and managed a football team at the city of Racine, and the members of the Legion have voluntarily and without compensation given their services as promoters, managers, officials, ushers, musicians, and in many other ways for the advancement of the sport and the entertainment of the citizens of Racine; and"

"Whereas each season of football has resulted in a heavy deficit because of expenses greatly exceeding revenue from the sale of tickets, which deficit has been covered by the members of the Racine Legion by solicitation, entertainment and otherwise; and"

"Whereas, we believe that football as conducted by the Legion at Racine is a substantial benefit to the community and the residents of the city and the business interests of Racine, because it is a clean, healthy manly sport; it provides wholesome outdoor entertainment for the people of Racine; It creates a strong civic and community spirit and interest in the city and its enterprises; and it results in valuable publicity for the city of Racine and the Racine Legion and it attracts the interest of the better class of young manhood to the city."

"Therefore, it is proposed to create a fund of $10,000.00, if possible and not less than $5,000.00 to be delivered to the board of directors of the Racine Legion for the purpose of being used with other income derived from the sale of tickets and other sources in connection with the football team, for the sole purpose of conducting a football team at the city of Racine in the season of 1924 and subsequent years upon the following conditions:"

"(1) All subscriptions to this fund to be paid to the Manufacturers National Bank to be held by said bank at 3% interest, until disposed of by the bank as follows:"

"(2) When a Legion football team for 1924 is assured the fund shall be delivered by the bank to the board of directors of the Legion, to be administered and used for the purpose of the payment of the necessary expenses of the team for the year 1924.

"(3) If a total sum of not less than $5,000.00 is not realized by the method on or before Feb. 1, 1924, or if a football team is not assured by May 15, 1924, all moneys to be returned by the board directly to the persons contributing the same."

"(4) This is proposed to be a contribution purely by persons interested in football for this city in the amount $10.00 each and carries with it no rights as to tickets or privileges and no compensation to the contributor except the satisfaction of doing something to further the sport and the interests of the city and of the Legion."

"I submit this proposed plan merely as my idea of the simplest, easiest and quickest method of raising funds for this purpose. I have no faith at this time and for this purpose in the success of the old style team and campaign method of raising funds, which came into existence during the war and has been to a considerable extent used for every purpose ever since."

"In this connection, I would not approve of any compulsory or bullying method of raising funds, whatsoever. I would not approve of any resident of Racine being told by a solicitor or committee that he should or must subscribe any sum of money, whatsoever for this purpose. On the contrary, I believe this is a proposition which

169

should be presented to the public and to the persons interested in football, entirely upon its merits. Therefore, I have eliminated the idea of having solicitors or teams or dinners or anything of the sort and have limited the plan merely to submitting it to the public, keeping it before them by the cooperation of the newspapers and accepting whatever, the general public desires to give to this fund, with one qualification of course, that subscriptions be a minimum of $10.00 and I believe that we should to stand entirely upon the results of this sort of a campaign."

"Of course, a campaign of this kind cannot be permitted to run itself entirely and I therefore, suggest that a committee of seven be appointed by the Chair to be the Racine Legion Football Fund committee, merely for the purpose of supervising the conduct of the campaign and the collection of funds. Also, I suggest that for the convenience of those, who are interested and who, desire to subscribe, that a few well known men in various portions of the city and connected with various of our larger industries be selected, so that the people in those particular portions of the city or employed in those particular plants can be more readily get information about the plan, if they desire it and get forms upon which, to enter their subscriptions and which, they can send to the bank with their remittance."

Following Knoblock's address, Toastmaster Attorney Walker appointed the following as a supervisory committee for the Football Fund Campaign: Max Zirbes, L.A. McDowell, Louis Homan, M.J. Knoblock, George Ruetz, G.W. Smith and Herbert F. Johnson.

The "Knoblock plan" was discussed and endorsed by several speakers of the evening. George Smith, who expressed himself as being highly in favor of the plan, offered to be one of the 1,000 men needed to back the plan.

The banquet wound down with Dr. Sidley proposing a toast to the team and Charles Nash sang a solo to end the banquet.

Photo of Racine Country Club – Racine, Wisconsin.
The 1923 Horlick-Racine Legion team banquet was held at the club.

LEGION FOOTBALL COUPON

Manufacturers National Bank,
Racine, Wisconsin.

I herewith send you $10 for the Racine Legion Football fund, upon the following conditions:

1. This fund is to bear interest at 3% until withdrawn for use by the Legion Athletic Association for a football team.

2. This fund is not to be used for any past expense but only for 1924 and future teams.

3. If no Legion football team is organized for 1924 this money is to be refunded to me.

4. If the total fund raised by this method is less than $5,000 this contribution is to be returned to me.

Signed ....

Address ....

Space contributed by The Journal-News for the American Legion

Coupon for Racine Legion Football Fund, which was printed in the Racine Journal News newspaper of Racine, Wisconsin

A CHAMPIONSHIP GRID TEAM FOR RACINE

How many people in Racine will support the American Legion in putting into the field a Championship Team for 1924.

We believe there are 1,000 people who will get back of the Legion to the extent of $10.00 each.

ARE YOU ONE OF THEM?

IF YOU ARE, send this form to the Manufacturers National Bank today. Manufacturers National Bank, Racine, Wisconsin.

I herewith send you $10.000 for the Racine Legion Football fund, upon the following conditions:

1. This fund is to bear interest at 3% until withdrawn for use by the Legion Athletic Association for a football team.

2. This fund is not to be used for any past expense but only for 1924 and future teams.

3. If no Legion football team is organized for 1924 this money is to be refunded to me.

4. If the total fund raised by this method is less than $5000.00 this contribution is to be returned to me.

Signed ....

Address ....

Coupon for the Racine Legion Football Fund, which was printed in the Racine Times Call newspaper of Racine, Wisconsin.

On Thursday December 29th, 1923, the Calhoun's National Pro Elevens selections were announced for the 1923 NFL season. G.W. Calhoun was a sports editor for the Green Bay Press Gazette. He released his NFL All-American Pro Player selections with the help of sports writers in the following cities: Pittsburgh, Milwaukee, Duluth, Minneapolis, Rock Island, Akron, Cleveland, Canton, Dayton, St. Louis and Green Bay. The selections appeared to have been biased as to the members of the media, who contributed. Surprisingly, Hank Gillo did not make this (Calhoun's National Pro Elevens) All Star team as well as other notable members of the 1923 Horlick-Racine Legion team. Hank Gillo was honored on the 1923 Collyer's All Star Pro Elevens Selection- First Team.

The National Football League
UNIFORM PLAYER'S CONTRACT

The ___Racine Legion Athletic Association Inc.___ _____, herein called the Club,
and _____ _Halliday_ _, of _Chicago Ill_ _____
herein called the Player.

The Club is a member of The National Football League. As such, and jointly with the other members of the League, it is obligated to insure to the public wholesome and high-class professional football by defining the relations between Club and Player, and between Club and Club.

In view of the facts above recited the parties agree as follows:

1. The Club will pay the Player a salary for his skilled services during the playing season of 192____, at the rate of $____ per game. As to games scheduled but not played the player shall receive no compensation from the Club, other than actual expenses.

_____

2. The salary above provided for shall be paid by the Club as follows:
Seventy-five per cent (75%) after each game and the remaining twenty-five per cent (25%) at the close of the season or upon release of the player by the Club.

3. The Player agrees that during said season he will faithfully serve the Club, and pledges himself to the American public to conform to high standards of fair play and good sportsmanship.

4. The Player will not play football during 192____ otherwise than for the Club, except in case the Club shall have released said Player, and said release has been approved by the officials of The National Football League.

5. The Player accepts as part of this contract such reasonable regulations as the Club may announce from time to time _of the Workmans Compensation Act of the State of Wisconsin_

6. This contract may be terminated at any time by the Club upon six (6) days' written notice to the Player.

7. The Player submits himself to the discipline of The National Football League and agrees to accept its decisions pursuant to its Constitution and By-Laws.

8. Any time prior to August 1st, 192_4_, by written notice to the Player, the Club may renew this contract for the term of that year, except that the salary rate shall be such as the parties may then agree upon, or, in default of agreement, such as the Club may fix.

9. The Player may be fined or suspended for violation of this contract, but in all cases the Player shall have right of appeal to the President of The National Football League.

10. In default of agreement, the Player will accept the salary rate thus fixed or else will not play during said year otherwise than for the Club, unless the Club shall release the Player.

11. The reservation of the Club of the valuable right to fix the salary rate for the succeeding year, and the promise of the Player not to play during said year otherwise than with the Club, have been taken into consideration in determining the salary specified herein and the undertaking by the Club to pay said salary is the consideration for both the reservation and the promise.

12. In case of dispute between the Player and the Club the same shall be referred to the President of The National Football League, and his decision shall be accepted by all parties as final.

13. Verbal contracts between Club and Player will not be considered by this League, in the event of a dispute.

Signed this ___twentieth___ day of ___October___, A. D. 192_3_

Witnesses: Racine Legion Athletic Assn. Inc
                                                                          (Club)
_____   By _____
                                                              Team Manager
_____   _____
                                                                    (Player)

Duplicate copy to be held by Player

NFL Player contract for Horlick-Racine Legion Player
Richard "Death" Halliday signed October 7th, 1923

Chapter 3:
Horlick-Racine Legion
1924 NFL season

The 1924 season for the Horlick-Racine Legion NFL football team would be filled with many changes in an effort to win a "State Championship" as well as an NFL League Championship. All of the players for the 1924 Legion team were expected to report to the first practice of the season on Saturday September 14th, 1924 at 2:00 pm as well as the second practice, which was to be held on Sunday at 10:00 am. Both practices were held at Horlick Athletic Field in Racine, Wisconsin. Five practices would be held each week until the first game of the season. Jack Melvin, newly elected Racine Legion Post No. 76 commander would be in charge of the publicity of the team, but not the personnel. Attorney Gwynette (George) Smalley was appointed as the new manager of the Legion team for the 1924 season and he would handle the personnel of the team. A meeting was held at the A.C. building in Racine on Thursday September 4th, 1924 in order to announce the players of the Legion team. G.E. Smalley, who was a city of Racine assistant district attorney was involved with the team as an advisor in 1923. The first game of the 1924 NFL season for the Legion was scheduled against the Hammond Pros at Horlick Athletic Field on Sunday September 28th, 1924 at 2:30 pm. Plans were made for a performance of the American Legion fife and drum corps to entertain the crowd. Smalley also announced a coaching change. Milton Romney, who played quarterback for the Legion in 1923 would be the coach for the 1924 season. Romney said that the first practice session would be devoted to looking over equipment, talking over plays, fixing up signal data as well as a light practice. In September of 1924, the team already had three players signed. Changes were still possible, due to three players still trying out for one of the end positions and eight players looking to try out for a back field position but the overall roster of the 1924 Horlick-Racine Legion professional football squad was near complete. The following was a tentative line-up that the team had in place at that time.

Tentative 1924 Horlick-Racine Legion Line-up:

Name	Position
Richard "Death" Halliday	Right End
Len "Fat" Smith	Right Tackle
Roman "Kibo" Brumm	Right Guard
Jack Mintun	Center
Jack Hueller	Left Guard
Don Murry	Left Tackle
Frederick "Fritz" Roessler	Left End
Wallace "Shorty" Barr	Quarterback
Al "Rowdy" Elliott	Left Halfback
Milton Romney	Right Halfback
Hank Gillo	Fullback
Al Benson	Guard

The American Legion Post No. 76 had a membership of over 1,300 during that time and Smalley said that he was certain that Racine professional football was in for a successful year, if all the members of the post would get out and boost the team. There would be no ticket drive that year but reservations were to be announced. At the season home opener, plans were made for a special presentation of a silver loving cup to be awarded to George Smith. This was a token of appreciation to his ticket team's success in the 1923 Legion football ticket sale. Also in the works, there was a plan to have a Ladies Day at one home game.

The Legion's first practice was attended by a large group of fans. The first task for the team was that the equipment needed to be looked over in order to determine, if any new items needed to be purchased. The Horlick-Racine Legion football team owned several thousands of dollars' worth of football equipment, at the time. Everything was determined to be in good shape.

Legion season football tickets went on sale exclusively from September 17th-23rd, 1924 at Rehl's Sixth Street Cigar Store in Racine, Wisconsin. Reserved box seats also went on sale exclusively at Rehl's Sixth Street location. The season individual game tickets were for five home games and they were offered at a total price of $7.50. Each individual game ticket(s) would be mailed out on the Tuesday prior to the Sunday's game that it would be used for, according to Jack Melvin, who was in charge of the project. Single game tickets for the first home game went on sale starting September 23rd, 1924 at the following locations: Rehl's Cigar Store at the 300 Sixth Street and 600 State Street locations, Monument Cigar Store-510 Monument Square, Smader's -331 Main Street. All located in downtown Racine, Wisconsin. The team was not offering a sale on season coupons, a ticket that included all the home games on one ticket for the 1924 NFL season and it was believed that was the best plan to offer by the new management.

Horlick-Racine Legion
1924 NFL Home game Schedule
All Home Games were played at Horlick Athletic Field

September 28th	vs	Hammond Pros
October 19th	vs	Kansas City
November 9th	vs	Rock Island Independents
November 27th	vs	Kenosha Maroons
November 30th	vs	Green Bay Packers

Ralph King was a 1923 center on the University of Chicago football team. He was signed to play for the Horlick-Racine Legion football team during the 1924 National Football League season. King, who weighed 240 lbs. was said to be one of the best at the center position in the BIG TEN conference during his last college season. He was a great addition to add strength for the Racine front line. It was reported that he was remarkably fast for a heavy man. Although, this was his first year in professional football, he had three years of being coached by Alonzo Stagg at the University of Chicago. Racine also signed John Webster, a halfback from California and Chuck Palmer, an end from Northwestern University. The signing of King, Webster and Palmer completed the line-up for Racine. In addition to those players, they had Len "Fat" Smith, Richard "Death" Halliday, Jack Mintun, Hank Gillo, Milt Romney, Al "Rowdy" Elliott, Frederick "Fritz" Roessler, Al Bentzin, Wallace "Shorty" Barr, Jack Hueller, Don Murry and Roman "Kibo" Brumm. Francis Russell played football in Illinois and he was also was a member of the famous Taylorville, Illinois team. He was trying out for a halfback position. Russell was employed by a local auto company in Racine. E.W. "Bill" Giaver, who played for Georgia Tech was another halfback trying to make the team. Earl "Bud" Gorman, a local boxer, who played with the team for the 1923 season, would serve as the team trainer. Cornelius "Pat" Hanley, who played for Marquette University and the famous 32D Army team during the World War, was trying out for the halfback

position, too. He had professional football experience from playing during 1922 with the Detroit Heralds and in 1923 with the Besser, Michigan pro team.

George "Babe" Ruetz, former team manager was out training and exercising with the team on Tuesday September 16th, 1924. He had dropped 50 lbs. in the last year and he was in top running condition.

The squad was working out 4:00 pm daily at Horlick Athletic Field as well as 9:00 am Sunday morning. In 1923, the Legion was forced to conduct practices at Lakeview Park because the new Horlick Athletic Field clubhouse was not completed.

Grandstand seating at Horlick Athletic Field

When the clubhouse was completed, it would have both dressing rooms and shower baths. The players would be able to get more acquainted with the field by holding practices on their home field. Mr. Horlick spent more than $50,000 on upgrades to Horlick Athletic Field. $30,000 was spent on the grandstand alone.

The Racine Legion Athletic Association, which was a subsidiary of the Racine Legion Post No. 76 was ready to back the team for another NFL season. The 1923 total paid admissions was 29,702. Total receipts for the 1923 season was $26,250.22. The 1923 average home attendance was 2,600. The average attendance at away games was 3,526. The average gate receipt for the 1923 Legion season was $2,965.62. The total cost for all games, less the amount paid to visiting teams, was $22,028.90.

In a comparison of attendance and cost for Horlick-Racine Legion's 1922 and 1923 seasons, it showed increases. The average home attendance in 1922 was 2,119 and in 1923, it increased to 2,609. That was 23% increase in attendance. The average 1922 Home game gate receipts was $2,618.58 and the average 1923 Home game receipts was $2,965.62. This was an increase of 12%. The average gate receipts at all games in 1923 was $2,625.02 compared to $2,474.83 in 1922. This was an increase of 6%. The average payroll in 1923 was $1,452.70 compared $1,256.78 in 1922. This was an increase of 15 ½ %.

The season opener for the Legion was expected to be a great matchup. The two teams did not play the previous season, but they played to 0-0 tie in 1922. Racine Legion Post No.76 Commander Jack Melvin, Team Manager G.E. Smalley and the entire athletic committee were expecting a large attendance for the Racine-Hammond game, based off a steady ticket sale. Special activities were planned for the 1924 NFL season opening game in Racine. The Racine Legion drum and bugle corps would provide the halftime entertainment. They would perform the same routine, which they used to win the National Championship in St. Paul, Minnesota, earlier in the summer of 1924. Miniature monuments

J I CASE T.M. Co. Racine, Wisc.

of the states were exhibited at the convention in St. Paul. The drum and bugle corps were awarded them as trophies and they were brought back to Racine. There was a plan to place one of these at each of the four corners of the Horlick Athletic Field football field. Fred Maxted was going to lead the Racine Legion drum and bugle corps during halftime, since Joseph Oliver was unable to be present. There was also a plan for a special promotion of a Ladies Day at Horlick Field. The promotion was to be as follows; each lady attending the game would receive a special souvenir (flower to wear) as well as being given a numbered program. Following a drawing at halftime, the lady having the correct number was going to receive a special prize. Season tickets would be given to one lucky lady at the game. Also, there was a plan to have a special loving cup trophy to be presented by L.A. Mc Dowell to the 1923 winning booster ticket sales team. George Smith (CASE T.M. Company) was the

Weigand Store-downtown Racine, Wisc.

team leader for the winning team. On this cup the following names were to be printed: G.W. Smith, Stephen Bull, John Carls, Soren Sorenson, H.C. Bowman, E.F. Russell, Herbert Morgan, E.F. Larke, Ralph Smith, William Albright and George Jorgenson. The 1923 cup was on display along with the 1922 cup in the window of Weigand's -a shop located in downtown Racine, Wisconsin. They planned to display the cups in downtown Racine and then after the completion of Memorial Hall, they would be displayed in the Hall's Legion trophy room. There was no competition for the 1924 season.

MAX ZIRBES

Max Zirbes

In an appeal to the people of Racine, Wisconsin for their support of the Horlick-Racine Legion professional football team, American Legion Post No. 76 Commander Max Zirbes wrote the following article, which appeared in both the Racine Times Call and Racine Journal News.

"By Max Zirbes Post Commander, American Legion

Sunday, Sept. 28 will open the football season in Racine. The Legion committees in charge of the different departments in producing a football team have spared no efforts to be able to give the people of Racine, a team they may well be proud of and everything possible is being done to provide every convenience for the spectators.

We appeal to the citizens of Racine for their co-operation and support to help make the Legion Football program a success. The Legion feels that Racine needs a team, and that the people want Racine to stay as one of the football leaders of the country.

The Legion football proposition is put right up to the people on its merits, the class of exhibition given are the best in the country and well worth the admission charged. The committees are giving every effort to make this season a financial success, the members of all committees giving their time and services free of charge. Mr. Horlick, dean of good sportsmen, has again placed Horlick Athletic Field stands, equipment and dressing rooms to the disposal of the Legion, free of charge.

Boxes and reserved seats may be reserved for the season at any of the ticket stations, but there will be no special booster ticket selling campaign organized this year.

The Legion believes Racine wants a football team. There will be only 5 or 6 games played here this year, and we feel sure that the fans will prove their support of the team by attending every game.

Sunday, Sept. 28, the Horlick-Racine Legion squad meets Hammond here. Let's pack the stands and show the team, we are with them. The team will play out of town, the following two Sundays, so don't miss the opening game.

Athletic Director L.A. McDowell has secured a wonderful schedule and built a fine organization to handle all drills. Team Manager Smalley will have a team in the field Sunday to make Racine, justly proud. Business chairman Melvin and field chairman Rundell are doing everything possible for the convenience of spectators.

Your only opportunity to support the team is by attending the games. Be there to greet the team for the opener next Sunday"

Horlick-Racine Legion Coach Milton Romney was putting the finishing touches on his 1924 grid machine on Thursday September 25th, 1924 for their game against Hammond, which was scheduled for the following Sunday. For three weeks prior, Romney and his staff of assistants were polishing up the crew, which was going to represent Racine, Wisconsin in the National Football League. He was well satisfied with the results that he was seeing from the squad. Romney was quoted as saying; *"We are entering the season with the finest jump-off team we ever had." "In former years, we were always strong in the backfield but rather weak in the line. This year, our line and backfield have equal strength and we have worked out a system of plays that is bound to carry us well up in the front."*

Halliday, Smith, Mintun, Hueller, Murray and Roessler were all veterans of the former Legion Lines. Bentzin, King and Palmer were the newcomers to the line and the team. They were expected to see playing time in the opener.

All of the newcomers to Racine team were stars from their respective college teams. Roman "Kibo" Brumm from University of Wisconsin, Al Bentzin earned his "M" with Golden Avalanche of Marquette University. Ralph King was with Chicago University and Chuck Palmer was known to be one of the finest tackles.

The returning veterans in the backfield were Hank Gillo, Al "Rowdy" Elliott, Milton Romney and Wallace "Shorty" Barr. Each of those players earned the respect of the Racine fans through their past performances. There was no better place kicker in professional football at the time than Hank Gillo. New additions to the Legion backfield included Bill Giaver, Chuck Palmer, John Webster and Richard Hanley. With these additions, Racine had a strong group of reserves.

Gillo stepped down as head coach for the 1924 season because of the continued increase of demand from his teaching career in Milwaukee, Wisconsin. He held the lead coaching position for the past two seasons.

The Legion was facing a tough opponent for their first game of the 1924 season. The Hammond Pros were loaded with former college star players including Frank Rydwesky (C) from Notre Dame and J. Witweiler (QB) from the University of Iowa. They had a great history against Racine. Two seasons prior, the two teams met and played to a 0-0 tie. They did not play again for the 1923 NFL season but Hammond was a strong team during that season. They were able to hold the 1924 NFL Champion Canton Bulldogs to a 3-0 loss. A history of Racine playing Hammond dated back to the days of the Racine Regulars semi pro football team.

179

No. 7 Don Murry Left Tackle   ***   No.4 Milton Romney Quarterback

Patronize the Merchants Who Advertise on This Page

Foot Ball Opens Tomorrow
Sunday, Sept. 28th

HORLICK ATHLETIC FIELD
Game Called at 2:30 O'Clock

HAMMOND VS. RACINE LEGION

HERE IS THE SCHEDULE FOR HOME GAMES

Sunday, Sept. 28 . . . . Hammond
Sunday, Oct. 19 . . . . Kansas City
Sunday, Nov. 9 . . . . Rock Island
Thanksgiving Day, Nov. 27 . . . . Canton
Sunday, Nov. 30 . . . . Green Bay

HERE'S THE FULL SCHEDULE

September 28th—Hammond at Racine.
October 5th—Racine at Rock Island.
October 12th—Racine at Chicago Bears.
October 19th—Kansas City at Racine.
October 26th—Racine at Milwaukee.
November 2d—Racine at Green Bay.
November 9th—Rock Island at Racine.
November 16th—Racine at Toledo.
November 23d—Racine at Chicago Cardinals.
November 27th—Canton at Racine.
November 30th—Green Bay at Racine.
December 14th—Racine at Kansas City.

NFL 1924 Season Openers

Saturday September 27, 1924
Rochester at Philadelphia

Sunday September 28, 1924
Hammond at Racine
Chicago Bears at Rock Island
Dayton at Akron
Cleveland at Columbus
Milwaukee at Chicago (Cardinals)
Green Bay at Duluth

Racine held a final practice before their first game on Saturday September 27th, 1924 at Horlick Athletic Field in Racine, Wisconsin. They were prepared for the 1924 NFL season opener. New cardinal jerseys with numbers were ordered for the Legion's 1924 season. Programs would be given out at the game, complete with player numbers from both teams in order for fans to know each player's name. Jack Melvin, who was in charge of the 1924 season ticket sales had reported a big advance distribution of tickets. A record crowd was expected. The main ticket reservations were made in the large grandstand at Horlickville. The smaller bleachers were switched over to the south end of the park. G.A. Malme, Legion official photographer was planning to be at the park to take pictures of the game as well as drum and bugle corps, with his motion picture layout.

** GAME DAY **

The 1924 NFL season opener between the Horlick-Racine Legion and the Hammond Pros was witnessed by a crowd of around 3,000 spectators. Rain on the prior day made Horlick Athletic Field difficult for the teams to establish a good running game and probably contributed to a decrease in attendance for fear of more bad weather. The lone touchdown of the game was scored by "Death" Halliday's sensational 25 yard run in the 1st quarter, which was followed with an extra point successfully kicked by Hank Gillo. A drop kick by "Shorty" Barr in the 4th quarter added to the scoring and gave the Horlick-Racine Legion a 10-0 victory over the Hammond Pros. Racine had a strong defensive line. They did not allow Hammond to gain any first downs, on the ground. Their three first downs came from pass completions. The Legion was able to gain five first downs by running the ball and the sixth one on a pass. The Racine defense was able to throw the Pro players, Dunc Annan, Sol Bulter and Guilford Falcon for losses during the game. The Legion was within striking distance of the goal line at several times during the game but they chose to attempt place kicks for field goals rather than try for touchdowns. Hank Gillo attempted a kick from around the 30 yard line and 40 yard line but both were unsuccessful.

182

PLAY BY PLAY: 1924 NFL SEASON HRL GAME 1
               HORLICK-RACINE LEGION VS HAMMOND PROS
               Sunday: September 28th, 1924   2:30 pm
               Horlick Athletic Field   Racine, Wisconsin

FIRST QUARTER:
  Gillo kicked off the ball to the Hammond Pros for start of the game. Falcon was back to receive the ball but the kick sailed over the goal post. It was considered a touchback by rule and Hammond started the game with the ball on the Pros 20 yard line. Hammond attempted to gain yardage on 3 downs but they were unsuccessful. The Pros choose to punt the ball on 4th down. Hammond punted the ball and it was received by Palmer on the Racine 40 yard line. He advanced the ball to the Hammond 40 yard line. The Legion fumbled the ball on first down but they were able to recover it. A run by Palmer through the line resulted in a 4 yard gain. Elliott ran the ball and it resulted in a 5 yard gain. Gillo attempted a place kick for field goal from the Hammond 40 yard line but it went wide of the goal post and resulted in no points. Hammond received possession of the ball. Racine's Halliday tackled the Pros Sol Bulter for a loss, back to the Hammond 10 yard line. They elected to punt the ball but only were able to get it to the Hammond 30 yard line. Racine took possession. Gillo ran the ball through the center of the line and it resulted in a 2 yard gain. A run attempt by Elliott resulted in no gain. Gillo ran the ball and it resulted in a first down. Elliott ran the ball and it resulted in a 4 yard gain. Romney ran the ball on a run around the end and it resulted in a first down for the Legion. The ball was placed near the Hammond 9 yard line. On the next play, Racine was penalized 15 yards for holding. This put the ball on about the 25 yard of Hammond. Elliott dropped back and tossed the ball 25 yards to Halliday. He swiftly ran the ball into the end zone for a Racine touchdown. Gillo successfully kicked the ball for an extra point. *Score: Racine 7, Hammond 0.* The Legion kicked the ball to Hammond. The Pros were unable to gain a first down. Hammond punted the ball to the Legion. Elliott ran the ball around the right end and it resulted in a 25 yard gain. A pass from Romney to Roessler gained 12 yards for Racine. Hammond intercepted a Racine pass. The ball was on the Pros 28 yard line. Hammond punted the ball to the Legion. Racine took possession of the ball on the Legion 12 yard line. They were able to gain yards. The ball was on the Hammond 40 yard line and the Legion had possession as the quarter ended.

SECOND QUARTER:
  The Legion was able to gain yards with a run by Murray. Racine was unable to gain a first down and punted the ball to the Pros. Hammond was unable to gain a first down and they punted the ball to the Legion. A run through the line by Halliday resulted in a gain. A run through the line by Elliott resulted in a gain. A run through the line by Gillo resulted in a gain. The Legion was unable to gain a first down and punted the ball to the Pros. A Hammond pass from Annan to Bulter resulted in a first down for the Pros. Racine substituted Webster in the game for Gillo and King in the game for Bentzin. Both substitutes played well and they were expected to be great additions to the team. The Legion regained possession of the

183

ball. Palmer ran the ball and it resulted in a gain of yards. Elliott ran the ball off the tackle and it resulted in a 25 yard gain for Racine. A pass from Elliott to Roessler resulted in a 12 gain for Racine. A run attempt by Webster resulted in no gain. A Legion pass from Elliott to Romney went incomplete. A Legion pass attempt was intercepted by Hammond on the Legion 30 yard line. The Pros were unsuccessful with gaining any yards. Annan punted for Hammond to the Racine 12 yard line. The second quarter ended.

THIRD QUARTER:

Racine kicked off the ball to Hammond. The Pros ran the ball and it resulted in a 1 yard gain. Sol Bulter was thrown for a loss by Halliday. Hammond punted the ball to the Racine 40 yard line. Racine took possession. Palmer gained 3 yards on a run attempt. Webster gained 4 yards on a run attempt. Elliott gained 1 yard on a run attempt. An attempt by Palmer resulted in no gain. Murray punted the ball to the Pros 20 yard line. After several Hammond attempts, they punted the ball to the Legion 30 yard line. A pass from Palmer to Roessler gained 25 yards for Racine. The Legion failed to make another first down. Gillo punted the ball to Hammond and it landed out of bounds at the 30 yard line. The Pros took possession of the ball but they were unable to advance it. Hammond kicked the ball to the Legion. Elliott received the ball and advanced it 2 yards. Racine was able to advance the ball to the Legion 48 yard line. The quarter ended.

FOURTH QUARTER:

Barr substituted in the game for Romney at quarterback. Barr attempted to pass the ball but it went incomplete. A Racine pass to Smith bounced off the shoulders off a Hammond defender and the ball was received by Brumm. He advanced the ball to the Hammond 45 yard line. Elliott ran the ball through the line and it resulted in a 2 yard gain. A strong rush by Hammond forced Barr to throw the ball for an incomplete pass. Romney punted the ball and it went out of bounds on the Pros 30 yard line. On first down, Hammond failed to gain any yards. Barr tackled Annan for a loss of yards. A Pros pass attempt to Butler went incomplete. Hammond punted the ball to Racine. Palmer received the ball and advanced it 8 yards. A run attempt by Romney resulted in no gain. Romney punted the ball to the Hammond 30 yard line. The Pros took possession. A Hammond run attempt by Annan around the end was stopped by Barr. Hammond punted the ball to Racine. Elliott received the ball on the Legion 40 yard line and he advanced it to the 48 yard line of Racine. Palmer ran the ball through the line and it resulted in a 1 yard gain. A Racine pass from Barr to Elliott gained 7 yards. Barr attempted a drop kick from the center of the field but the ball landed short on the Pros 10 yard line. Hammond took possession. A Pros pass from Butler resulted in a 9 yard gain. Another Butler run through the line resulted in a 6 yard gain and a Hammond first down. A Butler pass attempt went incomplete. A second pass attempt resulted in no yards gained. A third Hammond pass attempt was intercepted by Romney on the Racine 40 yard line. He advanced the ball to the Hammond 40 yard line. Barr ran the ball out of bounds and it resulted in no gain. A Legion pass attempt from Barr to Romney gained 8 yards. A Palmer run attempt resulted in a loss of yards. A Racine pass to Elliott went incomplete. The ball was on the Hammond 10 yard line.

184

A long drop back pass from Barr to Romney advanced the ball to Pros 5 yard line, where Romney was tackled by Williams. A run attempt by Palmer resulted in a loss. A pass from Barr to Romney resulted in a loss of yards for the Legion. Elliott ran the ball through the line and it resulted in a 3 yard gain. The ball was back on the Hammond 10 yard line. Barr drop kicked a successful field goal for 3 points from Pros 20 yard line. *Score: Racine 10, Hammond 0.* The Pros took possession of the ball. Hammond completed several passes. They were unable to gain any significant yardage. The ball was on the Racine 48 yard line when the whistle blew, which ended the game.

FINAL SCORE: HORLICK-RACINE LEGION 10, HAMMOND PROS 0

SCORE BY PERIODS:

	1st	2nd	3rd	4th	Final
Horlick-Racine Legion	7	0	0	3	10
Hammond Pros	0	0	0	0	0

TOUCHDOWNS: Racine- Halliday (1)
EXTRA POINT: Racine- Gillo, place kick (1)
FIELD GOAL: Racine- Barr, drop kick (1)

STARTING ROSTER:

RACINE		HAMMOND
Roessler	Left End	Williams
Murray	Left Tackle	Otiz
Bentzin	Left Guard	Barry
Mintun	Center	Rydesky
Brumm	Right Guard	Neal
Smith	Right Tackle	Usher
Halliday	Right End	Seyfert
Romney	Quarterback	Hess
Palmer	Left Halfback	Annan
Elliott	Right Halfback	Butler
Gillo	Fullback	Falcon

SUBSTITUTIONS: RACINE– Webster for Gillo, King for Bentzin, Gillo for Elliott, Barr for Webster, Giaver for Elliott. HAMMOND– Robertson for Butler, Bests for Falcon, Burton for Williams.

REFEREE: St. John
UMPIRE: Meyers
HEAD LINESMAN: Hoyt

Manager Smalley was content with his lead and he was able to give several players a chance to see playing time in the game. The Legion drum and bugle corps had performed the same drill at halftime, which won them honors in St. Paul, earlier in 1924. It was the first time that the Racine people had witnessed this championship performance in their nickel plated helmets. Racine Legion Post No. 76 Athletic Director L.A. McDowell was "Big Game" hunting in Canada but returned to Racine on Saturday to be able to attend the season opener for the Horlick-Racine Legion football team.

The Legion would have to travel for their next two games. Their next opponent was the Rock Island Independents from Illinois. Jim Thorpe, the famous Indian athlete was a player for the Independents. He was an exceptional halfback and great kicker. The team that he owned in the previous season, folded due to finances. He was joined on the roster with one of the greatest tackles in the game, Joe Little Twig. Another great tackle, Duke Slater (All-American, Iowa State University 1922) was the Rock Island Independents right tackle and another famous star player, who would be featured on the team. Rube Ursella was coaching the team as well as playing quarterback and halfback. He was a former quarterback for the Minneapolis Marines professional football team of the NFL. They also had Buck Gavin, Chicago University, "Terrible" Tommy Thompson, who played for the 1923 Nebraska Cornhuskers, Louis Kolls, who played several years of Illinois professional football. He divided his time playing football and chasing bootleggers as a member of the County Deputy Force. They were all on the Rock Island roster. Their roster was completed with a few other former college players.

Racine would practice all week at Horlick Athletic Field in preparation for their next game with their final practice of the week being on Friday October 3rd, 1924 at 4:00 pm. Coach Romney reported that the team came out of the game against Hammond without any significant injuries. He also mentioned that the team was in excellent condition and ready for Sundays' battle. The starting line-up was expected to be close to the same as the game against the Pros with the exception of Webster at fullback in place of Gillo. Romney would start at quarterback with Barr being available to substitute during the game. Palmer practiced at the end position and he would possibly see playing time at that position. Racine planned to pass the ball against Rock Island as they had against Hammond.

The Legion planned to leave Racine on Saturday to travel to Moline, Illinois and arrive on Sunday morning. The management informed the Legion players that they should meet at the train depot in Chicago at 10:30 pm. Team Chairman G.E. Smalley would oversee the team during the trip. They would have a chalk board meeting prior to boarding the train. They planned to travel via a midnight train out of Chicago and arrive at their destination at 5:00 am on Sunday. They would remain aboard the train until 8:00 am and then have breakfast in town. Racine would be staying at a local hotel and they described the accommodations as "Not the best". The Legion team would go through a light practice on Sunday morning in order to prepare for the game, which was scheduled to start at 2:30 pm, later that day. An announcement was made that a full report of the game would appear Monday in the Racine Journal News. The score of the game was going to be received via wire at the newspaper, after the game. Phone calls would be answered after 5:00 pm. Local Racine fans were planning to take trains to the game out of Beloit and Rockford in order to avoid the Chicago traffic, which they might experience traveling to the Chicago train station.

Rock Island had played the Chicago Bears to 0-0 tie in the week prior. The Rock Island Independent professional football team was formed by group in the early summer months of 1924 and local fans doubted that they would see professional football for the upcoming season. They organized and decided to put the best possible eleven on the field from old favorites and new players. The Independents chose green and white for their team colors.

PLAY BY PLAY: 1924 NFL SEASON HRL GAME 2
HORLICK-RACINE LEGION VS
ROCK ISLAND INDEPENDENTS
Sunday: October 5th, 1924   2:30 pm
Douglas Park   Moline, Illinois

GAME RECAP/PLAY BY PLAY:

FIRST QUARTER/SECOND QUARTER:
The game was an even battle for most of the game. The Independents had a slight edge because of the exceptional game, which Jim Thorpe played. Racine and Rock Island each moved their teams into scoring position during the first quarter but both were unable to capitalize. Rock Island was stopped on Racine's 9 yard line when "Rowdy" Elliott intercepted an Independents pass in the end zone. The Legion team was able to get down into scoring position, when Elliott broke through the line. This resulted in a long gain. The ball was on the Rock Island 30 yard line for Racine. The Legion attempted to run the ball but they were unable to get a first down. They lost possession of the ball to Rock Island. Thorpe successfully ran the ball several times through the line and around the end, while moving the ball down the field. The Independents were unable to score and Thorpe punted the ball to Racine. Racine was unable to score and Murray punted the ball to Rock Island. The second quarter ended with the ball on the Racine 30 yard line. The Legion had possession of the ball.

THIRD QUARTER:
There was an even exchange of possession of the ball and both teams successfully ran the ball. Neither team was able to score with possessions by both Racine and Rock Island. The ball remained around the 50 yard line.

FOURTH QUARTER:
A pass attack was forged by both the Racine and Rock Island. The Independents had possession of the ball. A pass from Armstrong to Wilson advanced the ball to the Racine 1 yard line. Gavin ran the ball through the line and scored a touchdown for Rock Island. The extra point attempt was unsuccessful. *Score: Racine 0, Rock Island 6.* On the next kick off, Thorpe received the ball on the Rock Island 5 yard line and he advanced it Racine 45 yard line. Thorpe made several successful runs

through the line to advance the ball. The Independents were able to move the ball down to the Legion 9 yard line. Racine was able to stop Rock Island from scoring a touchdown. Rock Island elected to attempt a field goal. Thorpe booted a successful drop kick for field goal. *Score: Racine 0, Rock Island 9.* Racine came back strong in the closing minutes of the game. They were able to advance the ball to the Rock Island 20 yard line by completing several pass attempts. The ball was intercepted by Rock Island. The game ended with the ball in the Independent's possession on the Racine 25 yard line.

FINAL SCORE: HORLICK-RACINE LEGION 0, ROCK ISLAND 9

SCORE BY PERIODS:

	1st	2nd	3rd	4th	Final
Horlick-Racine Legion	0	0	0	0	0
Rock Island Independents	0	0	0	9	9

TOUCHDOWNS: Rock Island-Gavin (1)
FIELD GOAL: Rock Island-Thorpe, drop kick (1)

STARTING ROSTER:

RACINE		ROCK ISLAND
Roessler	Left End	Thompson
Murray	Left Tackle	Twig
Bentzin	Left Guard	Kraker
Mintun	Center	Kolls
Brumm	Right Guard	Burton
Smith	Right Tackle	Slater
Halliday	Right End	Wilson
Romney	Quarterback	Ursella
Palmer	Left Halfback	Thorpe
Elliott	Right Halfback	Armstrong
Webster	Fullback	Gavin

SUBSTITUTIONS: RACINE– Giaver for Palmer, Hueller for King, Gillo for Elliott. ROCK ISLAND– Little Wig for Scott, DeClerk for Kolls, Scott for Little Wig.

REFEREE: St. John
UMPIRE: Morris
HEAD LINESMAN: Behnamann

"Rowdy" Elliott gained most of the yards for the Legion through the Racine run attack. Jim Thorpe was exceptional with how he advanced the ball for Rock Island. Palmer was injured during the game and he was replaced by Gillo. G.E. Smalley, chairman of the Legion football team said that he never saw the players of the Racine line play better than they did against Rock Island. The Independents had the ball on the Racine three yard line in the 1st quarter with four downs to go. The Racine defensive line not only stopped them from scoring but they moved the Independents back four yards and regained possession of the ball. This was due to the exceptional play by Smith in the middle of the line and Brumm containing the end.

A large number of fans accompanied the team to the game, cheering on the train ride to Illinois. It was estimated that a record crowd of 5,000 fans witnessed the game.

The Legion began practice immediately for their next road game against the Chicago Bears. Lights were added to Horlick Athletic Field and Coach Romney kept the team practicing late under the new lights. They expected a large number of Racine fans to take the trip to Chicago, to support the team against the Bears. The Legion organization was expecting to make a large amount of money from the gate of the game against the Chicago Bears, since the home team gave the option of sharing their gate revenue with the opposing team. The Green Bay Packers played the Chicago Cardinals in the week prior with only 2,500 paid admission but the low attendance was believed to be due to the Chicago Cubs vs. Chicago White Sox baseball game being played on the same day. Around 300 Green Bay fans accompanied their team to the game and Racine expected more fans to travel to Chicago for the Bears game. The Packers elected to take the "Guaranteed" gate money rather than a split of the paid admission.

Arrangements were made to take the American Legion drum and bugle corps to Chicago to play at halftime during the game against the Bears at Cubs Park. A special train was scheduled to Chicago on North Shore Line and it would leave Racine at 9:30 am on Sunday. The train would make a special stop at Wilson Avenue Station in Chicago, Illinois. Cubs Park was six blocks from that stop. The train was scheduled early in order to allow the fans to get lunch before the game, which was scheduled to start at 2:15 pm. A round trip train ticket to the game was sold for $3.20. The return tickets were good for any train returning to Racine, Wisconsin, so the fans could spend extra time in Chicago, if they chose to do so. There were 200 grandstand box ticket reserved seats for the Horlick-Racine Legion vs. Chicago Bears game at Cubs Park in Chicago, which were made available for sale in Racine. They were placed on sale along with the train tickets at Tom Smader's Place in downtown Racine. The game tickets were received by the Legion on Thursday October 9th, 1924 and they were sold for $2.00 each including the war tax. This was the regular price charged at all the Chicago Bears games for those seats. The tickets for the game sold fast in Racine and Legion officials were expecting to see a sell-out of the game down in Chicago. Many fans were planning to take the train and others were planning to drive to Chicago for the game.

Racine Coach Romney held the final practice of the week on Friday October 10th, 1924, as they prepared for a stiff battle against the Bears in the Windy City. Milt ran the team through one of the hardest practices of the season. Coach Romney made it clear to the team, in the future every player will report to scheduled practices or players, who do not attend practice would have their weekly pay cut considerably. He realized that he could not build a winning team, even with great star players unless they knew Racine's signals and plays, well. Romney was planning to start the same line up as he used against Rock Island with the exception of Gillo at fullback, to start in the game against the Bears. Racine signed former Legion halfback, Johnny Mohardt. He played his college football at Notre Dame under Coach Knute Rockne. After college, he signed different contracts and played on several professional football teams. He was a player for the Green Bay Packers and later, the Racine Legion in 1921. In 1922, he signed a contract to play for the Chicago Cardinals and he was playing there until the day he signed with Horlick-Racine Legion. The Legion would cut a player to make room for Mohardt on the roster.

** GAME DAY **

The Horlick-Racine Legion played the highly touted Chicago Bears to a 10-10 tie at Cubs Park in Chicago, Illinois on Sunday October 12th, 1924 before an estimated crowd of 10,000 fans. The Legion played their best game of the season on both the offensive and defensive side of the ball. Exceptional performances were made by Bill Giaver, "Kibo" Brumm, Len Smith and Hank Gillo for Racine. Coach Romney's team surprised the Bears, who were expecting to have an impressive victory in their first home game of the 1924 NFL season. One play that stood out in the first quarter of the game, came from Racine halfback Giaver. He received the ball on a punt from Duke Hancy and made a beautiful criss-cross run to the Chicago 8 yard line. The criss-cross run was said to be a thing of beauty to watch from the press box, which was located above the grandstand. It was reported that you could see him run his holes with the Racine players knocking down the Chicago players on both the left and right. Giaver started on the east side of the field and ran diagonally west, while he was heading south to the Chicago goal line. He was grabbed at the heel by Chicago Bears defender George Trafton, who appeared to be knocked out cold on the play. He was later revived and continued to play the game.

PLAY BY PLAY: 1924 NFL SEASON HRL GAME 3
      HORLICK-RACINE LEGION VS CHICAGO BEARS
      Sunday: October 12ᵗʰ, 1924 2:15 pm
      Cubs Park Chicago, Illinois

FIRST QUARTER:

 Chicago's Haney kicked off the ball to Racine. The ball went out of the back of the Racine end zone. The Legion took possession of the ball on the Racine 20 yard line. Racine elected to punt the ball. Murray kicked the ball to the Chicago 35 yard line. The Bears received the ball and the Chicago kick returner was tackled immediately by Brumm. Chicago took possession on the Bears 35 yard line. The Bears could not gain any yards. On third down, Chicago punted the ball back to the Racine 20 yard line. Giaver received the ball. On first down, Giaver ran the ball around the end and it resulted in a 1 yard gain. Gillo ran the ball off tackle and it resulted in a 6 yard gain. Giaver ran the ball and it resulted in a 10 yard gain as well as a Racine first down. Three attempts to run the ball by the Legion were unsuccessful. Racine punted the ball to Chicago. Three run attempts by the Bears were unsuccessful. The Bears punted the ball back to the Legion. Giaver received the ball on the 20 yard line for Racine. The Legion attempted to run the ball but it resulted in no gain. Gillo ran the ball through the line and it resulted in a gain of 25 yards as well as a first down. The Legion was unable to gain another first down and therefore, they punted the ball back to the Bears. Chicago could not get a first down and they punted the ball to Racine. Haney punted the ball to the Legion 40 yard line. Giaver received the ball and made a long run, criss-crossing the field to the Chicago 8 yard line, where he was tackled at the ankle by Trafton. On first down and goal to go, Gillo ran the ball through the line and it resulted in a 3 yard gain. On second down and goal to go, Elliott ran the ball and it resulted in a 1 gain. On third down and goal to go, Elliott ran the ball and again it resulted in another 1 yard gain. On fourth down and goal to go, the ball was on the Chicago 3 yard line. Gillo dropped back to the 18 yard line and drop kicked a successful field goal for Racine. *Score: Racine 3, Chicago 0.* Chicago again kicked the ball off to Racine. The Legion took possession of the ball on the Racine 20 yard line. The 1ˢᵗ quarter ended.

SECOND QUARTER:

 The quarter was filled with competitive football by both teams. Chicago outplayed Racine for most of the quarter by making the most of their possessions of the ball. The ball was on the Racine side of the field for most of the game. There was no scoring in the 2ⁿᵈ quarter. The Bears made 3 first downs and Racine was able to make only one first down in the quarter. Mohardt ran the ball through the line and it resulted in a 5 yard gain. Mohardt ran the ball through the line and it resulted in a 3 yard gain. Webster ran the ball and it resulted in a 2 yard gain as well as Racine first down. Racine had possession of the ball as the quarter ended.

THIRD QUARTER:

 Haney kicked the ball to Racine. The ball went out of the back of the Legion end zone. Racine took possession of the ball on the Legion 20 yard line. Gillo ran the ball and it resulted in a 1 yard gain. Giaver ran the ball through the line and it resulted in a 4 yard gain. Elliott was thrown for a loss of 9 yards. Murray punted the ball to the Chicago 40 yard line. Chicago took possession of the ball. A run attempt by Sternaman was stopped at the line. He was tackled by Smith. Lanum ran the ball through the line and it resulted in a 5 yard gain. A Bears pass attempt failed. It was 4th down and 5 yards to go. Chicago chose to punt the ball. Haney punted the ball to the Racine 30 yard line. The Legion took possession of the ball. Giaver gained 2 yards on a run through the line. Mohardt ran the ball and it resulted in a 1 yard gain. Giaver ran the ball through the line and it resulted in a 3 yard gain. On fourth down, Murray punted the ball to the Chicago 30 yard line. Joe Sternaman received the ball and he advanced it to the Bears 45 yard line. Lanum ran the ball and it resulted in a 5 yard gain. A successful Chicago pass from Lanum to Joe Sternaman resulted in a 20 yard gain. The ball was on the Racine 30 yard line. Joe Sternaman ran the ball through the line and he took the ball to the end zone for a touchdown. He also kicked a successful extra point for the Bears. *Score: Racine 3, Chicago 7.* Haney kicked the ball off to Racine. Bentzin recovered the ball on the Legion goal line and he advanced it to around the 30 yard line of Racine. He was tackled by a Chicago defender. A flag was thrown for the Bears being off sides on the kick off. It was a 15 yard penalty. After a discussion between Chicago Center Trafton and Referee Cahn, the penalty was reversed and the ball was spotted on the Legion 30 yard line. Racine had possession of the ball. A run through the line by Giaver resulted in no gain. A Racine pass attempt went incomplete. Another Legion pass attempt went incomplete. Murray kicked the ball to the Chicago 30 yard line. Joe Sternaman was back to receive the punt and he fumbled the ball. It was recovered by Racine. "Death" Halliday was running down to cover the punt when the ball was fumbled and it took a bounce. Halliday tried to scoop the ball up and advance it but he was unable to, so he fell on the ball. Racine had possession of the ball on the Chicago 13 yard line. Giaver ran the ball through the line and it resulted in a 5 yard gain. Gillo ran the ball through the center of the line and it resulted in a 4 yard gain. Giaver ran the ball through the line and it resulted in a 1 yard gain as well as a Legion first down. The ball was located around the Chicago 4 yard line. Racine set up a fake formation and the Chicago line was fooled by it, allowing Elliott to take a short run around the left end to score a touchdown for Racine. Gillo kicked a successful extra point. *Score: Racine 10, Chicago 7.* Sternaman kicked off the ball to the Legion. The ball was kicked out of the Racine end zone and therefore, they received possession of the ball on the Legion 20 yard line. Gillo gained 7 yards on a run through the center of the line. Giaver ran the ball and it resulted in a 2 yard gain. Another run by Giaver resulted in no gain. Murray attempted to punt the ball but it was blocked by Chicago. The Bears took possession of the ball on the Racine 20 yard line. Lanum ran the ball and it resulted in a 1 yard gain. Joe Sternaman was tackled for a 1 yard loss. Dutch Sternaman kicked a successful place kick for field goal from the Legion 20 yard line. The ball went sailing over the cross bar and the Bears had tied the score. *Score: Racine 10, Chicago 10.* Racine kicked off the ball to the Bears 10 yard line. Lanum received the ball and advanced it to the Chicago 25 yard line. He was tackled by Bentzin. The 3rd quarter ended.

FOURTH QUARTER:

Dutch Sternaman attempted a place kick for field goal from the center of the field. It was a long shot attempt at trying to win the game. He was unsuccessful. Haney punt the ball to the Legion. The ball landed out of bounds at the Racine 4 yard line. Racine took possession of the ball. They were able to advance the ball down field. Chicago was able to stop their drive. Murray punted to the Bears. The Bears were able to complete a pass and it resulted in an 8 yard gain. Further attempts to pass by Chicago went incomplete. The Legion took possession of the ball. Racine attempted to pass the ball but they were successful in moving the ball close enough to score. The Bears took possession of the ball. A Chicago pass was received by J. Sternaman at the 50 yard line. He advanced the ball to the 42 yard line of Racine. It resulted in an 8 yard gain. A run attempt by J. Sternaman resulted in a 2 yard gain. It was a first down for the Bears at the Legion 40 yard line. They attempted to run the ball 3 times and they were able to move the ball to the Racine 35 yard line. The Bears were preparing for a place kick for a field goal, when the whistle blew and the game ended.

FINAL SCORE: HORLICK-RACINE LEGION 10, CHICAGO BEARS 10

SCORE BY PERIODS:	1st	2nd	3rd	4th	Final
Horlick-Racine Legion	3	0	7	0	10
Chicago Bears	0	0	10	0	10

TOUCHDOWNS: Racine- Elliott (1) Chicago- J. Sternaman (1)
EXTRA POINT: Racine- Gillo, drop kick (1) Chicago- J. Sternaman (1)
FIELD GOAL: Racine- Gillo, drop kick (1) Chicago- E. Sternaman (1)

STARTING ROSTER:

RACINE		CHICAGO
Brumm	Left End	Haney
Murray	Left Tackle	Healy
Bentzin	Left Guard	Anderson
Mintun	Center	Trafton
King	Right Guard	McMillen
Smith	Right Tackle	Blacklock
Halliday	Right End	Halas
Romney	Quarterback	J. Sternaman
Giaver	Left Halfback	E. Sternaman
Elliott	Right Halfback	Armstrong
Gillo	Fullback	Knop

SUBSTITUTIONS: RACINE– Palmer for Giaver, Mohardt for Elliott, Webster for Gillo, Barr for Webster. CHICAGO– Bryan for E. Sternaman, Mullen for Halas, Kendrick for Walquist, LaFluer for Anderson, Lanum for Kendrick.

REFEREE: Cahn (Chicago)
UMPIRE: Unknown
HEAD LINESMAN: Whitlock

    The Racine Legion Post No. 76 drum and bugle corps marched around the field prior to the start of the game against Chicago and they also performed an exhibition drill during the halftime of the game. The drum and bugle corps from Racine performed at the request of the Chicago Bears and they were greeted with rounds of applause as they showcased the same maneuvers, which won them a National Championship at a recent convention in St. Paul, Minnesota.

    The Legion football team came out of the battle with Chicago without any serious injuries. They only significant injury of the game for Racine was to "Kibo" Brumm. He received a dislocated shoulder during the game against the Bears. He left the game until his arm was pulled back in position. Brumm returned to finish the game and he did not report any pain after that. Coach Romney expressed that team showed much improvement in the game against the Bears. He attributed this to the hard work at the practices that were held prior to the game and there would be no letting up in the next 5 days of practice. His lineman played better than they had against Hammond and Rock Island. He noticed a greater coordination and drive within the players. Plays from the Chicago game would be gone over to work through problems. New plays were introduced to Racine for the upcoming game against the Kansas City.

    Tickets went on sale for the next game at Tom Smader's – Main Street, Monument Cigar Store-Monument Square, and Rehl's Cigar Store-Sixth Street and State Street. The Horlick-Racine Legion would play the Kansas City Blues at Horlick Athletic Field in Racine, Wisconsin. The game was set for Sunday October 19th, 1924 at 2:30 pm

Kansas City played the Milwaukee Badgers, two weeks prior and the Green Bay Packers, the week prior to this upcoming game. They practiced in Green Bay, Wisconsin for the week and then headed to Racine, Wisconsin on Saturday for their game against the Legion. Curly Lambeau, manager of the Green Bay Packers informed G.E. Smalley, manager of the Horlick-Racine Legion about the fact that Kansas City did not have a good passing attack but they did have a strong running game as well as several former All-Conference college football players. Doc Andrews, manager of the Blues wrote to G. E. Smalley in order to let him know that they would arrive in Racine on either Friday or Saturday. They eventually communicated that they would arrive Saturday October 18, 1924, shortly after 12:00 noon.

Manager Andrews did not communicate this confirmed timetable to one of the owners of the Blues. This owner stopped in to the Racine Journal News in downtown Racine, Wisconsin looking for his team on Friday before their planned arrival. He arrived in Racine by automobile stating that he was to meet them on Friday but he could not locate them. He was told that the team sent word that they would arrive on Saturday.

Manager Smalley announced on Wednesday October 15th, 1924 that he was releasing two players from the Racine roster. Chuck Palmer and John Webster were released from the team due to the fact that continual missed practice. Both were members of the Legion backfield, who were college stars and played well for Racine. The players were warned about missing practices and Smalley was firm on his decision. Every player was paid to play for their respective clubs in the National Football League.

195

No.11 "Death" Halliday-Right End * No. 10 Bill Giaver-Left Halfback

No. 16 Bentzin-Left Guard   *   No. 18 "Shorty" Barr-Quarterback

No. 1 Hank Gillo-Fullback   *   No. 15 Smith-Right Tackle

No. 14 Jack Mintun-Center   *   No. 13 Kibo Brumm-Left Guard

No. 8 "Rowdy" Elliott-Right Halfback   *   No. 19 King-Right Guard

No. 7 Murry-Left Tackle

It was reported that the Waukegan (IL.) Elks were broadcasting (declaring) that Hank Gillo was trying to get a contract with the Elks and play for them in their game on Sunday October 19th, 1924, which was scheduled against a football team from Evanston, IL. Manager Smalley emphatically denied this report. He said that Hank had not been in communication with the Elks and he had no plans of quitting the Legion team. He said, Gillo played on the Racine team for the past three years and currently still was a member of the squad. Hank played for Racine Legion in 1921 and the Horlick-Racine Legion for 1922, 1923 and 1924 NFL seasons. It was thought that Waukegan was sending out this report to attract players and promote the team.

CAPT. HANK GILLO

Henry Charles Gillo
Horlick-Racine
Legion

FOOT BALL
Tomorrow
Sunday, October 19th

HORLICK ATHLETIC FIELD
Game Called at 2:30 O'Clock

HERE IS THE SCHEDULE FOR HOME GAMES

Sunday, Oct. 19 ....Kansas City
Sunday, Nov. 9 ....Rock Island
Thanksgiving Day, Nov. 27.........Canton
Sunday, Nov. 30 ....Green Bay

Kansas City   vs.   Racine

KANSAS CITY LINEUP	LINE-UP RACINE
No. 12, Corgan, R.E.	No. 11, Halliday, R. E.
No. 1, Bassett, R.T.	No. 15, Smith, R. T.
No. 9, Owens, R. G.	No. 13, Brumm, R. G.
No. 6, Peterson, C.	No. 16, Bentzin, R. G.
No. 17, Berquist, L. G.	No. 14, Mintin, C.
No. 10, Kroeger, L.T.	No. 12, King, L. G.
No. 8, Webber, L.E.	No. 17, Hueller, L. G.
No. 4, McElmore, Q.	No. 7, Murry, L. T.
No. 18, De Witz, R.H.	No. 3, Palmer, L. E.
No. 7, Hill, L.H.	No. 3, Palmer, L. E. or L.H.B.
No. 15, Strauss, F.	No. 5, Roessler, L. E.
	No. 4, Romney, Q. B.
	No. 18, Barr, Q. B.
	No. 8, Elliott, R. H. B.
	No. 10, Giaver, R. H. B.
	No 6, Webster, L.H.B. or F.B.
	No. 9, Hanley, L. H. B.
	No. 1, Gillo, F. B.

** GAME DAY **

Hank Gillo, who was a veteran of many hard fought football games was the lone scorer in the game against Kansas City. The Horlick-Racine Legion defeated the Kansas City Blues on Sunday October 19th, 1924 at Horlick Athletic Field by a score of 13 to 3. Gillo was able play exceptionally well despite a nagging cracked rib, which he received prior to the game. He was knocked around several times by the Blues but he was still able to excel. They were calling Gillo the "Red Grange" of the Legion team. Milton Romney played well on the defensive side of the ball for the

Legion. He had several tackles, which ended the Blues running attempts. Racine outplayed Kansas City during first half of the game. The Blues regrouped at halftime and ran the ball well but it didn't last. The Legion dominated the fourth quarter and Gillo was able to gain 10 or more yards on several carries. Racine was able to get fifteen first downs to ten by Kansas City. The Legion completed three of ten passes to the Blues completing five of eleven. Kansas City was able to pass the ball well throughout the game, which was contrary to what was reported by Curly Lambeau of the Green Bay Packers, prior to the game. The game was played before a disappointing low attendance on a day, which was considered a warm fall day.

PLAY BY PLAY: 1924 NFL SEASON HRL GAME 4
HORLICK-RACINE LEGION VS KANSAS CITY BLUES
Sunday: October 19th, 1924   2:30 pm
Horlick Athletic Field   Racine, Wisconsin

FIRST QUARTER:
Kansas City kicked off the ball to Racine. Giaver received the ball on the Racine goal line and he advanced it to the Legion 20 yard line. Elliott ran the ball and it resulted in a 1 yard gain. Gillo ran the ball and it resulted in an 11 yard gain and he was tackled by DeWitz at the Racine 32 yard line. It was a Legion first down. Romney ran the ball and it resulted in a 9 yard gain. The ball was on the Racine 41 yard line. The Blues substituted H. Hill in the game for Strauss. Elliott ran the ball around the right end and it resulted in a 15 yard gain. The ball was on the Blues 44 yard line. Gillo ran the ball and it resulted in a 1 yard gain. A pass from Romney to Giaver was completed for a 7 yard gain after it had been tipped by Kansas City. Gillo ran the ball through the line and it resulted in a Legion first down. A run attempt by Giaver resulted in no gain. A run attempt by Romney resulted in no gain. A run attempt by Elliott resulted in no gain. The ball was on the Kansas City 36 yard line. Gillo attempted a place kick for field goal but it was unsuccessful. The ball flew wide of the goal post. Kansas City took possession of the ball on the 20 yard line of Racine. A Blues run attempt through the line resulted in no gain. Another Kansas City run attempt resulted in no gain. The Blues punted the ball to the Legion. Giaver received the ball on the Racine 20 yard line. He advanced it to the Legion 32 yard line. Gillo ran the ball through the line and it resulted in a 9 yard gain. Elliott ran the ball and it resulted in a 2 yard gain as well as a Racine first down. A long pass to Halliday went incomplete. Another Racine pass to Murray went incomplete. Racine punted the ball to Kansas City. Hill received the ball and he was immediately tackled by Halliday on the Blues 10 yard line. On first down, Kansas City punted the ball to Racine. The Legion received the ball on the Racine 45 yard line. Romney ran the ball through the line and it resulted in a 3 yard gain. Gillo ran the ball and it resulted in a 5 yard gain. Elliott ran the ball through the line and it resulted in 2 yard gain as well as a Racine first down. The Legion fumbled the ball on first down but they were able to recover it and still gain 1 yard. A Racine pass went incomplete. Romney ran the ball around the left end and it resulted in a 20 yard gain. Gillo ran the ball through the line to the Kansas City 1

yard line. It was first down and goal to go on the 1 yard line. A Racine run attempt by Giaver failed to gain any yards. Gillo ran the ball through the line and it resulted in a Racine touchdown. Gillo successfully kicked the ball over the goal post for the extra point as the pistol sounded for the end of the quarter. *Score: Racine 7, Kansas City 0.*

SECOND QUARTER:

Gillo kicked the ball to the Blues. It went out of their end zone and the ball was placed on the Kansas City 20 yard line. It was a first down for the Blues. Kansas City ran the ball and made small gains of yardage. Hill punted the ball to the Racine 42 yard line. It was a first down for Racine. Giaver ran the ball and it resulted in a 1 yard gain. A Racine pass attempt went incomplete. Another Legion pass attempt went incomplete. Murray punted the ball to Kansas City. Hill received the ball for the Blues and he returned it to the 28 yard line. Two run attempts by the Blues resulted in a 4 yard gain. Kansas City punted to the 50 yard line. Racine was penalized 5 yards for being off sides. Four run attempts by the Legion resulted in no gain. The Blues took possession of the ball. Two run attempts through the line by Kansas City resulted in a first down. After several attempts, the Blues were unable to gain enough yards for a first down. The Blues punted to the Legion 20 yard line. It was a first down for Racine. Mohardt ran the ball through the line off the tackle. He gained 12 yards and a first down. Romney ran the ball around the end and it resulted in a 1 yard gain. Gillo ran the ball through the line and it resulted in a 6 yard gain. Gillo ran through the line and it resulted in a 3 yard gain and a Racine first down. A run by Mohardt resulted in no gain. A Legion pass from Mohardt to Romney resulted in a 13 yard gain. Gillo ran the ball through the line but it resulted in no gain. A Racine pass went incomplete. Murray ran the ball around the left end and it resulted in a 6 yard gain. Romney punted the ball Kansas City on the Blues 20 yard line. On first down, The Blues attempted a pass but it was intercepted by Romney. He advanced the ball to the Blues 30 yard line, where he went out of bounds. A Legion pass from Romney to Mohardt resulted in an 11 yard gain. It was another Racine first down. Gillo ran the ball and it resulted in a 2 yard gain. The ball was on the 18 yard line of Kansas City. Giaver was tackled for an 8 yard loss. Mohardt ran around the left end and it resulted in a 6 yard gain. Gillo kicked the ball successfully through the goal post to score points for a Racine field goal. *Score: Racine 10, Kansas City 0.* The Blues kicked the ball to the Legion. Romney received the ball on the kickoff. Barr, who substituted in the game for Gillo at fullback was unable to gain any yards on a run. He decided to pass the ball but it was intercepted by Corgan on the Racine 30 yard line. The second quarter ended.

THIRD QUARTER:

A Blues pass from Hill to Corgan resulted in a 20 yard gain. Kansas City ran the ball through the line and it resulted in a 3 yard gain. DeWitz ran the ball through the line and it resulted in a 7 yard gain as well as a Blues first down. Hill ran the ball and it resulted in a 3 yard gain. Hill ran the ball but he was tackled for a 3 yard loss. A Kansas City pass was knocked down by Mintun. Andrews attempted a place kick for field goal but it was unsuccessful. Racine took possession of the ball. Murray punted the ball to Kansas City. Corgan received the ball and he advanced it to the

Racine 40 yard line. Hill ran the ball through the line and it resulted in a 3 yard gain. Hill ran the ball through the line and it resulted in a 1 yard gain. A pass from Hill to Corgan resulted in a 20 yard gain and a Kansas City first down. The Ball was on the Racine 25 yard line. Another Kansas City place kick for field goal attempt by Andrews was unsuccessful. The Legion took possession of the ball. Murray punted the ball to the Blues. Kansas City took possession of the ball. Hill ran the ball through the line and it resulted in a 6 yard gain. Another pass from Hill to Corgan resulted in a 10 yard gain. The Blues ran the ball out of bounds and it was placed on the Racine 25 yard line at the middle of the field. A Kansas City pass was intercepted by "Death" Halliday. He advanced the ball to the 35 yard line of the Legion. Racine ran the ball and it resulted in no gain. They ran the ball again and it resulted in no gain. Murray punted the ball to the Blues 35 yard line. On the first play, DeWitz ran the ball around the left end and it resulted in a 17 yard gain. H. Hill ran the ball through the line and it resulted in a 9 yard gain. Corgan ran the ball and it resulted in a Kansas City first down. DeWitz ran the ball and it resulted in a 1 yard gain. H. Hill ran the ball and it resulted in a 9 yard gain as well as another Blues first down. At first, DeWitz was unsuccessful with running the ball through the line but he was able to break free from being tackled by the Racine defense. He ran around the left end and he was able to gain 20 yards. The ball was on the Legion 10 yard line. Hill ran the ball off the tackle for 2 yards but he was thrown for a 5 yard loss by the Racine defense. The Blues were penalized 5 yards for being off sides. The ball was on the Legion 20 yard line. Kansas City attempted a run, which resulted in no gain. They attempted another run, which resulted in no gain. Andrews attempted his fourth place kick for a field goal. This one was successful. _Score: Racine 10, Kansas City 3._
FOURTH QUARTER:
Kansas City kicked off to Racine. On first down, Gillo ran the ball for a 10 yard gain and a Legion first down. On the next play, Racine was penalized for being off sides. The ball was on the Blues 45 yard line. Gillo ran the ball through the line and it resulted in a 5 yard gain. Elliott ran the ball through the line and it resulted in a 2 yard gain. A Legion pass from Romney to Elliott resulted in a 20 yard gain. A Racine run attempt resulted in no gain. Another run attempt resulted in no gain. A Legion pass attempt was knocked down by Kansas City. Gillo dropped back and kicked a successful place kick for a field goal. _Score: Racine 13, Kansas City 3._ The Blues regained possession of the ball. They were on the Racine 40 yard line when the game ended.

FINAL SCORE: HORLICK-RACINE LEGION 13, KANSAS CITY BLUES 3

SCORE BY PERIODS:

	1st	2nd	3rd	4th	Final
Horlick-Racine Legion	7	3	0	3	13
Kansas City Blues	0	0	3	0	3

TOUCHDOWNS: Racine- Gillo (1)
EXTRA POINT: Racine- Gillo (1)
FIELD GOAL: Racine- Gillo, place kick (1) Kansas City- McElmore (1)

STARTING ROSTER:

RACINE		KANSAS CITY
Roessler	Left End	Webber
Murray	Left Tackle	Krueger
Bentzin	Left Guard	Berquist
Mintun	Center	Peterson
Hueller	Right Guard	Owens
Smith	Right Tackle	Bassett
Halliday	Right End	Corgan
Romney	Quarterback	Burquist
Mohardt	Left Halfback	Milton
Giaver	Right Halfback	Hill
Gillo	Fullback	Strauss

SUBSTITUTIONS: RACINE– Barr for Gillo, King for Hueller, Mohardt for Giaver, Giaver for Elliott, Elliott for Mohardt. KANSAS CITY- Choate for Strauss, Andrew for Choate.

FIRST DOWNS BY PERIODS:

	1st	2nd	3rd	4th	Total
Horlick-Racine Legion	7	3	0	5	15
Kansas City Blues	0	1	8	1	10

Giaver sustained a knee injury in the game against Kansas City. He was the only player to be injured. Manager Smalley secured Henry Garrity, who played football at Oregon University, to cover for the injured Giaver. "Kibo" Brumm was available to play after recovering from the shoulder injury, which he received against the Bears but Romney chose to rest him, since they did not need him for the game against the Blues. Practice resumed on Tuesday October 21st, 1924 at Horlick Athletic Field in preparation for their next game against the Milwaukee Badgers at Milwaukee, Wisconsin.

MILTON ROMNEY

No. 4 Milton Romney-Quarterback

Attorney G.E. Smalley, manager of the Horlick-Racine Legion football team made arrangements to get a block of 800 tickets in the stands to be reserved for the Legion fans at the next game in Milwaukee, Wisconsin. The Legion grid team was expecting several hundreds of fans to accompany them to Milwaukee for the game against the Badgers. The Legion played Green Bay and Milwaukee for two games each year and this was considered a race within a race. They were playing for the "State Title"- the best record of the Wisconsin teams, who played each other.

On Wednesday October 22nd, 1924, Attorney Smalley was in Milwaukee to complete the arrangements for the game on Sunday. A block of tickets in a section of the stands was reserved for the Racine fans. They were purchased and brought back to Racine, Wisconsin in order to sell them at Tom Smader's Place-Main Street, Racine, Wisconsin for the game. The tickets would remain on sale at Smader's until 11:30 am on game day. All of the seats were all located together and a cheer leader was going to be provided to pep up the crowd. Racine and Milwaukee had a strong rivalry and both had good teams. Red Dunn, former Marquette University captain was leading the Badgers team.

Coach Romney of the Horlick-Racine Legion eleven practiced regularly all week in preparation for their game against Milwaukee at Brewers Park (Athletic Park). Henry Garrity, who played 3 years for the University of Oregon was brought into Racine to tryout as a reserve fullback to replace Gillo, if necessary. Hank had a cracked rib injury from the previous game. Garrity played fullback and end for former Notre Dame Coach Darius, while at Oregon. Giaver, who suffered a knee injury would return to practice for the Milwaukee game. "Kibo" Brumm, who was out in the previous week with a bad shoulder returned to play one of the offensive (end) positions.

** GAME DAY **

Racine displayed a great team effort with solid individual contributions by Hank Gillo in their game against Milwaukee on Sunday October 26th, 1924. They were able to shut out the Badgers with a 10-0 victory. The Horlick-Racine Legion was known for a large number of assets, which gave them a good name. They had a good organization supporting the team along with a great fan base but they also had an exceptional All-American fullback named Henry Charles Gillo. He was able to score all the points against the Badgers, which included a 40 yard run that resulted in the only touchdown of the game. Hank and his gilded hoof (kicking foot) still showed exceptional form. Gillo was supported by a cast of players, who excelled the team to victory. The offensive line consistently blocked their opponents, which allowed Gillo, Elliott and Barr to advance the ball as well as protecting Murray to punt the ball. The Legion was able to make five first downs to the Badgers one in the second quarter. Milton Romney injured his knee and he was removed from the game during the first quarter. He returned to the game in the second quarter and he brought new energy to the field. Halliday, Smith and Murray were stars of the Racine defense in this game.

PLAY BY PLAY: **1924 NFL SEASON HRL GAME 5**
HORLICK-RACINE LEGION VS MILWAUKEE BADGERS
Sunday: October 26th, 1924   2:30 pm
Athletic Park   Milwaukee, Wisconsin

FIRST QUARTER:

The ball was exchanged between both teams at midfield. The Legion and Badgers exchanged punts as neither team was able to advance the ball. Murray (Racine) and Dunn (Milwaukee) were involved in a punting duel. Dunn punted the ball 55 yards to set the Legion back. Racine was penalized 5 yards for delay of game. Towards the end of the first quarter, Racine was able to advance the ball with a run and a pass completion. A Legion run by Barr advanced the ball for 10 yards and a Racine first down. A Racine pass from Barr to Elliott advanced the ball 10 yards and it was another Legion first down. Barr ran the ball through the line and it resulted in a 5 yard gain. Barr attempted to pass the ball but it was intercepted by Red Dunn on the Milwaukee 25 yard line. Milwaukee advanced the ball 5 yards to the Badgers 30 yard line as the quarter ended.

SECOND QUARTER:

Milwaukee was able to advance the ball 5 yards for a Badger first down. Gillo stopped Dunn from advancing the ball. Murray tackled Dunn for a loss. Milwaukee was penalized 5 yards for delay of game. Dunn punted the ball for Milwaukee and it landed out of bounds on the Racine 20 yard line. Gillo ran the ball through the line and it resulted in a gain. Gillo ran the ball around the end for a gain of yardage. Racine was unable to further advance the ball. Murray punted the ball to the 50 yard line. Milwaukee took possession. The Badgers were unable to advance the ball. They punted to Racine. Murray received the ball and he was tackled on the Racine 14 yard line. Barr ran the ball through the line and it resulted in a 2 yard gain. Elliott ran the ball through the line and it resulted in a 2 yard gain. Elliott ran the ball around the left end and it resulted in a 10 yard gain as well as a Legion first down. Gillo ran the ball off the left tackle and it resulted in a 40 yard gain. He was forced out of bounds at the 20 yard line. It was another Racine first down, which was deep in Milwaukee territory. Mohardt gained 2 yards on a run through the line. Romney, who had replaced Barr at quarterback tossed a short pass to Elliott, which resulted in a 10 yard gain. It was another first down for Racine. Gillo ran the ball through the center of the line and it resulted in a 4 yard gain. Mohardt twisted through the line to advance the ball for a 15 yard gain and a Legion first down. The ball was on the Milwaukee 10 yard line. Gillo ran the ball for a gain. Gillo ran the ball across the goal line to score a Racine touchdown. Gillo kicked the ball through the goal posts for a successful extra point. *Score: Racine 7, Milwaukee 0.* Gillo kicked off the ball to the Badgers. Conzelman received the kick off and he was immediately tackled by Brumm after receiving the ball. Milwaukee took possession of the ball. A Milwaukee pass was knocked down by the Racine defense. A Badgers pass from Conzelman to Winkelman netted only a small gain. After another attempt, the Badgers were unable to advance the ball. Dunn punted the ball to Racine 45 yard line. The Legion took possession of the ball. Elliott ran the ball and it resulted in a 5 yard gain. Elliott ran the ball around the right end and it resulted in a 15 yard gain as well as Racine first down. As the half was about to end, Gillo kicked the ball from the 50 yard line squarely through the uprights for a successful field goal. *Score: Racine 10, Milwaukee 0.* The Badgers took possession of the ball. A run attempt by Dunn was unsuccessful. The ball was on Milwaukee's 20 yard line as the quarter ended.

THIRD QUARTER:

Racine and Milwaukee exchanged the ball. Elliott intercepted a Milwaukee pass. The Badgers defense was constantly stopping the Legion offense. Neither team was able to significantly gain. "Death" Halliday of Racine sacked Milwaukee Quarterback Dunn for a loss. Dunn was removed from the game because of injury and he was replaced by Conzelman. Mooney was substituted in the game at left end. Racine took possession of the ball. The Legion could not advance the ball. Milwaukee took possession of the ball. The Badgers could not advance the ball. The Badgers dropped back for a punt and Racine broke through the line and blocked it. Milwaukee regained possession of the ball on the Racine 33 yard line. The Badgers were unable to advance the ball. Milwaukee attempted a pass, which was intercepted by Elliott for the Legion. The quarter ended.

FOURTH QUARTER:

Milwaukee regained possession of the ball. They began a passing attack in an attempt to move the ball. The Racine defense penetrated the Badgers offense line and broke up a pass play. Milwaukee attempted to pass the ball without success. The Badgers attempted another pass without success. A pass by Milwaukee resulted in a 10 yard gain. The pass also resulted in a Milwaukee Badgers first down. Milwaukee attempted to pass the ball without success. A Badgers pass went incomplete. The Legion defense penetrated the Badgers offensive line and a Conzelman pass attempt was unsuccessful. Milwaukee passed the ball and it resulted in a 20 yard gain. The pass completion resulted in another first down for the Badgers. Milwaukee was unsuccessful in advancing the ball. Racine took possession. The Legion advanced the ball. Barr ran the ball through the line and it resulted in a Racine first down. The ball was in Racine territory. The game ended.

FINAL SCORE: HORLICK-RACINE LEGION 10, MILWAUKEE BADGERS 0

SCORE BY PERIODS:

	1st	2nd	3rd	4th	Final
Horlick-Racine Legion	0	10	0	0	10
Milwaukee Badgers	0	0	0	0	0

TOUCHDOWNS: Racine- Gillo (1)
EXTRA POINT: Racine- Gillo (1)
FIELD GOAL: Racine- Gillo, place kick (1)

STARTING ROSTER:

RACINE		MILWAUKEE	College
Brumm	Left End	Neacy	Colgate
Murray	Left Tackle	Widerquist	W. & J.
Bentzin	Left Guard	Jean	Bethany
Mintun	Center	Larson	Notre Dame
King	Right Guard	McGinnis	Marquette
Smith	Right Tackle	Weller	Nebraska
Halliday	Right End	Swanson	Lombard
Barr/Romney	Quarterback	Dunn	Marquette
Mohardt	Left Halfback	Conzelman	W. & J.
Elliott	Right Halfback	Erickson	W. & J.
Gillo	Fullback	Winkelman	Arkansas

RESERVES:

Jack Hueller		Mooney	Georgetown
Fred Roessler		Madolney	Notre Dame
"Shorty" Barr		Foster	former HRL
Bill Giaver		Swanson	Lombard

SUBSTITUTIONS: RACINE– Hueller for King. MILWAUKEE- Madolney for McGinnis, Conzelman for Dunn, Mooney for Conzelman.

Referee: ST. John (Chicago)
Umpire: Meyers (Milwaukee)
Head linesman: Downer (Milwaukee).

The contest between Racine and Milwaukee developed into a rough battle, which featured neck tie tackles and hard hitting. At one point, "Death" Halliday hit "Red" Dunn, so hard on a quarterback sack that the Badger was removed from the game because he became dizzy. A crowd of about 4,000 fans witnessed the game and approximately a 1,000 were from Racine, Wisconsin. The victory gave the Legion a tie with the Packers in a battle for the "State Title". The Horlick-Racine Legion was in 3rd place of the National Football League standings.

Since, Green Bay began playing in the National Football League (known as APFA) in 1921, they have only lost four games at home. They were defeated at home by the Rock Island Independents in 1921, Horlick-Racine Legion in 1922 and the Chicago Bears and Horlick-Racine Legion in 1923. To date, the Green Bay Packers had not defeated Racine on their home playing field. The focus was now on the next game with the state rival, Green Bay Packers. The Legion was expecting that many fans would travel up to Green Bay to support Racine.

Arrangements were made to charter one of the T.M.E.R. & L. Co. white buses for the transport of 25 fans to the game. Fans were instructed to contact Harry

T.M.E.R & L Co. Office
Racine, Wisconsin

LePoidevin of the Racine Journal-News to reserve a seat on the bus, which was described as comfortable. The bus held 35 people but in order to insure comfort only 25 passenger tickets were going to be sold. A ticket for a seat on the round-trip bus from Racine, Wisconsin to Green Bay, Wisconsin was offered for $7.70. The fare to ride the train round trip to Green Bay was $10. Many other fans were expected to make the trip by automobile and motorcycle. The Legion expected at least 500 fans to make the long trip. This game was expected to be a sellout. Horlick-Racine Legion management asked for a block of tickets to be reserved for the Racine fans.

Milton Romney began preparing the team for one of the toughest battles of the season. Green Bay always brought good competition to the Legion and Racine expected that they sent scouts to analyze the game against Milwaukee. Milton was planning to add a new halfback, since the club gave releases to both Hanley and Palmer.

The football fans from Oshkosh, Wisconsin planned to travel to Green Bay, Wisconsin to see Len "Fat" Smith play for the Horlick-Racine Legion. Smith received his primary gridiron education at Oshkosh High and Normal schools. After graduation, he played football at the University of Wisconsin along with fellow Oshkosh Lineman Marty Below. Now, Smith was studying at a Chicago college and playing for the Legion.

The Packers players significantly outweighed the Legion players, especially for the lineman. Green Bay's line was 163 lbs. heavier than Racine's linemen. Racine manager Romney was not worried. They handled teams with bigger players in the past and he was preparing the team for the passing game of the Packers. The Green Bay Packers ended the week with a practice on Thursday, Friday morning and a blackboard talk at Continuation school on Friday night. Saturday morning would round out their practice preparation for the game, given by Captain Lambeau.

The Legion team would leave Racine by train on Saturday November 1st, 1924 at 6:30 pm. They planned to arrive in Green Bay, Wisconsin around 11:00 pm. The team would enjoy a good night of rest before the Sunday afternoon game. Fans were also planning to leave early for the game. Some would leave on Saturday at 12:00 noon, while a majority would leave Saturday night or early Sunday morning. Booble Cahn, who was rated as one of the best officials working in professional football was named by National Football League President Joe F. Carr to oversee the game between the Packers and the Legion. This game was considered to be a deciding factor of the best team in the state and many believed that the winner would be have a good chance to take a National Title. The game was going to be played at Bellevue Park in Green Bay, Wisconsin and it was scheduled to start at 2:00pm

Pro League Standings.				
Team	W.	L.	T.	Pct.
Duluth	3	0	0	1.000
Cleveland	3	0	1	1.000
Racine Legion	3	1	1	.750
Buffalo	3	1	0	.750
Rock Island	3	1	1	.750
Chicago Bears	2	1	2	.667
Chicago Cards	3	2	0	.600
Philadelphia	3	2	1	.600
Green Bay	3	2	0	.600
Dayton	2	2	0	.500
Columbus	2	2	0	.500
Milwaukee	2	3	0	.400
Akron	1	2	0	.333
Kansas City	1	3	0	.250
Minneapolis	0	3	0	.000
Rochester	0	5	0	.000
Kenosha	0	3	0	.000

Back Row:	Giaver-HB	Gillo-FB		Mohardt-HB	Elliott-HB
Front Row:		Romney-QB		Barr-QB	

** GAME DAY **

The Horlick-Racine Legion led the Green Bay Packers for three quarters by a margin of three points because of a field goal successfully booted by Hank Gillo in the first to minutes of the game. The Legion was defeated by the Packers, when Curly Lambeau completed a 40 yard pass to Tillie Voss in the back of the end zone. This was the first play of the fourth quarter and the final score of the game. The Packers defeated the Legion by a score of six to three. It was a hard fought game, which gave the fans a real football showing. This was the first time, which Green Bay had defeated Racine at their home field (Bellevue Park), since they joined the NFL in 1921.

PLAY BY PLAY: 1924 NFL SEASON HRL GAME 6
HORLICK-RACINE LEGION VS GREEN BAY PACKERS
Sunday: November 2nd, 1924   2:00 pm
Bellevue Park   Green Bay, Wisconsin

FIRST QUARTER:

Racine chose the north goal and elected to kickoff. Gillo kicked the ball to Green Bay and Voss received the ball on the Packers 20 yard line. Voss fumbled the ball and the Legion recovered it. Gillo ran the ball but it resulted in no gain. Gillo attempted to run the ball but it resulted in no gain, again. Gillo signaled for a place kick from the 30 yard line. Gillo kicked the ball and it successfully sailed clear over the crossbar. *Score: Racine 3, Green Bay 0.* The Packers received the ball. Several Green Bay attempts went unsuccessful. Green Bay punted to Racine. The Legion received the ball. Several Racine attempts were unsuccessful. The Legion punted to the Packers. Green Bay made a first down. The Packers were unsuccessful in moving the ball. Green Bay punted to Racine. The Legion made a first down. Racine was unsuccessful in moving the ball. The Legion punted to the Packers.

SECOND QUARTER:

The ball was on the Racine 20 yard line. Racine had possession of the ball. The Legion made several attempts to advance the ball. They could not make a first down. Murray punted to Green Bay on the Packers 25 yard line. Basing ran the ball and it resulted in an 8 yard gain. Hendrian ran the ball and it resulted in a 2 yard gain as well as a Green Bay first down. The Packers advanced the ball and it resulted in a 5 yard gain. Green Bay fumbled the ball. Giaver recovered the fumble on the Racine 40 yard line. The Packers and Legion exchanged punts as a result of not being able to advance the ball. Green Bay took possession of the ball. A Packers pass attempt resulted in a 2 yard gain. Another Green Bay pass resulted in a 2 yard gain. The Packers were unable to make a first down and Racine gained possession of the ball. Gillo ran the ball and it resulted in a gain of 10 yards as well as a Legion first down. Racine was unable to advance the ball. Gillo punted the ball to the Packers 20 yard line. The quarter ended.

THIRD QUARTER:

Racine gained possession of the ball. Gillo ran the ball through the left side of the line and it resulted in a 30 yard gain. The ball was on the Legion 45 yard line. Giaver ran the ball and it resulted in a 3 yard gain. Mohardt ran the ball and it resulted in a 2 yard gain. A Legion pass from Romney to Halliday was intercepted by Voss on the Green Bay 40 yard line. Lambeau ran the ball and it resulted in an 8 yard gain. Lambeau ran the ball and it resulted in a 2 yard gain. Green Bay had a first down on the 50 yard line. Lambeau ran the ball through the line and it resulted in a 3 yard gain. Hendrian ran the ball and it resulted in a 7 yard gain as well as a Packers first down. The ball was on the Racine 30 yard line. A Green Bay pass was intercepted by Romney on the Legion 7 yard line. Murray punted the ball. It was returned by the Packers to the 43 yard line. Woodin signaled for a place kick. The kick was blocked and Racine took possession of the ball. Murray punted the ball out of bounds at the Legion 40 yard line. The quarter ended.

FOURTH QUARTER:

Lambeau passed the ball to Voss. Voss fell down on the back of the end zone line but retained hold of the ball and he scored a Green Bay touchdown. The kick for an extra point was blocked by "Fat" Smith. *Score: Racine 3, Green Bay 6.* Green Bay kicked the ball off into the Racine end zone. The Legion took possession of the ball on the 20 yard line. Barr substituted in the game for Gillo by Racine. A Legion pass from Barr to Halliday resulted in a 15 yard gain. It was a Racine first down. A Legion pass from Romney to Brumm resulted in a 9 yard gain. Giaver ran the ball through the line and it resulted in a 1 yard gain as well as a Racine first down. Another Legion pass from Romney to Giaver resulted in an 8 yard gain. A run attempt by Elliott resulted in no gain. A Racine pass attempt was broken up. Murray punted the ball to the Mathys. Mathys received the ball on the Green Bay 8 yard line and he was immediately tackled by Halliday. On first down, Hendrian immediately punted to get the Packers out of their own territory. Racine took possession of the ball. Giaver gained 3 yards on a run through the line. A Racine pass from Romney to Halliday resulted in a 30 yard gain. The ball was on the Packers 30 yard line. Barr ran the ball and it resulted in a 1 yard gain. Another Racine pass from Barr to Mohardt was completed for a 2 yard gain. Mohardt ran the ball and it resulted in a 1 yard gain. Barr signaled for a drop kick for field goal. Barr attempted a drop kick for field goal from the 40 yard line of Green Bay. The kick missed by inches and did not go through the uprights. It rolled over the goal line, on the left side. The Packers took possession of the ball. Green Bay was unable to advance the ball. The Packers punted. Racine took possession of the ball. Barr completed a pass to Mohardt and it resulted in a 40 yard gain. The ball was on the 50 yard line. Racine attempted several passes but the ball ended up incomplete. Green Bay took possession of the ball. The Packers punted the ball to the Legion. The Legion took possession of the ball. A Racine pass attempt went incomplete. A Legion pass from Barr to Halliday resulted in a 20 yard gain. The ball was located near the 50 yard line as the game ended.

FINAL SCORE: HORLICK-RACINE LEGION 3, GREEN BAY PACKERS 6

SCORE BY PERIODS:

	1st	2nd	3rd	4th	Final
Horlick-Racine Legion	3	0	0	0	3
Green Bay Packers	0	0	0	6	6

<u>TOUCHDOWNS:</u> Green Bay- Voss (1)
<u>FIELD GOAL:</u> Racine- Gillo, place kick (1)

218

STARTING ROSTER:

RACINE		GREEN BAY
Brumm	Left End	Murray
Murray	Left Tackle	Buck
Bentzin	Left Guard	Woodin
Mintun	Center	Earp
King	Right Guard	Gardner
Smith	Right Tackle	Rosaiti
Halliday	Right End	Voss
Romney	Quarterback	Mathys
Mohardt	Left Halfback	Basing
Elliott	Right Halfback	Lambeau
Gillo	Fullback	Hendrian

SUBSTITUTIONS: RACINE– Barr for Romney, Romney for Barr, Barr for Gillo. GREEN BAY- Duford for Murray.

Referee: Cahn (Chicago) Umpire: Meyers (Milwaukee) Head linesman: Coffeen (Beloit)

   A close game was played between the Legion and Packers in front of 4,000 wildly excited fans. The scoring highlights of the game included a perfect field goal kick from Hank Gillo and a 40 yard game winning pass from Curly Lambeau to Tilly Voss in the back of the end zone. A potential game tying field goal sent thousands of fans to sit silent as a drop kick for field goal from Barr, rose in the air. The kick was unsuccessful by inches and the game was eventually lost by Racine. The Green Bay fans swarmed the field in a large mob after the final game whistles blew to congratulate their Packers after the hard fought game.
   Don Murry was recognized as playing an exceptional game against the Packers and especially Cub Buck of the Green Bay Packers. Buck was much larger than Murry but he was continuously able to get through to the Packers backfield to interrupt their plays. Murry also punted the ball very well. He averaged between 45 and 50 yards per punt.
   The next game for the Legion was scheduled to be at home against the Rock Island Independents. The independents were in third place of the National Football League standings. Rock Island defeated Racine by a score of 9-0 on the last time that they played each other. The team featured the great halfback Jim Thorpe, formerly of the Canton Bulldogs as well as Duke Slater- a 1922 All-American tackle from Iowa State. Thorpe also played professional baseball for the New York Giants. These two players were destined to have a place reserved for them in American football history. Rock Island officials were planning to have a special wire service to cover the game with a play by play coverage for the fans back in Rock Island. The Western Union was stringing a special wire to the Park in order to render this service.

November 2nd, 1924   Horlick-Racine Legion vs. Green Bay Packers

The Legion started preparing immediately Monday afternoon at Horlick Athletic Field for an exceptional Rock Island team. Elliott injured his knee but he expected to practice again by the end of the week. Gillo had a leg injury but he also expected to return to practice mid-week. The Horlick-Racine Legion organization was planning some special features for the upcoming game. A halftime parachute jump was planned as the entertainment feature of the game. Miss Ethel Dare, a nationally known aviatrix, was going to jump from a moving plane operated by Jim Duncan and attempt to land on the 50 yard line at the center of the Horlick Athletic Field football field. This was definitely both a dangerous and intriguing halftime entertainment for the return of the Legion to Horlickville.

Death Defying
Parachute Jump

THE most daring, hair-raising, spine-chilling flying stunt ever attempted in Racine. 1500 feet up in the air, with his airplane speeding over 100 miles an hour, Mr. Sam Duncan will throw himself off the right wing, drop like a rock until his parachute opens, and then attempt to land on the fifty yard line on Horlick's Football Field.

This will be followed by a very instructive exhibition of stunt flying at 1,000 feet over the field, portraying every trick used by our famous aces: The loop, Immelman-turn, falling leaf, tail spin, barrel roll and the dreaded spinning nose dive.

Nothing like it ever before seen in Racine. It may be years before you have another opportunity of witnessing such death defying feats of skill and nerve. Don't miss this thrilling acrobatic flying, which is the extraordinary added attraction at the great

Football Game

RACINE vs. ROCK ISLAND

Sunday, November 9th 2:30 P.M.
Horlick Athletic Field

2500 Good Seats at $1.00

Some especially good reserved seats can still be obtained if you decide early. Go to the stores shown below. They will be glad to help you select good seats. Do it now, and decide that everlasting problem of "What to do this Sunday."

THE LEGION

Best Seats Now on Sale at
Rehl's, Sixth St.   Rehl's, State St.
Smader's, Main St.   Monument Cigar

The team officials were making every effort to get a packed house for the game on Sunday. They issued around 6,000 tickets to members of the American Legion Post No. 76 in an effort to increase attendance to the game. A meeting was held on Thursday November 7th, 1924 with the Legion membership of the Post No. 76 at the Association of the Commerce building in Racine, Wisconsin. Vilas Whaley, former Wisconsin department commander, L.A. McDowell, athletic director, G.E. Smalley, team manager, Don Murry, left end for team and others sought to excite the membership about the team and hopefully boost attendance. Mr. Whaley said, outside of the drum corps, the Legion did not have a better asset than the Legion football team, which is giving the city of Racine valuable advertising. His speech went on to compare attendance at the Green Bay Packers game to the upcoming Horlick-Racine Legion game as a measure to exceed. He also said that the fate of pro football depended in a large measure on the attendance at the upcoming Sunday game against Rock Island. Whaley stated that every effort was being made to increase attendance at the games. Don Murry was introduced by L.A. McDowell. He said that Fred Maxted, champion new member associate of the Post No. 76 had signed Don up as a 1925 member. Murry said that there wasn't one player on the team, who would not have given all the money, which he made in the Green Bay game, if the Racine could have won that game. He added, the spirit on the Legion team was as close to college in which he ever saw on any other pro team. He went on to say that the players were not just out for the money, which they received although they could not afford to play without it, they were fighting for the honor of the Legion at all times. Mr. Smalley said that Racine was represented by the best team that ever played in this city. Smalley stated that it would take the support of the fans to make the season a success. He pleaded to the membership about attending the game. He said, *"I would give more for our chances of a win against Green Bay than I would for our chances against Rock Island." "Yet, we are going to win that game." "If you fellows will turn out and attend the game, you will help the team a lot."* Athletic Officer McDowell said that if the members attended the football games in as large numbers as they attend the post meetings, the season would be successful. McDowell went on to say that Murry may play as a fullback on Sunday, a position that he was known for as being a great ground gainer. He also individually outlined the Rock Island Independent players. Commander Melvin explained to every one of the great expense that the Legion was going to incur to get Ms. Ethel Dare, the female stunt performer, who would parachute jump from the plane at halftime. He concluded with a request to get full attendance at the game against Rock Island.

Tickets were also on sale at the usual outlets in Racine-Rehl's Cigar Stores on Sixth and Main streets, the Monument Cigar Store and Tom Smader's Place. The Legion officials announced on Friday that the advance sale of tickets was by far the largest of the year and it was even bigger than the sales before the Green Bay Packers game from last year, which was a sellout. Everything was pointing to a standing room only crowd for the Sunday battle (game), which promised to be one of the biggest attractions of the year.

MISS ETHEL DARE in

Death Defying

Parachute Jump!

THE most daring, hair-raising, spine-chilling flying stunt ever attempted in Racine, 1500 feet up in the air, with her airplane speeding over 100 miles an hour, Miss Ethel Dare will throw herself off the right wing, drop like a rock until her parachute opens, and then attempts to land on the fifty yard line on Horlick's Football Field.

This will be followed by a very instructive exhibition of stunt flying at 1,000 feet over the field, portraying every trick used by our famous aces: The Loop, Immelman-Turn, Falling Leaf, Tail Spin, Barrel Roll, and the dreaded Spinning Nose Dive.

Nothing like it ever before seen in Racine. It may be years before you have another opportunity of witnessing such death defying feats of skill and nerve. Don't miss this thrilling acrobatic flying, which is the extraordinary added attraction at the great

Football Game

RACINE vs ROCK ISLAND

2,500 Good Seats at...

$1

Sunday, Nov. 9th

Horlick Field, 2:30 p. m.

Some especially good reserved seats can still be obtained if you decide early. Go to the Stores shown below. They will be glad to help you select good seats. Do it now, and decide that everlasting problem of "What to do this Sunday,"

THE LEGION

Best Seats Now On Sale At—

REHL'S—SIXTH
REHL'S—STATE

MONUMENT CIGAR
SMADER'S

Romney and his team fully realized the strength of the team that they were about to play, but there was a lot of confidence among the players and they were ready to send them home with a loss.

** GAME DAY **

After all the preparation of the team, a controversial call decided the outcome of this game for Racine. The Legion went down to defeat by a score of 6-3. Early in the first quarter, Hank Gillo kicked a 30 yard field goal to give Racine their first and only points of the game because a Racine touchdown pass was ruled illegal.
"Shorty" Barr completed a 30 yard pass to "Death" Halliday in the end zone for a Racine touchdown but it was ruled no touchdown by an official. Shortly after the beginning of the second quarter, the Legion successfully ran the ball and moved it to the Rock Island 40 yard line. A long 30 yard pass completion from Barr to Halliday was completed to the 20 yard line and Halliday advanced it to the 10 yard line of the Independents. Gillo advanced the ball another 3 yards before the touchdown pass of the controversy.

CONTROVERSIAL PLAY: Barr threw the ball over the goal line into the arms of Halliday as he was standing in the end zone. The stands erupted and the fans roared in celebration until puzzled silence set in as the ball was given to Rock Island on the Independent 20 yard line. To the disbelief of many, Referee J. Holloway ruled that Halliday stepped out of bounds, while making the catch.

A fumble in the 3rd quarter gave the Independents field position close to the goal line. They were able to score the only touchdown of the game from this mistake and defeat the Legion.

FOOT BALL
Tomorrow
Sunday, November 9th

HORLICK ATHLETIC FIELD
Game Called at 2:30 O'Clock

HERE IS THE SCHEDULE FOR HOME GAMES

Sunday, Nov. 9 . . . . Rock Island
Thanksgiving Day, Nov. 27 . . . . Canton
Sunday, Nov. 30 . . . . Green Bay

Rock Island vs. Racine

ROCK ISLAND LINEUP	LINE-UP RACINE
Little Twig, L. E.	No. 11, Halliday, R. E.
Scott, L. T.	No. 15, Smith, R. T.
G. Thompson, L. G.	No. 13, Brumm, R. G.
Kollé, C.	No. 16, Bentzin, R. G.
Buland, R. G.	No. 14, Mintin, C.
Slater, R. T.	No. 12, King, L. G.
Wilson, R. E.	No. 17, Hueller, L. G.
Thorpe, L. H. B.	No. 7, Murry, L. T.
Bradshaw, R. H. R.	No. 5, Roessler, L. E.
Gavin, F. B.	No. 4, Romney, Q. B.
Armstrong, Q. B.	No. 18, Barr, Q. B.
	No. 8, Elliott, R H. B.
	No. 10, Giaver, R. H. B.
	No. 9, Hanley, L. H. B.
	No. 1, Gillo, F. B.

225

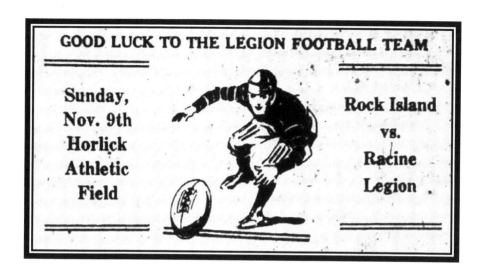

GOOD LUCK TO THE LEGION FOOTBALL TEAM

Sunday,
Nov. 9th
Horlick
Athletic
Field

Rock Island
vs.
Racine
Legion

PLAY BY PLAY: **1924 NFL SEASON HRL GAME 7**
HORLICK-RACINE LEGION VS
ROCK ISLAND INDEPENDENTS
Sunday: November 9th, 1924   2:30 pm
Horlick Athletic Field   Racine, Wisconsin

FIRST QUARTER:

Gillo kicked off the ball to the Rock Island. Bradshaw received the ball and returned it 20 yards to the 35 yard line. Thorpe ran the ball off the left tackle and it resulted in a 4 yard gain. Thorpe punted to Racine. Barr received the ball on the Racine 35 yard line. Mohardt gained 2 yards through the right end. Gillo ran the ball but it resulted in no gain. Barr passed the ball to Mohardt and it resulted in a 13 yard gain. It was a Racine first down and the ball was on the 50 yard line. Racine attempted to advance the ball but they were penalized for being off sides. The Legion was penalized 5 yards. Barr attempted to pass the ball but it went incomplete. Murry punted the ball to Bradshaw on the Rock Island 40 yard line. He advanced the ball 3 yards. Ursella ran the ball through the left guard and it resulted in a 4 yard gain. Ursella ran the ball off the left tackle and it resulted in a 3 yard gain. The ball was at the 50 yard line. Bradshaw ran the ball off the right tackle and it resulted in a 4 yard gain. Thorpe attempted to drop kick the ball for a field goal from the 50 yard line but he missed by inches. Racine took possession of the ball. Giaver gained 1 yard on a run through the right end. The ball was on the Racine 21 yard line. Barr ran the ball through the right tackle and it resulted in a 12 yard gain. Giaver ran the ball and it resulted in a 4 yard gain. He was tackled by Little Twig. Gillo smashed through the right tackle taking the ball to mid field. Giaver ran the ball but it resulted in no gain. Gillo plunged through the line for an 11 yard gain.

He was tackled by Ursella. It was a first down for the Legion. Barr passed the ball to Brumm and it resulted in a 6 yard gain. Barr plunged through the line and it resulted in a 5 yard gain. Gillo ran the ball off the left tackle and it resulted in a 5 yard gain. It was a first down for the Legion and the ball was on the Independents 25 yard line. Barr attempted a pass but it went incomplete. Barr passed the ball to Brumm and it resulted in a 1 yard gain. Gillo successfully drop kicked the ball over the goal post from the 31 yard line. _Score: Racine 3, Rock Island 0._ Thorpe kicked off the ball to Racine and it went over the goal post, landing into the end zone. Racine took possession of the ball on the Legion 20 yard line. Mohardt gained 2 yards on a run at the right end. Gillo gained 2 yards on a run at the right guard. Giaver gained 4 yards on a run around the left end. Murry punted the ball out of bounds on the Rock Island 40 yard line. Ursella attempted a run at the left tackle but it resulted in no gain. Thorpe was thrown for a 3 yard loss, when he attempted a criss-cross play from Ursella. Thorpe punted to the Racine 25 yard line and the ball was grounded. Barr ran the ball and it resulted in a 6 yard gain. The ball was located on the Legion 31 yard line. The quarter ended.

SECOND QUARTER:

Gillo plunged through the center of the line and it resulted in a 5 yard gain as well as a Racine first down. Barr smashed through the line and it resulted in a 2 yard gain. The ball was on the Legion 38 yard line. Goyer substituted in the game for Ursella. Armstrong substituted in the game for Bradshaw. A run attempt by Barr resulted in no gain. Barr dropped back to attempt a pass but George Thompson penetrated the line and threw Barr for a 15 yard loss. Barr was driven out of bounds with no gain. The ball was on the Racine 23 yard line. Murry punted the ball out of bounds on the Independents 46 yard line. Guyon attempted a run through the right end but he was tackled for a 3 yard loss. Thorpe plunged through the center of the line and it resulted in a 3 yard gain. A pass attempt by Thorpe went incomplete. Thorpe punted the ball out of bounds on the Racine 43 yard line. Gillo twisted through the line at the left guard and he gained 5 yards for the Legion. Barr smashed through the line at the right guard and it resulted in 3 yard gain. Gillo ran the ball for a 2 yard gain. Barr smashed through the line at the left guard and it resulted in a 3 yard gain as well as a first down for Racine. A run attempt by Mohardt resulted in no gain after he was stopped by Slater. Barr passed the ball to Mohardt and it resulted in a 4 yard gain. The ball was on the Rock Island 41 yard line. A 20 yard pass from Barr to Halliday resulted in a 31 yard gain after Halliday advanced the ball another 11 yards. The ball was on the Independents 10 yard line. It was another Racine first down. Giaver attempted a run through the left end, which resulted in no gain. Gillo ran the ball through the right guard and it resulted in a 3 yard gain. Barr passed the ball to Halliday in the end zone and it scored a Legion touchdown. Referee Holloway called the play illegal because he said that the Racine player was out of the end zone. He ruled that there was no touchdown and the ball was moved back to the 20 yard line. Rock Island was given possession of the ball. A run by Thorpe resulted in no gain. Thorpe punted the ball to the Racine 33 yard line and the ball was grounded. Giaver attempted to run the ball but he was tackled for a 3 yard loss. A run attempt by Gillo resulted in no gain. A long pass attempt by Barr went incomplete. Murray punted the ball to Rock Island and Guyon received it. He fumbled the ball and it was recovered by Racine on the Rock Island 41 yard line. Mohardt smashed through the line at the left guard and it resulted in a 2 yard gain. A Barr pass attempt went incomplete. Murry gained 3 yards on a fake punt formation. Gillo dropped back to kick a field goal but the kick was blocked. It was recovered by Racine on the Legion 47 yard line. A run attempt by Gillo resulted in no gain. A long pass attempt by Barr was intercepted by Guyon. Guyon advanced the interception 35 yards to the Racine 30 yard line. Thorpe gained 2 yards on a run through the right end. A run by Armstrong resulted in no gain. A pass attempt from Armstrong to Guyon was barely missed and resulted in an incomplete pass. A drop kick attempt for field goal by Thorpe from the 33 yard sailed wide right of the goal post. Racine took possession of the ball on the 20 yard line. Barr attempted to run the ball through the center of the line but it resulted in no gain. Barr plunged through the line at the left guard and it resulted in a 2 yard gain. The ball was on the Racine 33 yard line. The quarter ended.

THIRD QUARTER:

Thorpe kicked the ball off for Rock Island and it went over the goal line. Racine took possession of the ball on the 20 yard line. Giaver ran the ball through the left guard and it resulted in a 5 yard gain. Mohardt ran the ball at the left tackle and it resulted in a 4 yard gain. Giaver ran around the left end and it resulted in a 16 yard gain and the ball was advanced to the Racine 47 yard line. It was a first down for the Legion. Mohardt smashed through the line at the right guard and it resulted in a 5 yard gain. Mohardt gained 1 yard with a run at the right end. Barr advanced the ball to the Rock Island 25 yard line. Barr completed a 25 yard pass to Giaver. He was stopped on the goal line. A run attempt by Mohardt resulted in no gain. Barr ran the ball at the center of the line but it resulted in no gain. Barr dropped back for a pass to Mohardt from a spread formation and it was completed for 2 yards but he did not reach the end zone. Gillo attempted to place kick the ball for a field goal from the 30 yard line. It was low and unsuccessful. Rock Island took possession of the ball on the 20 yard line. Thorpe ran the ball through the line and it resulted in a 2 yard gain. Gavin plunged through the center of the line and it resulted in a 3 yard gain. Thorpe punt to the Legion. Barr received the ball and he was immediately tackled, at the Racine 33 yard line. Barr attempted a pass to Brumm but it was incomplete. Murray punted the ball to the Independents. Armstrong received the ball and he was immediately tackled at the Independents 35 yard line. Guyon attempted a run at the left end but he was tackled for a 1 yard loss. A Rock Island fumble from the center was recovered by Thorpe but it resulted in a 3 yard loss. Armstrong ran the ball around the left end and it resulted in a 9 yard gain. Thorpe punted the ball and it was received by Barr. He was immediately tackled by Fred Thompson on the Racine 21 yard line. The Legion fumbled the ball and it was recovered by Slater on the Racine 15 yard line. Gavin ran the ball through the center and it resulted in a 3 yard gain. Thorpe ran the ball through the left tackle and it resulted in a 1 yard gain. Rock Island set up a fake pass formation and Armstrong dodged through the Racine line to score a touchdown. Thorpe attempted a drop kick for the extra point but it was unsuccessful.

Score: Racine 3, Rock Island 6. Thorpe kicked off the ball to Racine and it sailed into the end zone. Racine took possession of the ball on the 20 yard line. Giaver ran the ball around the left end and it resulted in a 5 yard gain. Barr attempted a long pass but it went incomplete around the 50 yard line. Another long pass by Barr went incomplete. Murray punted to Armstrong on the Rock Island 38 yard line. Gavin ran through the center of the line and it resulted in an 8 yard gain. Armstrong ran off the right tackle and it resulted in a 1 yard gain. The quarter ended.

FOURTH QUARTER:

Rock Island was penalized 15 yards for roughing. The penalty moved the ball back to the 32 yard line. Thorpe punted the ball to the Legion. Barr received the ball and he was immediately tackled by Armstrong on the 20 yard line. A run by Giaver resulted in no gain. Another run attempt by Giaver resulted in no gain. A Legion pass from Barr to Brumm resulted in a 4 yard gain. Brumm was tackled by Kolle and Thompson. Murray punted the ball to the Independents. Thorpe received the ball and he returned the ball 8 yards to the Independent 37 yard line. Gillo smashed Thorpe to the ground. Both Gillo and Giaver were laid out. Gillo received a standing ovation as he was carried off the field. Romney substituted in the game for Gillo by Racine. Giaver remained in the game. On the next play, Rock Island punted the ball but they were penalized 5 yards for being off sides and the play was called back. The Independents punted to the Legion. The ball was on the Racine 25 yard line. Giaver ran the ball through the right tackle and it resulted in a 2 yard gain. Mohardt ran the ball through the right guard and it resulted in a 4 yard gain. The ball was on the Racine 31 yard line. Giaver ran the ball through the line and it resulted in a 4 yard gain. Barr ran the ball and it resulted in a 1 yard gain as well as Legion first down. Gavin slipped through the line but he was stopped Romney and it resulted in no gain. Mohardt ran the ball at the right end and it resulted in a 4 yard gain. Barr attempted a forward pass but it went incomplete. Rock Island was penalized 5 yards for holding. The ball was on the Legion 45 yard line. Barr smashed through the line and gained 4 yards for Racine. Mohardt ran the ball and it resulted in a 1 yard gain. He was tackled by Gavin at the line. Barr completed a pass but it was called back and Racine was penalized 15 yards for an illegal play. A long pass attempt by Romney went incomplete. Murray punted the ball to Rock Island. Armstrong received the ball and he was nailed on the Independents 22 yard line. Gavin ran the ball through the center of the line and it resulted in a 5 yard gain. Gavin ran the ball through the center of the line and it resulted in a 4 yard gain. Armstrong ran the ball but it resulted in no gain. Thorpe punted the ball to the Legion. Barr received the ball on the Racine 25 yard line. Barr returned the ball to the Legion 40 yard line. Barr pass the ball to Halliday and it resulted in a 10 yard gain. The ball was on the 50 yard line and it was a Racine first down. DeClerk substituted in the game for Kolle of Rock Island. Barr ran the ball off the left tackle and it resulted in a 1 yard gain. Romney smashed through the line and it resulted in a gain of 1 yard. A Barr pass attempt to Romney went incomplete. Another pass attempt by Barr was grounded and it went incomplete. A Barr pass attempt was intercepted by Wilson. He advanced the ball 10 yards to the 50 yard line. Guyon

229

plunged through the line at the right tackle and it resulted in a 5 yard gain. Gavin ran the ball through the center of the line and it resulted in a 2 yard gain. Armstrong ran through the line at the right tackle and he advanced the ball for a 10 yard gain. It was a Rock Island first down. The ball was on the Legion 32 yard line. Gavin was forced out of bounds with no gain. Guyon failed to gain any yards and Rock Island was penalized 15 yards for roughness on the play. The ball was on the Racine 47 yard line. Armstrong ran the ball around the end and it resulted in an 8 yard gain. Armstrong ran the ball and it resulted in a 3 yard gain. Armstrong was knocked out on the play. Ursella substituted in the game for Armstrong. Thorpe attempted a kick for field goal from the 45 yard line but it was unsuccessful as it went wide of the goal post. Racine took possession of the ball. The Legion attempted a long pass but it went incomplete and the gun sounded to signal the end of the game.

FINAL SCORE:
HORLICK-RACINE LEGION 3, ROCK ISLAND INDEPENDENTS 6

SCORE BY PERIODS:	1st	2nd	3rd	4th	Final
Horlick-Racine Legion	3	0	0	0	3
Rock Island Independents	0	0	6	0	6

TOUCHDOWNS: Rock Island- Armstrong (1)
FIELD GOAL: Racine- Gillo, place kick (1)

STARTING ROSTER:

RACINE		ROCK ISLAND
Brumm	Left End	Twig
Murry	Left Tackle	Scott
Bentzin	Left Guard	G. Thompson
Mintun	Center	Kolle
King	Right Guard	Kraker
Smith	Right Tackle	Slater
Halliday	Right End	F. Thompson
Romney	Quarterback	Ursella
Mohardt	Left Halfback	Thorpe
Elliott	Right Halfback	Bradshaw
Gillo	Fullback	Phelan

SUBSTITUTIONS: RACINE– Romney for Gillo. ROCK ISLAND- Armstrong for Bradshaw, Ryan for Ursella, Buland for Kraker, Gavin for Phelan, DeClerk for Kolle, Bradshaw for Armstrong.

Referee: Jim Holloway
Umpire: DeVinney

The Legion made twelve first downs in the game, while the Independents only had two. Barr completed nine of eleven pass attempts for Racine. The Legion had outplayed Rock Island but a fumble in the third quarter gave the Independents possession of the ball, near the goal line. Rock Island capitalized on this mistake and scored a touchdown. Also, the controversial touchdown call back would have given Racine enough points to win the game.

The attendance was estimated at 4,000 fans. This was the best crowd of the season. The fans expressed dissatisfaction in the work of the officials and there were several calls by the referees, which were viewed as questionable by the crowd. The halftime entertainment featured Miss Ethel Dare, who attempted to parachute from a plane onto the 50 yard of the Horlick Athletic Field football field. She missed her intended target by about 25 feet and landed a few feet outside the Park. Miss Dare was almost directly south of the middle of the field (50 yard line).

American Legion Post No. 76 Commander Jack Melvin wrote the following, Thank you letter to the fans. It was printed in the local Racine newspapers.

The Melvin Letter was as follows:

On behalf of the Racine Post of the American Legion and the Legion Athletic association, which is trying to give the city a high class brand of professional football, I want to thank the general public for the wonderful support given us on Sunday, when we played Rock Island here. Our appeal for support was more than met and we certainly appreciate this cooperation without which, it would be impossible for us to continue in the game. With the public backing of us in this loyal manner, we are going to continue in the fight and you can depend upon it that we will always be giving the best that is in us, at all times.
Jack Melvin, Post Commander.

The game, which was set in the schedule for the Sunday November 16, 1924 between the Horlick-Racine Legion and the new NFL Kenosha (WI) Maroons team was called off because of the lack of support by the Southport (Kenosha, Wisconsin) fans. The franchise moved to Kenosha, Wisconsin for a short time and they were formally the Toledo (OH) Maroons. The Maroons were supported by the Nash and Simmons companies and their manager was George Johnson. Johnson was former professional baseball umpire. A couple weeks prior, there had been speculation that the Kenosha team was going to fold. They were unable to attract fans at their home games in Kenosha, Wisconsin. The Maroon organization decided to cancel all their home games and only play away games for the 1924 season. The game with Racine was originally scheduled to be played at Simmons Field in Kenosha, Wisc. and the Maroons were scheduled to play Racine on Thanksgiving Day at Horlick Athletic Field. They later announced that the Duluth (MN) Kelleys football team would finish out their season wearing Maroons uniforms. The team would be officially disbanded for good on Wednesday November 19th, 1924, as announced by Team Manager George Johnson. Johnson proposed to bring in the Kelleys to play the Legion but he was unable to purchase the team. After a meeting with Johnson and having a consultation from NFL President Carr, the game was officially called off. Their (Kenosha Maroons) final 1924 NFL record was 0-4-1. The Duluth Kelleys approached the Horlick-Racine Legion via telegraph message on Thursday November 20th, 1924 with the offer to still travel to Racine. They Kelleys offered to play them on Thanksgiving Day for half of the gate receipts. Racine declined this offer because they were unsuccessful with their Thanksgiving Day attendance in the past and they did not want to take a chance on a financial deficit.

The Horlick-Racine Legion announced that they would fill the open date, left by Kenosha canceling the game in the Racine 1924 NFL schedule with a game against the Chicago Bears in Chicago. Earlier in the season on October 12th, the Legion battled the Bears in a game, which resulted in a 10-10 tie. The Bears management asked for the Racine Legion Post No. 76 drum and bugle corps to perform at halftime of the game as they did the previous game at Cubs Park. They would perform under the direction of Fred Maxted. A special train was scheduled to leave at 9:30 am-from Racine on Sunday over the North Shore Line and it would take the drum and bugle corps to the Windy City as well as any Racine fans, who wanted to make the trip. The special train was offered for a reduced rate of $3.00 for a round trip ticket. The last time that the two teams played in Chicago, it was attended by over 10,000 fans. Chicago Bears officials sent a block of 300 reserved box seat section tickets to be sold to the Legion fans. They would be sold at Smader's Place in Racine, Wisconsin. Also, a Racine yell leader was going to be sent to Chicago to pep up the Legion fans.

Pounding through a hard practice on a field that was soft and slippery from heavy rain on Monday, the Horlick-Racine Legion football team started preparations for the game against the Chicago Bears on Sunday November 16th, 1924 2:30 pm in Chicago, Illinois. All of the players reported to practice in good condition with the exception of Gillo. Hank still had an injured leg but he was hoping to heal enough to play against Chicago. "Rowdy" Elliott did not play against Rock Island because of the injury that he received in the game two weeks earlier against the Packers. He was expected to play against the Bears. Racine quarterback Romney had been feeling under the weather. He did not play in the previous week until he substituted into the game for Gillo in the fourth quarter. He was in good shape and ready for the game against the Bears. Racine was well aware of the tough Bears line and therefore, they would be perfecting their passing game. It was said that the Legion outplayed the Bears in their last meeting but Joe Sternaman broke through the line and scored a touchdown on a long run, late in the game to tie the score. Racine would have to control the Bears breakaway running plays in order to defeat Chicago.

** GAME DAY **

The game between the Horlick-Racine Legion and the Chicago Bears ended in another tie game. Both teams were able to score a field goal but neither team was able to capitalize on further opportunities. Hank Gillo was able to place kick a successful field goal in the first quarter after King recovered a Bears fumble on the

40 yard line for the Legion. Joe Sternaman tied up the game with a successful field goal kick in the second quarter. Neither team was able to score from then on. Hank tried two more place kicks for field goals, one from the Racine 45 yard line (55 yard attempt) and the other from the 35 yard line. Both kicks were unsuccessful due to the Chicago defense rushing through the line and disrupting the kicks. The 55 yard field goal attempt fell short of the goal post after Gillo was rushed and the ball was not able to be placed before he kicked it. The 35 yard field goal attempt was blocked after two Bears players rushed through the line and Hank was forced to kick the ball off the ground before Romney was able to get it in the set position for the place kick. The kick went wide of the goal post. In the third quarter, Joe Sternaman was knocked out of the game from a hard smashing hit by "Death" Halliday of the Legion. It was later reported that this was the first game, which J. Sternaman was ever pulled from a game for an injury. George Halas substituted in the game to replace Sternaman for the rest of the game. Gillo was able to get the Legion within field goal striking distance at the end of the game with a spectacular crowd pleasing 35 yard run toward the Bears goal line. Captain Romney decided to try to get the ball closer because Hank would be facing a strong south wind for a field goal kick attempt. Giaver was chosen to carry the ball and after an unsuccessful forward run, he scrambled around and he was tackled for a 15 yard loss. This took Racine out of reasonable field goal range. An estimated crowd of 8,000 fans braved the chilly winds that made Chicago famous, to witness the game of these two equally matched teams. They saw a great display of professional football. The Racine Post No. 76 drum and bugle corps marched about the field prior to the game. Their halftime performance, which was led by Fred Maxted was spectacular. They performed their difficult moves with military like precision. A touch of humor was added to the performance, when a young boy around 5 years old went onto the football field behind the drum and bugle corps. He marched around the sidelines with the corps and stood marking time as they went through their fancy steps. A policeman and stadium groundskeeper went after the boy to try to get him off the field, but he ignored their requests. Finally, a member of the corps grasped the protesting young boy by the arm and led him from the field. The boy was cheered by the thousands of fans attending the game.

PLAY BY PLAY: 1924 NFL SEASON HRL GAME 8
HORLICK-RACINE LEGION VS CHICAGO BEARS
Sunday: November 16th, 1924   2:30 pm
Cubs Park   Chicago, Illinois

FIRST QUARTER:
On the opening kickoff, Gillo booted the ball over the Bears goal line. Chicago took possession of the ball on the 20 yard line. E. (Dutch) Sternaman ran the ball twice and the total result was a 3 yard gain. Hanney dropped back and punted the ball to the Legion. Racine took possession on the Legion 20 yard line. Gillo ran the ball through the center of the line and it resulted in a 6 yard gain. Mohardt ran the ball through the line and it resulted in a 6 yard gain. It was a Legion first down.

233

Giaver ran the ball but it resulted in no gain. Mohardt ran the ball and it resulted in a 3 yard gain. Gillo ran the ball into the line but he was stopped with no gain. Murray punted the ball to Joe Sternaman and he was immediately tackled with a fine tackle by Bentzin. E. (Dutch) Sternaman ran the ball and it resulted in a 3 yard gain. Knop ran the ball and it resulted in a 4 yard gain. E. (Dutch) Sternaman ran the ball and it resulted in a 3 yard gain as well as a Chicago first down. The ball was on the 50 yard line. Joe Sternaman ran the ball around the right end and it resulted in a 5 yard gain. Little Joe Sternaman fumbled the ball on the next play. King recovered the ball for the Legion on the Racine 40 yard line. Romney attempt to advance the ball but it resulted in no gain. Gillo ran the ball and it resulted in a 4 yard gain. Gillo advanced the ball and it resulted in a 3 yard gain. Murray punted the ball to the Chicago 10 yard line. Chicago decided to immediately punt the ball. Hanney punted the ball out of bounds at the Bears 38 yard line. Romney gained 6 yards on a run off the far left side. Mohardt ran the ball around the left end and it resulted in a 4 yard gain as well as a Racine first down. Romney ran the ball and it resulted in a 1 yard gain. A Legion pass from Mohardt to Romney resulted in a 15 yard gain. The ball was on the Chicago 14 yard line. Morhardt ran the ball and it resulted in a 1 yard gain. Gillo ran the ball and it resulted in a 1 yard gain. Gillo dropped back to the 17 yard line and kicked a successful place kick for field goal. *Score: Racine 3, Chicago 0.* The Bears took possession of the ball but they could not advance it. Chicago punted to Racine. The Legion took possession of the ball. Racine could not advance the ball. The Legion punted to the Bears. Little Joe Sternaman ran the ball around the end and it resulted in a 10 yard gain as well as a Chicago first down. The ball was on the Racine 38 yard line. The quarter ended.

SECOND QUARTER:

E. (Dutch) Sternaman ran the ball and it resulted in a 2 yard gain. Joe Sternaman ran the ball and it resulted in a 3 yard gain. A Chicago pass was broken up and it went incomplete. Joe Sternaman attempted a place kick for field goal from the 49 yard line but it fell short and it was unsuccessful. Racine took possession of the ball on the Legion 20 yard line. A run attempt by Giaver resulted in a 1 yard loss. A run attempt by Gillo resulted in no gain. A run attempt by Mohardt resulted in no gain. Murray punted the ball to the Chicago 40 yard line. The Bears took possession of the ball. A run attempt by E. (Dutch) Sternaman was stopped without gain by a solid tackle from Bentzin. Dutch gained 6 yards on a run through the line. Knop ran the ball and it resulted in a 9 yard gain as well as a Bears first down on the Legion 45 yard line. E. (Dutch) Sternaman ran the ball and it resulted in a 4 yard gain. Joe Sternaman ran the ball and it resulted in a 1 yard gain. Knop ran the ball and it resulted in no gain. Joe Sternaman ran the ball around the end and it resulted in 12 yard gain. It was a first down for Chicago. Joe Sternaman ran the ball and it resulted in a 4 yard gain. He was tackled by Giaver. Knop plowed through the line and it resulted in a 5 yard gain. Knop ran the ball and it resulted in a 5 yard gain. Knop ran through the line and it resulted in a 3 yard gain as well as a Bears first down. Knop ran through the line and it resulted in a 3 yard gain. Joe Sternaman ran the ball and it resulted in a 2 yard gain. Knop ran through the center of the line and it resulted in a short gain. Joe Sternaman dropped by to the 17 yard line and

234

booted a successful kick for field goal to tie the game. *Score: Racine 3, Chicago 3.*
Gillo kicked off the ball to the Bears. E. (Dutch) Sternaman received the ball on the
Chicago 10 yard line. He advanced the ball to the Bears 30 yard line. E. (Dutch)
Sternaman ran the ball and it resulted in a 2 yard gain. E. (Dutch) Sternaman
attempted to run the ball but it resulted in no gain after he was immediately tackled
by King. Hanny punted the ball to the Racine 20 yard line. A Legion run attempt
resulted in no gain. Mohardt ran through the line and it resulted in a 9 yard gain.
Giaver advanced the ball and it resulted in a first down for Racine. Mohardt ran the
ball through the line and it resulted in a 1 yard gain. A Legion pass attempt went
incomplete. Bryant substituted in the game for E. (Dutch) Sternaman. A Mohardt
run attempt resulted in no gain. Gillo ran through the line and it resulted in 4 yard
gain. Murray punted the ball to the Bears 35 yard line. The Bears took possession.
Chicago was penalized 5 yards for being off sides. The Bears punted to the Legion.
Racine punted to Chicago. Chicago punted back to Racine. A Legion pass attempted
was intercepted by Trafton for the Bears. Chicago had possession of the ball on the
Racine 45 yard line. The quarter ended.

THIRD QUARTER:

   Gillo kicked off the ball to Chicago. The Bears returned the ball to the Legion 40
yard line. Chicago advanced the ball three times and it resulted in a Bears first
down. A Bears pass was completed for a short gain. Chicago was unable to advance
the ball. The Bears attempted to punt the ball to the Legion. The Legion was
penalized 5 yards for being off sides on the punt and it gave Chicago a first down on
the 50 yard line. Bryant ran the ball and it resulted in a 7 yard gain. Knop advanced
the ball and it resulted in a Bears first down. Lanum ran the ball and it resulted in a
7 yard gain and another Chicago first down. Knop ran the ball for a 3 yard gain. J.
Sternaman fumbled the ball on the Racine 20 yard line after taking a hard smashing
hit from "Death" Halliday. Halliday recovered the fumble for Racine. Joe
Sternaman was injured and he was removed from the game. E. (Dutch) Sternaman
was brought back into the game and Bryant substituted for Joe Sternaman. Gillo
ran the ball and it resulted in a 4 yard gain. Chicago was penalized for being off
sides. The penalty gave the Legion a first down. Racine was penalized 15 yards for
roughing. The ball was moved to the Legion 20 yard line. Giaver ran the ball and it
resulted in no gain. Mohardt ran the ball and it resulted in no gain. Murray punted
the ball to the Bears. Chicago took possession of the ball on the 50 yard line. The
Bears passed the ball and it resulted in a 2 yard gain. Chicago passed the ball but it
went incomplete. The Bears ran the ball and it resulted in a gain. Chicago passed
the ball again but it went incomplete. The Bears ran the ball and it resulted in a gain
as well as a Chicago first down. A Bears pass advanced the ball to the Racine 30
yard. A Chicago pass was intercepted by Mintun on the Racine 20 yard line. He
advanced the interception to the Legion 40 yard line. Gillo ran the ball through the
line and it resulted in a 5 yard gain. Giaver ran the ball and it resulted in a gain.
Gillo advanced the ball and it resulted in a Racine first down. Mohardt gained 5
yards on a criss-cross play. Gillo plunged through the center of the line and it
resulted in a short gain. Gillo attempted a kick for field goal from the Racine 45
yard line. The 55 yard field goal attempt fell short and it was unsuccessful. Chicago

caught the kick in the air and the Chicago player was tackled on the 10 yard line by Mintun. Hanny punted the ball to the Legion and it was received on the Racine 45 yard line. The Legion receiver fumbled the ball but it was recovered by Racine. There were 4 yards lost on the kick reception. The ball was on the Legion 41 yard line. The quarter ended.

FOURTH QUARTER:

Romney attempted to advance the ball but it resulted in no gain. Mohardt attempted to advance the ball but it resulted in no gain. Murray punted the ball to the Bears 18 yard line. Chicago received the ball and advanced it 2 yards to the Bears 20 yard. He was tackled by Bentzin. Chicago attempted a double forward pass but it went incomplete. Walquist fumbled the ball for the Bears and it was recovered by Mohardt on the Chicago 29 yard line. Gillo plunged through the line and it resulted in a 2 yard gain. A run attempt by Romney resulted in no gain. Gillo attempted a place kick for field goal from the Chicago 35 yard line but it was blocked by the Bears defense. The Bears took possession of the ball at the Chicago 20 yard line. Knop ran the ball and it resulted in a 3 yard gain. He was tackled by "Kibo" Brumm. Chicago ran the ball and it resulted in a 1 yard gain. Hanny punted the ball to the Racine 40 yard line. Racine took possession. Giaver ran the ball and it resulted in a 1 yard gain. Gillo ran the ball and it resulted in a 3 yard gain. Giaver ran the ball but it resulted in no gain. Murray punted the ball to the Bears 10 yard line. Chicago advanced the ball to the Bears 20 yard line. Bryant ran the ball and it resulted in a 3 yard gain. Bryant ran the ball and it resulted in a 2 yard gain. Knop ran the ball and it resulted in a 3 yard gain. Hanny punted the ball out of bounds, on the Racine 40 yard line. Halas substituted in the game for Mullen by Chicago. Mohardt ran the ball and it resulted in a short gain. Romney ran the ball and it resulted in a short gain. Murray punted the ball to the Chicago 25 yard line. The Bears advanced the ball on the kick to the Chicago 30 yard line. A Chicago pass attempt went incomplete. Another Bears pass attempt was knocked down incomplete by Giaver. Hanny punted to Mohardt and he received it on the Racine 30 yard line. A run attempt by Mohardt resulted in no gain. Gillo broke through the Chicago defensive line and ran the ball, which resulted in a 35 yard gain. The ball was on the Chicago 35 yard line. Giaver ran with the ball and after an unsuccessful forward run, he scrambled around and he was tackled for a 15 yard loss. The ball was on the 50 yard line. Gillo ran the ball through the line and it resulted in a 2 yard gain. Giaver ran the ball and it resulted in a 5 yard gain. Murray punted the ball to the Bears 16 yard line. The game ended.

FINAL SCORE: HORLICK-RACINE LEGION 3, CHICAGO BEARS 3

SCORE BY PERIODS:	1st	2nd	3rd	4th	Final
Horlick-Racine Legion	3	0	0	0	3
Chicago Bears	0	3	0	0	3

FIELD GOAL: Racine- Gillo, place kick (1) Chicago- Joe Sternaman, drop kick (1)

236

STARTING ROSTER:

RACINE		CHICAGO
Brumm	Left End	Hanny
Murray	Left Tackle	O'Connell
Bentzin	Left Guard	Anderson
Mintun	Center	Trafton
King	Right Guard	McMillen
Smith	Right Tackle	Blacklock
Halliday	Right End	Halas
Romney	Quarterback	J. Sternaman
Mohardt	Left Halfback	Walquist
Giaver	Right Halfback	E. Sternaman
Gillo	Fullback	Knop

RESERVES:

Hueller (G)	(QB, HB) Bryant
Roessler (E)	(HB) Kendrick
Barr (QB)	(RT) Scott
Elliott (RH)	(RE) Mullen
Croft (T)	(G) LaFluer
	(T) Healy
	(HB) Lanum

Referee: Jim Holloway (Great Lakes)

The Horlick-Racine Legion 1924 NFL season record was moved to 3-3-2 (.500) after their second tie of the season with the Chicago Bears. Racine began to prepare for a return to Chicago because their next game was against the Chicago Cardinals (NFL 5-3-0) at White Sox Park. They would have their hands full with the Cardinals star player, Paddy Driscoll. Driscoll was as famous for his place kicking as Gillo. A kicking duel would be expected for this game. Hank was known for his "Educated toe" and his ability to successfully run the ball. The Legion gained a following in Chicago. It was believed that there were more Cardinals fans, who attended the game against the Bears than there were at the Chicago Cardinals/Akron Indians game because that game was expected to be a sure victory. The Legion/Cardinals game was anticipating the opposite. Predictions were made to the effect that the upcoming game would draw many Bears fans over to White Sox Park to witness the match up.

Racine began practice to prepare for a tough Cardinals team. All of the players for the Legion team were left uninjured in the battle against the Bears and they were expected to play Sunday.

There were 200 box seat tickets placed on sale for $2.20 each at Tom Smader's Place (331 Main Street) in downtown Racine. They also could purchase round trip tickets on North Shore Line train (leaving on Sunday November 23, 1924 at 9:20 am) that would be for the game in Chicago. The Chicago Cardinals management, once again requested the Racine Legion drum and bugle corps perform at halftime of the game. They agreed to perform and traveled via the North Shore Line, as well.

** GAME DAY **

A large crowd of Legion fans attended the game. There was a group of Notre Dame College football players there, too. These players were known as Notre Dame coach Knute Rockne's "Four Horsemen". This famous Notre Dame backfield consisted of Harry Struhldreher (QB), Jim Crowley (LHB), Don Miller (RHB) and Elmer Layden (FB). They attended the game with Harold "Red" Grange-nicknamed the Galloping Ghost, a great football player from the University of Illinois. These players were there as guests of the Horlick-Racine Legion. Prior to the game, Racine American Legion Post No. 76 Athletic Director L.A. McDowell was standing at the pass gate letting in members of the drum corps, newspaper men, etc., when he was approached by Harry Struhldreher. Harry stepped up and said, *"We are the original four horsemen of Notre Dame and we want to attend this game."* Mac (L.A. McDowell) called Chris O'Brien, owner of the Chicago Cardinals over and introduced him to the notable visitors. They were given a place of honor on the bench. Harold "Red" Grange came in later and joined them. These special guests were introduced to the more than 4,000 fans present. This took place after the first half and it took several curtains calls. The well-known college players were seeing their first pro game. Grange and the "Four Horsemen" were quite excited, when Racine came from behind to tie the score.

The Horlick-Racine Legion staged a great comeback of a 10-0 deficit against the Chicago Cardinals but a fourth quarter potentially game winning perfect field goal kick was ruled no good by a controversial call from the Referee Jim Holloway. He was the same referee, who made a controversial call of a Legion touchdown, which ended up being called back in the game that the Horlick-Racine Legion played against the Rock Island Independents, in the week prior. The Legion would have to settle with a tie game after coming back from being down by ten points in the game against the Cardinals. In fact, there were two questionable calls made by Holloway in the game against the Cardinals, with the second of the two being the controversial call, which stood out the most. Both the Racine, Wisconsin and Chicago, Illinois sports writers told similar stories about the account of the event. The first call by Referee Holloway, which drew attention, was a kick attempted by Paddy Driscoll, after a Chicago touchdown. Driscoll drop kicked the ball for an extra point attempt and Umpire Dr. Rublee ruled that the ball went underneath the goal post and it was unsuccessful. He was located close to underneath the goal post and he was in a good position to make the call. Referee Holloway ruled that the kick was successful and it had sailed over the cross bar. Dr. Rublee strongly protested to Holloway. After a heated exchange, the Cardinals were awarded the extra point. Later in the game, the Legion scored a touchdown and extra point to tie the game at 10-10. Racine again took possession of the ball and they were able to advance the ball to the

238

Chicago 10 yard line. They were stopped by a strong Cardinals line. Gillo dropped back to the 21 yard line for a field goal attempt. The ball sailed through the goal post uprights and the umpire, who was located behind the goal post signaled his arms for a successful kick. The Legion supporters roared in delight, but that changed into a puzzled silence as Referee Holloway over ruled the umpires' signal. He ruled that they kick was not successful even after the umpire, who was located directly behind the goal post for the sole purpose judging the kick, signaled that is was successful. The following are statements made by sports writers regarding the game:

Riley Murray attended and covered the Horlick-Racine Legion vs. Chicago Cardinals game for the Chicago Tribune newspaper. He made the following statement about the disputed Hank Gillo field goal. *–Just before the final whistle Gillo booted, what looked from the stands, like a perfect goal from placement. For some reason, whoever, the referee refused to allow it and for a time things looked interesting but quiet was restored. –*

Tex Reynolds was a sports writer for the Racine Times Call newspaper. He wrote the following about Horlick-Racine Legion vs. Chicago Cardinals game:
The alibi about a bum referee or umpire's decision is timeworn and has been used since sports took a place in the life of the first nation. And in 99 out of 100 cases such complaints should be taken with a grain of salt.　But there are exceptions to every rule, and if a team was ever entitled to victory, it was the Racine squad Sunday. He was the same Referee, who handled the Rock Island game that was played in Racine. (This game was on Sunday November 9th, 1924 and it also had a Racine score (touchdown) that was overturn by Referee Holloway- To the amazement of those in attendance)

PLAY BY PLAY:　1924 NFL SEASON HRL GAME 9
　　　　　　　　HORLICK-RACINE LEGION VS CHICAGO CARDINALS
　　　　　　　　Sunday: November 23rd, 1924　2:30 pm
　　　　　　　　White Sox Park,　Chicago, Illinois

FIRST QUARTER:
　Racine kicked off the ball to Chicago. The Cardinals took possession of the ball. Paddy Driscoll tore through the line at the left end and it resulted in a 15 yard gain. It was a Chicago first down. Koehler ran the line and it resulted in a 10 yard gain as well as another Cardinals first down. Folz ran the ball around the end and it resulted in a 15 yard gain. It was a Chicago first down. Folz ran the ball around the left end but then he cut back and darted off the right tackle. It resulted in a 35 yard gain as well as a Chicago touchdown. Driscoll attempted a drop kick for extra point. Umpire Dr. Rublee, who was standing near to under the goal post ruled that the ball went under the goal post and he signaled the kick as being no good. Referee Holloway ruled that the ball was kicked over the goal and therefore, it was a

239

successful kick. A heated discussion, started by Dr. Rublee took place regarding the kick but Holloway made the final decision and the Cardinals were given the extra point. <u>*Score: Racine 0, Chicago Cardinals 7*</u>. The Cardinals kicked off the ball to the Legion. Racine took possession of the ball. The Legion advanced the ball and gained enough yards for a Racine first down. Racine could not gain enough yards to advance the ball for a first down. Murray punted the ball to Chicago. Driscoll was back to receive the punt and Romney immediately tackled him after he caught the ball. Chicago attempted to advance the ball on a run through the line. The Cardinals attempt to advance the ball on another run through the line. Chicago fumbled the ball on the Racine 40 yard line and it was recovered by King for Racine. The Legion began to advance the ball. The ball was advanced by Romney, Elliott and Giaver. Their total gains resulted in 2 first downs and a total of 30 yards for Racine. The ball was on the Cardinal 10 yard line. Racine advanced the ball for a total of 5 yards. The ball was on the Chicago 5 yard line but Racine was unable to get the ball into the end zone. The Cardinals took possession of the ball on the Chicago 5 yard line as the whistle blew to end the quarter.

SECOND QUARTER:

The Cardinals decided to immediately punt the ball for better field position. Racine received the kick and took possession of the ball. The Legion was unable to advance the ball and Chicago took possession. The Cardinals were able to successfully advance the ball to the Legion 20 yard line. Driscoll dropped back to attempt a drop kick for field goal from the 30 yard line. His kick attempt was unsuccessful. Racine took possession of the ball. The Legion was unable to successfully advance the ball for a first down. Chicago took possession of the ball. The Cardinals were unable to successfully advance the ball for a first down. The Legion was unable to successfully advance the ball for a first down. The Cardinals took possession of the ball on the Legion 40 yard line. Driscoll ran the ball and it resulted in a 20 yard gain as well as a Chicago first down. The ball was on the Racine 20 yard line. Paddy Driscoll dropped back to the 30 yard line and kicked a successful drop kick for field goal. <u>*Score: Racine 0, Chicago 10*</u>. Racine took possession of the ball. Barr passed the ball to Romney and it resulted in a 45 yard gain. The quarter ended.

THIRD QUARTER:

Chicago kicked the ball off to Racine. Gillo received the ball on the 10 yard line and he advanced it to the Legion 25 yard line. Romney ran the ball through the center of the line and it resulted in a 1 yard gain. Gillo gained 3 yards on a run through the line. A Racine pass attempt was unsuccessful. A Legion pass attempt went incomplete. Murray punted the ball to the Cardinals 10 yard line. Chicago took possession of the ball. Folz ran the ball and it resulted in a 2 yard gain. The Cardinals could not advance the ball. Driscoll punted the ball to Racine. Mohardt received the ball and advanced it to the 45 yard line. Gillo ran the ball through the center of the line and it resulted in a 10 yard gain as well as a Racine first down. Mohardt ran the ball around the right end and it resulted in a 10 yard gain as well as another Legion first down. The ball was on the Cardinals 25 yard line. A run attempt by Giaver resulted in a 1 yard loss. Gillo plunged through the line and it resulted in a 4 yard gain. Mohardt passed the ball to Romney and he advanced it to the Chicago 5 yard line. It was another first down for the Legion. Gillo plowed through the center of the line and scored a touchdown for Racine. Gillo successfully kicked a place kick for the extra point. *Score: Racine 7, Chicago 10.* Gillo kicked off the ball to the Cardinals. Driscoll received the ball on the goal line and advanced it 15 yards. He was tackled by Romney. Driscoll ran the ball around the right end and it resulted in a 2 yard gain. A run attempt by the Cardinals resulted in no gain. Driscoll punted the ball to the Legion. It was received by Mohardt on the 50 yard line. Hartong substituted in the game for Smith by the Legion. Gillo bucked (ran) the ball and it resulted in a 9 yard gain. A run attempt by Mohardt resulted in less than a yard gain. It was just short (inches) of a first down. A Racine run attempt resulted in no gain. Gillo ran the ball and it resulted in a Legion first down. The ball was on the Chicago 35 yard line. Romney gained 4 yards on a plunge (run) through the line. Buckeye went out of the game for Chicago. Mohardt ran the ball around the left end and it resulted in a 6 yard gain. A Racine pass was broken up and it went incomplete. Gillo stepped back to the 40 yard line. He attempted a place kick for field goal but it fell short. Chicago took possession of the ball on the Cardinals 4 yard line. Gilles ran the ball and it resulted in a 4 yard gain for Chicago. Driscoll punted the ball to the Legion 44 yard line. Racine took possession of the ball. Gillo ran the ball through the line and it resulted in a 6 yard gain. Holloway signaled a penalty against the Legion. Racine was penalized 15 yards for roughing. This placed the ball on the Racine 35 yard line. A pass from Romney to Halliday resulted in a 16 yard gain. Gillo ran the ball through the line and it resulted in a 9 yard gain. Despite the added penalty yards, Racine was able to make a first down. A run attempt by Mohardt resulted in no gain. Mohardt passed to Romney and it resulted in a 9 yard gain. Gillo advanced the ball 5 yards and it resulted in a Legion first down. The ball was on the Chicago 26 yard line. The Legion was unable to advance the ball. Gillo ran the ball through the center of the line and it resulted in a 4 yard gain. Mohardt ran the ball and it resulted in a 1 yard gain. Gillo dropped back to place kick for field goal as the quarter ended.

FOURTH QUARTER:

Gillo set up again at a difficult angle. He booted (kicked) a successful place kick for field goal over the knot (cross bar) from around the Cardinals 21 yard line. *Score: Racine 10, Chicago 10.* Gillo kicked off the ball to Chicago. Driscoll received the ball on the goal line and he advanced it to the Cardinals 24 yard line. Gilles ran the ball and it resulted in a 2 yard gain. A run attempt by Paddy (Driscoll) was unsuccessful and it resulted in no gain. Gilles ran the ball off the left end and it resulted in a 3 yard gain. Driscoll kicked the ball to the Racine 20 yard line. Mohardt received the ball and returned it to the Legion 40 yard line. Giaver ran the ball and it resulted in a 3 yard gain. Romney completed a pass to Mohardt, which resulted in a gain from the Racine 40 yard line to the Chicago 30 yard line. It was a first down for the Legion. Gillo ran the ball through the line and it resulted in a 4 yard gain. Gillo ran the ball through the line and it resulted in a 5 yard gain. The Chicago defense were grabbing at the ball in attempt to cause a Racine fumble. A Legion run attempt resulted in no gain. Gillo broke through the line and advanced the ball to the Chicago 10 yard line. It was a first down for the Legion. In three attempts, Romney was unable to advance the ball. Gillo dropped back to the Cardinals 20 yard line and kicked, what appeared to be a successful place kick for field goal. Umpire Dr. Rublee signaled the kicked as a successful kick. Referee Holloway ruled that the kick was no good. Chicago took possession of the ball on the Cardinal 20 yard line. The Cardinals ran the ball and advanced it to around the Chicago 30 yard line. Koehler ran the ball around the end and it resulted in a 20 yard gain. It was a Cardinals first down with the ball located around the 50 yard line. Driscoll attempted a drop kick for field goal but it was unsuccessful. The kick was partially blocked and the ball landed on the goal line. Racine recovered the ball. The game ended.

FINAL SCORE: HORLICK-RACINE LEGION 10, CHICAGO CARDINALS 10

SCORE BY PERIODS:

	1st	2nd	3rd	4th	Final
Horlick-Racine Legion	0	0	7	3	10
Chicago Cardinals	7	3	0	0	10

TOUCHDOWNS: Racine- Gillo (1) Chicago- Folz (1)
EXTRA POINT: Racine- Gillo, place kick (1) Chicago- Driscoll, drop kick (1)
FIELD GOAL: Racine- Gillo, place kick (1) Chicago- Driscoll, drop kick (1)

STARTING ROSTER:

RACINE		CHICAGO
Brumm	Left End	McNulty
Murray	Left Tackle	Smith
Bentzin	Left Guard	Buckeye
Mintun	Center	McInerney
King	Right Guard	Brennan
Smith	Right Tackle	Gilles
Halliday	Right End	Anderson
Romney	Quarterback	McMahon
Mohardt	Left Halfback	Folz
Giaver	Right Halfback	Driscoll
Gillo	Fullback	Koehler

RESERVES:

RACINE	CHICAGO
Croft	Clark
Barr	DeStefano
Hartong	

SUBSTITUTIONS: RACINE– Racine-Hartong for Smith CHICAGO- Clark for Buckeye
Referee: Jim Holloway (Great Lakes) Umpire: Dr. Rublee (Michigan) Head Linesman: Moore (Boston)

   The game drew many questions regarding the seemingly standard kicks, which were over turned by Referee Holloway. It looked like a bad afternoon for the Legion fans. The Cardinals were frequently ripping through the Racine line but the game would change in the second half. Racine went on to outplay the Cardinals and the score reflected it.

   The Legion would return home to play their final home game of the 1924 NFL season. Racine had an open date on their 1924 schedule for December 7th. Arrangements were developing to play an away game against the Hammond Pros or an eastern NFL team (Buffalo or Philadelphia) as well as the scheduled game against Kansas City on December 14th. The Green Bay Packers would invade Horlickville to clash with the Horlick-Racine Legion on Sunday November 30th, 1924. This was a game that the Legionnaires (Racine fans) were looking forward to watching, since Racine lost the previous matchup by a close score (HRL 3- GBP 6) at the Bay City (Green Bay, WI.). Green Bay Packer Curly Lambeau hurled a long pass to end Tillie Voss. He grabbed the pass and scored the winning touchdown in the 4th quarter of the game. The "State Pro Title" was on the line and Green Bay was no stranger with eight years as State Champions. Among the stars on the Packers squad, there was Captain Curley Lambeau, who played right halfback and Dutch Hendrian, who played fullback. Lambeau was a powerful man with a great plunging (running) ability and a knack for throwing passes. He gave the Packers the aerial attack, which helped them win many of their games in the 1924 NFL season. Hendrian was a fullback that opposing lines had many problems trying to stop his run attack. He gained many yards for the Packers during the 1924 season. These two players were exceptional members, who added to a strong Packers team.

   Racine prepared for this game with a team practice on Tuesday night at Horlick Athletic Field. "Rowdy" Elliott was injured again (knee) in the game against the Chicago Cardinals and they expected him to be out for the rest of the season. There were rumors that Harry Thomas, a star football player from Chicago University was going to sign with the Legion to replace the injured Elliott. Racine Manager G. E. Smalley confirmed that brothers, Harry, who finished the 1924 season with Chicago University as 1924 All-Conference player and John (1922 All-American) Thomas visited Racine Legion Athletic Director L.A. McDowell in the Racine dressing room after the game against the Cardinals. A deal was discussed and Harry was supposed to report to the Legion team on Tuesday. He never did report to the team or sign a contract.

   Captain Romney executed a stiff workout for the team behind locked gates on Tuesday evening. Several new plays were introduced for Gillo and company in order to use for a defeat of the Green Bay Packers.

   NFL President Joe Carr sent a wire to Racine Legion Athletic Director L. A. McDowell stating that he was sending NFL Official Dr. Frank. A. Lambert (Columbus, Ohio) to oversee the officiating of the Legion-Packers game on Sunday.

243

Lambert was regarded as one of the best officials in the National Football League.

  The Packers would play a game at home on Thursday (Thanksgiving Day) against the Kansas City Blues prior to playing the Horlick-Racine Legion in Racine on Sunday. Green Bay practiced every day of the week and fines were assessed against players, who failed to report. Every Monday, they had a blackboard talk to pick out flaws in the game from the previous Sunday.

Will We Win?

Our team and Green Bay's aren't exactly "Friendly Enemies"! But somewhere between that and "Bitter Enemies" lies the correct description. So we promise you a royal battle, a nip and tuck jovial fight, packed with more thrills than a bull fight, more interest than a movie, more courage than a melodrama, more pep, scrap, and action than you have ever before seen on any gridiron anywhere.

For a supreme exhibition of America's greatest game, see

Racine *vs.* Green Bay

SUNDAY, NOV. 30th, 2:00 P. M.

Please decide early what you will do this Sunday. This is a word to the wise. Because seats are going fast. Red-blooded Racine has taken the Legion team to its heart and the Green Bay rivalry is intense.

That means the biggest crowd of the season. You will have lots of company if you go. But you won't be able to go, if you don't get you seats soon. Many will wait and be disappointed. The early birds will get the good tickets.

Tonight, seats are on sale at

REHL'S—SIXTH

REHL'S—STATE

MONUMENT CIGAR

SMADER'S

Why wait until the choicest tickets are gone? You pay no more RIGHT NOW, yet get better seats. The demand is great. The supply is limited. That's why we say "Buy Tickets Today."

2,500 Good Seats at $1

THIS IS THE LAST HOME GAME OF THE SEASON

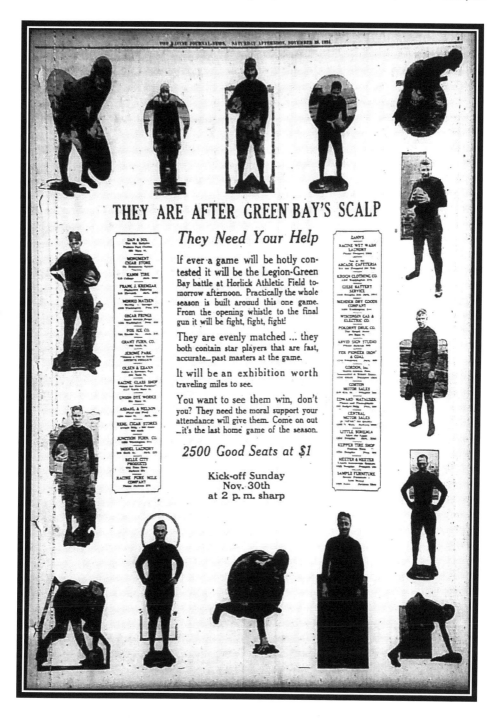

** GAME DAY **

This matchup had all the makings of a classic rematch football game. These teams were showing their best football skills at the end of the 1924 season. A light covering of snow fell in Racine, Wisconsin on Friday November 28th, 1924 and a chill was in the air. Tickets for the game were selling fast. Legion officials were hoping for warmer weather to help boost ticket sales. A large profit from the sale of those ticket sales would give the team financial stability for the 1924 NFL season. The game had created an interest from not only Racine and Green Bay but also Milwaukee and Kenosha. Many out-of-town fans were expected to attend the game. A week earlier, odds of 7-5 were in favor of Green Bay predicted from odds makers in Milwaukee, Wisconsin. Those odds later shifted to even up that Racine would win the game.

The Packers were scheduled to arrive in Racine, Wisconsin at noon on Saturday November 29th, 1924. They would stay in a hotel and workout early Sunday morning at Lakeview Park in preparation for the game at Horlick Athletic Field.

There were over 3,500 fans, who braved the winter atmosphere to watch the Horlick-Racine Legion battle their state rival. Many Packers fans did not make the trip because of a snow storm that developed in Green Bay. The scene at Horlick Athletic Field included prepared fans with blankets, fur coats and galoshes (rubber boots). They were stamping their feet to keep warm. The football field was lightly covered with snow prior to the game but it was brushed off by the groundskeepers. The cold weather was ideal for the players as it made the field hard for fast running. Earlier on November 2nd, the Packers defeated the Legion by a score of 6-3 in a close game that went to the wire with a missed field goal by Racine. These teams exhibited their best brand of football for the 1924 NFL season. Racine was able to pass the ball effectively. Johnny Morhardt (Racine LHB) completed 6 of 8 passes for a total of 140 yards. Morhardt even completed a long pass to Romney and he intercepted three Green Bay passes as well. He played an exceptional game. One of those passes was completed for the lone touchdown of the game. The Legion offense was able to make ten first downs to the Packers four. Green Bay made two of those first downs off of Legion penalties. Racine defeated Green Bay by a score of 7-0. The crowd was treated to a football game, which included long and short passes with some being intercepted. There were also end run attempts and line plunges (running plays), which contributed to a game full of excitement. The Legion defense played exceptionally well against the Green Bay offense, which was known for winning games by successfully passing the ball. The Packers offensive play was uncharacteristic of the aerial team, which they were known as with Curly Lambeau only completing 5 of 17 passes with 5 interceptions. The Legion offense was twice penalized fifteen yards for holding and they were penalized four times for being off sides. Racine outclassed Green Bay and the victory in the State Champion bragging rights became more equalized. Green Bay and Racine split with one win and one loss. Green Bay defeated Milwaukee twice and Racine defeated them once but they only played once. Additional games would be needed to have an equal determination.

247

PLAY BY PLAY: 1924 NFL SEASON HRL GAME 10
HORLICK-RACINE LEGION VS GREEN BAY PACKERS
Sunday: November 30th, 1924   2:00 pm
Horlick Athletic Field   Racine, Wisconsin

FIRST QUARTER:

Racine kicked off the ball to Green Bay. Gillo kicked the ball and it went out of bounds on the Packers 20 yard line. The ball was brought back by rule for Racine to kick the ball again. On the second kick, Gillo kicked the ball over the goal line and the ball was placed on the 20 yard line. Green Bay took possession of the ball. Lambeau gained 3 yards on a run around the left end. The next play, Buck punted the ball to the Racine 5 yard line. Morhardt received the ball and he was immediately tackled by O'Donnell. Gillo plowed (ran) through the line and advanced the ball for a 6 yard gain. Giaver ran the ball and it resulted in a 3 yard gain. Hank (Gillo) ran the ball through the Packers line and it resulted in a 3 yard gain. This was a first down for the Legion on the Racine 18 yard line. Mohardt attempted a run around the left end and it resulted in a loss of 1 yard. A run attempt by Gillo resulted in no gain. Giaver gained 4 yards off a fake punt formation by Racine. Murray punted the ball for Racine. The Packers took possession on the Green Bay 35 yard line. Basing ran the ball through the right tackle and it resulted in a 2 yard gain. A run by Lambeau gained 1 yard for the Packers. The next play, Lambeau fumbled the ball. He recovered it but lost 6 yards for Green Bay. The ball was located on the Racine 38 yard line. Lambeau drop kicked the ball to the Legion 10 yard line. The ball was received by Mohardt. He advanced it to the Racine 20 yard line. Giaver gained 1 yard with a run through the line. Giaver gained 5 yards with a run around the right end. He was forced out of bounds on the 26 yard line of the Legion. Mohardt ran the ball and he circled around the left end for a 10 yard gain. This gave Racine a first down on the Legion 36 yard line. Romney gained 3 yards on a run through the right guard. Giaver attempted a run, which resulted in a 1 yard loss. A successful pass from Romney to Mohardt resulted in a 15 yard gain. Gillo bucked (ran) the ball through the center of the line and it resulted in a 2 yard gain. The next play Gardner broke through the line and tackled Giaver for a 10 yard loss. A successful pass from Mohardt to Romney resulted in a 13 yard gain. Murray punted the ball for Racine to the Packers. Green Bay was penalized for being off sides on the punt and the Legion was given possession with a first down on the 40 yard line after the 5 yard penalty was assessed. Gillo ran the ball and it resulted in a 1 yard gain. Gillo attempted another run and it resulted in no gain. A pass attempt by Romney went incomplete. Gillo attempted a place kick for field goal from the 43 yard line. The boot (kick) was unsuccessful. It fell short and the ball was received by Mathys. He advanced the ball and Mathys was tackled on the Packers 15 yard line. On the first play, Buck punted the ball for Green Bay. The ball was received by Gillo on the Racine 40 yard line and he was unable to advance it. The quarter ended.

248

SECOND QUARTER:

Giaver attempted a run around the left end but it resulted in a 3 yard loss. Mohardt ran the ball around the right end and it resulted in a 3 yard gain. Murray punted the ball to the Packers. It went out of bounds at the Green Bay 15 yard line. Lambeau gained 2 yards on a buck (run) through the line. Basing ran the ball around the right end and it resulted in a 3 yard gain. Buck punted the ball to the Legion. Giaver received the ball on the 45 yard line and he advanced it 5 yards. A run attempt around the right end by Giaver resulted in no gain. Another run attempt by Giaver was stopped as Earps broke through the line to make the tackle. A successful pass from Mohardt to Romney resulted in a 15 yard gain and a Racine first down. A run attempt through the line by Gillo resulted in a 1 yard gain. The Legion received penalty of 15 yards for holding. The ball was moved back to the 50 yard line. Gillo gained 4 yards on a run through the line. A pass attempt from Mohardt to Halliday went incomplete. A pass attempt from Romney to Giaver resulted in a 20 yard gain. Racine had a first down on the Green Bay 23 yard line. Gillo ripped (ran) through the center of the line and it resulted in a 4 yard gain. Mohardt ran the ball off the tackle and it resulted in a 4 yard gain. The ball was on the Packers 15 yard line. A pass attempt from Mohardt to Romney resulted in a 5 yard gain. This was a Legion first down on the Green Bay 10 yard line. Gillo ran the ball off the left guard and it resulted in a 1 yard gain. Gillo attempted a run through the center of the line but it resulted in a 1 yard loss. Mohardt completed a pass to Romney. Romney received the ball, shook off a couple would be tacklers and plunged into the end zone for a Racine touchdown. Gillo kicked a successful point after touchdown. *Score: Racine 7, Green Bay 0.* The Packers kicked off the ball to the Legion. Halliday received the kick and he fumbled the ball. Green Bay recovered the ball on the Legion 20 yard line. An attempted Green Bay line buck (run through the line), but it resulted in no gain. A run through the line by Hendrian resulted in a 4 yard gain. The ball was on the Racine 16 yard line. A pass attempt by Lambeau was intercepted by Halliday. Halliday advanced the interception back to the Racine 30 yard line. Murray punted the ball for the Legion on first down. The ball landed and rolled out of bounds at the Legion 47 yard line. Green Bay took possession of the ball. Another Green Bay pass attempt was intercepted by Romney on the 47 yard line. The Legion decided to punt and Romney kicked the ball to the Packers 20 yard line. Lambeau received the ball and he was immediately tackled by "Kibo" Brumm. Basing ran the ball through the center of the line and it resulted in a 1 yard gain. A Lambeau pass attempt went incomplete. Racine was penalized for pass interference. The Packers were given 15 yards and the ball was placed on the Green Bay 36 yard line. It was a first down for the Packers. A pass from Lambeau to Mathys resulted in a 5 yard gain. A Green Bay pass went incomplete. Lambeau punted the ball to Racine and it went out of bounds at the 27 yard line. Gillo ran the ball and it resulted in a gain of 1 yard. Mohardt attempted to run the ball but it resulted in a 1 yard loss. Gillo ripped (ran) through the center of the line and gained 10 yards for the Legion. Racine was penalized 15 yards for holding. The ball was moved to the Legion 19 yard line. Gillo ran the ball through the center of the line and it resulted in a 2 yard gain. Romney

249

punted the ball to the Packers and it went out of bounds at the Racine 43 yard line. A pass attempt by Lambeau went incomplete. A pass attempt from Lambeau to O'Donnell resulted in a 7 yard gain. The quarter ended.

THIRD QUARTER:

Lambeau kicked off the ball to Racine. Murray received the ball and he advanced it 10 yards to the 30 yard line. A run attempt by Gillo resulted in no gain. A run attempt by Gillo through the line resulted in a 2 yard gain. Romney punted the ball to the Packers. Lambeau received the ball on the Green bay 38 yard line. Basing ran the ball off the right tackle and it resulted in a 1 yard gain. A pass attempt from Lambeau to Voss went incomplete. Basing attempted a run through the right tackle, which resulted in no gain. Buck punted the ball to the Legion. The punt sailed 50 yards to the Racine 20 yard line, where it was downed. The Legion took possession of the ball. Gillo ran the ball through the right side of the line and it resulted in a 2 yard gain. Mohardt attempted a run through the left end but it resulted in no gain. Romney punted the ball to the Packers and it was downed on the 50 yard line. Green Bay took possession of the ball. Hendrian gained 1 yard on an off tackle smash (run). Liewellen substituted in the game for Green Bay. A pass attempt from Liewellen to Lambeau went incomplete. A pass attempt from Lambeau to Mathys went incomplete. Racine was penalized again for illegal interference with the attended receiver of the pass. Green Bay was awarded 15 yards and a first down on the Legion 25 yard line. Hendrian ran the ball through the line and it resulted in a 1 yard gain. Hendrian gained 2 yards on a run through the line. Hendrian ran the ball through the line and it resulted in a 5 yard gain. It was 4th down and 2 yards to go with the ball on the Racine 17 yard line. Liewellen attempted to run and jump through the line but he was stopped by the Racine defense. The Legion took possession of the ball on downs. Elliott substituted in the game for Giaver at right halfback for Racine. Elliott ran the ball around the right end and it resulted in a 4 yard gain. A play fake attempt by Racine resulted in Murray being tackled for a 4 yard loss. Murray punted the ball to the Packers and they took possession at the Green Bay 38 yard line. Hendrian ran the ball through the line and it resulted in a 2 yard gain. Liewellen bucked (ran) through the line and it resulted in a 3 yard gain. A run attempt by Liewellen resulted in no gain. Buck punted to Racine. O'Donnell downed the ball on the Legion 3 yard line. Racine took possession. Racine decided to punt the ball. The Legion by rule was allowed 10 yards to kick. The allowed 10 yards would be assessed on the return. Murray kicked the ball out of bounds at the 33 yard line. The officials moved the ball back 10 yards to the Racine 22 yard line. Green Bay took possession of the ball. A run attempt by Liewellen resulted in no gain. A pass attempt from Lambeau to O'Donnell resulted in a gain. The ball was on the Racine 8 yard line. Hendrian ran the ball and it resulted in a 1 yard gain. Lambeau ran the ball and it resulted in a 1 yard gain. A pass from Lambeau was received by Voss and he took it over the goal line for a touchdown. The Packers were penalized for being off sides on the play and the touchdown was no good. A pass attempt from Lambeau to Voss went incomplete. Racine took possession of the ball. Romney punted the ball to the Packers. Green Bay took possession of the ball on the Packers 25 yard line. The quarter ended.

FOURTH QUARTER:

Racine substituted Barr in the game for Elliott at right halfback. The Packers had possession of the ball. Hendrian attempted a run through the center of the line but it resulted in no gain. A pass attempt from Lambeau to Liewellen resulted in a 10 yard gain and a Packers first down. Liewellen gained 1 yard on a run around the End. A Lambeau pass attempt was broke up by Brumm and it went incomplete. Another Lambeau pass attempt was intercepted by Romney on the Racine 45 yard line. Barr gained 2 yards on a plunge (run) though the line. A Barr pass attempt went incomplete. Gillo gained 5 yards on a run through the line. Racine was penalized 5 yards for being off sides. A run attempt by Barr resulted in no gain. Murray punted the ball to the Packers. Green Bay took possession of the ball. Lambeau attempted a run around the left end and it resulted in a 1 yard gain. He was tackled by Gillo. A Green Bay pass was completed to Hendrian. After the catch, he fumbled the ball but Hendrain was able to recover it. A pass attempt from Lambeau to Mathys went incomplete. Buck punted the ball to the Legion. Barr received it for Racine and he was tackled on the Legion 40 yard line. Gillo gained 3 yards on a line plunge (run). A Racine fumble was recovered by Rosaiti for Green Bay. A Packers pass from Lambeau to Mathys resulted in a 20 yard gain, bringing the ball to the Racine 20 yard line. A pass attempt by Lambeau was intercepted by Romney for the Legion. Racine took possession of the ball on the 5 yard line. A run attempt by Gillo resulted in no gain. Another run attempt by Gillo resulted in no gain. A run attempt by Gillo resulted in a 1 yard gain. Murray punted the ball to the Packers. The receiver fumbled the ball and Halliday recovered the ball for Racine. Barr ran the ball through the left tackle and it resulted in a 2 yard gain. A pass from Romney to Barr resulted in a 25 yard gain. It was a first down for the Legion. A run attempt by Barr resulted in a 2 yard gain. A run attempt by Barr resulted in no gain. The snap from the center was fumbled by Romney. Barr recovered the ball for Racine. The Legion lost 6 yards on the fumble recovery. Gillo attempted a place kick from the 35 yard line. The ball fell short. Green Bay took possession of the ball on the 25 yard line. A pass attempt by Lambeau was intercepted by Mohardt for Racine. Gillo plowed (ran) through the left tackle and it resulted in a 3 yard gain. Mohardt attempted a run around the right end but it resulted in no gain. Barr ran through the center of the line and it resulted in a 10 yard gain. The Legion had a first down at around the 50 yard line. The game ended.

FINAL SCORE: HORLICK-RACINE LEGION 7, GREEN BAY PACKERS 0

SCORE BY PERIODS:	1st	2nd	3rd	4th	Final
Horlick-Racine Legion	0	7	0	0	7
Green Bay Packers	0	0	0	0	0

TOUCHDOWNS: Racine- Romney (1)
FIELD GOAL: Racine- Gillo, place kick (1)

STARTING ROSTER:

RACINE		GREEN BAY
Brumm	Left End	O'Donnell
Murray	Left Tackle	Buck
Bentzin	Left Guard	Gardner
Mintun	Center	Earp
King	Right Guard	Woodin
Croft	Right Tackle	Rosaiti
Halliday	Right End	Voss
Romney	Quarterback	Mathys
Mohardt	Left Halfback	Lambeau
Giaver	Right Halfback	Basing
Gillo	Fullback	Hendrian

SUBSTITUTIONS: RACINE– Elliott for Giaver, Smith for Croft, Barr for Elliott. GREEN BAY- Liewellen for Basing.

Referee: Dr. Frank Lambert (Ohio)

   The victory over the Packers set the win loss-tie-record at 4-3-3 for the Horlick-Racine Legion. Dr. Lambert was quoted as saying in regards to the Racine vs Green Bay game; *"It was the best game of football, I have seen this year and I was mighty glad of a chance to come out here and officiate at such a contest."* Dr. Lambert was a friend of former Racine Mayor William Thiesen. During his stay in Racine, he stopped to visit Mr. Thiesen at his home at 920 Lake Ave on the weekend. Dr. Lambert expressed that he was greatly surprised over the high class brand (quality) of football that he witnessed in the Midwest. This was Lambert's first time officiating in the Midwest as he usually oversaw eastern US games. Dr. Lambert was sent to Racine by NFL President Joe Carr. Following the game, Green Bay Packer players said, they were satisfied with the way that the game was handled in Racine. Mr. Thiesen said that Dr. Lambert greatly enjoyed his visit and that he hoped to return next season.
   Racine was able to defeat Green Bay by outperforming them through using the very technique that made the Packers successful. Green Bay attempted twice as many passes as the Legion but Racine was to complete the same amount as the Packers. Green Bay attempted twenty one passes but only completed six. Racine attempted ten passes and completed six. Another loop sided statistic was the amount of passes intercepted. The Packers had a total of five passes intercepted in the game and the Legion had zero. In the first quarter, Green Bay did not attempt any passes. Racine attempted three and completed two. In the second quarter, the Packers threw the ball eight times but only completed two. Racine intercepted two of those passes. One interception was by Halliday and the other was by Mohardt. The Legion threw four passes and completed three. In the third quarter, the Packers continued to pass the ball. They threw six passes but only completed two. Racine did

not throw a pass in third quarter. In the fourth quarter, Racine threw the ball three times with one completion. Green Bay threw the ball seven times with two completions and three interceptions. Mohardt intercepted the ball twice and Romney had the other one.

Pass records for the game:

1st Quarter	Pass Attempts	Completions	Interceptions	Incomplete
Racine	3	2	0	0
Green Bay	0	0	0	0

2nd Quarter

	Pass Attempts	Completions	Interceptions	Incomplete
Racine	4	3	0	1
Green Bay	8	2	2	4

3rd Quarter

	Pass Attempts	Completions	Interceptions	Incomplete
Racine	0	0	0	0
Green Bay	6	2	0	4

4th Quarter

	Pass Attempts	Completions	Interceptions	Incomplete
Racine	3	1	0	2
Green Bay	7	2	3	2

Totals

	Pass Attempts	Completions	Interceptions	Incomplete
Racine	10	6	0	4
Green Bay	21	6	5	10

On Tuesday December 2, 1924, a statement was made by Horlick- Racine Legion Manager G.E. Smalley. He stated that there are no further games booked by the Legion other than the game against Kansas City. He further stated that there were negotiations pending with the management of several teams. Smalley went on to say that it was unlikely, the Legion would play any more home games for the 1924 season but more likely that they would still play more away games. A report had been circulating with regard to the Kansas City team, who Racine still had a game scheduled with on December 14th, 1924, saying they had disbanded. If that was true, the Legion game at Kansas City would be cancelled. At that point, there was nothing officially received by the team regarding a cancellation. The team received notice on the next day that game against Kansas City was officially cancelled for December 14th because they were experiencing financial trouble. It was also reported that only 1,500 fans attended the game between Green Bay and Kansas City on Thanksgiving Day. The game cost the Kansas City management over $3,000. Efforts were still being made by the Horlick-Racine Legion team management to schedule an eastern trip, which would include games against the Philadelphia Yellow Jackets and the Buffalo Bisons. The Legion did not have a game scheduled for December 7th, 1924 but they would attempt to play on the 7th and stay out there to play again on December 14th. (This was the Official date that the 1924 National Football League schedule ended) There was also a potential that the Legion would play the Chicago Bears. The Bears were scheduled to play against the Cleveland Bulldogs on December 7th and on December 14th against the Rock Island Independents. In 1924, the Bears played two games against both Rock Island and Racine. All of those games ended in a tie. The Legion management discussed with George Halas and the Bears about playing a third game in order to break the tie for 1924. Up to that date, three games, which Racine played in Chicago against the Bears resulted in a tie. It was expected that another matchup would draw a large crowd. Legion Post No. 76 Athletic Officer, L.A. McDowell

PRO LEAGUE STANDING	W.	L.	T.	Pct.
Cleveland	7	1	1	.875
Chicago Bears	6	1	4	.855
Philadelphia	11	2	1	.846
Duluth	5	1	0	.831
Rock Island	6	2	2	.750
Green Bay	7	4	0	.636
Buffalo	6	4	0	.600
Racine	4	3	3	.571
Chicago, Cards	5	4	1	.555
Columbus	4	4	0	.500
Hammond	2	2	1	.500
Milwaukee	5	8	0	.385
Akron	2	6	0	.250
Kansas City	2	7	0	.222
Dayton	2	7	0	.222
Kenosha	0	5	1	.000
Minneapolis	0	6	0	.000
Rochester	0	7	0	.000

telegraphed the Yellow Jackets management, a day earlier and he expected an early reply. If the Romney satellites (Horlick-Racine Legion team) made the eastern jump (travel to eastern US) to play those teams, they would need to get prepared early in the week to travel and therefore, needed to know right away.

  The administrative success of the 1924 Horlick-Racine Legion was credited to the work of L.A. McDowell. The success of the strength, of the 1924 team that was assembled, was a credit to Messrs.' McDowell and Melvin. The Horlick-Racine Legion record was 4 wins, 3 losses and 3 ties but there was a strong belief that 2 games were lost because poor officiating. If those games had resulted in wins, the Legion team record would be at the top of the NFL standings with the Chicago Bears.

The Legion organization was expecting a larger crowd from the previous game to help clear up their debt. If Sunday had been warmer, attendance at the game more than likely would have been closer to 5,000 fans because of the highly anticipated end of the season rematch of Racine and Green Bay.

The Packers had several hundred dollars in the bank before they left to play a 3 day away game stretch. This ten day trip included games against the Chicago Bears, Kansas City Blues and the Horlick-Racine Legion at their respective fields. The Green Bay Packers had their coffers enriched by the "Guarantee" of money to play against each team. They also saved money by traveling and stopping at each destination along the train route. The Legion was hopeful that by playing several away games, the financial gain would do the same for them. However, they would be contacted by both Philadelphia and Buffalo and told that those teams would not be interested in playing because of the fact that late season games had the potential for bad weather. Both teams felt that they did not want to risk the "Guarantee" pay out that the Racine officials were seeking to make the trip.

A Banquet was planned for Tuesday December 9th, 1924 in order to honor the Horlick-Racine Legion football team. It was going to be held that Tuesday night, starting at 7:00 pm at the Racine Country Club. A number of Racine football enthusiasts were promoting the event and all the American Legion Post No. 76 members were invited. The banquet committee, who were in charge of arrangements was listed as the following members: George W. Smith, chairman of the committee along with: Milt Knoblock, Steven Benisch, William Horlick, Sr., Arthur Modine, Nate Silver, Harold Pugh, Henry Keefe, Joseph Rehl and Frank Miller. Reservations were offered to 200 guests and the cost of each ticket was $5. The banquet was set up to honor the Legion players and what they did for the city of Racine. All of the Racine players expressed their desire to attend and there were plans to award trophies to the players. Tickets were almost sold out as of the prior Sunday and the final remaining tickets were placed on sale at the Rehl's Cigar Stores in Racine.

An NFL game, which was being played between the Chicago Bears (6-1-4) and the Cleveland Bulldogs (7-1-1) was considered a post season exhibition game because it was not part of the official 1924 NFL schedule. Those teams met on Sunday December 7th, 1924 at Cubs Park in Chicago and it was attended by Hank Gillo along with several Legion organizational personnel/ players. A win by Chicago would have meant another shot at playing the Bears for Racine on December 21st. The Bears defeated the Bulldogs but they would lose to Rock Island by a score of 7-6 on the following Sunday after a failed point after touchdown kick by Joe Sternaman. The Bears vs Independents game was attended by more 18,000 fans. On Tuesday morning December 16th, 1924, a tentative game with the Horlick-Racine Legion was cancelled by George Halas, manager of the Chicago Bears. Halas told Legion Manager Smalley that his reason for cancelling the game was that weather conditions were too uncertain for playing that late in the year and he felt it would not be well attended by Chicago fans. The Legion finished with a 4-3-3 (.571) record and placed 7th in the National Football League for 1924

1924 Final Game Scores Horlick-Racine Legion

Date	Team	Score		Opponent	Score
October 5th	Horlick-Racine Legion	0	vs.	Rock Island Independents	9
October 12th	Horlick-Racine Legion	10	vs.	Chicago Bears	10
October 19th	Horlick-Racine Legion	13	vs.	Kansas City Blues	3
October 26th	Horlick-Racine Legion	10	vs.	Milwaukee Badgers	0
November 2nd	Horlick-Racine Legion	3	vs.	Green Bay Packers	6
November 9th	Horlick-Racine Legion	3	vs.	Rock Island Independents	6
November 16th	Horlick-Racine Legion	3	vs.	Chicago Bears	3
November 23rd	Horlick-Racine Legion	10	vs.	Chicago Cardinals	10
November 30th	Horlick-Racine Legion	7	vs.	Green Bay Packers	0
Totals	**Horlick-Racine Legion**	**69**		**Opponents**	**47**

1924 Horlick-Racine Legion Roster

No.	Name	Pos.
1	Gillo	HB
3	Romney	QB
5	Roessler	E
7	Murray	LT
8	Elliott	HB
9	Mohardt	HB
10	Giaver	HB
11	Halliday	RE
13	Brumm	LE
14	Mintun	C
15	Smith	RT
16	Bentzin	LG
17	Hueller	LG
18	Barr	QB
19	King	RG
26	Croft	T

256

Arrangements were completed for the football banquet to honor the 1924 Horlick-Racine Legion. The banquet committee asked that reservations be received by Saturday December 6th, 1924. Tickets were offered for sale by the following Ticket Committee members: Nate Silver, Frank Miller, Henry Keefe, George W. Smith, Bernie Miller, Art Modine, Charles Tiede, Ernest Mrkvicka, Joseph Rehl, Art Loeb, Jack Melvin, Steve Benish, Harold Pugh, Oscar Fringe, Thomas Smader, Harry Herzog, Peter Wherie, Edward Zahn, Jr., George Connolly, Harry Anderson and Joseph Jagersberger.

On Thursday December 4th, 1924, a meeting was held at A.C. Hall by the American Legion Post No. 76 of Racine, Wisconsin, which was scheduled by Post No. 76 Athletic Officer L.A. McDowell. Mr. McDowell said that there was a big deficit that they were facing regarding the Horlick-Racine Legion football team, despite the fact that those in charge had assembled the finest eleven (team) that ever represented the city. He was quoted as saying; *"I do not know whether or not the American Legion will have a football team in the field next year, but I do know that we can never go through a season in which we depend upon the gate unless we can sell 2,500 season tickets previous to the opening game."* McDowell went on to say the following regarding the 1924 season; *"It is doubtful, if a better team than the one we have assembled could be put into the game, yet we are running behind financially. The support has not been anywhere near up to expectations. Take the Kansas City game on Oct. 19 for example. Here was one of the best games of the season, yet we ran $2,600 in the hole because fans did not know anything about Kansas City. It was a strange team and had dropped two games, one to Green Bay and one to Milwaukee. Both of these games were lost by narrow margins. Since then, the Kaws have been going strong and they are ending the season with a good record. We lost money on a game that we played in Milwaukee and with the Cardinals in Chicago at both of which games, we expected to make a killing. A year ago we cleaned up $500 on the Milwaukee game and $1,000 on the Cardinal game. These were serious blows to the team, which is not well financed enough to carry along a deficit from one game to another. Those who have been in charge of the team have given much of their time and all of their ability to making the team a success. I think the Post as a whole approves of what we have done"*

The banquet was sold out. It was attended by 200 Racine grid fans. It was held at the Racine Country Club, as planned in order to pay tribute to the grid squad (1924 Horlick-Racine Legion team). Those in attendance experienced several speeches from members of the Legion Football team. The unanimous opinion of those speakers was that the Horlick-Legion team of 1924 was the best football team that ever represented Racine, Wisconsin. Several members of the team were unable to be present but all those who were able to attend, gave short speeches. Everyone was united in agreeing that the support given as well as the spirit shown by local fans, had much to do with the success of the team. Ever speaker also expressed the wish that they could continue playing under Legion standards. Mort Walker acted as toastmaster of the evening event. He opened the banquet with a short speech. Walker said that the assembly of the banquet had not occurred for any propaganda but rather to pay tribute to the team. Mort spoke of the beginning of organized athletics and the coordination, as it was represented by the Racine team and how they worked to increase the efficiency of the athletic organization. Following Walker's opening speech, he called upon George Ruetz, former team manager, who worked for 3 years to build an efficient Legion football organization. It was said that he deserved credit for contributing toward building the organization, up to the present high state of efficiency. Ruetz stated that it was his belief that the Legion team in 1924 was better than previous years. He congratulated the present management of the team for the success, which they had enjoyed during the season. Ruetz was followed by Milton Romney, captain of the 1924 Horlick-Racine Legion team. Romney related several anecdotes in connection with different individuals of the Racine squad. He expressed his appreciation of the manner in which Racine fans had supported the Legionnaires (Legion football team) during the 1924 campaign (season). The next speech was given by L.A. McDowell, athletic director of the Legion. McDowell was called upon to speak and he spoke of what the Legion team had done to give Racine desirable publicity throughout the country. He also expressed the wish that the Legion could continue to support a team of high caliber. He explained the reason for a deficit during the 1924 season was related to two or three games that were played out of town, which were expected to pay big dividends but were failures from the attendance standpoint. McDowell went on to say that the team should be self-supporting and this could only be accomplished by the advance sale of season tickets, so that a good crowd would be guaranteed at every home game. He then spoke of the assistance that William Horlick, Sr. had rendered to the team with his generous use of Horlick Athletic Field for the season. In addition, he said that Horlick gave further financial aid to the team. A Resolution of Appreciation, which was read at the banquet and it was met with a rising vote as well as being backed up by three cheers. He said that William Horlick, Sr., dean of sportsmen was the main supporter of the Horlick-Racine Legion during the prior three years. Not only did he allow the team, the free use of Horlick Athletic Field but he also covered all debts on the organization's financial ledger. Those debts were described as healthy ones. Without the assistance of Mr. Horlick, the first Legion NFL team would have been the last one. Horlick took care of the $2,500 of debt at the end of the 1923 season and he covered the $3,500 deficit, which accumulated after the 1924 season. It took around $30,000 to operate the team for one season. The team was debt free going forward because of Mr. Horlick. The future of the Horlick-Racine Legion football team was in question because of the continued inability to be financially stable. McDowell introduced the following resolution, which was unanimously approved by a rising vote of those present.

William Horlick, Sr.

258

Resolution

"*Whereas , We, the citizens of Racine, have assembled together on this 9th day of December 1924 , for the purpose of fostering and promoting in the city of Racine clean athletic sports, and particularly the great game of football: and,*"

"*Whereas, we realize and fully appreciate, the splendid assistance and support, which has been given to this sport by Mr. William Horlick, Sr., by his ready and willing assistance, to the Racine Legion football team, in many ways and particularly, by his contributing to them the use of Horlick's Athletic field.*"

"*Now, therefore, be it resolved, that we on our own behalf and on behalf of all other citizens of Racine, who are followers of this great sport, express to Mr. Horlick, Sr. our appreciation and gratitude for his outstanding support of this game and it's success in this community: and,*"

"*Be it further resolved, that a copy of this resolution be delivered to Mr. Horlick in evidence of our gratitude and appreciation.*"

(Signed), 200 Racine Grid Fans

William Horlick, Sr. - Owner   ***   Henry Gillo – Star Fullback
Horlick-Racine Legion NFL football franchise

G.E. Smalley, manager of the team was the next to speak. He spoke of the success that the organization had during the season. He attributed much of the success to the able leadership of the team on the field. He said that the credit of the winning attitude belonged to the team and further stated that there had been no let-ups during the entire campaign (season). Smalley stated that the squad (players) put forth their best effort in every game. Following Smalley's speech, Vilas Whaley, former state commander of the American Legion Post No. 76 gave a short speech. Whaley spoke of the future of the American Legion activities. He went on to say that the completion of the new half of a million dollar Memorial Hall in Racine would give the organization opportunity for boxing and professional basketball. He stated that they currently had a Boxing License. Vilas said that the success of Legion activities combined with the great showing of the drum corps was the combination, which had much to do with putting Racine and the American Legion Post No. 76 on the map. He appealed to the business owners in attendance to help the Legion continue the success of their athletics. Whaley said that the backing of business men was needed in the Legion's efforts to make Racine, the athletic center of the state. There were also short speeches given by Max Zirbes, Bill Hayman, Johnny

Mohardt, Pete Herman, George W. Smith, Thorwald Beck, M. Buelow, Frank Miller, Atty. Charles Bergener, Jack Melvin, Dip Sondergard, Atty. Charles Wratten, Raymond Weins, Nate Silver, James Allan (president of the Racine Midwest Baseball Association), Harry Cohen, Don Murry, William Giaver, Roman "Kibo" Brumm, Al Bentzin, Jack Hueller, Len "Fat" Smith, Al "Rowdy" Elliott, Richard "Death" Halliday, Wallace "Shorty" Barr and Hank Gillo.

Johnny Mohardt was introduced as the greatest forward passer in the nation. Mohardt said that he played on several other pro grid teams since his college days but he would sooner be a member of the Horlick-Legion squad than play for any other team. Frank Miller said that he felt that he voiced the sentiments of the city by saying, they wanted to see a Legion team on the field next year. Gillo received an exceptionally loud applause, when he was introduced indicating that the veterans popularity was increasing every year that he was with the Racine team. Gillo said that in the past, he talked about each season being his last at the start of the season but each year he found himself playing again. He said that he has been playing so long that most people in Milwaukee, where he lives, thought that he was a Racine man. Hank thanked the citizens for their support on behalf of the team members. Gillo said that he hoped to see the Legion team back on the field next year. He was the idol of the area grid followers. Gillo was dedicated to winning and he ran the ball with successful gains. His golden toe booted over many field goals and extra points to score for Racine. The final speaker of the banquet was Milton Knoblock. After lauding the work of the squad (team) for 1924, he expressed hope that next year, he would see the same personnel back on the team. Knoblock presented every player, who attended the banquet, a watch as a token of appreciation from the followers of the team. There were 16 watches, which were given out to the players. Gillo received a special watch, which was more ornate than the other ones of those awarded. During the evening, the American Legion Post No. 76 drum corps quartet played several fine selections. The quartet was repeatedly encored. The banquet was declared to have been one of the most successful events that had been held there. Most of the credit was given to the banquet committee headed by George W. Smith.

The 1924 Calhoun Eleven (NFL All Star) team was announced. Ralph King (No. 19) and Hank Gillo (No. 1) were Third team selections. The selection of the All-American pro football teams was based off of replies from a dozen sports writers of the cities that had teams in the National Football League. Also, there was input from six officials, who worked the games during the past season.

Calhoun's Eleven
1924 NFL All-American Pro Teams

First Team
Little Twig, Rock Island –LG
Healy, Bears-LT
Youngstrom, Buffalo-LG
Trafton, Bears-C
Muirhead, Dayton-RG
Petcoff, Columbus-RT
Voss, Green Bay-RE
J. Sternaman, Bears-QB
Way, Philadelphia-LHB
Boyton, Buffalo-RHB
Elliott, Cleveland-FB

Second Team
Anderson, Cardinals-LE
Lyman, Cleveland-LT
Williams, Duluth-LG
Nemecek, Columbus-C
McMillin, Bears-RG
Slater, Rock Island-RT
Goebel, Columbus-RE
Driscoll, Cardinals-QB
Nobie, Cleveland-LHB
Lambeau, Green Bay-RHB
Hamer, Philadelphia-RHB

Third Team
Chamberlain, Cleveland-LG
Buck, Green Bay-LT
Nesser, Akron-LG
Peterson, Kansas City-C
King, Racine RG
Gulian, Philadelphia-RT
Christianson, Minneapolis-RE
Winters, Columbus-QB
Guyon, Rock island-LHB
Brenkhert, Columbus-RHB
Gillo, Racine-FB

262

Those three mythical pro grid teams were ultimately selected by G.C. Calhoun, sports writer of the Green Bay Press-Gazette. He was considered one of the best authorities in professional football. Editor Calhoun said that he obtained his input from sport writers and officials throughout the league and based his selections off of their input. Questions were raised from Racine sports writers, as to why the Legion did not have any players on the first team and also the absence of Milton Romney as well as Richard "Death" Halliday. There was a belief that Hank Gillo should have been a first team selection because of the fact that Racine tied the Chicago Bears twice and defeated the Green Bay Packers. They believed that this showed that these players exhibited a high caliber brand of football. It was expressed that the Racine players deserved more recognition from Calhoun.

Al "Rowdy" Elliott (No. 8) leaping to receive a Horlick-Racine Legion pass from Milton Romney (No. 4) in a game against the Green Bay Packers on November 2nd 1924 at Bellevue Park in Green Bay, Wisconsin

Chapter 4:
Racine Legion
1925 NFL season

On Saturday August 1ˢᵗ and Sunday 2ⁿᵈ, 1925, there was a two day League meeting held by the National Football League in Chicago, Illinois. Commander Jack Melvin and Athletic Director L.A. McDowell of the American Legion Post No. 76 attended the two day meeting on behalf of the Racine Legion football team. An announcement was made at the meeting stating that NFL President Joe Carr would appoint all of the officials, who would be in charge of the NFL games. They hoped that this would eliminate the controversies that arose during in the 1924 NFL season. The work of 1924 NFL referees and umpires was said, to not be of the highest caliber. Racine management announced that they secured the following schedule for the 1925 NFL season.

<u>1925 Racine Schedule</u>

September 27th	Racine at Rock Island Independents
October 4th	Hammond Pros at Racine
October 11ᵗʰ	Chicago Bears at Racine
October 18ᵗʰ	Racine at Chicago Cardinals
October 25ᵗʰ	Green Bay Packers at Racine
November 1ˢᵗ	Racine at Chicago Bears
November 8ᵗʰ	Rock Island Independents at Racine
November 15ᵗʰ	Racine at Green Bay Packers
November 22ⁿᵈ	Racine at Hammond Pros
November 29ᵗʰ	Milwaukee Badgers at Racine
December 6ᵗʰ	Racine at Milwaukee Badgers

Their schedule wasn't considered to be an "easy" schedule with "soft spots" but rather Racine would play good competition throughout the 1925 NFL schedule. The Legion squad opened the 1925 NFL schedule at Rock Island, since the Horlick Athletic Field was being used by the baseball team on September 27ᵗʰ, which was the League opening date. The team would play a rotation of home and away games regularly throughout the schedule. Hammond, who was expected to be their easiest team on the schedule but they gave the Legion a great battle in 1924. The Chicago Bears was expected to be the toughest opponent on their schedule. The Bears did not travel to Racine in the previous year but the two teams played both of their games to a tie in that year.

American Legion Post No. 76 Commander Jack Melvin announced on the morning of August 3ʳᵈ, 1925 that Milton Romney had agreed to lead the team, again. Romney was a great leader with the ability to bring the team together. Jack Hueller, a Racine guard in 1924, who was the only Racine native on the team, announced his to return to uniform for Racine. He was in Chicago at the time of the Melvin announcements. While, there was no definite plans regarding the return of the players from the 1924 squad, Melvin said that he expected most of them to return. The exceptions were Len "Fat" Smith, who left the country and Al "Rowdy" Elliott. Elliott re-injured his leg in the final game of 1924 against the Green Bay Packers. He announced his retirement from professional football. Therefore, his return was never expected.

With the details of the 1925 NFL schedule in place, attention of the local Legion officials would turn to the matter of organizing to secure financial support of the professional football team in Racine. Vilas Whaley was appointed to be in charge of this organized effort. Whaley said that (August 25th, 1925) morning, nothing definite had been done yet, but he expected to hold a meeting some time that week, when an organized effort would be inaugurated. Commander Jack Melvin had not yet appointed an athletic officer for the year. L.A. McDowell, who held the position for the previous two years was still acting in that capacity. Melvin refused to state the person, who he would appoint but indicated that it was not improbable that McDowell would receive the position again for the upcoming season.

Vilas Whaley called a meeting of the Racine football fans at the Elks club in downtown Racine, Wisconsin for Friday August 7th, 1925. The meeting would start at 8:00 pm and they intended to have about 50 football fans, who were outside of the Legion organization members, who planned to attend. The plan was to organize an association to be known as the Racine Football Fans Association. The meeting was intended to devise ways and means of obtaining the necessary financial backing to continue to field a Racine professional football team in the National Football League for the 1925 season. An announcement was made several weeks earlier that American Legion Post No. 76 of Racine, Wisconsin decided that it would abandon professional football. After the announcement was made, a suggestion was brought from the Racine Times-Call newspaper personnel, it was a suggestion that the Legion organization ban together with a group of Racine football fans in order to work toward continuing forward with professional football in the NFL. The meeting, which was scheduled at the Elks Club was an outgrowth of that suggestion. When it was clear that Legion would give up their franchise in the National Football League, several fans came forward with an offer of assistance in an attempt to keep Racine in the League. Since the Legion reconsidered and they kept their franchise, they believed that these fans would cooperate in helping to get this sport financially stable. There was an estimate of 1,300 to 1,400 fans, who regularly attended the Legion football games. The Legion officials felt that the assurance of fan support was necessary to make the team self-supporting in Racine. It was expressed that all those interested in Racine being represented on the gridiron for the 1925 NFL season should attend the upcoming scheduled meeting on Friday.

Johnny Mohardt, "Death" Halliday and Don Murry were definitely expected to be back in a Racine Legion uniform, when the 1925 Pro Grid season started, according to Commander Jack Melvin. Those three players contributed to the success of the team in 1924 and the news of their return was welcomed by the Racine fans. He stated on August 4th, 1925, that all of the mentioned players, told him that they would be back. Although, nothing definite was reported about any other players returning from last year's squad, officials expected that the majority would return for the 1925 campaign. All of the 1924 Horlick-Racine Legion players were bound by contracts, which stipulated that the players must return to Racine, if they wanted to play in the National Football for 1925. They each had yet to sign a contract but these players were bound by the renewal clause in the previous year's contract. Re-signing them was just a formality. This was contingent on Racine wanting them back to play for their team. There were notices sent out to all of the players, who were under contract for the 1924 season with the Legion. Each of those players would have a conference with either Jack Melvin or the Legion athletic officer before the start of the season and new contracts were expected to be signed at that time.

On Thursday night August 6th, 1925, L.A. McDowell resigned from his position as athletic officer at a meeting held for the American Legion Post No. 76. He addressed those who attended the meeting with the explanation that the pressure of Business duties made it impossible for him to devote the necessary time to do the work of the athletic officer and this was his reason for resigning. McDowell also stated that he told Commander Nevin of his intention of resigning, earlier that year but he had agreed to act in that athletic officer capacity until after the August National Football League meeting in Chicago.

L.A. McDowell explained the Legion's attitude towards professional football by briefly recounting the events, which lead to the board of governor's decision to retain the franchise in the NFL. He said that the officials were reluctant to renew the franchise because of the heavy expense that was involved in operating a pro grid team but after learning of the desire of the many fans for a team in the National Football League, the board voted to retain the franchise and give the fans another chance to back the team. The Legion's present position at the time in regards to the NFL franchise was the following: *If enough fans can be secured and who are willing to lend material aid, so that the Legion is guaranteed against loss as well as any deficit, which might exist at the end of the season, that can be met without further solicitation, then the Racine Post No. 76 is willing to get behind the proposition and field a team for 1925.*

The meeting at the Elks Club went on as planned. Racine football fans and members of the American League Post No. 76 met to discuss the future of the Racine, Wisconsin NFL franchise. The consensus at the meeting was that Racine wanted football and several speakers agreed that by supporting a team in the National Football League, it assumed the character of a civic proposition. Some of the key points made were that of the benefits derived from professional football on national level being played in Racine, Wisconsin. These benefits were that of entertainment, advertising and prestige for the city of Racine. Vilas Whaley, former State Commander of the Legion explained the following in regard to the Legion organization's attitude toward continuing with the professional football franchise: *"Pro football has been a big expense to the Legion. We have gone along for several years, facing an average deficit of about $5,000 at the end of each season. It has come to the point, where the local post feels, it can no longer carry this big burden unaided. 1. Both as a member of the Legion and a citizen of Racine, I would hate to see this city lose it's franchise in the National league. The circuit of which Racine has been a member constitutes real "Big League" football. Racine is a growing city,-a city, which I believe is now big enough to support that class of football and there should be some method of putting the game Over here."*

The question arose about the amount of money, which would be required to continue to finance a team in the NFL. L.A. McDowell, who resigned as athletic officer of the Legion read a budget prepared to show the maximum amount, which it would cost to support a team for the 1925 season. McDowell read the report and quoted the total expenses as $29,416. He also told the group of the anticipated gate receipts (money brought in from ticket sales). The resulting deficit of about $6,500 was the worst, which could be expected, McDowell explained. He went on to say that he felt expenses would be hardly as high as he quoted and that the income would be more than he listed. The figures had been prepared to show the "darkest" side of the proposition, he said. He also believed that the deficit would be much less. Some of those present expressed the belief that the team could break even, provided that a group of interested fans would support the proposition and a good energetic season ticket sale campaign was administered. The suggestion was that industrial conditions were improved and therefore, the support for a pro grid pastime would be greater than any other year since, Racine became a member of the NFL. It was also presented that there was more money per capita in Racine at that time than there had been for several years. Milton Knoblock, who was a Racine business man and interested in the well-being of Racine football suggested that another meeting of the group be set for Monday August 10th, 1925. At that time, a committee would direct the organization and discuss the best methods for arranging support of the team. This new committee would later hold another meeting on the following Friday night (Friday August 14th, 1925 at 8:00 pm Elks Club in Racine, Wisconsin) to give a report on the progress of the actions. It would be at this meeting that the fate of NFL pro football in Racine would be decided. It was agreed by all in attendance, if there wasn't sufficient interest from the Racine business community, then it would be unadvisable to start the 1925 season. They did not want to risk incurring a big deficit from the necessary startup costs of operating the team. According to the plans that were discussed at the meeting, the proposed citizen's group would back the team financially but the actual football operations would be administered by the American Legion Post No. 76. The Legion commander and athletic officer would be in charge of assembling the team and conducting it on the field. The sentiment at the meeting was that there was little time to waste, since most of the other NFL teams already signed players to contracts and started preparing to sell tickets for the season. If reports made at the next meeting were satisfactory, the group planned to start selling tickets on September 1st. The majority of those present at the meeting agreed, the best plan was to sell season tickets, which would be good for all of the 1925 home games on their schedule. It was stated at the meeting, if 1,000 tickets could be sold than the organization would have gone a long way toward financing the team for the season. The consensus of opinion seemed to be that the ticket prices should remain the same as the 1924 season, which was a $1.00 for general admission seat, $1.50 for a reserved admission seat and $2.00 for reserved box seat admission.

The meeting, which was scheduled to take place on Friday August 14th, 1925 at the Elks Club was cancelled. Vilas Whaley reported that there was not enough interest for financial backing of the team. He said that a report would be given to the American Legion Post No.76 on the following Monday, as to this affect. George Ruetz had offered to take over the franchise after the original announcement, which was made by Legion that they would not field a team for 1925. Ruetz was approached about taking over the franchise after the meeting was cancelled. He stated on the following Saturday morning that it was too late for him to try to operate the team for the upcoming season. After a meeting of the American Legion Post No. 76 board of directors was held on that Monday, it was decided that they would hold their NFL franchise in hopes of a Racine team being fielded in 1926. Commander Melvin was instructed to continue to work with those from Racine, who were interested in fielding the NFL team. They would be open to giving them the opportunity to take over the franchise.

It was said that throughout the past three seasons, the respectability and upstanding reputation of the Horlick-Racine Legion football team was made possible by the generosity of William Horlick, Sr. to cover all the debts that were incurred each season as well as the hard work of George Ruetz, Dr. Arthur J. Morrissey, Charles Wratten, Max Zirbes, Jack Melvin, G.E. Smalley, L.A. McDowell, Hank Larsen, and others. They devoted their time and labor to the success of the team without any compensation.

Racine, Wisconsin would not field a team for the 1925 NFL season.

Chapter 5:
Racine Tornadoes
1926 NFL season

On August 2nd, 1926, it was announced that George G. Ruetz had been working with others to form a group in Racine, Wisconsin within the American Business Club (A.B.C.) of Racine, Wisconsin. This new Association was going to operate the NFL franchise, which was held by the American Legion Post No. 76 of Racine, Wisconsin. Ruetz had already started contacting former Legion players in an attempt to get them to play for this yet to be named 1926 Racine, Wisconsin NFL team. Hank Gillo and Milton Romney were immediately asked to rejoin the Racine roster and they accepted the invitation. Gillo was up in the northern woods of Wisconsin clearing land and building a cabin, at the time. He said that he was in the best physical shape of his football career and would be ready to start playing football, immediately. Hank had been a football coach and teacher at Bayview high school in Milwaukee, Wisconsin for the previous year. After the decision was made by the Legion to not field an NFL team for 1925, Gillo played for the NFL Milwaukee Badgers. George also secured a 1926 NFL schedule of opponents in preparation for this new team. Ruetz was notified by the National Football League that in order for the American Business Club of Racine, Wisconsin to move forward with participating in the 1926 NFL season, they would have to pay $1,900. This money needed to be paid by a certain date or they would lose the rights to the franchise. George immediately informed the rest of the club members. The club quickly took this matter under advisement and they arrived at the conclusion, it would be functioning within its intended scope as a civic body by giving Racine a football team, which would advertise the city as well as provide a popular form of entertainment for the local fans. Bob Bushell, Bob Johonnott, George Pendall, Ray Kitchingman, Hymen Davidson and J.C. Kolinski formed a committee to consult with George "Babe" Ruetz as to the feasibility of the team. These members immediately decided to borrow the $1,900 needed to secure the Racine NFL franchise from a local bank. Ruetz was sent to make a payment to the NFL office.

The American Business Club of Racine, nicknamed the "ABC club" filed the necessary paperwork to incorporate an association to be known as the "Racine Fan Athletic Association". A meeting was planned for Thursday night August 12th, 1926 at Little Bohemia in Racine, Wisconsin. The approved copy of the Articles of Incorporation, which were filed for the Racine Fan Athletic Association were expected to be received on Thursday Aug 12th, 1926 at 12:00 noon.

The meeting on Thursday took place as planned. George Pendall, head of the committee for the ABC club announced at the meeting that the necessary incorporation paperwork was received and it completed the formation of the Racine Fan Athletic Association, Inc. George Ruetz addressed the group regarding the status of the football operations. Ruetz said that he was discussing with Bob Johonnott about becoming the team manager. George expressed that he planned to assist him and share his experience of the position. Ruetz said that Bob had been a long follower and keen student of the game and he was destined to make a capable team manager. He approached H.F. Hansen, Georgia Tech assistant coach about coaching the team for the upcoming season. Hansen was a well-respected coach and very sought after. Ruetz laid out details about Hansen's family and the idea of him assuming the coaching role for the team. It would be announced later that H.F. Hansen accepted another offer

269

coach an eastern professional team, which paid more than the Racine offer. George said that Hank Gillo, "Kibo" Brumm and Jack Mintun would be returning to play for the team. Gillo was at the end of his career. He announced his retirement several times and the team did not plan to use him regularly but rather as a utility back and assistant coach. Hugh Blacklock and Milton Romney (former HR Legion player) were under contract with the Chicago Bears but they potentially would be signed to a Racine contract. Don Murry, Johnny Mohardt and several other Horlick-Racine Legion players were under contract with other NFL teams. Ruetz said that he wanted to re-sign those players but it was highly unlikely that he could get them back in a Racine uniform. There were 70 men, who applied to try out for the Racine team, Ruetz said. The possible prospects included a few former University of Wisconsin stars as well as Marquette University All-American Lavvy Dilweg. Dilweg lived in Milwaukee, Wisconsin but he wanted $250 per game and the Racine organization did not want to pay that much. The pick of star players was getting smaller because time was running out before the first 1926 NFL game. Several star players were eliminated from the list because they were unable to get to Racine to attend practice. Ruetz declared that all of the players would have to attend practices, regularly. The group also decided that the officers and directors of the Racine Fan Athletic Association, Inc. would be selected at a meeting of the ABC club on Monday August 14th, 1926. There would be six members from the ABC Club and five individuals from outside the club, who would be selected as the board of directors of the Racine Fan Athletic Association, Inc. The board of directors would vote on the members, who would be the officers. This would be a non-profit association and any profits, which were made would be turned over to a local charity. The 1926 NFL game schedule was presented was as follows:

1926 Racine Schedule

September 26th	Hammond Pros at Racine
October 3rd	Racine at Chicago Cardinals
October 10th	Milwaukee Badgers at Racine
October 17th	Duluth Eskimos at Racine
October 24th	Racine at Green Bay Packers
October 31st	Louisville Colonels at Racine
November 7th	TBD
November 14th	Green Bay Packers at Racine
November 21st	Racine at Milwaukee Badgers
November 28th	Dayton Triangles at Racine

******** The plan was that after the November 28th game, Racine, Milwaukee and Green Bay would play for the championship of Wisconsin.

270

At the Friday meeting, which took place as scheduled, the incorporators of the Racine Fan Athletic Association, George Pendall, Bob Bushell, Bob Johonnott, Joe Kolinski, Ray Kitchingman and George G. Ruetz appointed five more members to the Racine Fan Athletic Association board of directors. The five members, who they appointed were E.L. Mrkvicka, G.W. Smith, M.J. Knoblock, Nate Silver and L.S. Browne. These were the eleven board members, who voted to elect the following officers: George G. Ruetz was elected as president. M.J. Knoblock was elected as vice president. G.M. Pendall was elected as secretary, and E.L. Mrkvicka was elected as treasurer.

George Pendall, board secretary was placed in charge of the Drive for Funds. L.S. Browne was appointed as trustee of the funds by the RFAA board of directors. The campaign for the financing of the football team was explained by Pendall: *The drive will be divided into three phases, which will include a drive among the Racine manufacturers along with the sale of a combined season ticket and honorary membership card to both business men. Also, a subscription list will be placed in factories and various other establishments around the city.* The Racine Fan Athletic Association (RFAA) was planning to seek aid from the Racine manufacturers similar to how the Racine baseball club did in the spring of 1926. They would ask for 1/3 of the amount that the baseball club was seeking. The organization that was backing the Racine Belles baseball team asked for $1 from each man on the plant's payroll. The gridiron group (RFAA) planned to only seek 33 $^{1/3}$ cents per person. By doing this, they hoped to raise $5,000. They started campaigning immediately for these funds. They offered season ticket books, containing game tickets for all 5 home games, at a cost of $2 per game. These sold for $10. They also offered a booklet for $20. For that amount you received the season tickets along with an honorary membership card. Those card holders would become honorary members of the Racine Fan Athletic Association. They would be allowed to attend meetings and voice their opinions. The board of directors would take those opinions into consideration. The $20 booklets were intended to be sold to merchants, business and professional men. The season ticket honorary membership mirrored the plan that was already proven successful for several seasons with the Green Bay Packers. The Packers charged more for their booklets. The subscription lists that were to be placed in the Racine, Wisconsin factories were offered for those who did not feel that they could contribute $20 or buy a season ticket book but wanted to do their part toward continuing to give Racine a professional football team in the National Football League.

Several of those offerings sold right away. Joseph Luxem of the Frank Luxem Company was the first to purchase one of the booklets.

There were six newly printed and unsigned football contracts, which started their journey to six grid stars in various cities on the morning of Friday August 27th, 1926. Officials of the Racine Fan Athletic Association would not say who the six contracts were mailed to but they assured the fans that only stars of the highest caliber would be signed for the upcoming season. Robert Johonnott, Racine team manager said that more contracts would go out over the weekend.

HE'LL STAR FOR RACINE!

Formation Y—27, 43, 19—Zowie!
This is Mr. Wallie McIlwain, former running mate of the famous Red Grange, who has signed with the Racine pro team this year. There are those that say Wallie was the main reason for Red's success, and they may not be far from wrong. Anyway, local fans are depending on him to smash many a hole through the opposing lines this fall.

Wallie McIllwain- Racine Tornadoes

On Tuesday August 31st, 1926, an announcement came from the Racine Fan Athletic Association headquarters that Wallie McIllwain had signed a contract with the team. McIllwain was a star player from the University of Illinois. He was a starter in his sophomore year and he complimented another famous college legend, Harold "Red" Grange as they made up the Illinois backfield in 1924. McIllwain coached the backfield of Illinois in 1925. He was working as a student engineer for the International Harvester company in Milwaukee, Wisconsin. Wallie was 5'9" and he weighed 169 lbs. The Milwaukee Badgers tried to sign him but he chose to play for Racine, instead. Bob Johonnott and George "Babe" Ruetz were not idle. They were planning a football team capable of handling the 1926 NFL teams. Directors of the organization were working quietly to revive a professional football team in Racine, Wisconsin.

The signing of players was not the only task necessary; they needed to gather costs regarding the operation of the team and figure out ways to cover those costs. It was estimated that it would cost around $4,000 before the team even played a game. They needed to purchase all new equipment including uniforms because there was none left over from the previous years. It was determined that adequate new equipment would cost about $1,000. Next, there was the insurance protection of the players. This would cost about $1,350. The insurance, which was required by the State of Wisconsin law provided full protection to all of the players in case of an injury. It also covered the Racine Fan Athletic Association from any legal responsibility related to their injuries. Besides the cost of the equipment/uniforms and insurance, they would incur expenses involved with the players reporting for the start of practice and the increased practice schedule prior to the game. They planned to have all of the players in Racine, Wisconsin for the first practice on September 15th, 1926. They would practice steadily until the first game against the Hammond Pros on September 26th, 1926. Manager Johonnott said that railroad fare and miscellaneous expenses involved with the players at the beginning of the season would cost about $600. There was also the cost of printing, advertising, telegraph, telephone, supplies and other miscellaneous items, which would have to be paid out and it would total around $1,000 for the season. To get a further idea of the amount of money that it cost to operate a 1926 NFL team for the season, you would take into account the fact that visiting teams were "Guaranteed" $1,200 with the privilege of taking 40% of the receipts (game tickets sold for that game). If you add the player salaries paid to the home team players along with the other expenses, it was determined that Racine would average a cost of $3,800 per home game throughout the 1926 season. An overall home game attendance estimate for the 1926 season was calculated at 3,200 paid admissions. If this estimate was achieved, then the franchise would be sustainable. When George Ruetz and the American Business Club of Racine decided to bring back the Racine NFL team for 1926, they realized that they would be tackling a big proposition. They also believed that the fans of Racine, Wisconsin wanted another NFL team and enough could be counted on to make it a success. The plan for financing the team moved steadily forward, while detailed plans for the operation of the team, both on and off the field, were being completed. RFAA President George G. Ruetz said, *"We have one big advantage"* He remarked about the finances of the organization.

Ruetz went on to say, *"There will be no one on the payroll but the players and the caretaker of the park. The directors and management are giving their time and effort without remuneration (compensation) and members of the A.B.C. club have pledged their services gratis as ushers, ticket sellers, ticket takers, etc. thus eliminating all this additional expenses."* George believed that there would be a record attendance at the Racine professional football games in the fall of 1926. He based this theory from the fact that there was increased popularity of pro football, all around the country. He felt that there was a big demand for the games in Racine, Wisconsin during the 1925 NFL season but there was no team to meet this demand. Ruetz said, *"Last season was indisputably, the greatest season of pro football ever enjoyed. A glance at the waiting lines around the Chicago parks was sufficient evidence of this fact. Racine, unfortunately, wasn't represented in the circuit. But interest in the game did not die here, for several hundred local fans attended most of the games at Chicago. One time, in particular, I remember seeing between 200 and 300 Racine fans on a train coming home from a certain game. How many there were on other trains or who drove down in autos, can only be estimated. With these followers of the game, and the new friends pro football made, there seems no reason to doubt that crowds here this season will exceed those of other years."* The average attendance at the NFL Horlick-Racine Legion home games was estimated at 2,600 in 1922 and 2,900 for 1923. Ruetz was not involved with the team for the 1924 season and he was not certain about the average home attendance for that season. The average attendance goal for 1926 was 3,200.

The new Racine NFL team needed a nickname. It was announced that the board of directors for the Racine Fan Athletic Association planned to hold a naming contest for the team and the winner would receive a 1926 season pass to all of the home games plus a membership to the RFAA. Residents were instructed to send their suggestions to the sports editor of the Racine Times Call newspaper. He would forward those suggestions to the RFAA. In the event that there were two entries with the same name, the first entry that was sent in would be selected. A name would be chosen and announced right after the first practice of the season on September 15th, 1926. Edward Klingenberg 910 Augusta Street Racine, Wisconsin was the first to send in a suggestion. Klingenberg thought that Racine Bearcats would be appropriate. The contest was in full swing.

The focus continued on signing players for the new squad. Racine Team Manager Johonnott had this to say, *"Youth must be served"*. In the process of building this new club; they were keeping an eye on the future. The management of the Racine NFL team was adding young players to the roster, who had just finished their college football careers. Bob went on to say; *"We realize the need for experienced performance-men, who thoroughly know the ins and outs of professional football. We are going to have enough of those men to stabilize our machine-to furnish the experience. But the majority of our players will be young men between 23 and 24, who played their last year of college football in 1925 and who are just ripe for the professional game."* The Racine team manager continued; *"Fans like to see a fighting crew-a football aggregation full of pep and out there battling for every foot. And it is the young huskies that furnish that kind of game. All of the players with whom, we are negotiating and whom, we expect to sign have earned their reputations at college and have been carefully chosen from a large list of applications. They are just in the prime of their football careers and have several years of good gridiron work ahead of them."*

Those involved with the RFAA organization, who was backing the team, believed that professional football in Racine, Wisconsin was going to be around for a long time and these young players would be the future of the franchise. All the players, who were signed to the Racine team were under contract exclusively with them and unless they were released or the contract was bought out through an agreement with another NFL team.

The Racine team wanted their former star quarterback, Milton Romney back on the team. He was under contract with the Chicago Bears but he expressed that he wanted to return to the new Racine team. He was especially important to the team, since H.F. Hansen turned down the coaching offer. Romney was the coach of the team in 1924 and he would be offered that position again upon his return. The Racine Fan Athletic Association management was told by George Halas, manager of the Chicago Bears, that if he was able to sign "Paddy" Driscoll, he would release Romney to play for them. On Friday September 10th, 1926, the organization received the information that Driscoll signed a Bears contract. Driscoll was going to make the second highest salary in professional football. The Racine team management wired George Halas regarding the proposition to get Milton Romney

Adolph Bieberstein

back. Halas told them that they changed their minds and they would not release him. The Racine team would sign several players in the weeks leading up to the first practice. The second player to sign a contract with the Racine team was Barney Mathews. He played end for the Northwestern University Wildcats. Mathews was in his early 20's and weighed about 190 lbs. Bob Johonnott, manager of the Racine pro football team received the third signed contract. The player was Charles Reichow. He was a 1924 captain of the St. Thomas college football team located in St. Paul Minnesota. Reichow was also in his early 20's. The theme of signing young players to build for the future seemed to be prevalent. The fourth player to sign a Racine contract was Adolph Bieberstein. He weighed about 200 lbs. and played his collegiate football at the University of Wisconsin as a lineman. Bieberstein was "Big Ten All-Conference team" starter during the UW 1923 and 1924 seasons. They would also sign Raymond "Champ" Boettcher, (QB/HB- Lawrence College), Chester Gay, (6'1" 198 lbs.- Tackle 1924 University of Minnesota) as well as Roman "Kibo" Brumm (Tackle, End-1924 NFL Horlick-Racine Legion, University of Wisconsin) and George Burnsite (Quarterback- University of Wisconsin, South Dakota University, U.S. Marines, Iron Mountain pro football team). The management of the Racine Fan Athletic Association said a few

275

days earlier, they had another big player announcement to make. They announced that the Racine team had signed contract from Graham Kernwein (halfback-1925 University of Chicago). They also had signed contracts with Jack Mintun (center-1924 Horlick-Racine Legion, 1925 NFL Kansas City Blues) and Fred Hodscheid (tackle-1925 University of Chicago). Furthermore, the following players would be at the first practice to try out for the team. Frank Linnan (tackle-1923 Horlick-Racine Legion, Marquette University), Joe Bush (end-1925 Loyola University), Jim Murphy (Hamline University), Ed A. Sparr (Carroll College), Jim "Red" Oldham (University of Arizona) and Sven Sadelin (Racine, Wisconsin-Played for Iron Mountain pro football team).

Graham Kerwein

The first official practice was scheduled to take place at Lakeview Park in Racine, Wisconsin on September 15th, 1926 at 4:00 pm. The players were issued their equipment in the afternoon prior to that practice session. There were twenty men, who were expected to participate but not all of them would be make the Racine roster. It was likely that other players would join the team at a later date. Ten of the anticipated reporting players were linemen, while eight of them including Gillo and Barr played the quarterback, halfback or fullback position. Twelve colleges would be represented by those twenty players. Those schools were University of Wisconsin, University of Chicago, University of Minnesota, University of Illinois, Northwestern University, Colgate University, St. Thomas University, Hamline University, Lawrence University, Carroll College, Marquette University and University of Arizona.

In a meeting scheduled on Tuesday September 14th, 1926, the management chose a new nickname from the suggestions that they received. The name chosen was the Tornadoes and the Racine, Wisconsin NFL franchise would be known as the Racine Tornadoes. Joe Laurent of 709 Hamilton Ave. Racine, Wisconsin submitted his name suggestion of Tornadoes on the second day from the start the contest. Laurent would receive a season ticket for all the 1926 home games that would be played by the Racine Tornadoes.

"Kibo" Brumm

TORNADOES

RACINE HAS WON!!
A PLACE IN THE
NATIONAL FOOTBALL LEAGUE

Racine has been greatly honored and is very fortunate in having successfully affiliated with the greatest group of professional football teams in the country.

RACINE NOW HAS AN ALL-STAR WINNING FOOTBALL TEAM

The Racine Fans' Athletic Association and the American Business Club have worked hard to save the franchise and build a powerful team.

NOW WE NEED YOUR HELP
THE DRIVE FOR FUNDS BEGINS TOMORROW, SEPTEMBER 15th

LET'S GO! BOOST THE TEAM!
BOOST RACINE AND FOOTBALL IN RACINE
"AMERICA'S GREATEST SPORT"

The smallest donations will be appreciated. Subscription lists are at the various factories and stores throughout the city.

MEET THE TEAM at the Big FOOTBALL DANCE at the SURF, Friday Evening, Sept. 24th

The Tornadoes management announced that "Shorty" Barr would assume the role of coaching the team with the assistance of Hank Gillo because Milton Romney would not be released by George Halas to rejoin the Racine team.

The first practice of the 1926 season was attended by 14 players. Thirteen of those players were in uniform and participated in the practice. The players, who practiced that day were Chuck Riechow, Jim Oldham, Wallace "Shorty" Barr, Hank Gillo, George Glennie, Joe Bush, Champ Boettcher, Wallie McIllwain, Sven Sandelin, Jim Murphy, Frank Linnan, Barney Mathews and George Burnsite. Bill Abbott attended the practice but he was unable to participate because he did not have any football shoes. Adolph Bierberstein, Kibo Brumm, Graham Kernwein and Jack Mintun did not appear, but they were expected to attend the following day. The team went through light signal calling, a few passes and general instruction. Several dozen fans attended the practice to observe, despite the uncertainty as to where it would be held. Several players had to serve as linemen with the absence of a few, who were to be in those positions.

After the practice was over, "Shorty" Barr said that he was well pleased with what he had seen of the players. Barr stated, *"We have a bunch of scrappy fellows, and if we can develop the sort of team I'm hoping for, we'll give them a run for their money."* Coach Barr was hampered by the lack of an opposing team to scrimmage but he was trying to find a solution for the need of the team. The next team practice was planned for the following day at Racine College. Daily workouts would be moved to

Horlick Athletic Field, after that. The first two practices were held in other locations because of the condition of Horlick Athletic Field. William Horlick, Sr. donated the free use of the park to the team for the duration of the season. The Racine Tornadoes would prepare every day for their first game of the 1926 NFL season.

THREE MORE RACINE STARS

HANK GILLO.   SHORTY BARR.

Here are three more reasons why the Racine pro football team is expected to be a success this year.

Gillo and Shorty Barr are well known to Racine fans, having played here on the old American Legion team. They will act as coaches for this year's aggregation. Champ Boettcher is a former Lawrence college star and those who have seen him in action say he is a real player.

CHAMP BOETTCHER.

The practice held on Thursday evening at the Racine College grounds allowed Coach "Shorty" Barr, a chance to send the players charging through a few plays and passing drills. Graham Kernwein and Bill Abbott were able to attend this practice, but Beiberstein, Brumm and Mintun were not expected until the end of the weekend. Mintun would later announce that he would not play for the Racine Tornadoes because he was unable to get a leave of absence from his job in Decatur, Illinois except for the two days on the weekend. The Racine management wanted the players to attend all of the practices that were held during the week. The Tornadoes players had their pictures taken before the practice started at the Racine College. After moving their practice to Horlick Athletic Field on Friday, they would practice there on Saturday at 3:00 pm and Sunday at 10:30 am. More than 300 fans witnessed those practices, which the organization believed was a good indicator of Racine's growing interest in the sport. The Tornadoes would hold practice sessions on every day of the week at 4:00 pm during the week before the first game. They planned to do scrimmages on Thursday and Friday night. The following was a list of numbers that each player wore at the second practice.

Racine Roster:

No.	Name
9	Wallace "Shorty" Barr
3	George Glennie
12	Jim Oldham
19	Chuck Reichow
4	Joe Bush
2	Champ Boettcher
23	Wallie McIllwain
22	Sven Sandelin
11	Jim Murphy
15	Frank Linnan
14	Barney Mathews
7	George Burnsite
13	Bill Abbott
20	Graham Kernwein

With only a week before their 1926 NFL debut at Horlick Athletic Field, every effort was being made to start the season with a capacity crowd at the opening game. In an attempt to boost sales, the officers of the Racine Fan Athletic Association announced a ticket selling campaign. The following announcement was made on Saturday September 18th, 1926: Any individual or organization selling the largest number of single admission tickets between now and the next Sunday (September 26th, 1926) would receive a high grade Atwater Kent radio set-complete from the Foster Battery Company. The Radio was placed on display at Monument Cigar Store in downtown Racine. Game tickets were being sold for $1 and they were good for general admission. Those interested in participating were instructed to get in touch with George Pendall at Jackson 6553. Pendall, one of the directors of the RFAA pointed out that this was a fine opportunity for a club or individual to get a nice radio set for the winter. A group of girls decided to take the challenge in an effort to win the radio set, so they could donate it to the Taylor Orphanage in Racine, Wisconsin. The advance sale of the tickets for the opening game of the 1926 NFL season for the Racine Tornadoes, who would be playing against the Hammond Pros was reported to be doing well. George Pendall, who was in charge of the sale of the ducats (tickets) said; *"The sale is most assuring and many fans have been calling up for tickets and offering their assistance in promoting the sale. We are expecting a capacity crowd when the whistle blows to open the season Sunday."* The sale of the reserved seat tickets for the game on the upcoming Sunday went on sale Wednesday at Rehl's Cigar Stores, Monument Cigar Store, Smader's, Harry Cohen's store, Avenue Drug Store and the Northside Drug Store. The sale of the box seat tickets would go on sale at Office Supply and Equipment company office at the Arcade building on Main Street in downtown Racine, beginning at noon. Lester Kennedy, who was a member of the American Business Club of Racine and manager of the Christensen Hardware Store on Taylor Ave in Racine arranged a unique window display at the store. The display was described as being a football game shown in progress. There was a scoreboard displaying a third quarter score of Racine 6, Hammond 3. (This was displayed before the game was ever played and surprisingly, it would be the actual final score of the game). There was a football field with players lined up in formation against each other. Officials could be seen on the field as well as the football in the hands of the center. There were linesman displayed along the sidelines and the grandstand was packed with fans. The window display opened on Thursday September 23rd, 1926 and many football fans were visiting the store to see what became known as "The Game".

Officers of the Racine Fan Athletic Association organized a "Booster Football Dance" to be held at *The Surf* in Racine, Wisconsin in order to promote the team and increase fan support. The Dance was planned for Friday evening September 24th, 1926 in *The Surf* ballroom and those attending would be able to meet the team in person. The Tornadoes were introduced at the dance.

NFL President Joe Carr announced the officials that he chose for the Racine Tornadoes vs Hammond Pros game. They were as follows; Referee-R.G. St. John (Chicago), Umpire-Katz (Chicago), and Head Linesman-A.A. Engel (Chicago). The American Business Club of Kenosha offered to help the American Business Club of Racine with the operation of the game against the Hammond Pros. The team was ready from preparing for the past two weeks and the Tornadoes were working under the direction of Coaches Barr and Gillo. They had perfected their passes, signals, interference and the finer points of the game. George "Babe" Ruetz said that they had not selected the jersey numbers for the Racine Tornadoes players as of Saturday but the numbers would be announced by megaphone at the game on Sunday in order for the fans to be able to identify them. The Racine Tornadoes average weight for their line was 203 lbs. The starting line-up with player weight for the first game of their 1926 NFL season against the Hammond Pros on Sunday September 26th, 1926 at 2:30 pm was as follows:

Racine Tornadoes
Kibo Brumm-C-188 lbs.
Adolph Bieberstein-LG-210 lbs.
Fred Hobscheid-RG-215 lbs.
Dick Hardy-LT-220 lbs.
Ed Sparr-RT-210 lbs.
Jim Oldham-LE-195 lbs.
Barney Mathews-RE-186 lbs.
George Burnsite-QB-153 lbs.
Chuck Riechow-FB-187 lbs.
Graham Kernwein-LHB-185 lbs.
Wallie McIllwain-RHB-168 lbs.
Reserves
Wallace "Shorty" Barr-Head Coach-QB-210 lbs.
Hank Gillo-Coach-FB-195 lbs.
"Champ" Boettcher-LHB-195 lbs.
Frank Linnan-205 lbs.
George Glennie-186 lbs.
Jim Murphy-185 lbs.
Godfred F. "Fritz" Heinisch-173 lbs.

FOOTBALL SUNDAY

HAMMOND

VS.

RACINE A. B. C. "TORNADOES"

AT

Horlick's Athletic Field

Kick Off at 2:30 P.M.

General Admission $1.00   Reserved Seats $1.50

Boxes $2.00

Reserved Seats on Sale at the Following Stores—

Tom Smader's   ACE Billiard Parlor
Monument Cigar Store   Office Equipment &
Rehls Cigar Store   Supply Co.
Sixth Street
Avenue Drug Store   North Side Drug Store

Professional football, after a year's absence made its 1926 NFL debut at Horlick Athletic Field on Sunday afternoon September 26th before a crowd of over 2,000. The Racine Tornadoes defeated the Hammond Pros by a score of 6 to 3.

** GAME DAY **

Hammond was the first to score at the opening of the second quarter. Walt Secrest sent the football through the uprights for a successful place kick, worth three points. The Pros were in the lead but not for long. Toward the end of the second quarter, the Tornadoes were able to move the ball near the end zone. Coaches Barr and Gillo entered the game. It wasn't long before they made their presence on the field, known. Gillo ran the ball for several gains of yardage. "Shorty" Barr heaved a pass to Jim Oldham, over the goal line. Barr's touchdown pass was made under the pressure of two defenders rushing at him. They scored the only touchdown of the game. Hank Gillo was not successful with the kick for extra point, but the touchdown was enough

283

to win the game for Racine. The young Tornadoes team showed future promise in the talents that they displayed in the game. A fourth quarter pass from Barr to Kernwein resulted in a twenty five yard gain after Graham maneuvered his way through the opposing team. The way that he zig-zagged through the Hammond players was exciting for the fans to watch his ability to play the game of football with style.

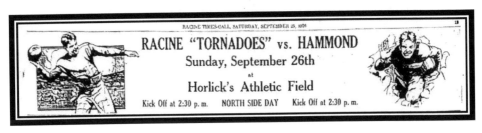

RACINE TIMES-CALL, SATURDAY, SEPTEMBER 25, 1926

RACINE "TORNADOES" vs. HAMMOND
Sunday, September 26th
at
Horlick's Athletic Field
Kick Off at 2:30 p. m.   NORTH SIDE DAY   Kick Off at 2:30 p. m.

PLAY BY PLAY: 1926 NFL SEASON RT GAME 1
                    RACINE TORNADOES VS HAMMOND PROS
                    Sunday: September 26th, 1926   2:30 pm
                    Horlick Athletic Field   Racine, Wisconsin

FIRST QUARTER:

Hammond took possession of the ball. Hammond was stopped by Racine. The Pros could not advance the ball. Hammond fumbled the ball. Riechow recovered the fumble for Racine on the Hammond 25 yard line. Kerwein ran the ball around the right end and it resulted in a 4 yard gain. Riechow ran the ball through the line and it resulted in a 1 yard gain. Riechow gained 1 yard on a plunge through the center of the line. Racine called a timeout. A drop kick attempt from the 25 yard line by Burnsite was unsuccessful. Hammond took possession of the ball on the 20 yard line. Three line plunges by the Pros resulted in a total of a 6 yard gain. Racine was penalized twice for being off sides. The Tornadoes call a timeout to discuss things over with their players. A run attempt by the Pros resulted in no gain. A fake punt formation with a run attempt resulted in a 1 yard gain. Annan punted for Hammond and Riechow received the ball for Racine on the 36 yard line. He advanced to the 42 yard line and he was tackled. A Kernwein run attempt around the left end resulted in no gain. McIllwain ran the ball around the right end and it resulted in a 3 yard gain. Racine fumbled the ball and Hammond recovered it on the 43 yard line. On first down, the Pros gained 3 yards. Another Hammond attempt resulted in a 2 yard gain. A run attempt by Gavin was stopped by Brumm and it resulted in a 1 yard loss. A place kick attempt for field goal by Curzon was unsuccessful. It was nowhere near the goal post. The Tornadoes took possession of the ball on the 20 yard line. A run attempt around the left end by Kernwein resulted in a 1 yard gain. McIllwain ran the ball off the left tackle and it resulted in a 2 yard gain. Kernwein punted the ball to "Ink" Williams on the Hammond 40 yard line. Williams advanced the kick to the 45 yard line, where he was tackled by Brumm. Racine called a timeout. Hudson attempted to advance the ball by circling around the right end but he was tackled for a 2 yard loss by Reichow. A 35 yard pass attempt from Curzon to Williams barely

284

went incomplete. Burnsite was penalized on the play for interference. The penalty moved the ball to the 20 yard line for Hammond. The Pros gained a total of 5 yards on first and second down. The quarter ended with Hammond having possession of the ball.

SECOND QUARTER:

Hammond has possession of the ball on third down with 5 yards to go for a first down. Annan ran the ball and it resulted in no gain. Secrest successfully place kicked the ball for a field goal from the 20 yard line. *Score: Racine 0, Hammond 3.* Nelson substituted in at the game at the center position for Rydewski. Secrest kicked the ball off to Mathews, who received the ball for Racine on the 20 yard line. Mathews advanced the ball to the 41 yard line. On first down, Reichow ran the ball through the line and it resulted in a 5 yard gain. The Tornadoes were penalized 5 yards for being off sides on the play. Riechow ran the ball and it resulted in a 1 yard gain. McIllwain ran the ball and it resulted in another 1 yard gain. Kerwein punted the ball to the Pros. It was received by Annan on the 30 yard line and he was immediately tackled by Mathews. Secrest punted the ball to Racine. Burnsite received the ball on the 45 yard line and he returned it 5 yards. Kernwein ran the ball and it resulted in a 2 yard gain. Kernwein completed a low pass to Reichow but he was tackled with no gain. A Kerwein pass to Burnsite went incomplete. Kernwein punted the ball to the Hammond 5 yard line and it was downed by Oldham. Hammond was able to gain on first down. Curzon punted the ball from inside the end zone. Burnsite received the ball for Racine. Barr substituted in the game for Burnsite. Gillo substituted in the game for Riechow. Kernwein ran the ball through the right tackle and it resulted in a 6 yard gain. Gillo ran the ball off the left tackle and it resulted in a 4 yard gain plus a first down for the Tornadoes. Hammond called a timeout. Kernwein ran the ball through the right tackle and it resulted in a 10 yard gain as well as another first down for Racine. Hammond substituted Neal for Usher at the tackle position. A run by Gillo resulted in no gain. A run by Kernwein resulted in a 1 yard loss. A run attempt by Barr resulted in a tackle for a 1 yard loss. A Barr completed pass to Oldham in the end zone resulted in a touchdown for Racine. Gillo was unsuccessful in an attempt to kick the ball for the extra point. *Score: Racine 6, Hammond 3.* Gillo kicked to Neal on the Pros 30 yard line. He returned the ball to the 38 yard line. A Hammond double pass was broken up by Barr and McIllwain. Kernwein intercepted a Pros forward pass on the Racine 45 yard line. Racine substituted Boettcher in the game for Kernwein at left halfback. A run by Gillo through the center of the line gained 2 yards for the Tornadoes. Racine was penalized 15 yards for roughness. A pass from Barr to Gillo resulted in a 2 yard gain. A pass attempt from Barr to Oldham went incomplete. Barr passed the ball 35 yards to Oldham but it went incomplete. Barr punted the ball to the 10 yard line. Hammond took possession of the ball. The Pros were penalized 5 yards for being off sides. Annan ran the ball through the line and it resulted in a 6 yard gain. Secrest ran the ball and it resulted in a 1 yard gain. Racine was penalized for being off sides on third down and the penalty resulted in a first down for Hammond. Annan ran the ball and it resulted in a 2 yard gain. Secrest ran the ball and it resulted in a 2 yard gain. The ball was around the 30 yard line as the quarter ended.

THIRD QUARTER:

Annan kicked off the ball for Hammond and McIllwain received the ball for Racine on the 10 yard line. McIllwain advanced the ball to the 30 yard line and he was tackled on the kick return. Reichow, who was in again at fullback ran the ball and it resulted in a 2 yard gain. Kernwein ran the ball around the left end and it resulted in a 3 yard gain. Kernwein fumbled the ball on the 30 yard line. He was able to recover the ball and advance it to the 45 yard line, where he went out of bounds. Kernwein ran the ball but he was tackled with no gain. A Racine pass over the line went incomplete. McIllwain was stopped on a run attempt and it resulted in no gain. Kernwein punted the ball to Hammond. Annan received the punt on the 30 yard line and he advanced the ball to the 45 yard line. Annan ran through the line and it resulted in a 3 yard gain. A run attempt by Williams resulted in no gain. Annan advanced the ball for a 2 yard gain. A place kick for field goal attempt by Secrest was unsuccessful. The ball rolled to the 20 yard line and Hammond recovered the attempted field goal kick. The Pros took possession of the ball. Hammond gained a total of 2 yards in 3 downs. Secrest attempted another place kick for field goal but it was blocked by Mathews. Secrest recovered the blocked kick behind the line of scrimmage and therefore Racine gained possession of the ball. It was a first down for the Tornadoes on the 26 yard line. Reichow ran the ball through the center of the line and it resulted in a 3 yard gain. Kernwein was tackled for a 3 yard loss. Reichow went out of bounds without gaining any yards. Kernwein punted the ball to Annan and he received it on the Pro 38 yard line. A Hammond pass to Williams resulted in no gain. Mathews was injured but he remained in the game. Williams ran the ball and it resulted in a 3 yard gain. A Pros pass attempt went incomplete. Annan punted the ball to Reichow. He received the ball on the 20 yard line and advanced it 5 yards. Reichow ran the ball and it resulted in a 1 yard gain. A run attempt by McIllwain resulted in no gain. Kernwein punted the Annan on the 45 yard line and he was immediately tackled by the Tornadoes. A run attempt by Annan resulted in no gain. A Hammond pass went incomplete. A Pros pass was intercepted by McIllwain on the 48 yard line. He advanced the ball to the Pros 25 yard line. Racine took possession of the ball. Williams substituted in the game for Hahn. A run by Kernwein resulted in a 2 yard gain. A Tornadoes pass went incomplete. A run attempt by Kernwein resulted in no gain. Mathews was injured and he was removed from the game. Murphy substituted in for Mathews. Kernwein punted the ball to Hammond. Williams received the ball on the 22 yard line and he advanced it 2 yards. Williams ran the ball through the line for a 2 yard gain as the quarter ended.

FOURTH QUARTER:

A Hammond pass was intercepted by McIllwain on the 30 yard line and he advanced it 5 yards. Rydewski substituted in the game for Neal. Hardy was injured but he remained in the game. Reichow attempted to run the ball twice and it resulted in a total of 3 yard gain. Gillo was substituted in the game for Glennie. Reichow moved to the end position. Gillo attempted a place kick for field goal but it was unsuccessful. Hammond took possession of the ball on the 20 yard line. "Fritz" Heinisch substituted in the game at the end position. Reichow moved back to the fullback position and Hank Gillo came out of the game. On first down, the Pros were able to gain 1 yard. A

Hammond pass went incomplete. A Pros pass went incomplete. Annan punted the ball to McIllwain. He received the ball on the 38 yard line and he was immediately tackled. A run attempt by McIllwain resulted in a 4 yard loss. A Racine forward pass attempt was intercepted by Mageda on the 28 yard line. Nelson substituted into the game for Secrest. A Hammond pass went incomplete. A Pros pass attempt went incomplete and they were penalized 5 yards on the play. A run attempt by Annan resulted in no gain. Annan punted the ball to the Tornadoes. McIllwain received the ball on the 50 yard line and he advanced it 8 yards. A Racine pass went incomplete. Kernwein ran the ball around the right end and it resulted in a 9 ½ yard gain. He was just shy of a Tornadoes first down. Barr substituted in the game for Heinisch by Racine. Barr took the quarterback position and Oldham moved to the end position. Reichow ran the ball and it resulted in a gain as well as a first down for Racine. McIllwain ran the ball and it resulted in a 2 yard gain. A Tornadoes pass went incomplete and Racine was penalized 5 yards for being off sides. A pass from Barr to Oldham resulted in a 10 yard gain. Another Tornadoes pass went incomplete. A run attempt by McIllwain resulted in a 4 yard loss. A place kick for field goal by Barr was unsuccessful. Hammond took possession of the ball on the 20 yard line. Annan ran the ball and it resulted in a 2 yard gain. A run attempt by Hudson was stopped without any gain. Annan circled around the right End and he advanced the ball for a Pros first down. A run attempt by Annan resulted in no gain. A Curzon pass attempt was intercepted by Barr on the 40 yard line and he returned it to the 47 yard line. A Racine pass attempt went incomplete. Barr completed a pass to Kernwein. He zig-zagged through the Hammond players and gained a total of 25 yards before he went out of bounds. McIllwain ran the ball through the tackle position and it resulted in a 2 yard gain. A pass from Barr to Murphy resulted in a 9 yard gain and a Racine first down. Kernwein ran the ball around the end and it resulted in a 10 yard gain as well as another Tornadoes first down. Kernwein was injured on the play and he protested to the referees about being roughed up by the Hammond players. Racine was penalized 50 yards on the play for roughness and the ball was moved back to the 48 yard line. Racine took Kernwein out of the game and he was replaced by Boettcher. Boettcher ran the ball and it resulted in a 2 yard gain. A Racine pass went incomplete. A Tornadoes pass went incomplete and they were penalized 5 yards on the play for holding. Another Racine pass went incomplete and they were penalized another 5 yards for holding. Barr punted the ball to Annan and he received the ball on the 30 yard line, where he was immediately tackled by Murphy before he could advance it. Curzon gained 3 yards on plunge through the line. A completed pass by the Pros resulted in a 4 yard gain. McIllwain intercepted a pass on the 35 yard line and he returned it to the 15 yard line of Hammond. Barr ran the ball around the end and it resulted in a 5 yard gain as the game ended.

<u>FINAL SCORE:</u> RACINE TORNADOES 6, HAMMOND PROS 3

SCORE BY PERIODS:

	1st	2nd	3rd	4th	Final
Racine Tornadoes	0	6	0	0	6
Hammond Pros	0	3	0	0	3

TOUCHDOWNS: Racine- Oldham (1)
FIELD GOAL: Hammond- Secrest, place kick (1)

STARTING ROSTER:

RACINE		HAMMOND
Oldham	Left End	Williams
Hardy	Left Tackle	Oshigren
Bieberstein	Left Guard	Neale
Brumm	Center	Rydewski
Hodscheid	Right Guard	Secrest
Sparr	Right Tackle	Usher
Mathews	Right End	Hahn
Burnsite	Quarterback	Annan
Kernwein	Left Halfback	Corzon
McIllwain	Right Halfback	Hudson
Reichow	Fullback	Gavin

SUBSTITUTIONS: RACINE- Barr for Burnsite, Gillo Reichow, Murphy for Mathews, Hardy for Bieberstein, Sparr for Hardy, Glennie for Hodscheid, Riechow for Gillo, Gillo for Riechow, Heinisch for Gillo. **HAMMOND-** Nelson for Rydewski, Rydewski for Neale, McKetas for Robtenson, Robtenson for Hudson.

Referee: Moore (Chicago)
Umpire: Katz (Chicago)
Head Linesman: Engle (Chicago)

The Racine Tornadoes made seven first downs and the Hammond Pros had four for the game. The Tornadoes attempted eighteen passes and completed eleven of those with six incomplete and one interception for the game. Hammond attempted thirteen passes and completed one of those with seven incomplete and five interceptions.

The game had to be stopped because of a unique situation that happened during the game at Horlick Athletic Field. Frank Linnan of the Racine Tornadoes had three of his molar teeth knocked out during the game and the players had to search the field for them. They did not find them and Linnan continued to play. Here is how the incident was described:

There was a delay out at the football game at Horlick Park Sunday that wasn't on the books. It was caused by a tooth hunt. Frank Linnan of the Racine eleven got his face in front of a flying number eleven and the result was disastrous. Players searched the greensward for a few of Mr. Linnan's teeth that failed to withstand the onslaught. A check up after the game found that three of his best and most useful chewing molars were among the missing. Anybody finding any stray teeth is asked to communicate with Mr. Linnan. Frank, who hails from Marquette University, showed an example of real spirit by refusing to come out of the game, despite the incident.

The American Legion Post No. 76 drum and bugle corps performed during halftime of the game. George Ruetz declared that the game attendance was around 2,000. This was far short of the 3,200 fans that they were attempting to draw. Even with the win, the youthful roster was in need of improvement, if they expected to continue to win. Coaches Barr and Gillo let it be known that they were not pleased with the performance of the Tornadoes. They were especially concerned with the offensive display. The play signals did not go smoothly for the team and Barr expressed that the passing techniques needed to be worked on. He felt that two passing opportunities were missed in the game against Hammond because of poor catching by the players.

George "Babe" Ruetz and Bob Johonnott of the Racine Tornadoes traveled to the Windy City (Chicago) on Monday September 27th, 1926 to complete the arrangements for their game with the Chicago Cardinals on the following Sunday. Contracts were signed by officials from both teams. The Cardinals management requested that Racine Legion drum corps accompany the team and the Chicago Cardinals management would cover the expenses for them to appear.

At 4:00 pm on Tuesday September 26th, 1926, all the players were in full uniform for a practice, which was held at Horlick Athletic Field. Another practice would be held at Horlick Athletic Field on Friday at the same time. There were no injuries as a result of the game, which were bad enough to keep anyone out of practice. Linnan was minus a few teeth but he jokingly remarked that he would be at practice, since he doesn't expect to bite anyone, anyway. Graham Kerwein would miss the Tuesday practice because he became ill, so he remained in Chicago, where he lived. The severity of his illness wasn't known at the time but he was believed to have an "Attack of the Grippe". Manager Johonnott would know more after he received a later wire (telegram) about his condition. The Tornadoes brought in two players to work out with the team at their Tuesday practice. The two players were Gilbert "Pee Wee"

Steer, a quarterback from Carroll College and George Bernard, who was a lineman from DePauw University. Steer was a small and light player, while Bernard tipped the scales at 200 lbs. Tornadoes Team Manager Bob Johonnott stated that the two players would probably take the trip to Chicago to play the Cardinals and one or both, may have a steady job here, later.

The Tornadoes were preparing to play the Chicago Cardinals on the upcoming Sunday at 2:15 pm. The game would be played at Normal Park Stadium, which was located at 6100 South Racine Avenue in Chicago, Illinois. George "Babe" Ruetz secured a block of 100 choice box seat tickets for the Racine Tornadoes fans, who wanted to make the trip. They would receive those tickets on Wednesday in Racine, so they could sell them before the game. Those tickets would be available for sale at Smader's and the Monument Cigar Store. A large crowd was expected for the game, since around 7,500 people attended the Cardinals game on the previous week. While in Chicago, the Racine Tornadoes team and the Racine Legion drum corps would stay at the Hallwood Hotel 740 West 52nd Place. To get to Normal Park by train, fans were instructed to take the Englewood "L" from the North shore to 63rd and Halsted. From there, they were told that they could walk a half mile to the park. Joe Kolinski, a member of the Racine Tornadoes Football Club board of directors was working on special arrangements for the trip to Chicago on the North Shore line train with special reduced rates. Several specials cars would be chartered to leave Racine, Wisconsin at 10:00 am on the Sunday, when they played against the Cardinals. They would arrive with plenty of time to make the 2:15 pm start of the game.

The Tornadoes had received good news regarding Kernwein. Hodscheid telephoned from Chicago on Friday morning and said that Graham was feeling better. He speculated that he would be good enough to play for a half of a game or at least a quarter. The team planned to play "Champ" Boettcher in his place until they could evaluate Kernwein's condition. The rest of the starting line-up would remain the same. Linnan and Sparr were fighting for the right tackle position. The tackle position was extra important in the upcoming game against the Cardinals, as they had All-American tackles and they were known to break up many plays before they had a chance to get started.

Tornadoes Coaches Barr and Gillo put there Mud Horses (players) into action on Friday afternoon with a rain or shine determination for a final practice before the game Sunday against Chicago. They mainly devoted the practice to signal calling in order to get the offense to run more smoothly. There was a report that Coach Barr had accepted a position as a tutor at Carroll College and it gave some of the fans the impression that he would leave the team. Coach Barr confirmed that it was true but he had made scheduling arrangements, so that he would only work at the college for three days a week. This would enable him to be able to attend all the Racine Tornadoes practices and be able to participate in all the games.

The starting line-up for the game against the Cardinals would most likely be Burnsite at quarterback, Boettcher and McIllwain at halfback position, if Kernwein does not play, Riechow at the fullback position, Oldham and Mathews in the end positions, Hardy and Sparr at the tackle positions, Bieberstein and Hodscheid at the guard positions and Brumm at the center position.

The Chicago Cardinals no longer had "Paddy" Driscoll, since he signed to play with Chicago Bears. He was their leading performer in the prior season, but the Cardinals still was able to assemble a team, which was ranked with the best in pro football. If the Tornadoes could show a credible performance against them, their reputation would be firmly established in the National Football League.

** <u>GAME DAY</u> **

Playing on a mud-soaked field and hampered by injuries and illness, the Racine Tornadoes suffered a 20 to 0 defeat by the Chicago Cardinals at Normal Park in Chicago, Illinois on Sunday afternoon October 3rd, 1926 before a crowd of around 3,500. To date, the defeat was one of the most humiliating a Racine, Wisconsin professional football team had ever suffered.

The conditions of the field were said to be anything but good for playing a football game. The central portion of the field was described as being under water and the sides of the field were ankle deep in mud. George "Babe" Ruetz said that those conditions accounted for the poor play of the Tornadoes, as they were not equipped with mud cleats. The Cardinals had those cleats, as that was their home field and they knew what to expect.

Several hundred Racine fans made the journey to Chicago, as the sky appeared to show rain, to cheer on their team but they did not expect the Cardinals to defeat the Tornadoes in the way

PRO LEAGUE STANDING	W	L	T	Pct.
Chicago Cards	2	0	0	1000
New York	1	0	0	1000
Buffalo	1	0	0	1000
Providence	1	0	0	1000
Racine	1	0	0	1000
Duluth	1	0	0	1000
Green Bay	1	0	1	1000
Chicago Bears	1	0	1	1000
Columbus	1	1	0	500
Milwaukee	1	1	0	500
Dayton	.	.	.	...
Louisville	.	.	.	...
Pottsville	.	.	.	...
Philadelphia	0	0	1	000
Akron	0	1	1	000
Canton	0	1	0	000
Los Angeles	0	1	0	000
Kansas City	0	1	0	000
Hammond	0	1	0	000
Brooklyn	0	1	0	000
Hartford	0	1	0	000
Detroit	0	2	0	000

Last Saturday's Result
Philadelphia, 6—Akron, 6.
Last Sunday's Result
Bears, 6—Packers, 6.
Milwaukee, 6—Detroit, 0.
Columbus, 14—Canton, 2.
Cardinals, 15—Los Angeles, 0.
Buffalo, 7—Akron, 0.
Racine, 6—Hammond, 3.
New York, 21—Hartford, 0.
Providence, 13—Brooklyn, 0.
Next Saturday's Game
Hartford at Philadelphia.
Next Sunday's Games
Racine at Chicago (Cards).
New York at Providence.
Louisville at Canton.
Chicago Bears at Detroit.
Columbus at Pottsville.
Dayton at Buffalo.
Hammond at Akron.
Duluth at Green Bay.
Philadelphia at Hartford.
Los Angeles at Milwaukee.

that they did. The Chicago Cardinals made thirteen first downs, while the Racine Tornadoes did not make any. Racine attempted ten passes with one completion. Chicago attempted seven passes, completed four and had two intercepted. The highlight for the Tornadoes came when "Shorty" Barr attempted a place kick for field goal from the 50 yard line. The kick missed by only inches. Barr and Gillo went into the game at the end of both halves and attempted to stage some of the great passes, which they were known for. The Cardinals capitalized on a Racine fumble in the first quarter. They took possession of the ball on the Tornadoes 38 yard line and drove the rest of the way to get their first score of the game. A second fumble, in the second quarter allowed the Cardinals to get their second score of the game. The ball was recovered on the six yard line and advanced into the end zone for a second touchdown.

The extra point was not good and the score was thirteen to zero at that point. While the ball was in Racine territory for most of the third quarter, the Tornadoes were able to stop Chicago from scoring. In the fourth quarter, Chicago took possession of the ball on the Cardinals 20 yard line and drove down the field for the final touchdown.

PLAY BY PLAY: 1926 NFL SEASON RT GAME 2
　　　　　　　RACINE TORNADOES VS CHICAGO CARDINALS
　　　　　　　Sunday: October 3rd, 1926   2:15 pm
　　　　　　　Normal Park Stadium   Chicago, Illinois

FIRST QUARTER:
　The Racine Tornadoes chose to defend the north goal. Brumm kicked off for the Tornadoes and the ball was received by McInerney of the Chicago Cardinals, who was immediately tackled on the 20 yard line. A run attempt by Francis resulted in no gain. A run attempt by Lamb around the left end resulted in a 7 yard gain. McDonnell ran the ball through the left guard and it resulted in 5 yard gain as well as a first down for Chicago. Lamb ran the ball through the left end and it resulted in a 1 yard gain. Chicago was penalized 5 yards for being in motion. McDonnell ran the ball through the right tackle and it resulted in a 10 yard gain as well as another Cardinals first down. Lamb ran the ball through the center and it resulted a 5 yard gain. In an attempt to run the ball through the right end, McDonnell fumbled the ball and Brumm recovered it for Racine. McIllwain ran the through the center of the line and it resulted in no gain. Reichow ran the ball and it resulted in a 1 yard gain. Kernwein punted the ball to the Chicago 3 yard line. It was received by Mahoney of the Cardinals and he was immediately downed by Mathews. Lamb attempted to run the ball through the center of the line but it resulted in no gain. "Kibo" Brumm was injured on the play and he went out of the game. Murphy substituted in the game for him. McDonnell gained 7 yards on a run around the right end. Weller punted to Racine and it was received by Burnsite on the Tornadoes 45 yard line. The ball was fumbled by Racine on the 35 yard line and it was recovered by McInerny of Chicago. Lamb ran the ball through the left end and it resulted in a 5 yard gain. Mahoney ran through the right end and it resulted in a 7 yard gain. It was a first down for the Cardinals. Francis ran through the center of the line and it resulted in a 4 yard gain. McDonnell ran the ball around the right end and it resulted in a 15 yard gain. The ball was on the Racine 5 yard line. Lamb ran the ball through the left end for about 5 yards but the Cardinals were penalized 5 yards for being off sides on the play. The ball was moved back to the Tornadoes 10 yard line. Lamb attempted the same play and he was able to gain 6 yards. Francis ran through the center of the line and he gained 3 yards. Lamb ran the ball through the center of the line and scored a touchdown for Chicago. The kick for the extra point after touchdown was missed by Mahoney but Racine was penalized for being off sides and the Cardinals were therefore awarded the Point. *Score: Racine 0, Chicago 7.* Weller kicked off for the Cardinals. His kick went out of bounds at the Racine 20 yard line, so he had to kick

the ball again. In his second kick, Weller booted the ball to the Tornadoes 5 yard line. Racine received the ball and advanced it to the 25 yard line of the Tornadoes. On first down, Kernwein ran the ball around the right end and it resulted in a 1 yard gain. Reichow ran the ball through the center of the line and it resulted in a 2 yard gain. A run attempt by McIllwain resulted in no gain. McIllwain punt the ball to Chicago. Lamb received the ball for the Cardinals on the Chicago 25 yard line and he advanced it to the 40 yard line. On the first play, the Cardinals were penalized for being off sides. Chicago punted the ball to Racine. Oldham received the ball on the Tornadoes 35 yard line. The Tornadoes punted the ball to the Cardinals. On first down, Lamb ran the ball for Chicago and it resulted in a 1 yard gain. Racine substituted in the game, Sparr for Hardy. McDonnell ran the ball off the tackle and it resulted in a 6 yard gain. Weller punted the ball to the Tornadoes. Burnsite received the ball on the Racine 10 yard line. He slipped and fumbled the ball. Chicago recovered the fumbled ball on the Racine 5 yard line. The quarter ended.

SECOND QUARTER:

   McDonnell ran the ball through the right end and it resulted in a 2 yard gain. McDonnell ran the ball through the center of the line and scored a touchdown for Chicago. Mahoney attempted a drop kick for extra point after the touchdown but it was unsuccessful. *Score: Racine 0, Chicago 13.* Weller kicked off for the Cardinals and McIllwain received the ball for Racine on the Tornadoes 5 yard line. He advanced the ball to the 30 yard line of Racine. On first down, Reichow ran the ball and it resulted in a 1 yard gain. Kernwein ran the ball through the center of the line and it resulted in a 2 yard gain. McIllwain ran the ball and gained 1 yard. Kernwein punted the ball to the Cardinals 45 yard line and it rolled out of bounds. Chicago took possession of the ball. Lamb ran the ball through the left end and it resulted in a 1 yard gain. Racine was penalized on the play for being off sides. Francis ran the ball and it resulted in a first down for the Cardinals. McDonnell ran the ball and it resulted in a 3 yard gain. Lamb ran the ball through the left end and he made a spectacular 35 yard gain. The ball was on the Tornadoes 15 yard line. Racine substituted Bernard in the game for Linnan. Lamb ran the ball through the line and it resulted in a 3 yard gain. Chicago was penalized for being off sides. Mahoney ran the ball through the center of the line and it resulted in a 6 yard gain. The ball was located on the Tornadoes 1 yard line. A run attempt by Lamb was stopped by Racine and it resulted in no gain. On a run attempt, Mahoney fumbled the ball. Murphy recovered the ball for Racine, just outside the goal line. Chicago made substitutions. McInerney substituted in the game for McDonnell and Connell substituted in the game for Lamb. From behind the Racine goal line, Kerwein punted the ball to the Chicago 45 yard line. The Cardinals took possession. On first down, McInerney ran the ball and it resulted in a 5 yard gain. Francis ran the ball through the center of the line and it resulted in a 4 yard gain. On third down, a Chicago pass attempt was intercepted by Reichow on the 45 yard line. He advanced the ball back to the Cardinals 40 yard line. A pass attempt by Kerwein went incomplete. The Tornadoes substituted in the game, Barr and Gillo for Burnsite and Reichow. After side stepping two players, Barr attempted a pass but it went incomplete. Racine was penalized 5 yards. Another Tornadoes pass attempt went incomplete. Barr punted the ball from the 25 yard line to the 14 yard line. Mahoney received the punt for Chicago and advanced it back to the 35 yard line. A run attempt by Francis resulted in no gain. Weller attempted to run the ball but it resulted in no gain. A pass from Mahoney to McInerney resulted in a 3 yard gain. Weller kicked the ball to the Racine 40 yard line. The Tornadoes took possession of the ball. A Racine pass attempt went incomplete. A pass from Barr to McIllwain resulted in a 7 yard gain. The quarter ended.

THIRD QUARTER:

Kohler went into the game at the fullback position for the Cardinals. Oldham went into the game at the quarterback position and Glennie went in the game at an end position. Weller kicked off the ball for Chicago. Reichow received the ball for Racine on the 10 yard line of the Tornadoes and he advanced it to the 31 yard line. Boettcher ran the ball through the center of the line and it resulted in a 1 yard gain. Boettcher ran the ball around the left tackle and it resulted in a 3 yard gain. McIllwain punted the ball to the Cardinals 25 yard line. Mahoney received the ball for the Cardinals and advanced it to the Tornadoes 45 yard line. McInerney ran the ball through the right tackle but it resulted in no gain because Chicago was penalized for being off sides. McInerney ran the ball through the left tackle and it resulted in a 3 yard gain. Mahoney ran the ball through the center of the line and it resulted in a 1 yard gain. A pass from Weller to Connell was completed for an 18 yard gain. Mahoney ran the ball through the center of the line for another 1 yard gain. Connell ran the ball through the left tackle but it resulted in no gain because the Cardinals were penalized for being off sides. The ball was on the Tornadoes 20 yard line. McInerney attempted to run through the left tackle but he was stopped with no gain. A McInerney pass went incomplete. Mahoney attempted a drop kick for field goal. It was blocked by Boettcher, who took the ball and it advanced it 1 yard. Racine had possession of the ball. A run by McIllwain resulted in no gain. Boettcher ran the ball through the center of the line and it resulted in a 3 yard gain. Kernwein punt the ball to the Cardinals 45 yard line. Chicago took possession of the ball. A run by Kohler through the center of the line resulted in a 2 yard gain. The Cardinals were again penalized for being off sides. Kohler gained 3 yards on a run through the tackle. A Chicago pass attempt was intercepted by Reichow on the 30 yard line and he advanced the ball to the 35 yard line. A pass by Murphy was fumbled. Riechow recovered the ball on the 10 yard line after a 25 yard loss. McIllwain punted the ball to the 50 yard line. The Cardinals took possession. Kohler ran the ball through the line and it resulted in a 2 yard gain. Connell was penalized for being off sides. Connell ran the ball and it resulted in a 7 yard gain. A run attempt by Kohler was stopped at the center of the line with no gain. Chicago was again penalized for being off sides. The quarter ended.

FOURTH QUARTER:

Chicago substituted Lamb in the game for Connell, McDonnell into game for Kohler and McInerney was put in the game for Green. McIllwain attempted a pass but it went incomplete. A pass from McIllwain to Oldham resulted in a 4 yard gain. McIllwain kicked the ball to the Cardinals. Lamb received the ball on the Chicago 12 yard line. On first down, Lamb ran the ball through the left end and it resulted in a 1 yard gain. Lamb ran the ball through the right tackle and it resulted in a 2 yard gain. McInerney kicked the ball to the Tornadoes. Reichow received the ball on the Racine

37 yard line and he advanced it to the 50 yard line. "Shorty" Barr and Hank Gillo substituted into the game. A Racine pass went incomplete. A run attempt by Barr through the right end resulted in no gain. Another Tornadoes pass attempt went incomplete. Barr punted the ball to the Cardinals. The ball went under the goal post and into the end zone. Chicago took possession of the ball on the Cardinals 20 yard line. On first down, McInerney ran the ball through the left tackle and it resulted in a 3 yard gain. Lamb ran the ball through the line and it resulted in a 7 yard gain and a first down. Lamb ran the ball through the center of the line and it resulted in a 3 yard gain. Lamb ran the ball through the left end and it resulted in a 1 yard gain. A Chicago pass from McInerney to Lamb resulted in a gain of 20 yards. The Cardinals were penalized 5 yards for being off sides. A pass from Lamb to McDonnell moved the ball from the 47 yard line to the Racine 15 yard line. Kohler ran the ball through the line and it resulted in a 1 yard gain. Lamb ran the ball around the left end and it resulted in a 3 yard gain. Kohler ran the ball through the line and it resulted in a 2 yard gain. McInerney ran the ball through right guard and it resulted in a first down for the Cardinals. McInerney ran the ball through the right end and into the end zone for a Chicago touchdown. Lamb place kicked the ball for a successful extra point. *Score: Racine 0, Chicago 20.* Weller kicked off the ball to the Tornadoes. McIllwain received the ball on the Racine 3 yard line. He advanced the ball to the 27 yard line. Two Racine pass attempts were completed but they resulted in a total of a 5 yard loss. Gillo ran the ball through the line and it resulted in a 6 yard gain. Barr punted the ball to the Cardinals. Lamb received the ball 35 yard line as the gun sounded for the end of the game.

FINAL SCORE:
RACINE TORNADOES 0, CHICAGO CARDINALS 20

SCORE BY PERIODS:	1st	2nd	3rd	4th	Final
Racine Tornadoes	0	0	0	0	0
Chicago Cardinals	6	7	0	7	20

TOUCHDOWNS: Chicago- Lamb (2) McDonnell (1)
EXTRA POINT: Chicago- Mahoney, place kick (1) Lamb, place kick (1)

STARTING ROSTER:

RACINE		CHICAGO
Oldham	Left End	Blumer
Hardy	Left Tackle	Weller
Bieberstein	Left Guard	Lunz
Brumm	Center	Claypool
Hodscheid	Right Guard	Brennan
Sparr	Right Tackle	Ellis
Mathews	Right End	McInerney
Burnsite	Quarterback	Mahoney
Kernwein	Left Halfback	Lamb
McIllwain	Right Halfback	McDonnell
Reichow	Fullback	Francis

SUBSTITUTIONS: RACINE- Murphy for Brumm, Sparr for Hardy, Bernard for Linnan, Gillo for Reichow, Barr for Burnsite, Glennie for Oldham, Burnsite for Barr, Oldham for Gillo, Barr for Oldham, Gillo for Boettcher. **CHICAGO-** McInerney for Lamb, Connell for McDonnell, Kiley for Lunz, Green for McInerney, Kohler for Francis, Lamb for Connell, McDonnell for Mahoney, McInerney for Claypool, Claypool for McInerney.

Referee: George Lowry (Chicago) **Umpire:** G.A. Brown (Chicago) **Head Linesman:** Hodgson Jolly (Chicago)

   Brumm, Hardy and Bieberstein were forced out of the game because of the injuries, which they sustained during the game. Kerwein, who was ill all week prior to the game did not see any action in the second half. The extent of the Racine Tornadoes player injuries were not immediately known after the game but the management feared that an x-ray examination would reveal a fractured shoulder for Brumm and Hardy with a cracked rib. They hoped that Bieberstein would recover and be able to play on the following Sunday.

   The Racine fans left the park in Chicago with their "flags flying high" despite the defeat. Their hearts were swelled with pride as the white clad Racine Legion drum corps took to the muddy field and went through maneuvers at halftime of the game. It was a performance, which took the crowd by storm and it was a powerful statement, which went towards putting Racine on the map. Under the leadership of Fred Maxted, the drum corps circled the playing field in squads with a roll of a double beat on the drums and the blare of their trumpets. Their exciting performance was heard throughout the surrounding neighborhood. The music was so appealing that the roof tops of neighborhood houses were soon packed with people, who had passed on the opportunity to take in the grid game but did not want to miss the halftime performance. When the drum corps went through a series of formations, it brought the spectators to their feet and they remained standing for fifteen minutes. The people of Racine, Wisconsin were used to these spectacular performances but they were new to the people of Chicago. They showed their appreciation by the wave after wave of applause, which greeted the steps of the performance. In a description of the performance, it was said that not a man lost his step despite the ankle deep mud. If the American Legion Post No. 76 drum corps performed as well at the Philadelphia competition on the following week, then they would certainly bring home another performance victory, which would be their fifth consecutive. Game officials were very vocal in their praise of the Racine Legion drum corps. Referee George Lowry said that he had never seen anything like it in his life, despite the fact that he traveled considerably. He went on to say, he was not surprised that Racine had taken national honors at the Legion conventions for four straight years and felt certain that they would repeat again that season. In regards to the Racine Legion drum corps, Lowry said; *"Nothing can beat that body of men. It would be a shame if the drum corps was ever to break up as every kid in the country should have an opportunity to see what a real drum corps looks like."*

George Ruetz said that the young Racine Tornadoes players needed more practice and practice is what they would do. Following their disastrous performance against the Cardinals, it was apparent that Racine's weaknesses were at the quarterback and center positions. As soon as Brumm became injured during the Chicago game, they were unable to be effective at the center position. They needed to prepare for their next game against the Milwaukee Badgers on Sunday October 10th, 1926 at Horlick Athletic Field but they also needed to adjust their roster. Team Manager Johonnott announced that George Burnsite was given his release from the Tornadoes following his performance against the Chicago Cardinals. Frank Linnan asked for and received his release from the team. Although, he would appear in the game against the Milwaukee Badgers before he left the team. Don Curtin, 1925 Marquette University Golden Avalanche quarterback would join the Tornadoes practice on Tuesday October 5th, 1926. Several teams were after him to play for them but he was practicing law in Rhinelander, Wisconsin and he was not interesting in playing. Curtin would change his mind about playing professional football after the Racine Tornadoes made him a good offer. He was described as being rated as one of the best field generals ever turned out at the institution. Besides being known as a smart player, he was said to be a great open field runner, who was dependable on defense and a good kicker. This was the quarterback that the team management expected to fill the gap of the starting Racine Tornadoes quarterback spot, which was believed to be a weakness of the team. It was expressed that Burnsite, though a hard worker did not measure up to the standards, which were required in professional football. "Kibo" Brumm was expected to be out for 8 to 10 days because of the torn shoulder ligament that he sustained in Chicago. Team Manager Bob Johonnott announced that every attempt was being made to fill the center position with an experienced and capable performer. They found someone to fill that position. At the start of the season, Ruetz and Johonnott attempted to bring Jack Mintun (Horlick-Racine Legion 1923, 1924) back to the Racine roster. Mintun was willing to come back but the officers of the Staley Manufacturing Company would not give him a leave of absence to play in Racine. On Tuesday October 6th, 1926, officers of the American Business Club-Racine went to the Staley Manufacturing Company in Decatur, Illinois and negotiated to get them to allow Mintun to play football for the Racine Tornadoes. Mintun would arrive in

297

Racine, Wisconsin on Friday.

Tickets went on sale for the Milwaukee Badgers vs Racine Tornadoes game on Wednesday October 6th, 1926 at the following locations: Ace Billard Parlor, Smader's, Rehl's Cigar Store and Monument Cigar Store. A special block of 200 tickets for the newly erected and arranged seats that were along the south side of the field would be placed on sale at the Monument Cigar Store. There was a "Letter to the Editor" published in one of the Racine newspapers saying that hundreds of fans were forced to stand up at the 1926 Tornadoes season opener against Hammond. According to A.B.C. of Racine, Wisconsin President Pendall, he said that it could not be true, since they only sold 1,100 general admission tickets and there were seating arrangements made for 3,500. He went on to say that anyone who stood at the Hammond game was doing it because he would rather do so than sit down. There was a further complaint about the Horlick Athletic Field seating conditions. Some of the local football fans said that they refused to further occupy the grandstand seats because of the wire screen in front of the stands, which they said interferes somewhat with the view of the field. The team management would announce later that the wire had been taken down thus furnishing a clear view of the game. They were 200 tickets sent to Milwaukee and they expected at least that many to follow the Badgers to Racine. It was believed that the game would draw a good number of fans. Milwaukee and Racine were natural rivals and the game against Milwaukee always drew well, in the past.

After a complete count from the results of the ticket selling contest from the opening game against Hammond, George Pendall, president of the A.B.C. of Racine announced that the group of girls, who were selling tickets for the Taylor Orphanage in Racine, Wisconsin won the radio that was offered as first prize. The radio set would be presented at a radio party to be held at the Taylor home orphanage on October 12th, 1926. The presentation of the first place prize would be made by Mr. Pendall at the radio party on that Tuesday evening. All of the members of the A.B.C. organization would be out to assist in the celebration as well as Santa Claus, who was getting ready for the upcoming Christmas season.

The Tornadoes were expecting a good battle from the Badgers. Team Manager Bob Johonnott was doing everything possible to make sure his players were in the finest condition possible for the game. He was familiar with most of the players on the Milwaukee team, since he watched them play in their first game of the 1926 season because Tornadoes did not have a game on that Sunday. He also had the opportunity to see some of them play, while they were in college. Most of the Badgers were big players, who weighed in at about 205 to 225 lbs. Bob said that the ends were the players to watch and he described them as being the best pair of wing men in the pro game today. Those two players were Lavy Dilweg, a 195 lb. former Marquette University player, who played left end and Clem Neacy, a 205 lb. former Colgate University player, who played right end. John Bryan, the Badger leader also had played in college. Stanley Kuick would be playing right guard, he was a former Beloit college star and they also had Duke Slater, who was a great fullback.

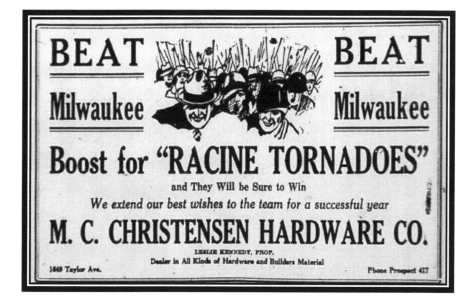

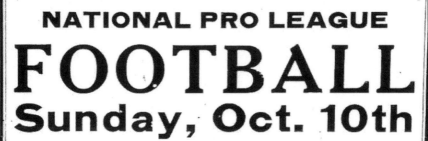

SEE
LAVVIE
DILWEG
THE
FORMER
MARQUETTE
STAR

WATCH
HANK
GILLO
RIP
'EM UP

Milwaukee Badgers

vs.

Racine Tornadoes

HORLICK ATHLETIC FIELD
Kickoff at 2:30 p. m.

*Reservations for seats may be had
at any of the following places:*

SMADER'S
331 Main St.

REHL'S
300 Sixth St.

Monument Cigar Store
510 Monument Square

ACE BILLIARDS
519 Monument Square

Box Seats on Sale at Office Equipment and Supply Co., Arcade Building

The Tornadoes held their final practice before the game against Milwaukee at Horlick Athletic Field on Friday. It was described as a heavy drill with a dummy scrimmage. Don Curtin was on hand to learn the signals but he did not participate in the heavy workout because he was not feeling well. Tornadoes Manager Johonnott said that Curtin probably would not be in any condition to play Sunday against Milwaukee but he would be in uniform. If Curtin did not see any action in the game, the plan was to play either Oldham or Steer at quarterback. Steer was an exceptionally fast shifty open field runner. He was playing well in practice. Coach "Shorty" Barr declared that he was pleased with results of the drill that night. Regarding the Friday practice, Bob Johonnott commented on Saturday; *"We're all pepped up over the team after seeing it go through last night's practice."* Coach Barr wasn't giving out any information regarding the strategy of the team but those, who were attending the practice sessions frequently at Horlick Athletic Field, said that the team was working a lot on the aerial (passing) attack. They predicted that Racine would attempt more passes than they had against the Cardinals. Passes were always a feature of the Racine games and they were missing on the previous Sunday.

** GAME DAY **

The Racine Tornadoes had the wind taken out of them by the Milwaukee Badgers on Sunday afternoon October 10th, 1926 at Horlick Athletic Field in a National Football League game. The Tornadoes were defeated by a score of 13 to 2. A safety, which was scored in the first quarter of the game gave Racine their only points of the afternoon. Johnny Heimsch scored a touchdown for Milwaukee in the second quarter and Johnny Bryan added another touchdown in the fourth quarter to seal the Badgers victory. A hard battle was expected by the fans but no one expected the on slaughter of the flashy Badgers. They presented the strongest line-up of a Milwaukee pro grid team that ever played in Racine. Lavvy Dilweg and Stanley Kuick both lived up to their college star reputations, while Heimsch and Bryan did their part to solidify the win over the Tornadoes. Racine did show some flashy signs of good form, especially in the third quarter, when they exhibited some exciting executions. Hank Gillo entered the game in the second quarter. He suffered a broken rib but he still continued to play. He was running the ball well. Kernwein, who was playing left halfback was carried off the field in the 4th quarter after an injury. The Tornadoes made only five first downs, while the Badgers had thirteen. Racine attempted eighteen passes, while only completing four but they did not throw any interceptions. Milwaukee attempted eighteen passes, while completing seven and four interceptions were thrown by the Badgers. Racine did not flow very well in their pass attempts as the ends were not getting down the field into receiving territory. Several times, the Tornadoes caught passes but then they fumbled the ball. There were also fumbles from their running plays and that proved to be costly. Milwaukee was able to score their touchdowns after they moved the ball down to the end zone through long and beautifully executed passes. A crowd of about 1,500 witnessed the game under ideal football conditions.

RACINE TIMES-CALL, SATURDAY, OCTOBER 9, 1926

FOOTBALL

National Pro. League

Milwaukee Badgers

vs.

Racine Tornadoes

Kick Off 2:30   Horlick Athletic Field   Admission $1.00

PLAY BY PLAY: 1926 NFL SEASON RT GAME 3
RACINE TORNADOES VS MILWAUKEE BADGERS
Sunday: October 10th, 1926   2:30 pm
Horlick Athletic Field   Racine, Wisconsin

FIRST QUARTER:

Racine elected to defend the east goal. The Tornadoes kicked off to the Badgers. Owell received the kick off on the Milwaukee 10 yard line and he advanced the ball to the 20 yard line, where he was tackled. On first down, Heimsch ran the ball through the line and it resulted in a 2 yard gain. Owell ran the ball around the right end and it resulted in a 2 yard gain. Heimsch lost 6 yards on a fumble, which was recovered by Milwaukee. Hallquist attempted to punt the ball but the kick was blocked. Mathews almost recovered the ball in the end zone for a touchdown but the blocked ball was quickly jumped on by Dilweg in the back of the end zone. Racine was awarded a 2 point safety on the play. *Score: Racine 2, Milwaukee 0.* Milwaukee kicked off the ball to Racine. Oldham received the kickoff for the Tornadoes on the Racine 30 yard line and advanced the ball to the 30 yard line of the Badgers before being tackled. On first down, a run attempt by Reichow resulted in no gain. A pass attempt from Kerwein to Mathews was completed and then Mathews fumbled the ball. Dilweg recovered the fumble and he was tackled by Hardy. A run attempt by Hallquist resulted in no gain. The Badgers punted the ball to the 50 yard line, where it was received by Kernwein for the Tornadoes. On first down, a run through the line by Kernwein resulted in no gain. A run attempt by Kernwein resulted in a 5 yard loss after he was tackled by Dilweg. Reichow ran the ball and it resulted in a 4 yard gain. Kernwein punted the ball to Milwaukee. Hallquist received the ball on the Badgers 20 yard line. On first down, a run attempt by Heimsch resulted in no gain. Heimsch bucked through the center of the line and it resulted in a 3 yard gain. A run attempt by Abel resulted in no gain. Hallquist punted the ball to Racine. Reichow received the ball on the Tornadoes 40 yard line and he fumbled the ball. It was recovered by Ashmore for Milwaukee. On first down, Heimsch attempted a pass but it was blocked by Reichow. A pass attempt from Hallquist to Heimsch was completed and it resulted in a 15 yard gain. The ball was on the Racine 30 yard line. A Badgers run attempt around the left end resulted in no gain. A pass attempt from Heimsch to Neacy resulted in a 12 yard gain. Heimsch ran through the line and it resulted in a 3 yard gain. Hallquist fumbled the ball but Heimsch recovered it after an 8 yard loss. A Milwaukee pass attempt was intercepted by Reichow on the Tornadoes 12 yard line. Racine substituted Linnan in the game for Bernard. Reichow ran the ball and it resulted in a 3 yard gain. Racine attempted to run the ball but it resulted in no gain. Kernwein punted the ball to the Badgers. Beiberstein downed the punted ball on the 40 yard line. Milwaukee took possession. Owell attempted a triple pass but it was broke up by McIllwain. Heimsch attempted another pass but it was intercepted by Reichow at the 30 yard line. On first down, Kernwein attempted to run the ball but he was tackled for an 8 yard loss. A run attempt by Reichow was stopped with no gain. Kerwein punted the ball to Milwaukee and it was downed on the 43 yard line as the quarter ended.

SECOND QUARTER:

Heimsch attempted a pass for Milwaukee but it was broken up by McIllwain. A pass from Owell to Hallquist advanced the ball to the Tornadoes 20 yard line. Heimsch ran the ball around the left end and it resulted in a 5 yard gain. A pass from Heimsch to Neacy resulted in a 12 yard gain. The ball was on the Racine 15 yard line. The Tornadoes were penalized 5 yards for being off sides. A run by Hallquist resulted in a 2 yard gain. Heimsch ran the ball and it resulted in a gain of 4 yards. A run by Hallquist advanced the ball to the 1 yard line. A run by Hallquist scored a touchdown for Milwaukee. Ashmore kicked a successful extra point. _Score: Racine 2, Milwaukee 7_. Racine substituted Gillo in the game for Reichow. Neacy kicked the ball to the Tornadoes. Hodscheid received the ball on the 30 yard line and it advanced it 6 yards. A run attempt by McIllwain resulted in no gain. Gillo bucked through the line and it resulted in a 2 yard gain. Kernwein punted the ball to the Badgers. Abel received the ball on the 38 yard line and he advanced it to the 40 yard line of Milwaukee. The Badgers were penalized 10 yards for delay of game. Heimsch punted the ball to the Tornadoes. Oldham received the ball on the Racine 35 yard line. On first down, Gillo plunged through the center of the line and it resulted in a 10 yard gain and a Racine first down. Gillo was injured on the play and it was believed that he broke a rib. Gillo ran the ball and it resulted in a 4 yard gain. Racine fumbled the ball and Gillo recovered it for the Tornadoes. A pass from Kernwein to Glennie resulted in a 10 yard gain but Glennie fumbled the ball. It was recovered by Heimsch for Milwaukee. On first down, Abel ran the ball through the center of the line and it resulted in a 5 yard gain. Heimsch ran the ball and it resulted in a 3 yard gain. The Tornadoes substituted Murphy in the game for Glennie. A Milwaukee pass attempt went incomplete. A pass from Heimsch to Neacy was completed for a 9 yard gain. Heimsch ran the ball and it resulted in a 3 yard gain as well as a Badgers first down. Owell ran the ball through the left end and it resulted in a 2 yard gain. A Badgers pass attempt went incomplete. A delayed pass attempt by Heimsch resulted in a tackle for a 10 yard loss. Ashmore attempted a place kick for field goal but it was blocked. Hardy recovered the ball. Racine substituted Barr in the game for Oldham. Milwaukee substituted Burks in the game for Gay and Slater in the game for Heimsch. Gillo ran the ball around the end and it resulted in a 2 yard gain. A Tornadoes pass went incomplete. Another Racine pass went incomplete. The Tornadoes were penalized 5 yards on the play. Kernwein punted to Milwaukee. The ball was received by Murphy of the Badgers. Murphy kicked the ball for Milwaukee from the Badgers 5 yard line and the ball was downed on the Racine 10 yard line. On first down, Gillo ran the ball but it resulted in no gain. Gillo ran the ball and it resulted in a 3 yard gain. Kernwein punted the ball to Milwaukee and it went out of bounds at the 45 yard line. A Milwaukee pass was intercepted by Barr on the Racine 18 yard line as the quarter ended.

THIRD QUARTER:

Racine substituted Sterr in the game at the quarterback position. Milwaukee kicked the ball to the Tornadoes. Kernwein received the ball on the Racine 10 yard line. He advanced the ball to the 18 yard line. On first down, Kernwein attempted to run the ball through the center of the line but he was tackled for a 5 yard loss. Reichow ran the ball and it resulted in a 3 yard gain. Kernwein punted the ball to Milwaukee. The Badgers took possession on the 40 yard line. On first down, Murphy ran the ball through the right tackle and it resulted in a 6 yard gain. Heimsch ran the ball around the left end and it resulted in a first down for Milwaukee. Slater ran the ball through the center of the line and it resulted in a 3 yard gain. Heimsch ran the ball through the line and it resulted in a 2 yard gain. A Milwaukee pass was intercepted by McIllwain on the Racine 10 yard line and he advanced the ball to the 30 yard line. Kernwein gained 15 yards on a run around the end. Reichow ran the ball through the center of the line and it resulted in a 3 yard gain. Reichow ran the ball around the left end and it resulted in a 4 yard gain. The ball was on the 50 yard line. Kernwein ran the ball and it resulted in a Tornadoes first down. A run by Kernwein around the left end resulted in a 3 yard gain. A run attempt by Sterr resulted in a 3 yard loss. Kernwein ran the ball through the left end and it resulted in a 1 yard gain. Kerwein punted the ball to the Badgers 5 yard line and the ball was downed. Murphy punted the ball from the behind the Badgers goal line to Racine. McIllwain received the ball on the Milwaukee 43 yard line and he was tackled by Dilweg. A run by Reichow through the center of the line resulted in no gain. Another run attempt by Reichow resulted in no gain. A run attempt by Sterr resulted in no gain. Kernwein punted the ball to the Badgers and Milwaukee took possession on the 20 yard line. Murphy punted the ball back to the Tornadoes. Steer received the ball on the 48 yard line of the Tornadoes and he advanced it to about the 45 yard line of Milwaukee. A Racine pass attempt went incomplete. Another Tornadoes pass attempt was received by Reichow and he advanced the ball 13 yards with the ball located on around the 32 yard line. A Tornadoes pass went incomplete. A run by Riechow through the left tackle resulted in a 2 yard gain. A pass attempt from Kernwein to Reichow resulted in a 5 yard gain. Racine substituted Oldham in the game for Glennie. A Tornadoes pass went incomplete and the ball was turned over to Milwaukee around the 26 yard line. Bryan gained 1 yard on a run around the right end. A run attempt by Heimsch resulted in a 1 yard loss. Murphy punted to Racine. The ball was received by Sterr on the 20 yard line of the Tornadoes and he advanced it to the 29 yard line. Kernwein ran the ball through the center of the line and it resulted in a 1 yard gain as the quarter ended.

FOURTH QUARTER:

Reichow ran the ball through the center of the line and it resulted in a 1 yard gain. Another run by Reichow through the left tackle resulted in a 3 yard gain. Kernwein punted the ball the Badgers. Bryan received the ball on the Milwaukee 30 yard line. On first down, Bryan ran through the center of the line and it resulted in a 15 yard gain. Heimsch ran the ball for two plays and he gained a total of 8 yards. Slater ran the ball through the line for a 25 yard gain but the play was brought back and the Badgers were penalized 15 yards for clipping. A Milwaukee pass went incomplete. Murphy punted the ball to the Tornadoes and it went out of bounds on the Racine 45 yard line. A run attempt by Kernwein through the right end resulted in no gain. Kernwein was injured on the play and he had to be carried off the field. Racine substituted Barr in the game for the injured Kernwein. A pass by the Tornadoes went incomplete. A pass was completed from Barr to Sterr and the ball was advanced to the Milwaukee 38 yard line. Barr advanced the ball to the Badgers 25 yard line and he was tackled. Milwaukee was penalized 5 yards for being off sides. A run attempt by McIllwain resulted in a 15 yard loss. A Racine pass attempt went incomplete. Another Tornadoes pass attempt went incomplete. Racine was penalized 5 yards on the play. Racine attempted another pass but it went incomplete. Milwaukee took possession of the ball on downs. Murphy ran the ball through the right end and it resulted in a 3 yard gain. A run attempt by Bryan resulted in no gain. Bryan punted to the Tornadoes and the ball was downed on the Racine 25 yard line. Racine substituted Heinisch in the game for Mathews. Milwaukee substituted Hallquist in the game for Heimsch. Reichow ran the ball through the left end and it resulted in a 3 yard gain. A run attempt by Steer resulted in a 2 yard loss. A Tornadoes pass went incomplete. Barr punted the ball and Milwaukee took possession on the Badgers 35 yard line. Bryan ran the ball around the left end and it resulted in a 4 yard gain. A Milwaukee pass attempt was completed to Murphy and the ball was on the Tornadoes 30 yard line. Slater ran through the center of the line and it resulted in a 2 yard gain. A Milwaukee pass went incomplete after it was broken up by McIllwain. A run by Slater resulted in a 2 yard gain. A pass from Bryan to Dilweg gained 13 yards and advanced the ball to the Racine 14 yard line. Slater ran through the center of the line and it resulted in a 5 yard gain. A run by Slater resulted in a 2 yard gain. A run attempt by Slater was stopped by Bieberstein and it resulted in no gain. A pass attempt was completed from Bryan to Dilweg. The ball was on the Racine 2 yard line and it was a first down for the Badgers. A run by Bryan went into the end zone and scored a touchdown for Milwaukee. Ashmore attempted to kick the extra point but it was unsuccessful. _Score: Racine 2, Milwaukee 13._ The Badgers substituted Gay in the game for Lane. Milwaukee kicked off to the Tornadoes. Reichow received the ball on the Racine 15 yard line and advanced it to the Tornadoes 38 yard line. A run by McIllwain resulted in no gain. A Racine pass attempt went incomplete. Milwaukee substituted Hertz in the game for Dilweg. Barr punted the ball to the Badgers. It was downed by Hodscheid on the Milwaukee 35 yard line. The Badgers took possession of the ball. A Badgers pass went incomplete. Another Milwaukee pass went incomplete. The game ended.

FINAL SCORE: RACINE TORNADOES 2, MILWAUKEE BADGERS 13

SCORE BY PERIODS:	1st	2nd	3rd	4th	Final
Racine Tornadoes	2	0	0	0	2
Milwaukee Badgers	0	7	0	6	13

TOUCHDOWNS: Milwaukee- Heimsch (1), Bryan (1)
SAFETY: Racine- Dilweg (1)
EXTRA POINT: Milwaukee- Ashmore, place kick (1)

STARTING ROSTER:

RACINE		MILWAUKEE
Glennie	Left End	Dilweg
Hardy	Left Tackle	Lane
Bieberstein	Left Guard	Kuick
Mintun	Center	Gay
Bernard	Right Guard	Donnigan
Hodscheid	Right Tackle	Ashmore
Mathews	Right End	Neacy
Oldham	Quarterback	Hallquist
Kernwein	Left Halfback	Abel
McIllwain	Right Halfback	Orwell
Reichow	Fullback	Heimsch

SUBSTITUTIONS: RACINE- Linnan for Bernard, Gillo for Reichow, Murphy for Glennie, Barr for Oldham, Glennie for Gillo, Sterr for Barr, Reichow for Gillo, Barr for Kernwein, Heinisch for Mathews. MILWAUKEE- Burks for Gay, Slater for Heimsch, Heimsch for Orwell, Bryan for Hallquist, Murphy for Abel, Hallquist for Heimsch, Gay for Lane, Herts for Dilweg.

Referee: George Lowry (Chicago) Umpire: G.A. Brown (Chicago) Head Linesman: Hodgson Jolly (Chicago)

The Racine Tornadoes needed to put this loss behind them, since they were facing one of their toughest opponents of the season on the following Sunday. The Duluth Eskimos were coming to Racine, Wisconsin. They featured Ernie Nevers and several other great players.

The Racine Fan Athletic Association held a special meeting on Monday night October 11th, 1926 to discuss the state of the organization. They realized that without a better attendance at their games, they could not continue in the National Football League. They were banking on a large crowd to attend the game coming up on the following Sunday at Horlick Athletic Field against Ernie Nevers and the Duluth

Eskimos. Several of the members of the American Business Club of Racine had signed the bank note, which brought in the original $1,900 to get the franchise into operation and they would be responsible to pay that money back. They were starting to see little hope in being able to satisfy this debt unless attendance increased at the games. There were fewer fans attending the games than two years ago, when the American Legion operated the team. The American Business Club of Racine even secured the return of the $1,000, which the American Legion Post No.76 paid for the forfeiture fee to the NFL and they were attempting to organize a good team. After the meeting, Manager Johonnott said that there would be more roster changes to the team and he also announced that "Kibo" Brumm would be returning to the line-up after fully recovering from his injury.

The organization was expecting a large turnout for the game, since the Eskimos were drawing well in their other away games that they had played already that season. This was due to the hype created by their roster. A ticket drive was launched with a committee, which was headed by Hyman Davis. Davis planned to canvas the city of Racine in an effort to build a large advance sale. Three thousand tickets were distributed to two teams that were competing in a ticket selling contest. One of the teams was headed by Mike J. Becker and the other headed by Elmer Hermes. The rivalry was strong between the two groups and the losing team would be obligated to furnish a banquet with all the trimmings for the winning team. Overall ticket sales were reported to be going well for the organization. There was also a ticket selling drive going on in Kenosha, Wisconsin. J. Hymen Davidson was in charge of both the ticket sale and publicity for the Tornadoes vs. Eskimos game. He made arrangements for a parade and demonstration on Saturday afternoon during the evening in both Racine and Kenosha, Wisconsin. The Duluth Eskimos and Racine Tornadoes would both participate. He planned to have a parade and bonfires as part of the festivities. The parade would consist of five or six cars carrying both the Racine and Duluth teams. The cars would go through Kenosha, Racine and more than likely Burlington, Wisconsin on Saturday afternoon with the bonfires planned for that night. Mr. Nevers was expected to be in the lead car.

The Racine Tornadoes made more changes in an attempt to field a winning team. They announced that Wallace "Shorty" Barr had been released from the team on Tuesday and his coaching position was replaced by Tornadoes player, Wallie McIllwain. McIllwain was a star player at the University of Illinois. He played alongside Red Grange in 1923 and 1924, while being instructed by Coach Bob Zuppke. He was considered by Coach Zuppke to be one of the smartest football minds at the University and that was why he retained McIllwain to be his backfield coach, the year following his graduation. Wallie would have most likely have stayed on the Illinois coaching staff but his work as an engineer brought him to Milwaukee, Wisconsin. McIllwain immediately took charge of practice on Tuesday night. He directed the team with new plays and instructed them how to execute them. Coach McIllwain immediately instructed his tackles and ends to rush the Blonde Giant (Ernie Nevers) and he told his secondary defense to watch for his passes. All of the Tornadoes players were in attendance for that practice session. Hank Gillo would continue his position as advisory coach. Frank Linnan was released from the roster

307

as planned. Johonnott also released Ed Sparr and he went on to say that a prominent player announcement would be happening soon. The team would add extra practice sessions in order to better prepare for the changes as well as the game against Duluth. They were planning to have extensive workout practices on every night of that week except Wednesday.

The Duluth Eskimos arrived in Racine, Wisconsin on Wednesday October 13th, 1926 and stayed at Hotel Racine. The Racine Tornadoes welcomed the team and accommodated the Eskimos need for team practices. The Racine Tornadoes offered to adjust their practice time, so that the Duluth Eskimos could practice at Horlick Athletic Field. The Eskimos practiced at 2:30 pm on Thursday and later changed to 1:30 pm, each day leading up to the game. The Tornadoes practiced at 4:00 pm.

Racine announced that they added John Fahey, an end from Marquette University to their roster. He weighed a 186 lbs. and he was considered a strong defensive performer as well as a good pass receiver. Team Manager Johonnott announced the starting line-up on Thursday morning. It was as follows:

Quarterback: Sterr, Halfback: McIllwain, Halfback: Kernwein, Fullback: Reichow, Center: Mintun, Guard: Bieberstein, Guard: Brumm Tackle: Hodscheid, Tackle: Hardy, End: Mathews, End: Fahy. Reserves included Murphy, Bernard, Heinisch, Oldham, Boettcher, Glennie and Gillo.

It was not anticipated that Gillo would play in the game because of his injury. The Racine Tornadoes had 18 players on their 1926 NFL roster with the release of three players and the addition of one. NFL rules stated that the team was allowed to carry as many players as they wished for the first three games but after that the League rule required that their squad be cut to 18 players. NFL President Carr announced that the referees for their upcoming game would be: Referee: Heldcamp (Chicago), Umpire: Malloy (Chicago), Head Linesman: Engel (Chicago)

Eskimos Team Manager Dewey Scanlon scoffed at a suggestion that Ernie Nevers would not play in the game on Sunday. He was quoted as saying; *"Nevers has played in five games this year and has only missed four minutes playing time."* He went on to say that he would be on the job and ready to show his wares for Racine, never fear."

The Eskimos team would wear their unique football uniforms, which featured pure white jerseys with the numerals in the color jet black. Across the front chest of the jersey was the team logo, which was an igloo. Scanlon commented, while we may have the neatest looking uniforms, we also have the greatest dry cleaning bill in the game.

Hotel Racine- Main Street Racine, Wisconsin

Football Sunday

One of the Biggest
Games of the Year

Ernie Nevers' Duluth Eskimos
will play
The Racine Tornadoes

SEE THE IMPROVED
RACINE SQUAD --- SEE
FOOTBALL'S GREATEST
STAR --- ERNIE NEVERS

KICK-OFF AT 2:30 PROMPTLY

*Better Get Your Seats Now Before
All the Good Ones Are Gone*

TO THE PUBLIC

Hundreds of football fans flocked to Chicago last season to witness

"RED" GRANGE

in action and those same fans will have the first opportunity of seeing in action his equal—

ERNIE NEVERS

considered by many authorities as the greatest football star of the day.

5000 Attendance

is necessary Sunday to root and cheer the Racine team and to welcome a truly great football star.

National Pro League
FOOTBALL
Sunday, October 17

Red Grange
AND
Ernie Nevers

are the two greatest football players in America today.

Tributes to Nevers

Nevers is the greatest backfield man on record.
Knute Rockne, Notre Dame.

The greatest football player I have ever seen in action, barring none.
"Pop" Warner

My choice of All-American Fullback.
Walter Eckersall

LET'S GO--5,000 STRONG AND SEE NEVERS
AND HIS
Duluth Eskimos
vs.
Racine Tornadoes

HORLICK ATHLETIC FIELD
Kickoff at 2:30 p. m.

Reservations for seats may be had at any of the following places:

SMADER'S
331 Main St.

REHL'S
300 Sixth St.

Monument Cigar Store
519 Monument Square

Ace Billiards
519 Monument Square

Box Seats on Sale at Office Equipment and Supply Co., Arcade Building

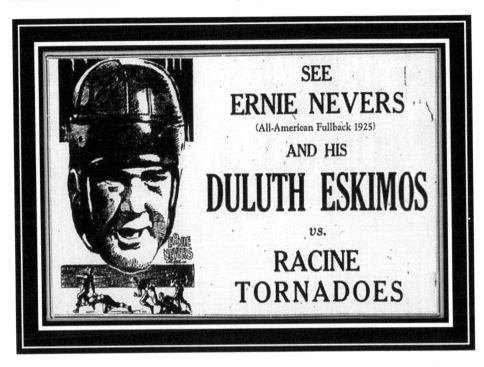

** <u>GAME DAY</u> **

Ernie Nevers swung around the ends, ran through the line, forward passed the ball, punted and place kicked goals on that Sunday afternoon at Horlick Field in Racine, Wisconsin. Nevers lived up to his reputation as the Duluth Eskimos defeated the Racine Tornadoes by a score of 21 to 0 in front of a disappointing crowd of 2,600 fans.

Despite the fact that the Tornadoes were beaten, they displayed their best game of the season, which showed more fight and all around football than any game that they played in 1926. Racine and Duluth, both had eleven first downs in the game. The Tornadoes attempted twenty three passes and completed ten, while throwing two interceptions. The Eskimos attempted twenty one passes and completed eight, while throwing three interceptions. Nevers zipped a long looper pass, which set up the first of three touchdowns in the game.

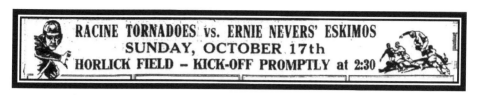

RACINE TORNADOES vs. ERNIE NEVERS' ESKIMOS
SUNDAY, OCTOBER 17th
HORLICK FIELD – KICK-OFF PROMPTLY at 2:30

PLAY BY PLAY: 1926 NFL SEASON RT GAME 4
RACINE TORNADOES VS DULUTH ESKIMOS
Sunday: October 17th, 1926   2:30 pm
Horlick Athletic Field   Racine, Wisconsin

FIRST QUARTER:

Racine elected to receive the ball. Ernie Nevers kicked off the ball to the Tornadoes. The kick sailed over the goal line and therefore, Racine took possession of the ball on the Tornadoes 20 yard line. Reichow ran the ball at the left side of the line and it resulted in a 2 yard gain. Another run by Reichow at the left side of the line resulted in a 2 yard gain. Reichow ran the ball through the right end and it resulted in a 3 yard gain. McIllwain missed a bad snap and Duluth recovered the ball on the Racine 7 yard line. Blood ran the ball through the center of the line and it resulted in no gain. Nevers attempted to run the ball through the line but it resulted in no gain. Nevers attempted a pass that went over the goal line but the pass was incomplete and Racine was given possession of the ball on the 20 yard line. Reichow ran the ball through the line but it resulted in no gain. Boettcher ran the ball through the line but it resulted in no gain. Duluth was penalized for being off sides. Reichow ran the ball through the right guard and it resulted in a 4 yard gain. McIllwain punted the ball to the Eskimos and it was downed on the Duluth 38 yard line. Nevers attempted a pass to Blood but he was tackled for a 7 yard loss by Reichow. Nevers punted to Racine. Sterr received the ball on the Tornadoes 35 yard line, where he was able to advance the ball for 10 yards and he was tackled. A pass by Reichow went incomplete. Duluth was penalized for 5 yards. A pass from Reichow to Sterr resulted in a 12 yard gain and a Racine first down. Boettcher ran through the center of the line and it resulted in a 2 yard gain. A Reichow pass attempt went incomplete. Reichow ran the ball through the right end and it resulted in a 4 yard gain. It was 4th down and 3 yards to go for the Tornadoes. Sterr dropped back and attempted a drop kick for field goal. It was blocked by the Eskimos and Duluth took possession of the ball. A pass from Nevers to Blood resulted in a 9 yard gain. Nevers ran the ball through the center of the line and it resulted in a 2 yard gain as well as a Duluth first down. Nevers completed a pass to Method but he fumbled the ball, while he was being tackled. Sterr touched the ball, before it went out of bounds. Racine was given possession of the ball on the 50 yard line. This was a new NFL rule. Boettcher ran the ball and it resulted in a 1 yard gain. Reichow ran the ball and it resulted in a 1 yard gain. McIllwain attempted a pass but it went incomplete. The Eskimos took possession of the ball on downs. Murray was injured on the play, he had wrenched (twisted) knee. Duluth substituted Fitzgibbons in the game for the injured Murray. Blood ran the ball through the left guard and it resulted in an 8 yard gain. A run by Nevers resulted in a 3 yard gain and

345

a first down for the Eskimos. Fitzgibbons was tackled for a loss by Bieberstein on a run attempt. Blood ran the ball around the left flank and it resulted in a 1 yard gain. A pass from Nevers to Fitzgibbons was completed and it resulted in a 5 yard gain. A place kick for field goal by Nevers from the 39 yard line was not successful. Sterr caught the ball on the 5 yard line and he returned it the back to the 20 yard line. Racine took a timeout. Reichow slammed through the right tackle and it resulted in a 2 yard gain. Boettcher rushed the ball through the center of the line and it resulted in a 6 yard gain. A run attempt through the center of the line by McIllwain resulted in no gain. McIllwain kicked the ball 20 yard to the Duluth 45 yard line. The Eskimos took possession of the ball. Blood muffed (fumbled) the ball but he was able to recover it. A Nevers pass went incomplete. The Tornadoes substituted Brumm in the game for Bernard. A Nevers pass was intercepted by Sterr on the Racine 20 yard line and he advanced it to the Tornadoes 27 yard line. Reichow ran the ball through the right end and it resulted in an 11 yard gain as well as a first down for Racine. Sterr ran the ball out of bounds without gaining any yards. McIllwain attempted to advance the ball through the end but it resulted in no gain. The ball was on the Tornadoes 35 yard line as the quarter ended.

SECOND QUARTER:

Reichow ran the ball through the line and it resulted in a 1 yard gain. McIllwain punted the ball to Duluth. Fitzgibbons received the ball for the Eskimos and he returned it 19 yards to the Racine 45 yard line. He was tackled by Boettcher. Two run attempts by Nevers through the line resulted in a total of a 7 yard gain. Nevers ran the ball through the left guard and it resulted in a 5 yard gain as well as an Eskimos first down. A run attempt by Blood through the left tackle resulted in no gain. Blood attempted a trick play but Mintun tackled him and it resulted in no gain. Nevers zipped a long looper pass to Blood and it resulted in a 33 yard again. Blood was tackled on the long pass by Sterr at the Racine 1 yard line. Nevers plunged through the center of the line and over the goal line for a Duluth touchdown. Nevers place kicked the ball for a successful Extra Point. *Score: Racine 0, Duluth 7.* Nevers kicked off and the ball went out of bounds, so he had to kick the ball again. Nevers kicked the ball off to the Tornadoes. Boettcher received the ball and advanced it 6 yards to the Racine 22 yard line. McIllwain ran the ball through the right guard and it resulted in a 13 yard gain as well as a first down. Boettcher ran the ball through the center of the line and it resulted in a 2 yard gain. Sterr plowed through the left tackle and he advanced the ball 10 yards, which was a Racine first down. A run attempt by McIllwain resulted in no gain. A Reichow pass from the 40 yard line to McIllwain was completed for a 20 yard gain. Racine substituted Murphy in the game for Mathews. Boettcher ran the ball through the left guard and it resulted in a 1 yard gain. A Reichow pass to McIllwain resulted in a 7 yard gain. A Racine pass went incomplete. A Tornadoes pass went incomplete. Duluth took possession of the ball on downs. A run attempt by Blood was stopped with no gain by Boettcher. A criss-cross play from Nevers to Blood resulted in a 5 yard gain with a run around the left end. Nevers circled around the right end and advanced the ball 4 yards. Nevers punted the ball to the Tornadoes. The ball was downed by Duluth on the 40 yard line. Racine took possession. A run by Boettcher through the center of the line resulted in no gain. A

316

Reichow pass went incomplete. A McIllwain pass was intercepted by Nevers on the 50 yard line and he returned it to the 44 yard line, where he was tackled by Hardy. A Nevers pass to Method resulted in a 34 yard gain. A Nevers pass went incomplete. A Nevers pass was completed from the 25 yard line to Blood, who was in the corner of the field and outside of the goal. Blood received the pass and ran the ball into the end zone for an Eskimos touchdown. Nevers successfully place kicked the ball for the extra point. *Score: Racine 0, Duluth 14.* A Reichow run attempt through the center of the line resulted in the loss of 1 yard. A Reichow run attempt run through center of the line resulted in no gain. A bad snap to McIllwain resulted in a 10 yard loss for Racine. Mac (McIllwain) punted the ball from the 10 yard line to Duluth. Fitzgibbons received the ball and ran out of bounds at the 32 yard line of Duluth. A pass from Nevers to Blood went incomplete. Another Nevers long pass went incomplete. A third pass by the Eskimos went incomplete and they were penalized 5 yards on the play. This was from a new NFL rule, which stated the backfield could not be in motion before the ball was snapped. Nevers punted the ball from the Duluth 42 yard line to Racine and it went over the goal line, therefore they took possession of the ball on the Tornadoes 20 yard line. A long pass from Boettcher to Murphy resulted in a 65 yard gain for Racine. The ball was on the Duluth 30 yard line as the quarter ended.

THIRD QUARTER:

Nevers kicked off to the Tornadoes. McIllwain received the ball and advanced it 30 yards to the Racine 35 yard line. Reichow ran the ball through the right end and it resulted in a 7 yard gain. A run by Boettcher through the left tackle resulted in a 3 yard gain and a Tornadoes first down. Stein was injured on the play. A Racine run attempt through the center of the line resulted in no gain. McIllwain kicked the ball to the Duluth 35 yard line. The Eskimos took possession. Fitzgibbons ran the ball through the right end but it resulted in no gain. Duluth was penalized 5 yards, which resulted from their backfield being in motion on the play. Nevers ran the ball through the left tackle and it resulted in a 5 yard gain. Nevers ran the ball and it resulted in a 20 yard gain but it was called back because they were again penalized for their backfield being in motion. Nevers briefly went out of the game because of a hit he took from Murphy on the tackle but then he came back onto the field to play. Nevers ran the ball through the right end and it resulted in a 5 yard gain. Nevers punted the ball from the Duluth 20 yard line and it went out of bounds on the Tornadoes 30 yard line. Racine took possession of the ball. McIllwain ran the ball through the left end and it resulted in no gain. Reichow ran the ball through the right end and it resulted in a 1 yard gain. Boettcher ran the ball through the left guard and it resulted in a 3 yard gain. McIllwain attempted to punt the ball to Duluth. The punt was blocked by Keisling and the ball was downed. The Eskimos took possession of the ball on the Tornadoes 21 yard line. A pass attempt by Nevers resulted in no gain. A Nevers run through the right guard resulted in a 9 yard gain. Blood ran through the left tackle and it resulted in a 6 yard gain. Nevers attempted a run through the right tackle and it resulted in a 1 yard loss. Nevers ran the ball through the right guard and it resulted in a 1 yard gain. The ball was on the Racine 4 yard line. A Nevers pass was blocked by the Tornadoes and Racine took possession of the ball. McIllwain punted the ball from the Racine end zone and the ball went out of bounds at the Tornadoes 13 yard line. It was a poor punt in a critical place. On first down, Fitzgibbons ran a delayed run play through the right tackle and it resulted in a 4 yard gain. Nevers ran the ball and it resulted in a 4 yard gain. Nevers ran the ball through the center of the line and it resulted in an Eskimos first down. Nevers ran the ball through the right guard and it resulted in a 2 yard gain. Duluth executed a fake play with a concealed ball and Fitzgibbons carried the ball over the goal line for an Eskimos touchdown. Nevers kicked a successful extra point. *Score: Racine 0, Duluth 21.* Nevers kicked off the ball to Racine. Hardy received the ball for the Tornadoes and advanced the ball to the Racine 38 yard line. A Racine pass was intercepted by Nevers and he was tackled by Brumm on the Tornadoes 41 yard line. Blood ran the ball through the right tackle and it resulted in a 6 yard gain. Duluth had the ball on the 35 yard line as the quarter ended.

FOURTH QUARTER:
Fitzgibbons ran the ball through the right tackle and it resulted in a 6 yard gain and a first down. Blood ran the ball and it resulted in a 5 yard gain. Duluth was penalized for being in motion in the backfield on the play. An Eskimos pass was intercepted by Sterr and he advanced the ball 10 yards to the Racine 30 yard line. Reichow ran the ball through the right end and it resulted in 3 yard gain. A pass from Reichow to McIllwain resulted in a 6 yard gain. Boettcher ran the ball through the right guard and it resulted in a 4 yard gain and a first down. A run attempt by Reichow resulted in no gain. A pass from Sterr to Murphy went incomplete. A pass from Boettcher to Sterr resulted in a 10 yard gain and a first down. Boettcher ran the ball through the center of the line and it resulted in a 2 yard gain. A Racine pass attempt went incomplete. A completed pass from McIllwain to Reichow resulted in no gain. McIllwain punted the ball to the Eskimos. Fitzgibbons received the ball and he advanced it 14 yards to the Duluth 29 yard line. Racine called a timeout. The Tornadoes substituted Bernard in the game for Hardy. A completed pass from Nevers to Underwood resulted in a loss. A Duluth pass attempt was blocked by Murphy. Nevers punted the ball to the Eskimos 49 yard line. Racine took possession of the ball. Reichow ran the ball through the right end and it resulted in a 10 yard gain as well as a first down. McIllwain ran the ball through the line but it resulted in no gain. A Boettcher pass attempt was intercepted by Nevers and he advanced the ball 30 yards to the Tornadoes 35 yard line, where he was tackled by Bernard. Racine called a timeout. The Tornadoes substituted Glennie in the game for Hardy. A Nevers pass attempt went incomplete. A run by Blood through the left end resulted in a 5 yard gain. Duluth was penalized 15 yards for holding. A Nevers pass attempt went incomplete. Nevers punted the ball 35 yards to the Tornadoes 10 yard line. Racine took possession of the ball. Reichow ran the ball around the end and gained 20 yards as well as a Tornadoes first down. Racine ran the ball out of bounds on the 28 yard line. Reichow ran the ball through the left end and it resulted in a 3 yard gain. A pass from Reichow to McIllwain was completed for a 27 yard gain and it was a Tornadoes first down on the Eskimos 48 yard line. Duluth called a timeout. Reichow attempted a delayed run, which resulted in a little gain. A McIllwain pass attempt fell short and it was incomplete. A completed pass from Boettcher to Murphy gained 14 yards and a Tornadoes first down on the Eskimos 34 yard line. A Racine pass attempt went

318

incomplete. Reichow crashed through the left tackle and gained 2 yards on the run. Racine was penalized for being off sides on the play. A Tornadoes pass went incomplete. Duluth took possession of the ball on downs and it was on around the Eskimos 32 yard line. A Nevers pass went incomplete. Nevers punted the ball to the Tornadoes. Racine took possession of the ball on the Tornadoes 10 yard line. Reichow ran the ball around the right end and it resulted in a 20 yard gain as well as a Racine first down. The Tornadoes carried the ball out of bounds on the 30 yard line. Reichow ran the ball through the left end and it resulted in a 3 yard gain. A pass from Reichow to McIllwain was complete and he advanced the ball 27 yards. Duluth called a timeout. Reichow attempted a delayed run on the short side of the field and he carried the ball out of bounds at the Eskimos 45 yard line. A completed pass from Boettcher to Murphy resulted in a 14 yard gain and the ball was on the 31 yard line. Reichow was able to gain 2 yards on a run through the right tackle. A pass attempt from Boettcher to McIllwain went incomplete. A Racine pass went incomplete and the Tornadoes were penalized 5 yards on the play. Duluth took possession of the ball on the Eskimos 36 yard line. Fitzgibbons gained 15 yards on a run through the right tackle. A Nevers pass attempt was intercepted by McIllwain on the Duluth 48 yard line. Racine called a timeout. A Boettcher pass attempt went incomplete. McIllwain ran the ball through the right guard but he was stopped with no gain. A run attempt by McIllwain was fumbled and recovered with a 5 yard loss. Reichow punted the ball from the Racine 40 yard line to Duluth 20 yard line. The Eskimos took possession of the ball. Nevers ran the ball through the center of the line and it resulted in a 3 yard gain as the game ended.

FINAL SCORE:
RACINE TORNADOES 0, DULUTH ESKIMOS 21

SCORE BY PERIODS:

	1st	2nd	3rd	4th	Final
Racine Tornadoes	0	0	0	0	0
Duluth Eskimos	0	14	7	0	21

TOUCHDOWNS: Duluth- Nevers (1) Blood (1) Fitzgibbons (1)
EXTRA POINT: Duluth- Nevers, place kick (3)

STARTING ROSTER:

RACINE		DULUTH
Mathews	Left End	Murray
Hardy	Left Tackle	Keisling
Bernard	Left Guard	Manion
Mintun	Center	Carlson
Bieberstein	Right Guard	Rundquist
Hodscheid	Right Tackle	Goyer
Fahey	Right End	Underwood
Sterr	Quarterback	Method
Reichow	Left Halfback	Rooney
McIllwain	Right Halfback	Blood
Boettcher	Fullback	Nevers

SUBSTITUTIONS: RACINE- Brumm for Bernard, Murphy for McIllwain, Bernard for Hodscheid, Glennie for Hardy. DULUTH- Fitzgibbons for Murray, Stein for Manion

Referee: Heldcamp
Umpire: Malloy
Head Linesman: Engel

It would be reported that the reason why Graham Kernwein did not play in the game, was because he was ill. Under new Coach McIllwain, Racine showed a surprisingly amount of improvement. He had only a few days to install his new system but even in that little time, it seemed to be effective. Despite the hard slashing battle put up by the Racine Tornadoes, no one was hurt in the game. Boettcher had reported a stiff neck but he was healed by the Tuesday practice. Every player attended that practice, which was the team's first workout, since the defeat by Ernie Nevers Duluth Eskimos. The players were in good condition and the Green Bay Packers was their next opponent. The game was scheduled to be played in Green Bay, Wisconsin and several car loads of Racine fans were expected to make the trip. As in the past, some would leave early Saturday afternoon and others would travel late Saturday night, leaving late, so they would arrive early Sunday morning. A block of 80 tickets were ordered by George Ruetz and they were expected to arrive in Racine and go on sale Wednesday October 20th, 1926. They would be sold at Ace Billard Parlor, Monument Cigar Store, Rehl's Cigar Store on Sixth Street and Smader's. The tickets would be left on sale at those locations until Saturday. The general impression in the Tornadoes camp was that the Packers had the best team of any in recent seasons. The Tornadoes were considered underdogs and they knew that they had a difficult proposition ahead. They planned accordingly.

There was a rivalry between the two teams, which dated back to 1921. The Racine professional football teams always had success playing the Packers at their home field.

In fact, the past records indicated that the only team to date to defeat Green Bay twice at their home game was Racine. Gridiron hostilities between the teams began in 1921, when they played a neutral game in Milwaukee, Wisconsin. Thanks to a last minute field goal by Hank Gillo, the game ended in a 3-3 tie. In 1922, the teams played three games against each other. Racine played up in Green Bay and handed them a 10-6 loss. The second game of 1922 was played in Horlickville (Horlick Athletic Field) and it ended in another 3-3 tie, as Gillo scored in the last seconds of the game, once again. The teams would meet again in a post season game in Milwaukee with the Packers winning with a 14-0 victory. In 1923, Racine would split the two games against Green Bay. Racine handed the Packers a 24-3 defeat and Green Bay would even the series with a 16-0 defeat of Racine. 1924 would produce the same outcome. Racine was defeated the Packers in Green Bay with a 6-3 thriller. Gillo scored a place kick for field goal but Tillie Voss would make a circus catch of a Packers pass to score the winning touchdown in the fourth quarter of the game. Late in that season, Green Bay would invade Horlicktown (Racine, Wisconsin) and be handed a 7-0 defeat upset in a cold weather game. Since, Racine did not field a professional team for 1925, the teams did not meet. The meeting on Sunday had the Green Bay fans wondering if the Racine Tornadoes would give the same match up as with the past Racine professional teams.

Hank Gillo was reported to be out for the season and possibly for his career because of the broken rib that he suffered in the game against Milwaukee. The veteran fullback was only being used occasionally and he was placed on the disability list with the team. He would no longer practice with the team. Jack Mintun left the team for good as part of the agreement that brought him back for a few games. The Tornadoes picked up a new player. Roy Longstreet, who was 6"1" and a 195 lbs. He would practice with the team and they planned to play him at center against the Packers on Sunday.

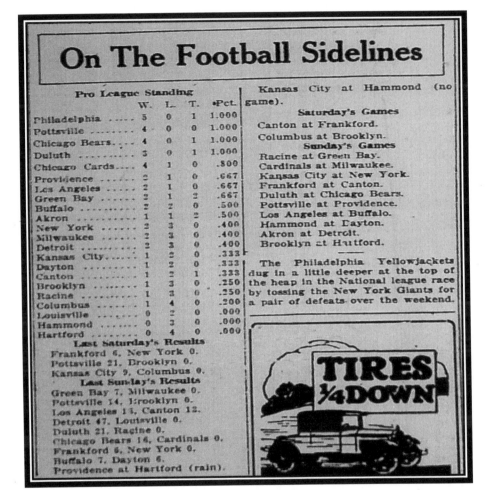

On The Football Sidelines

Pro League Standing

	W.	L.	T.	Pct.
Philadelphia	5	0	1	1.000
Pottsville	4	0	0	1.000
Chicago Bears	4	0	1	1.000
Duluth	3	0	1	1.000
Chicago Cards	4	1	0	.800
Providence	2	1	0	.667
Los Angeles	2	1	2	.667
Green Bay	2	1	2	.667
Buffalo	2	2	1	.500
Akron	1	1	2	.500
New York	2	3	0	.400
Milwaukee	2	3	0	.400
Detroit	2	3	0	.400
Kansas City	1	2	0	.333
Dayton	1	2	0	.333
Canton	1	2	1	.333
Brooklyn	1	3	0	.250
Racine	1	3	0	.250
Columbus	1	4	0	.200
Louisville	0	2	0	.000
Hammond	0	3	0	.000
Hartford	0	4	0	.000

Last Saturday's Results
Frankford 6, New York 0.
Pottsville 21, Brooklyn 0.
Kansas City 9, Columbus 0.
Last Sunday's Results
Green Bay 7, Milwaukee 0.
Pottsville 14, Brooklyn 6.
Los Angeles 13, Canton 12.
Detroit 47, Louisville 0.
Duluth 21, Racine 0.
Chicago Bears 14, Cardinals 0.
Frankford 6, New York 0.
Buffalo 7, Dayton 6.
Providence at Hartford (rain).

Kansas City at Hammond (no game).
Saturday's Games
Canton at Frankford.
Columbus at Brooklyn.
Sunday's Games
Racine at Green Bay.
Cardinals at Milwaukee.
Kansas City at New York.
Frankford at Canton.
Duluth at Chicago Bears.
Pottsville at Providence.
Los Angeles at Buffalo.
Hammond at Dayton.
Akron at Detroit.
Brooklyn at Hartford.

The Philadelphia Yellowjackets dug in a little deeper at the top of the heap in the National league race by tossing the New York Giants for a pair of defeats over the weekend.

The Tornadoes held a Friday evening practice, which was a hard and fast one with the concentration being on the development of new plays. That development took up most of the time. The forward pass was also a feature of the practice. Reichow and Boettcher were doing most of the passing with Mathews, Murphy, and the rest of the ends and backs doing the receiving.

Graham Kernwein did not attend the practice session. Team Manager Johonnott explained that Kernwein had an exam to take and that he was notified long before that practice. He went on to say that Graham would be present at the Green Bay game.

The Racine Tornadoes would travel in private cars to the game and stay at Beaumont Hotel on Saturday night in Green Bay, Wisconsin. The Tornadoes were accompanied by some Racine fans, who left the city of Racine after lunch at noon on Saturday October 23rd, 1926 and headed to Green Bay.

** GAME DAY **

The Green Bay Packers had no trouble in administering a 35-0 defeat of the Racine Tornadoes. The Packers went through the Racine team like a clown through a paper hoop at the circus. With the exception of Bieberstein and Boettcher, who each played an acceptable game, the rest of the team was simply among those who were present at the game. The Tornadoes were outplayed in every aspect of the game and the Racine line held off Green Bay like a row of bottles in front of a steam roller. Green Bay was able to get twenty five first downs, while Racine only had three. The Packers attempted twenty six passes and completed thirteen with one interception. The Tornadoes attempted twelve passes and one was completed and they had a total of three interceptions. There were about 2,600 fans, who attended the game.

PLAY BY PLAY: 1926 NFL SEASON RT GAME 5
RACINE TORNADOES VS GREEN BAY PACKERS
Sunday: October 24th, 1926   2:30 pm
City Stadium   Green Bay, Wisconsin

FIRST QUARTER:

Gardner kicked off for the Packers. The ball went rolling over the goal line and into the end zone. Racine took possession of the ball at the 20 yard line of the Tornadoes. Kernwein went back to punt the ball on first down but the snap from the center was poor and the kick was blocked. Green Bay recovered the ball on the Racine 20 yard line. On first down, Basing ran the ball through the left guard and it resulted in a 3 yard gain. McAuliffe ran the ball and circled around the right end for a gain of 2 yards. A short pass from McAuliffe to Flaherty was advanced across the goal line for a Green Bay touchdown. Purdy drop kicked a successful point after touchdown. *Score: Racine 0, Green Bay 7.* Gardner kicked off the ball for the Packers. Sterr received the ball for the Tornadoes on the 20 yard line and he advanced it to the 30 yard line of Racine. Kerwein ran the ball around the right end and it resulted in a 1 yard gain. McIllwain ran the ball through the left tackle and it resulted in a 5 yard gain. McIllwain ran the ball through the right tackle and it resulted in a **5 yard gain** and a Racine first down. The Packers intercepted a Tornadoes pass and advanced the ball to the Racine 20 yard line. Kotel ran the ball for a Green Bay gain. Basing was able to run the ball over the goal line and in the end zone for a touchdown. Purdy successfully kicked the point after touchdown. _Score: Racine 0, Green bay 14_. There was no more scoring during remainder of the quarter. The Packers had the ball in Racine territory at this point and continued to threaten to score. A Green Bay fumble on the 20 yard line was recovered by the Tornadoes. Reichow punted the ball to get the Packers into their own territory but it wasn't long before they were back on the Tornadoes 20 yard line. In this quarter, Kernwein was taken out the game because of badly slashed lip injury. His absence during the remainder of the game left Racine without the services of a good punter and hurt them because he was also one of their best halfbacks. End of quarter.

SECOND QUARTER:
A pass from McAuliffe to Kotel was completed over the goal line and they scored another touchdown for the Packers. Woodin kicked a successful extra point. _Score: Racine 0, Green bay 21_. During the remainder of this quarter, the Tornadoes were fighting off the rushing attack of Green Bay with their back against their own goal line. On one series, the Packers advanced the ball down to the Tornadoes 1 yard line. Racine held off the Packers and they were able to get the ball back on downs. The ball was on the Tornadoes 6 yard line as the quarter ended.

THIRD QUARTER:
The Packers sent Rex Enright (Notre Dame) in the game at the fullback position and Jack Harrison (University of Wisconsin), from Racine, Wisconsin into the game to play at the end position. Harris caught several passes, while Enright repeatedly ripped through the Racine line to keep the ball down in Tornadoes territory. This was the only quarter that Green Bay did not score.

FOURTH QUARTER:
Harris would caught long passes and score two touchdowns in this quarter. The ball was on the Racine 5 yard line. On the second play, Harris ran the ball through the left tackle and scored another touchdown for the Packers. Purdy successfully kicked the point after touchdown. _Score: Racine 0, Green bay 28_. After the Packers took possession of the ball again, Sterr was able to intercept a Green Bay pass on the 50 yard line. The Tornadoes attempted to pass the ball on every play but the Packers seemed to break up each attempt. Green Bay would again take possession of the ball and get into Racine territory. The time keeper was ready to end the game. Enright was able to plow through the Tornadoes line for three consecutive times and it resulted in a 25 yard gain. The ball was on the Racine 1 yard line. Harris ran the ball smashing through the left tackle and scored the final touchdown of the game. Purdy successfully kicked the point after touchdown. _Score: Racine 0, Green bay 35_. The game ended.

FINAL SCORE: RACINE TORNADOES 0, GREENBAY PACKERS 3

SCORE BY PERIODS:

	1st	2nd	3rd	4th	Final
Racine Tornadoes	0	0	0	0	0
Green Bay Packers	14	7	0	14	35

TOUCHDOWNS: Green Bay- Gardner (1) Flaherty (1) Kotel (1) Harris (2)
EXTRA POINT: Green Bay- Purdy, drop kick (3) Woodin (1)

STARTING ROSTER:

RACINE		GREEN BAY
Fahey	Left End	Harris
Hardy	Left Tackle	Cahoon
Bieberstein	Left Guard	Woodin
Longstreet	Center	Earp
Bernard	Right Guard	Gardner
Hodscheid	Right Tackle	Rosatti
Mathews	Right End	Flaherty
Sterr	Quarterback	Purdy
McIllwain	Left Halfback	Kotal
Kernwein	Right Halfback	McAuliffe
Reichow	Fullback	Basing

SUBSTITUTIONS: RACINE- Murphy for Mathews, Brumm for Bernard, Boettcher for Kernwein, Oldham for Boettcher. GREEN BAY- Jean for Rosatti, Mathys for Purdy, Cyre for Jean, Jean for Earpe, Lambeau for Kotal, Purdy for Mathys, Gardner for Woodin, Enright for Basing, Kotal for Lambeau, Basing for McAuliffe, Lewellen for Kotal, Woodin for Carlson.

The loss was devastating to the Racine Tornadoes. Not only did the team suffer a large defeat, but the fate of the Racine Tornadoes professional football team hung in the balance. The officials of the team held a meeting on Monday evening October 25th, 1926 to discuss the possibility of dropping, the remaining games on the 1926 Racine Tornadoes NFL schedule. The organization was facing a deficit because of the inability to draw well at their home games. The largest crowd of the season was 2,600 fans, who witnessed the game against the Duluth Eskimos and it was an expensive game to host. Another meeting was planned for Tuesday October 26th, 1926 to decide, if they would drop out of the league to avoid any further deficit. A game was scheduled to be played in Racine, Wisconsin at Horlick Athletic Field against the Louisville Colonels on Sunday October 31st, 1926.

An announcement was made on Wednesday October 27th, 1926 by George "Babe" Ruetz, president of the Racine Fan Athletic Association that the Racine Tornadoes was offered for sale and negotiations would take place with a Chicago group, who wanted to purchase the team on Thursday. Ruetz said; *"This means the end of pro football in Racine, at least as far as the National League goes."* George went on to *say, "After dropping out one year, we had plenty of difficulty getting the franchise for this year and would stand a very slim chance of even getting another after we have again given up the ship." "A pro football team cannot be operated with the amount of support received by the club here this season. Fans clamored for the game, when we were not represented in the League, but only a minority actually contributed to its support when we finally assembled a team and tried to give the public what it wanted."*

George Pendall, president of the American Business Club of Racine, Wisconsin had this to say; *"We are faced with a deficit that the sale of the Franchise will hardly clear up. But we hope to see that the creditors receive all that they have coming."*

The game against Louisville, which was set to be played at Horlick Athletic Field on Sunday October 31st, 1926 was definitely cancelled but scheduled games still remained with Milwaukee, Green Bay and Dayton as opponents. Ruetz wrote to the manager of the Colonels and the game was called off by mutual consent, as it was figured that the game would not be a drawing card. Tornadoes Manager Johonnott had this to say; *"Whether we keep the football team or not is as much of mystery to you as it is to me." "The club has held no meeting in regard to the matter and nothing can be done until several important deals that are hanging in the fire are decided. We should definitely know in a day or two what the fate of the local outfit will be."*

There was a hope that someone would buy the franchise and continue to operate it in Racine, Wisconsin. Anyone purchasing the team would have to complete the 1926 NFL schedule in order to be able to obtain the franchise for the following year. National Football League rules stated that to hold a franchise, a club must play all games on the schedule unless a cancellation can be brought about by mutual agreement between the clubs involved. Contracts of the players would stay with the team, when it was sold. Professional football was one of the most rapidly growing sports in America in 1926 and many agreed that pro football was destined to become one of the major sports of the fall season. It was also believed that the gridiron sports league would find itself on the same level as baseball.

The information was brought out that there were Chicago men, who wanted to purchase the team and they were planning to move the franchise to Indianapolis. The Racine Tornadoes were in debt for between $800 and $1,000.

GRID FRANCHISE IS SOLD

On Wednesday November 3rd, 1926, George "Babe" Ruetz announced that the NFL Racine Tornadoes franchise had been sold. He said that the deal had been completed but he had no further information to offer. The deal was believed to be closed over long distance telephone. Ruetz explained that there would be Chicago men coming to

Racine, Wisconsin on Thursday October 4th, 1926 in order to sign the papers for the purchase of the franchise. George declared that the new owners met his terms in regard to the sale of the club rights but that the Racine Fan Athletic Association would be left with a small deficit after the sale. Fred Ahlgrimm, who was a Racine lawyer was retained to draw up the Articles of Incorporation for the new organization. It was stated that the Racine Fan Athletic Association would definitely go out of existence after making up any deficit that still existed. The new club would be known as the Racine Tornadoes Athletic Association. When asked, Attorney Ahlgrimm had this to say about the question, if he could give any information about the sale of the Racine Tornadoes. He said; *"No, I am not at liberty to tell who the new purchasers of the club are but I will say this: the team will continue here and will play out its schedule. Then, if Racine shows a reasonable support towards the pro game, I might even go as far to state that the franchise will be kept right here another year."* It was believed that the one of the "Prime Movers", who was involved with the purchase of the franchise, was a man, who was well known in the league circles and he managed another club a year or so ago. He would be the manager of the Tornadoes. It was further reported that the new management would keep four or five of the current players but the remainder of the squad would be made up of prominent performers brought in by the organization, who purchased the franchise.

The Racine Tornadoes were supposed to host the Green Bay Packers in Racine on the upcoming Sunday.

An announcement was finally made that the "mysterious Chicago interest" in the team was Ambrose McGurk. McGurk, who previously was the owner of the NFL Milwaukee Badgers but was forced to sell his team after he was caught violating NFL rules regarding players, which he used in a game against the Chicago Cardinals. NFL President Joe Carr conducted an investigation and determined that Ambrose violated League rules. He ordered him to sell his franchise. Ambrose was permanently banned from the league after the sale of the Milwaukee franchise. McGurk later told Ruetz that he decided rather suddenly that he did not want the franchise. It was more likely that Carr found out that he was attempting to purchase the team. NFL President Carr would have been against the sale to him for two reasons; one was related to the McGurk being banned from the league, which was later lifted. The other reason was that McGurk planned to use stars from the defunct Cleveland club but he was soon to find out that some of them were ineligible to play in the NFL. With all this against him, Ambrose McGurk, who was represented by a local Racine, Wisconsin attorney decided to pull up stakes on the purchase of the Racine Tornadoes. Ruetz said that he had received a wire from the president of the National Football League and it was asking him, whether the Racine franchise had been sold or not? The wire said nothing about McGurk, according to George. The officials of the Racine Tornadoes organization said that they understood that Ambrose McGurk was the person representing the Chicago interest, who wanted to buy the Franchise. They expressed that they were under the impression McGurk did not intend to run or own the club himself.

The Racine Tornadoes needed to play their game Sunday. It was a scheduled game and the $1,500, which was paid to the NFL as forfeiture would be lost, if they did not play. George Ruetz announced on Friday November 12th, 1926 that the game with the Green Bay Packers had been cancelled. Ruetz declared that arrangements had been made with Green Bay, whereby this week's game was "cancelled" and Green Bay has completed plans to play Louisville. Further efforts were being made to cancel the other two remaining games and Ruetz was confident this would happen. Reports that Bieberstein's contract had been sold to Green Bay were denied by Ruetz. He said that the Packers asked for Bieberstein but that nothing had been done in the matter.

Racine was experiencing snow and zero weather temperatures. The snow and frozen condition of the field would make playing nearly impossible and keep the fans away from the game. It was pointed out that if snow and ice melted in time for the game, it would leave the gridiron (field) a sea of mud, anyway.

The Racine newspapers reported this view of the Racine professional football situation: *Professional football had proved a losing proposition in Racine, Wisconsin from the beginning. The crowds at the game were mere handfuls of the number that should been attending for a city of its size and the losses of team as of recent made it worse. The American Business Club of Racine, Wisconsin put forth the effort in an attempt to give professional football to the fans of Racine. It seemed that the interest was not there after the club worked long and hard as well as spent money on the proposition. They deserve a great deal of credit for their effort.*

Tex Reynolds, a Racine newspaper journalist, who appeared as "On the Sport Trail with "Tex" Reynolds" wrote the following in his column of the 1926 Racine Times Call newspaper: *How vividly those immortal lines are recalled to the minds of Racine football fans nowadays when they pick up newspapers and read headlines similar to these:*

"Johnny Mohardt stars for Chicago Bulls"

"Milton Romney plays stellar role at quarterback for the Bears"

"Don Murry, regular with the Bears, rated on a par with any Tackle in the National Pro League"

In 1924, the above players and several others of note were members of the Racine professional team. Then, came the Legion's decision to drop out of the League for the year 1925. And all of these star players were released without provision. So they became property of other clubs, and when pro football came movement was started this spring, the local club was faced with the necessity of building an entirely new team.

What a difference it would have made if strings had been kept on Mohardt, Romney and Murry! What a swell nucleus this would have been around, which to build the 1926 eleven.

Yes, it might have been.

The Racine Fan Athletic Association was still in possession of their NFL franchise as of Thursday November 11th, 1926 and Ruetz stated that there was a meeting of the National Football League in New York that was set for early next year. He also said, at that time, the franchise would be disposed of, providing that the cancellation of the Tornadoes 1926 remaining games was completed.

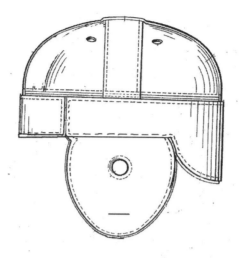

www.RacineLegion.com

After Word

There was an NFL League meeting, which was held in New York, New York at the Astor Hotel on February 5th and 6th of 1927. At that time, the owners of the Racine Tornadoes franchise were given the option of either fielding a team for the 1927 NFL season or forfeit their franchise to the League. The Racine Tornadoes had disbanded. The Racine, Wisconsin NFL franchise was forfeited back to the National Football League.

George "Babe" Ruetz passed away on Tuesday May 24th, 1927 at the age of 33 years old.

William Horlick, Sr. died on Friday September 25th, 1936 at the age of 90 years old.

George G. Ruetz

William Horlick, Sr.

Henry Charles Gillo (above) passed away on Monday September 6th, 1948 at the age of 53 years old.

The following are quotes that were made by George Halas and Curly Lambeau after the death of Hank Gillo:

George Halas (Chicago Bears) said;

"Gillo would stack up with the great fullbacks-Nagurski, Hinkle, Battles. What a line plunger that fellow was! He'd bow that back of his and plow in and keep his knees churning. Hard to stop. And I speak from experience because I tried to tackle him more than once. And he was a terrific placekicker too." Beat us one year 3-0."

Curly Lambeau (Green Bay Packers) said;

"He was the same type of player as Ernie Nevers. A hard runner and a great line bucker. No matter what you did, you couldn't stop him short of two or three yards. He just bowled em over. "

The following is a quote made by Wallace "Shorty" Barr (Horlick-Racine Legion quarterback) regarding the playing technique of Hank Gillo:

Wallace Barr (Legion quarterback) said;

"Gillo had it on Joesting and Manders. Nagurski was a different type. Hank drove in very low and went lower just before he hit. Then he would come up. Lots of times, his head would come up under a tacklers chin and just about knock the player out. He was one of the best, all right!

George G. Ruetz obituary

Babe Ruetz, Best Friend of Clean Sport, Dies Here

GEORGE RUETZ

Was Well Known Young Businessman and Promoter of Baseball and Football

George G. (Babe) Ruetz, 33, young Racine businessman who attained wide prominence as a promoter of sports here, died Tuesday night at his home, 1407 Superior street. Death came suddenly as a climax to months of illness, during which time he spent several weeks at a northern Wisconsin sanitarium and later at St. Mary's hospital. Until recently he was able to retain charge of the grocery business which he had conducted for the last six years.

George Ruetz was born in Racine, Sept. 23, 1893, the son of Mr. and Mrs. Peter Ruetz. He attended St. Frederick's and the Racine high school, later taking a course in a local business college. He was employed in the general offices of the Mitchell Motors company for several years.

Served in War

When the United States entered the World war, Ruetz joined the army and was sent to Camp Hancock, Ga., July 6, 1918. At camp he took an active part in athletics, was appointed instructor, and managed and played on football and baseball teams. After his discharge on March 15, 1919, "Babe" returned to Racine and opened a grocery store.

Ruetz started his football career with the old Racine Regulars in 1911. He was prominent as a member of that eleven until 1917, when the Battery C team, (first Racine professional club) was organized.

After the war, the professional league movement began to gain headway, and "Babe" was instrumental in getting Racine a berth as associate member of the national circuit in 1920. The next year, this city obtained a regular franchise and Ruetz managed the team that put Racine in the national limelight. For three years he piloted the Legion eleven, retiring in 1924. The following year, Racine dropped out of the circuit, and there was no professional football here in 1925. But in 1926 there was a renewed demand for a team and again it was "Babe" who was called upon to help put the game back on its feet. He was named president of the Racine Fans' association, which backed the project and was a prime mover in assembling the eleven that played under the name, "Racine Tornadoes."

Backed Baseball, Too

But while Ruetz was best known as the "father of professional football" in Racine, the gridiron sport was not alone in occupying his attention. He was one of the incorporators of the baseball club here in 1925, and acted as secretary, working many weeks on the project and serving without remuneration.

As one of the first delegates to attend a meeting of the National Professional Football league, "Babe" was active in its organization and proposed several of the measures which now control the circuit—an organization governing a sport that has grown rapidly in recent years.

He was known in the sporting world as a "square shooter", and throughout this section of the country the name "Ruetz" was synonymous with Racine athletics.

Ruetz was an active member of the Racine American Legion post, Elks, Eagles and Knights of Columbus. He was also a member of St. Patrick's Catholic church.

He is survived by his wife, a son, George, Jr.; his parents, Mr. and Mrs. Peter Ruetz; one sister, Miss Emily Ruetz; and five brothers, Clarence, Edward, Paul, Jerome and Lawrence.

The funeral services will be held Friday at 8:30 a. m. from the Krug Funeral home, on Lincoln street and at 9 a. m. from the St. Patrick's Catholic church. Burial will be in the Catholic cemetery.

Article written about George G. Ruetz after his death.
By Tex Reynolds

Death Crosses Goal Line Of George (Babe) Ruetz

Prominent in Athletics Here for Many Years, and Known as Father of Racine Pro Football—Hundreds Pay Tribute as His Passing Becomes Known

BY TEX REYNOLDS

Death, that unbeatable foe, last night crossed the last goal line of George (Babe) Ruetz, taking a man who had been prominent in athletics here for a decade, "father of professional football" in Racine and identified with progress of the National Pro league from its infancy.

For months "Babe" had been waging a losing battle with ill health. He spent several weeks in a sanitarium last winter, returning to his home apparently somewhat improved. But his condition later grew worse and he was taken to St. Mary's hospital, again improving sufficiently to return home, where death suddenly overtook him last night.

Many Pay Tribute to Ruetz

Prominent men in the city today paid tribute to Ruetz. Known as a "square shooter" and a tireless worker, he spent months working in the interests of Racine sports without profit to himself. Assuming responsibilities and labors when others hesitated, he played a major part in putting this city on the national football map, and he did it when at times his support wavered. But "Babe" was not alone interested in football, and was always ready to lend a helping hand in any movement for the good of Racine. He was one of the incorporators of the baseball club here in 1925, when things looked dubious, and it began to appear as though this city would be without a team. And he put in many hours of work on the proposition without a nickel of remuneration for himself.

Ruetz was a star player in his time, and he picked up his knowledge of football without the aid of college coaches. "Babe" started with the old Racine Regulars back in 1911, playing guard. This team was in existence until 1917, when the Battery C eleven, first pro crew in Racine history, was organized by Fred Maxted.

Starred on Army Eleven in Georgia

Later Ruetz entered the army and was sent to Camp Hancock, Ga., where he was one of the outstanding players on the army team. Weighing between 260 and 270 pounds, he was a bulwark of strength in the forward wall and pronounced by nationally-known players at the army camp as one of the best linemen they had ever seen in action.

Returning from the army, and becoming one of the first members of the Racine American Legion post, "Babe" was one of the organizers of the first Racine pro league team in 1920. Racine was an associate member of the league that year, but in 1921 was given a regular franchise and became one of the strongest clubs in the circuit.

Ruetz managed the team in 1922 and 23, retiring in the latter year while the club was run by Manager L. A. McDowell. The next year, Racine dropped out and the Legion team disbanded.

In 1926 there was a demand for a professional team here, and "Babe" got behind a movement which ended with the Racine Fans' association being organized and a club put in the field.

Prominent in National League Councils

One of the first delegates to sit in a meeting of the new national football circuit, Ruetz was one of its active members and several of the measures later adopted by the fast-growing and now popular league are the results of his efforts. President Joe Carr, a close personal friend of the Racine man, has given "Babe" credit for being one of those largely instrumental in the success of professional football from its small beginning.

Racine owes a debt to George Ruetz which can now be paid only in the tribute which is his honest due.

333

William Horlick, Sr. Obituary

Feb. 23, 1846 --- William Horlick --- Sept. 25, 1936

This is a recent photograph of William Horlick, who died at his home here Friday morning.

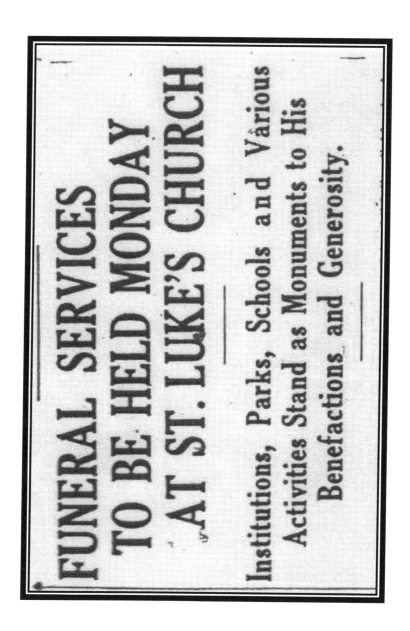

FUNERAL SERVICES
TO BE HELD MONDAY
AT ST. LUKE'S CHURCH

Institutions, Parks, Schools and Various Activities Stand as Monuments to His Benefactions and Generosity.

William Horlick, Sr. obituary continued 2

Gave Freely to City.

Mr. Horlick presented to the city the 11 acres of land which form the site on which the Horlick high school was built and six additional acres to provide for an athletic field for the school.

His most recent gift to the city, and one of the most outstanding, is Horlick Athletic field to be used for the promotion of athletic sports in which he always took a keen interest, at one time having been quite an expert in cricket. His original gift to the Racine park system of Island park and assistance in securing Washington park for the public, has made Racine's extensive park system possible.

He always took great interest in young boys. He was appointed an honorary vice president of the Racine Council of Boy Scouts of America, in appreciation of his interest and gifts, among which latter was a handsome library room and staff headquarters for Scout leaders.

The monument and large lot in Graceland cemetery of the American Legion, Post 76, are other gifts by Mr. Horlick.

Contributor to Science.

Mr. Horlick gave freely in the cause of science. The rank of Knighthood in the Royal Norwegian Order of St. Olaf was conferred upon him by King Haakon of Norway in 1922 in recognition of assistance given by him to Norwegian expeditions, particularly the polar explorations of Capt. Roald Amundsen and the scientific expeditions of Dr. Carl Lumholz.

The seaplane with which Admiral Richard Byrd explored the previously unknown regions of the Antarctic was christened the "William Horlick" in appreciation of the assistance rendered by Mr. Horlick to the Byrd expeditions. Mr. Horlick had long been a close personal friend of Admiral Byrd as he was also of Capt. Roald Amundsen.

Mr. Horlick was the first honorary life member of the Order of Sons of St. George and a member of the Union League clubs of New York and Chicago and of the Milwaukee club.

Married in Racine.

His marriage in this city to Miss Arabella R. Horlick was solemnized Nov. 16, 1870.

Surviving are his widow, two sons, A. J. Horlick and William Horlick Jr.; one daughter, Mrs. Mabelle Horlick Sidley, all of Racine; a grandson, William Horlick Sidley, of Racine; two granddaughters, Mrs. Helen Horlick Bond and Mrs. Jeannette Horlick Simmons of Greenwich, Conn.; a great grandson, James Bond, and two great granddaughters, Jeannette and Patricia Simmons.

Funeral Services Monday.

There will be private funeral services Monday forenoon at the residence for members of the family. Public services will be held in St. Luke's Episcopal church at 2 p. m. Monday and an opportunity will be given all those who desire to view the remains at the church from noon until 2 p. m.

Bishop Harwood Sturtevant, Fond du Lac, will officiate and he will be assisted by Dean Henry W. Roth, Milwaukee. Burial will be in Mound cemetery.

Pallbearers will be selected from the older employes of the office and the plant.

William Horlick, Sr. obituary continued 3

William Horlick, president of the Horlick Malted Milk corporation, whose death occurred at 8:15 a. m. Friday at his residence on Northwestern avenue, charted his life's voyage along the lines of the morning prayer and benediction by Bishop Vincent and which constantly was before him on his desk.

"I will try this day," reads the prayer, "to live a simple, sincere and serene life, expelling every thought of discontent, self-seeking and anxiety; cultivate magnanimity, self-control and the habit of silence; practicing economy, cheerfulness and helpfulness. And as I cannot on my own strength do this, or even with a hope of success attempt it, I look to Thee, O Lord my Father in Jesus Christ, my Savior, and ask for the gift of the Holy Spirit."

Mr. Horlick was born in Gloustershire, Eng., Feb. 23, 1846, the son of James and Priscilla Horlick.

Educated in England.

Mr. Horlick grew to manhood in England and received his education there. He came to the United States in 1869, becoming naturalized a few years later. He began the manufacture of food products in Chicago in 1873, with his brother, James. The business later was moved to this city, the small frame building in which it was begun and which still stands being occupied in 1875.

It was in that small building Mr. Horlick began the production of his malted food products and which institution, as a result of his origination and discovery of Horlick's malted milk, has developed into one of Racine's outstanding and most stable industries and which has carried the name of Horlick to every corner of the earth.

In order to care for the constantly increasing foreign trade Mr. Horlick caused to be erected a branch establishment in England, selecting a site at Slough, near Windsor, where is operating today another outstanding industry for the production of Horlick's malted milk. The plan of architecture of that plant follows the Old English style of the original Racine plant with its square towers.

Mr. Horlick continued as head of this great institution from its inception until the time of his death.

Benefit to Communities.

Not only have the city and farming districts of the community in which he lived benefited from the success of a successful business, but his personal benefactions throughout the years have indicated his desire to have his fellowmen enjoy fully the fruits of his successful career.

Mr. Horlick was a lifelong member and supporter of St. Luke's Episcopal church of which he long was a warden. The site on which the parish house is located was a gift to that congregation.

That gift was only one of his many benefactions. Among them were the Alice Horlick Memorial hospital and the Alice Horlick Maternity hospital, two units of St. Luke's hospital. Others were the Horlick refectory, the addition to the Western Theological seminary at Evanston, Ill., a large subscription to the Y. M. C. A., and a generous contribution to the fund which helped build Memorial hall.

Mr. Horlick also was a liberal supporter of the Grand Army of the Republic and of the Spanish-American War Veterans.

His benefactions included also gifts to St. Mary's hospital and various other institutions of the city.

337

Henry Charles Gillo
May 1920

Henry Charles Gillo article, in regards to his death notice, from the Milwaukee Journal on September 8th, 1948.

Maybe I'm Wrong

By R. G. LYNCH
(Sports Editor)

Gillo, One of Greatest, Came Along Too Soon

JUST seven lines of type went over the Associated Press wires to inform the nation that Hank Gillo had died. This is not written as a criticism of the AP but to emphasize the fickleness of fame, for Gillo was one of the greatest football players who ever drew on a cleated shoe; he simply had the misfortune to reach his collegiate heyday while sports were curtailed in the first World war and to achieve professional stardom before the play for pay sport grew up.

Football history dismisses Gillo with mere mention as one of Colgate's all-time greats and as a third string halfback on the all-American team of 1919. Yet. no less a gridiron light than George Halas. coach and owner of the Chicago Bears, told the writer Tuesday:

"Gillo would stack up with the great fullbacks—Nagurski, Hinkle. Battles. What a line plunger that fellow was! He'd bow that back of his and plow in and keep his knees churning. Hard to stop, and I speak from experience because I tried to tackle him more than once. And he was a terrific place kicker, too. Beat us one year, 3-0."

And Curly Lambeau of the Green Bay Packers said, "He was the same type of player as Ernie Nevers, a hard runner and a great line bucker. No matter what you did you couldn't stop him short of two or three yards. He just bowled 'em over."

The Line Bulged

BOTH Halas and Lambeau should remember Gillo, for Hank was the mainstay of the Racine Legion team in the early days of the National league and both of them played against him. We recall a game in Chicago against the original Bear line-up operated by the firm of Halas. Stincomb & Sternaman. The Bears had a great line. When Gillo hit it — and he carried into the line time and again that day—he would come to a stop, but his legs would be going up and down. Then the line would budge at the rear and out would come Hank. carrying two or three men. Once he kept on churning away for 30 yards with his head down, unaware that he was in the clear, until most of the Bear team caught up with him and bore him down

Shorty Barr, who quarterbacked the Racine team, once said:

"Gillo had it on Joesting and Manders. Nagurski was a different type. Hank drove in very low and went lower just before he hit. Then he would come up. Lots of times his head would come up under a tackler's chin and just about knock the player out. He was one of the best, all right!"

339

Henry Charles Gillo article-Milwaukee Journal September 8ᵗʰ, 1948- continued.

What a Kicker!

GILLO'S name does not appear in the list of great field goal kickers, but he was among the greatest of drop kickers and place kickers. Apparently, he did not demonstrate this prowess in college as he had in high school and did later as a pro.

As a high school boy, he kicked a 53 yard field goal. Charley Kahle, former East Division coach, tells about it:

"Gillo seldom used to punt at any time. He drop kicked. Against Oshkosh high school, he kicked what I think is the longest drop kick on record in Milwaukee. Standing on his own 47 yard line, 53 yards from the goal posts, he put the ball through the uprights."

Hank turned from the drop kick to the place kick in his pro days. Nowadays, much ado is made over a goal made from anywhere near mid-field. Such kicks were commonplace for Gillo. The writer saw him beat Akron, Ohio, at Racine by kicking goals from 50, 45 and 30 yards out. Barr tells of holding the ball when Gillo put it between the uprights from 48 and 50 yards out.

Some years ago we asked Gillo what his longest field goal was and he said it was a 56 yard place kick against the Green Bay Packers at Borchert field, when it was called Athletic park.

If the old South Division star had come along 20 years later, he might have spent most of his time on the bench as a pro, for he was just about as deadly on points after touchdown as Automatic Jack Manders. In Hank's time, kicking extra points was an incidental chore. In Manders' day, it was a specialists' job.

Hank Gillo Fact Sheet

Henry Charles Gillo
Born: October 5th, 1894 Milwaukee, Wisconsin
Died: September 6th, 1948 Manchester Township, Wisconsin
Height: 5' 10" Weight: 195 lbs.
College: Colgate University

Professional Football Career
Positions: Coach, Captain, Fullback, Kicker, Quarterback
Nicknames: "Line Plunging Hank" "Gillobird"

Player information

League	Year	Team	Ttl Game	Starts	Position	Ttl Pts
APFA	1920	Hammond Pros	7	3	Fullback	
APFA	1921	Hammond Pros	1	1	Fullback	
Indep.	1921	Racine Legion	2*	2*	FB/Kicker/Quarterback	
NFL	1922	Horlick-Racine Legion	11	10	Fullback/Kicker	52
NFL	1923	Horlick-Racine Legion	10	10	Fullback/Kicker	44
NFL	1924	Horlick-Racine Legion	10	9	Fullback/Kicker	48
NFL	1925	Milwaukee Badgers	2	0	Fullback	
NFL	1926	Racine Tornadoes	4	0	Fullback/Kicker	

*=Total game information is incomplete.

NFL Records

Record		1922	Team
Rushing Touchdowns	5	3rd National Football League	HRL
Field Goals	6	2nd National Football League	HRL
Total Points League	52	1st National Football League	HRL
		1923	
Extra Points	8	2nd National Football League	HRL
Field Goals	8	3rd National Football League	HRL
Total Points League	44	4th National Football League	HRL
Longest Field Goal	50 yd	1st National Football League	HRL
		1924	
Field Goals	8	2nd National Football League	HRL
Total Points League	48	4th National Football League	HRL

Awards

Year	No./Rank	NFL Record/All Star team name	Team
1922/23	3	Most Field Goals in a Game	HRL
1923	First Team	Collyer's All Star Pro Elevens Selection	HRL
1924	7	Most Consecutive Games w-Field Goal	HRL
1924	Third Team	Calhoun's Eleven All-Pro Team Selection	HRL

341

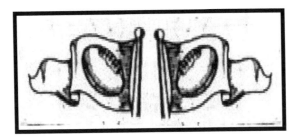

The following individuals have been nominated to the Pro Football Hall of Fame in Canton, Ohio by Matthew C. Snyder:

1. William Horlick, Sr. as owner (co-owner) of the Horlick-Racine Legion NFL 1922 1923 1924 for the category of Contributor-Team owner

2. George G. "Babe" Ruetz as NFL scheduling committee NFL 1922 1923, Team Manager of Horlick of the Horlick-Racine Legion 1922 1923, and owner (co-owner) of the Racine Tornadoes NFL 1926 for the category of Contributor-Team administrator.

3. Henry Charles Gillo as coach/player (fullback/kicker) Hammond Pros APFA 1920 1921, coach/player (quarterback/fullback/kicker) Independent Racine Legion 1921, coach/team captain/player (fullback/kicker) Horlick-Racine Legion NFL 1922 1923 1924, player (fullback) Milwaukee Badgers NFL 1925, coach/player (fullback/kicker) Racine Tornadoes NFL 1926 for the category of Player-Fullback.

"Preserve the History"
-Matthew C. Snyder

About the Author

Matthew C. Snyder is a lifelong resident of Racine, Wisconsin. His education consists of the following; 1987 graduate of St. Catherine's High School- Racine, Wisconsin and a 1992 graduate of the University of Wisconsin- Parkside- Kenosha, Wisconsin. Matthew is married and he has three children. Snyder is the owner of the Racine Legion Football Club and he is a board member of the United States Football Federation.

The above logos are protected by Trademark laws and may not be reproduced

343

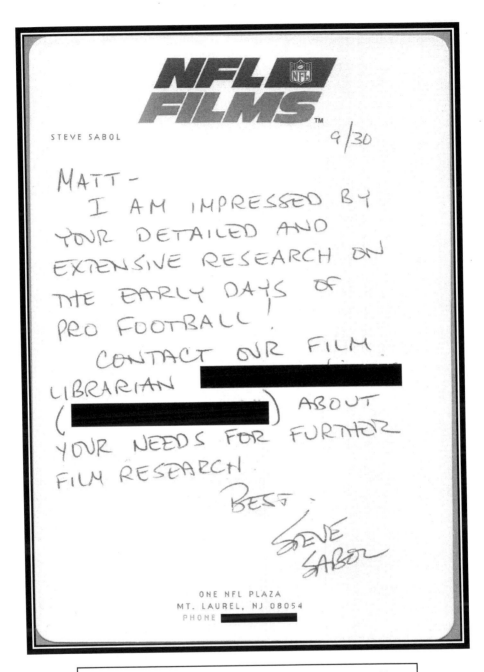

NFL FILMS™

STEVE SABOL   9/30

MATT —
    I AM IMPRESSED BY
YOUR DETAILED AND
EXTENSIVE RESEARCH ON
THE EARLY DAYS OF
PRO FOOTBALL!
    CONTACT OUR FILM
LIBRARIAN ▮▮▮▮▮▮▮▮▮▮▮
(▮▮▮▮▮▮▮▮▮▮) ABOUT
YOUR NEEDS FOR FURTHER
FILM RESEARCH.
                    BEST,
                    STEVE
                    SABOL

ONE NFL PLAZA
MT. LAUREL, NJ 08054
PHONE ▮▮▮▮▮▮▮▮▮

Letter to Matthew C. Snyder from Steve Sabol of NFL films.

344

Game Results

Records

Year	Team	Record (W-L-T)
1922	Horlick-Racine Legion	6-4-1
1923	Horlick-Racine Legion	4-3-2
1924	Horlick-Racine Legion	4-3-3
1925	Racine Legion	*Did Not Play/Suspended operations*
1926	Racine Tornadoes	1-4-0

Racine, Wisconsin NFL franchise season schedule/results

1922 Game/Final Score/Location

Game 1-HORLICK-RACINE LEGION 0 VS CHICAGO BEARS 6
Sunday: October 1st, 1922   2:30 pm   Horlick Athletic Field   Racine, Wisconsin

Game 2-HORLICK-RACINE LEGION 10 VS GREEN BAY PACKERS 6
Sunday: October 8th, 1922   2:30 pm   Hagemeister Park   Green Bay, Wisconsin

Game 3-HORLICK-RACINE LEGION 0 VS MILWAUKEE BADGERS 20
Sunday: October 15th, 1922   2:30 pm   Athletic Park   Milwaukee, Wisconsin

Game 4-HORLICK-RACINE LEGION 0 VS TOLEDO MAROONS 7
Sunday: October 22nd, 1922   2:30 pm   Horlick Athletic Field   Racine, Wisconsin

Game 5-HORLICK-RACINE LEGION 9 VS ROCHESTER (NY.)JEFFERSONS 0
Sunday: October 29th, 1922   2:30 pm   Horlick Athletic Field   Racine, Wisconsin

Game 6-HORLICK-RACINE LEGION 57 VS LOUISVILLE COLONELS 0
Sunday: November 5th, 1922   2:30 pm   Horlick Athletic Field   Racine, Wisconsin

Game 7-HORLICK-RACINE LEGION 26 VS COLUMBUS PANHANDLES 6
Saturday: November 11th, 1922   2:30 pm   Horlick Athletic Field Racine, Wisconsin

Game 8-HORLICK-RACINE LEGION 3 VS GREEN BAY PACKERS 3
Sunday: November 19th, 1922   2:15 pm   Horlick Athletic Field   Racine, Wisconsin

Game 9-HORLICK-RACINE LEGION 6 VS HAMMOND PROS 0
Sunday: November 26th, 1922   2:15 pm   Horlick Athletic Field   Racine, Wisconsin

Game 10-HORLICK-RACINE LEGION 3 VS MILWAUKEE BADGERS 0
Thursday: November 30th, 1922   2:15 pm   Horlick Athletic Field Racine, Wisconsin

Game 11-HORLICK-RACINE LEGION 3 VS GREEN BAY PACKERS 0
Sunday: December 3rd, 1922   2:15 pm   Athletic Park   Milwaukee, Wisconsin

1923 Game/Final Score/Location

Game 1-HORLICK-RACINE LEGION 7 VS TOLEDO MAROONS 7
Sunday: September 30th, 1923   2:30 pm   Horlick Athletic Field   Racine, Wisconsin

Game 2-HORLICK-RACINE LEGION 0 VS CHICAGO BEARS 3
Sunday: October 7th, 1923   2:30 pm   Horlick Athletic Field   Racine, Wisconsin

Game 3-HORLICK-RACINE LEGION 7 VS MILWAUKEE BADGERS 7
Sunday: October 14th, 1922   2:30 pm   American Association Baseball Park
Milwaukee, Wisconsin

Game 4-HORLICK-RACINE LEGION 9 VS AKRON PROS 7
Sunday: October 21st, 1923   2:30 pm   Horlick Athletic Field   Racine, Wisconsin

Game 5-HORLICK-RACINE LEGION 24 VS GREEN BAY PACKERS 3
Sunday: October 25th, 1923   2:30 pm   Bellevue Park   Green Bay, Wisconsin

Game 6-HORLICK-RACINE LEGION 6 VS MINNEAPOLIS MARINES 13
Sunday: November 4th, 1923   2:30 pm   Nicolet Park   Minneapolis, Minnesota

Game 7-HORLICK-RACINE LEGION 0 VS GREEN BAY PACKERS 16
Sunday: November 11th, 1923   2:30 pm   Horlick Athletic Field   Racine, Wisconsin

Game 8-HORLICK-RACINE LEGION 10 VS CHICAGO CARDINALS 4
Sunday: November 25th, 1923   2:15 pm   Comiskey Park   Chicago, Illinois

Game 9-HORLICK-RACINE LEGION 0 VS MILWAUKEE BADGERS 16
Thursday: November 28th, 1923   2:15 pm   Horlick Athletic Field Racine, Wisconsin

Game 10-HORLICK-RACINE LEGION 23 VS MINNEAPOLIS MARINES 0
Sunday: December 2nd, 1923   2:15 pm   Horlick Athletic Field   Racine, Wisconsin

1924 Game/Final Score/Location

Game 1-HORLICK-RACINE LEGION 10 VS HAMMOND PROS 0
Sunday: September 28th, 1924   2:30 pm   Horlick Athletic Field   Racine, Wisconsin

Game 2-HORLICK-RACINE LEGION 0 VS ROCK ISLAND INDEPENDENTS 9
Sunday: October 5th, 1924   2:30 pm   Douglas Park   Moline, Illinois

Game 3-HORLICK-RACINE LEGION 10 VS CHICAGO BEARS 10
Sunday: October 12th, 1924   2:15 pm   Cubs Park   Chicago, Illinois

Game 4-HORLICK-RACINE LEGION 13 VS KANSAS CITY BLUES 3
Sunday: October 19th, 1924   2:30 pm   Horlick Athletic Field   Racine, Wisconsin

Game 5-HORLICK-RACINE LEGION 10 VS MILWAUKEE BADGERS 0
Sunday: October 26th, 1924   2:30 pm   Athletic Park   Milwaukee, Wisconsin

Game 6-HORLICK-RACINE LEGION 3 VS GREEN BAY PACKERS 6
Sunday: November 2nd, 1924   2:00 pm   Bellevue Park   Green Bay, Wisconsin

Game 7-HORLICK-RACINE LEGION 3 VS ROCK ISLAND INDEPENDENTS 6
Sunday: November 2nd, 1924   2:30 pm   Horlick Athletic Field   Racine, Wisconsin

Game 8-HORLICK-RACINE LEGION 3 VS CHICAGO BEARS 3
Sunday: November 16th, 1924   2:30 pm   Cubs Park   Chicago, Illinois

Game 9-HORLICK-RACINE LEGION 10 VS CHICAGO CARDINALS 10
Sunday: November 23rd, 1924   2:30 pm   White Sox Park   Chicago, Illinois

Game 10-HORLICK-RACINE LEGION 7 VS GREEN BAY PACKERS 0
Sunday: November 30th, 1924   2:00 pm   Horlick Athletic Field   Racine, Wisconsin

1925 /Suspended operations-did not play

1925 Racine Legion Schedule

September 27th	Racine at Rock Island Independents
October 4th	Hammond Pros at Racine
October 11th	Chicago Bears at Racine
October 18th	Racine at Chicago Cardinals
October 25th	Green Bay Packers at Racine
November 1st	Racine at Chicago Bears
November 8th	Rock Island Independents at Racine
November 15th	Racine at Green Bay Packers
November 22nd	Racine at Hammond Pros
November 29th	Milwaukee Badgers at Racine
December 6th	Racine at Milwaukee Badgers

1926/Game/Final Score/Location

Game 1-RACINE TORNADOES 6 VS HAMMOND PROS 3
Sunday: September 26th, 1926   2:30 pm   Horlick Athletic Field   Racine, Wisconsin

Game 2-RACINE TORNADOES 0 VS CHICAGO CARDINALS 20
Sunday: October 3rd, 1926   2:15 pm   Normal Park Stadium   Chicago, Illinois

Game 3-RACINE TORNADOES 2 VS MILWAUKEE BADGERS 13
Sunday: October 10th, 1926   2:30 pm   Horlick Athletic Field   Racine, Wisconsin

Game 4-RACINE TORNADOES 0 VS DULUTH ESKIMOS 21
Sunday: October 17th, 1926   2:30 pm   Horlick Athletic Field   Racine, Wisconsin

Game 5-RACINE TORNADOES 0 VS GREEN BAY PACKERS 35
Sunday: October 24th, 1926   2:30 pm   City Stadium   Green Bay, Wisconsin

Team Manager/Coach/Captain

1922
Manager- George Ruetz (10)
Coach- Bill Hollenback (1) / Hank Gillo (10)
Captain- Hank Gillo (10)

1923
Manager- George Ruetz (9)
Coach- Hank Gillo (9)
Captain- Irv Langhoff (4) / Hank Gillo (5)

1924
Manager- G.E. Smalley (10)
Coach- Milton Romney (10)
Captain- Milton Romney (10)

1926
Manager- Bob Johonnott (5)
Coach- Wallace Barr (3) / Wallie McIllwain (2)
Asst. Coach- Hank Gillo (5)

( ) = number in parenthesis equals games in position.

Main Ticket Outlets

All located in downtown Racine, Wisc.

**Rehl's Cigar Store- 300 Sixth Street,
600 State Street**

Smader's Place -331 Main Street

**Monument Cigar Store-510
Monument Square**

349

This page intentionally left blank

References

Milwaukee Journal 1948
NFL Films
Pro Grid Forces © 2008 Matthew C. Snyder
Racine Journal News Newspaper 1921, 1922, 1923, 1924, 1925, 1926, 1927, 1936
Racine Times Call Newspaper 1921, 1922, 1923, 1924, 1925, 1926, 1927, 1936

This page intentionally left blank

©2014 Matthew C. Snyder

Glossary of Terms

Educated toe- a descriptive name for the kicking foot of Hank Gillo.

Gilded hoof- a description of Hank Gillo's kicking foot.

Gillobirds- a descriptive name for the Horlick-Racine Legion name, who were led by Hank Gillo.

Gillomen- a descriptive name for the Legion team, who were led by Hank Gillo.

1924 grid machine- a descriptive name for the Horlick-Racine Legion football team.

Horlick Athletic Field– This was the official name of the football field, where the Racine, Wisconsin NFL franchise played their home games. This field was originally designed by Walter Dick in 1909 and the baseball field was known as the Northside baseball park. William Horlick, Sr. purchased the field in 1919 and he renamed it Horlick Athletic Field. The land is surrounded by a stone wall and access is gained through wrought iron fence gates. There was originally a large covered wood grandstand with folding chairs to accommodate spectators. It was designed for the game of baseball and adapted to accommodate the game of football. Mr. Horlick spent many thousands of dollars to add bleacher seating, locker rooms and press box above the grandstand. He also had the first known NFL Premium boxes built for spectators to see the game up close with a field level view of the game. Horlick Athletic Field- Home of the Horlick-Racine Legion (1922, 1923, 1924) and the Racine Tornadoes (1926).

Horlick-Racine Gridders- another name for Horlick-Racine Legion football players.

Horlick-Racine Legion- Official name of the Racine, Wisconsin National Football League franchise from 1922-1924.

Horlick's Crew- A name used to describe the men, who worked on the grounds of Horlick Athletic Field, hired by William Horlick, Sr. and his company.

Horlick Eleven- another name for Horlick-Racine Legion football team.

Horlicktown- another name for Racine, Wisconsin.

Horlickville– another name for Horlick Athletic Field in Racine, Wisconsin.

Legion gridders- another name for Horlick-Racine Legion football players.

Legionnaires- a name used to describe the Horlick-Racine Legion fans.

Line Plunging Hank- a descriptive name for Henry Charles Gillo, who was one of the few men in early football, who had developed the twisting run and spiral jump.

Racine Gridiron– another name for Horlick Athletic Field in Racine, Wisconsin.

Racine Legion- Nickname used for the NFL Horlick-Racine Legion football team. Also, official name of the team, who represented the American Legion Post No. 76 professional team prior to 1922.

Racine Tornadoes- The official name of the 1926 Racine, Wisconsin National Football League franchise football team.

Romney satellites- Horlick-Racine Legion team.

Ruetzmen- a descriptive name for Horlick-Racine Legion football team, who were managed by George "Babe" Ruetz for the 1922 and 1923 season.

Horlick Athletic Field Historical Photos

Aerial photo of Horlick Athletic Field

Home Field
Horlick Athletic Field 1648 Forest Street
Racine, Wisconsin 53402

Horlick Athletic Field
Home of the NFL Horlick-Racine Legion (1922-1924) and Racine Tornadoes (1926)

354

Above: Horlick Athletic Field original grandstand seating. Box seating was located in front of the reserved seating of the grandstand. William Horlick, Sr. would increase the amount and location of the boxes as well as improvements to the grandstand prior to the 1922 NFL season. The new Premium box seats were built and located along the sidelines of the football field at Horlickville.

Circa 1920's Close up view of the reserved seating in the main grandstand at Horlick Athletic Field

355

2014 Horlick Athletic Field main entrance

Horlick Athletic Field
Total Seats

1920 1,300
1921 2,500
1922 3,500
1923 5,000
1924 5,000
1926 5,000

5,000 Horlick Athletic Field seats
was made up of 1,907 General
Admission seats, 1,337 reserved
seats and 256 Premium box seats.
Lighting was added in 1924.

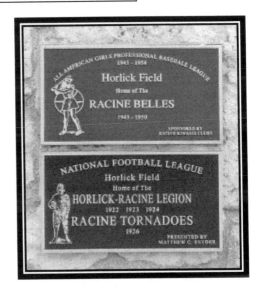

Plaques located on the front of the ticket
booth at Horlick Athletic Field
aka Horlickville.

This page intentionally left blank

Team Uniforms

1922 Horlick-Racine Legion
Helmet: Black leather four strap
Jersey: Crimson red with 8" White numerals
on the back only
Alternate Jersey: Khaki brown with 8" White
numerals on the back only
Shoulder pads: Leather with wool liner
Pants: Khaki brown canvas pants
Socks: Black wool long socks with 3 White stripes
Shoes: Stacked leather football cleats

1922 HRL
Stripes
on socks

1923 Horlick-Racine Legion
Helmet: Black leather four strap
Jersey: Olive drab green with 8" White numerals on the back only
Shoulder pads: Leather with wool liner
Pants: Khaki brown canvas pants
Socks: Olive drab green wool long socks
Shoes: Stacked leather football cleats

1924 Horlick-Racine Legion
Helmet: Black leather four strap
Jersey: Original cardinal red with 8" White numerals on the back only
Shoulder pads: Leather with wool liner
Pants: Khaki brown canvas pants
Socks: Black wool long socks with 3 White stripes
Shoes: Stacked leather football cleats

1926 Racine Tornadoes
Helmet: Black leather four strap
Jersey: Maroon red with 8" White numerals on the back only
Shoulder pads: Leather with wool liner
Pants: Khaki brown canvas pants
Socks: Black wool long socks with 3 White stripes
Shoes: Stacked leather football cleats

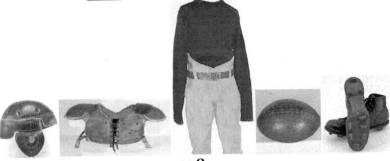

**Horlick-Racine Legion NFL 1922 1923 1924
Professional Football Racine, Wisconsin**

To get your Gear go to:
www.RacineLegion.com